# BARDEN IN WHARFEDALE

## The Place and its People

# BARDEN IN WHARFEDALE
## The Place and its People

Brontë Bedford-Payne

HAYLOFT PUBLISHING LTD.

First published by Hayloft 2016


Hayloft Publishing Ltd, Cumbria


tel: 07971 352473
email: books@hayloft.eu
web: www.hayloft.eu


ISBN 978-1-910237-13-7

Copyright © Brontë Bedford-Payne, 2016


Brontë Bedford-Payne has asserted her right to be identified
as the Author of this Work



This book is sold subject to the condition that it shall not, by way of trade or otherwise, be lent, resold, hired out, or otherwise circulated without the publisher's prior consent in any form of binding or cover other than that in which it is published and without a similar condition including this condition being imposed on the subsequent purchaser.


A CIP catalogue record for this book is available
from the British Library


Papers used by Hayloft are natural, recyclable products made from wood grown in sustainable forests. The manufacturing processes conform to the environmental regulations of the country of origin.


Designed, printed and bound in the EU


*Frontispiece, Barden Tower with Billy Mason from a postcard by Walter Scott, Bradford*

To my sister, Elisabeth, June 2014

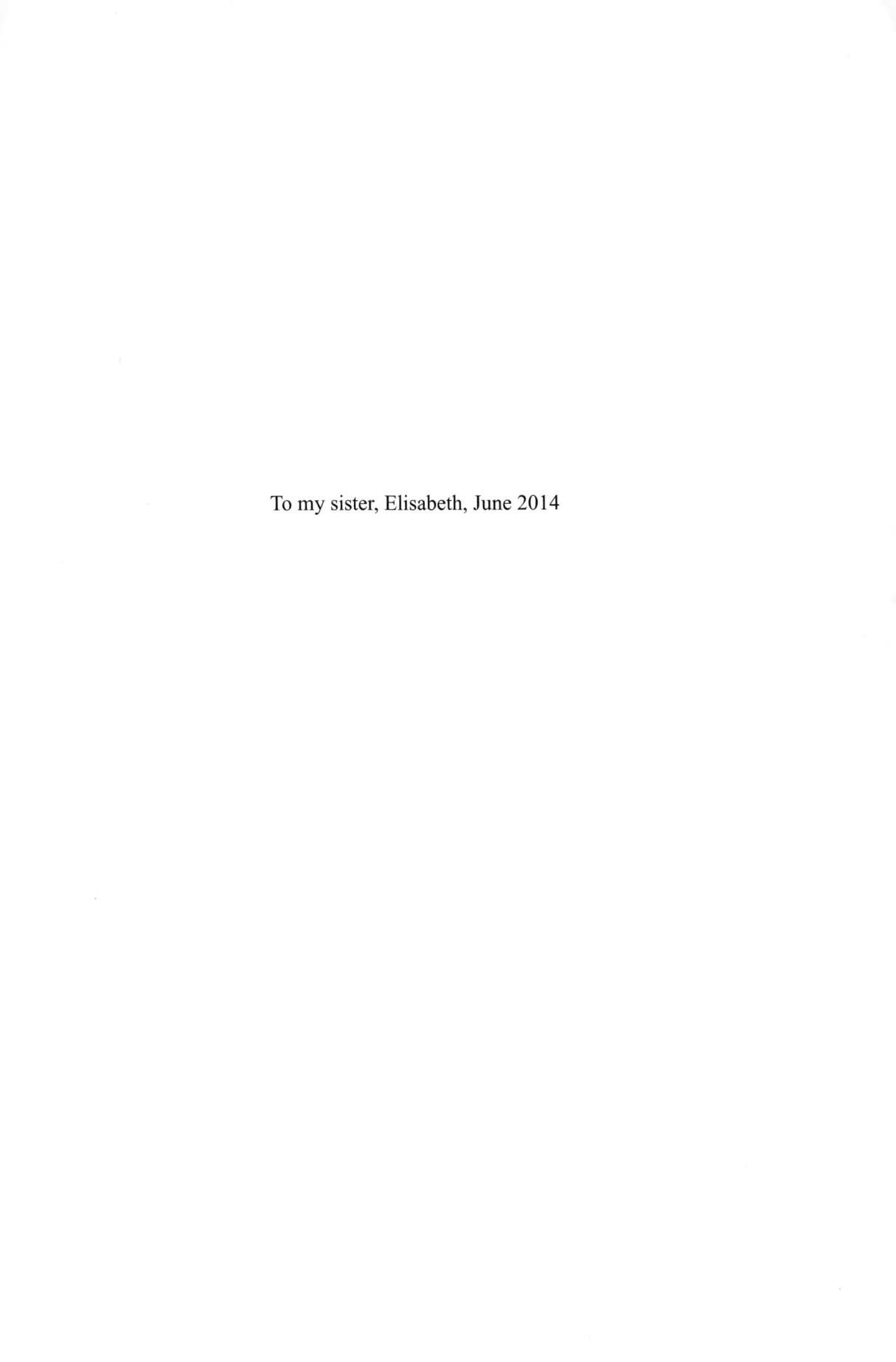

*However skilful a man may be in writing – however natural his style – no one can write history naturally. The array of facts which the historian has first to collect is far too great. In my own work I generally find that for perhaps a simple paragraph I may have four or five hundred typed or hand-written scripts of paper – extracts and notes from letters and books and documents. And the sense and truth of all these have somehow to be worked into that paragraph. It's like a jig-saw puzzle. However carefully one may have arranged one's material, however thoroughly one has mastered it, to get it all down in the right and natural order is a most difficult business. That is the fun of writing history – it's a test, like everything else worth doing, of effort and endurance.*

Sir Arthur Bryant,
*The Story of England, Makers of the Realm*, 1955

# Contents

|   | Contributors and Illustrators | 8 |
|---|---|---|
|   | Preface and Acknowledgements | 9 |
|   | Foreword by the Duke of Devonshire | 13 |
| 1 | Early Settlement in Barden | 15 |
| 2 | Barden Tower – History and Architecture | 22 |
| 3 | Routeways | 34 |
| 4 | Buildings in Barden | 58 |
| 5 | Farms | 74 |
| 6 | Drebley | 78 |
| 7 | Chapel, School, Hough Mill and various other buildings | 112 |
| 8 | Social History in Barden | 255 |
|   | Bibliography | 268 |

# BARDEN IN WHARFEDALE, THE PLACE AND ITS PEOPLE

### CONTRIBUTORS:

| | |
|---|---|
| Brontë Bedford-Payne | Upper Wharfedale Field Society. |
| | The Local History, Vernacular Buildings and |
| | Medieval Landscape of Barden, |
| | Social History including Schools and Chapels |
| Dr Heather Beaumont | Upper Wharfedale Field Society. |
| | The Local History and the Medieval Landscape of |
| | Upper Wharfedale |
| Arnold Pacey | Cruck buildings, Barns and Farmhouse surveys |
| Architectural Historian | The buildings of Barden Tower including the Chapel |
| | Barden Bridge and Hough Mill |
| Alison Armstrong | Vernacular Buildings |
| | Medieval Stone Walls Survey |
| Dr David Johnson | Archaeology, Geology, Trackways, Stone Walls |
| Les Bloom, C.Eng | Hon. Life Member: Upper Wharfedale Field Society and |
| | retired Consulting Engineer (Mechanical & Engineering) |

### ILLUSTRATIONS:

I acknowledge and am grateful to the Trustees of the Chatsworth Settlement for permission to reproduce maps from manuscripts at Bolton Abbey. I thank the following friends for the use of photographs, old postcards and other illustrative memorabilia:

Jane Hargreaves, Chris Lunnon, Alan Stockdale.
Rosemary Lodge for the reproduction of her painting of Woodend Farm, near Burnsall.
Andrew C. Boult for the reproduction of photographs of the bridges over Barden Beck
   from his book *A Walk in the Past*
Julian Royle (Royle Publications Ltd.) for permission to reproduce two paintings by
   John Atkinson Grimshaw
Many of the black and white photographs were taken by Herbert Chester during his
   tenancy of Drebley Farm 1929-57; some photographs of wartime farming at
   Drebley were taken by Dr Ian Hay, Agricultural Department, University of Leeds.

# Preface and Acknowlegements

This collection of articles has been written not only as a result of a lifetime's interest in Barden, on the estate of the Duke of Devonshire at Bolton Abbey, but also to put together the information I have gleaned from the many sources described in the text. I have not attempted to write a definitive history of Barden, but to arouse in the reader an interest in the many historical aspects and features which can still be discerned in the rich palimpsest of the landscape and its buildings. I also hope to introduce some of the people who over the centuries created this uniquely preserved little Lordship.

In 2010 I was joined in compiling this history of Barden by Arnold Pacey, David Johnson and Alison Armstrong, whose writings are included in the sections concerning Barden Tower and Barden Bridge, Barden Scale, Club Nook and other farmsteads, the *Road to Burnsall, Kettlewell and Buckden*, and the survey of medieval stone walls. During the time of writing, David Johnson's report *Excavation of a series of earthworks at Bumby Laithe, Drebley* (2010) was deposited at the estate office in Bolton Abbey, with the Trustees of the Chatsworth Estate. I thank Arnold Pacey for his help, and also thank Heather Beaumont and Les Bloom for their work on Hough Mill.

I am indebted to the Trustees of the Chatsworth Estate Settlement, to the retired Agent for the Duke of Devonshire at Bolton Abbey John Sheard, and to the present Agent Ben Hayes. In particular I am grateful to the late Peter Watkins, Honorary Archivist at Bolton Abbey, who made his office, the papers and the maps from the Chatsworth Collection Manuscripts (Barden Box) available to me and to my colleague Heather Beaumont. My thanks also go to the late Hugh Stele-Smith, honorary research assistant at Bolton Abbey who, while sorting the manuscripts, selected and showed us relevant Barden papers.

Especial thanks to the late Heather Beaumont, through whom I was introduced to the archives at Bolton Abbey, to The Yorkshire Archaeological Society in Leeds, to the Borthwick Institute of Historical Research in York, and to a map of the Lordship of Barden in the West Riding of the County of York copied by Matthew Oddie in 1778 from the plan drawn by Ed Beckwith in 1731. I was first shown this map as it lay on the dining table of Peter Watkins' house in Skyreholme. I could see that it was hand-drawn and coloured, but I did not then realise how it would open up to me a new concept of the history of Barden.

The first thing I noticed was the road past Barden Tower… it was not the same as the road I knew so well, and along which we all travel today. Then I noticed a trackway marked 'Road to Burnsall, Kettlewell and Buckden', which led northward from Barden Scale in the direction of Burnsall along the edge of the moor. There is no such road today. From the evidence of Beckwith's survey of 1731, it appears that many of the Barden enclosures and the building of the associated walls still standing today, took place for Richard Boyle, third Earl of Burlington 1694-1753, during the reign of George II 1727-60. This was generally before Parliamentary Enclosures were being carried out in the rest of the country.

From these revelations, my interest was nurtured by many regular visits to Peter's archive office, together with Heather Beaumont. This was situated at the back of the Rectory, and overlooked by the newly restored stonework for the Pugin windows in the nave of the Priory church at Bolton Abbey. Heather and I combed the Barden archives, and from these we published our book describing the history of Barden School in 1997. Meanwhile, Heather continued with her interpretation of the landscape for an article entitled *Settlement and land usage in an upland estate: Barden in Wharfedale*, which in May 1996 she published in the journal of the British Association for Local History.

Since these early days, we continued to trace our history of Barden through a remarkable series of records as listed below:

Firstly, the Skipton archives held by the Yorkshire Archaeological Society (YAS) in Leeds; these documents came to light in 1802, through Thomas D. Whitaker, the nineteenth century historian who not only transcribed the documents for his publication, *History and Antiquities of the Deanery of Craven*, first published in 1805, but he also arranged for the archives to be removed from Skipton Castle and deposited with the Yorkshire Archaeology Society. He wrote:

> In the second great rounder from the entrance is the muniment room of the Cliffords; a place of impenetrable security from everything but mice and damp, which, as it has not been opened more than twice in the last forty years, have been carrying on their depredations during all that time with uninterrupted perseverance. In one drawer had been deposited the ancient charters of the Romillies, Albemarles, Percys, and earlier Cliffords, of which nine parts out of ten I found in 1802 gnawed to fritters; of the remainder, I have not failed to avail myself in this work. The compotuses, house books, etc. of the later Cliffords, being written principally on paper, are in somewhat better preservation.

In the library we met Richard (Dick) Spence, whose knowledge and published work concerning the Clifford family (including Lady Anne and the Earls of Cumberland) was unsurpassed, and it was he who introduced us to a series of abstracts from the Clifford papers by W. E. Preston 1953-4.

These papers include leases issued by the Earls of Cumberland and their successors to named individuals on the Barden estate from 1632-57 onwards; reading the transcripts enabled us to gain (for the first time) an insight into which families had lived at each of the farmsteads, and occasionally to gain a sense of how they inter-relate with today's tenants. We were unable to decipher the script for any of the earlier papers, and this inevitably influenced the scope of this book.

At the Borthwick Institute in the University of York we found a few wills, probates and inventories, from which we gleaned a little further insight into the lives of some tenant farmers in Barden.

Included in the archives of the Chatsworth Estate Settlement at Bolton Abbey are rent books, cash books, maps and other material concerning the history of the estate during the

## PREFACE AND ACKNOWLEDGEMENTS

seventeenth, eighteenth and nineteenth centuries. These invaluable documents enabled us to follow through the named tenancies of each farmstead, and it was here that we found such comments as 'Old decrepit or thatched buildings, in need of repair,' and so on, or 'newly built. In good repair.' In addition a collection of about twenty unsigned architectural drawings, dating from around 1862, show plans for the building of new farmsteads on the Bolton Abbey estate. Amongst these, for instance, are plans for a new, model farmyard at Drebley.

These records, combined with parish records and nineteenth century census returns, revealed to us how, over a period of some 350 years, generations of the same families inhabited the same steadings, farming the same land as had their forefathers. Once having settled, many of these tenant farmers built their own houses and their barns; their families were born, baptised, married and died in the homes of their forefathers. Many now lie before stone headstones in the churchyard at Bolton Priory.

In the early 1990s, I joined classes tutored by Steven Moorhouse, under the auspices of the Workers Educational Association (WEA), and later, the University of Leeds School of Adult Education. It was through these classes and the associated days spent field walking in Wharfedale that I grew to see and appreciate the medieval landscape in Barden, my sense of nostalgia having been replaced with a keen desire to understand its many facets. I do not claim to have interpreted all this information correctly, and I apologise for errors and omissions. I trust that in the future, further knowledge will be revealed by those more experienced in understanding the remarkable features of this seigneurial landscape, where, since its earliest settlement, many periods of history are represented, and where it has remained entire, in the possession of descendants of the same family since 1310, when the Plantagenet King Edward II reigned over England.

I would like to thank everyone who has helped with this book which could not have been created without my friend, Ryan, whose patience and ingenuity knew no bounds. Thanks are due to everyone who assisted with illustrations – in all cases we have tried to find copyright owners and would like to thank everyone for the use of the images. Finally to all those who have helped, too numerous to mention individually, who made this book possible, my heartfelt thanks.

Brontë Bedford-Payne, Spring 2016

# BARDEN IN WHARFEDALE, THE PLACE AND ITS PEOPLE

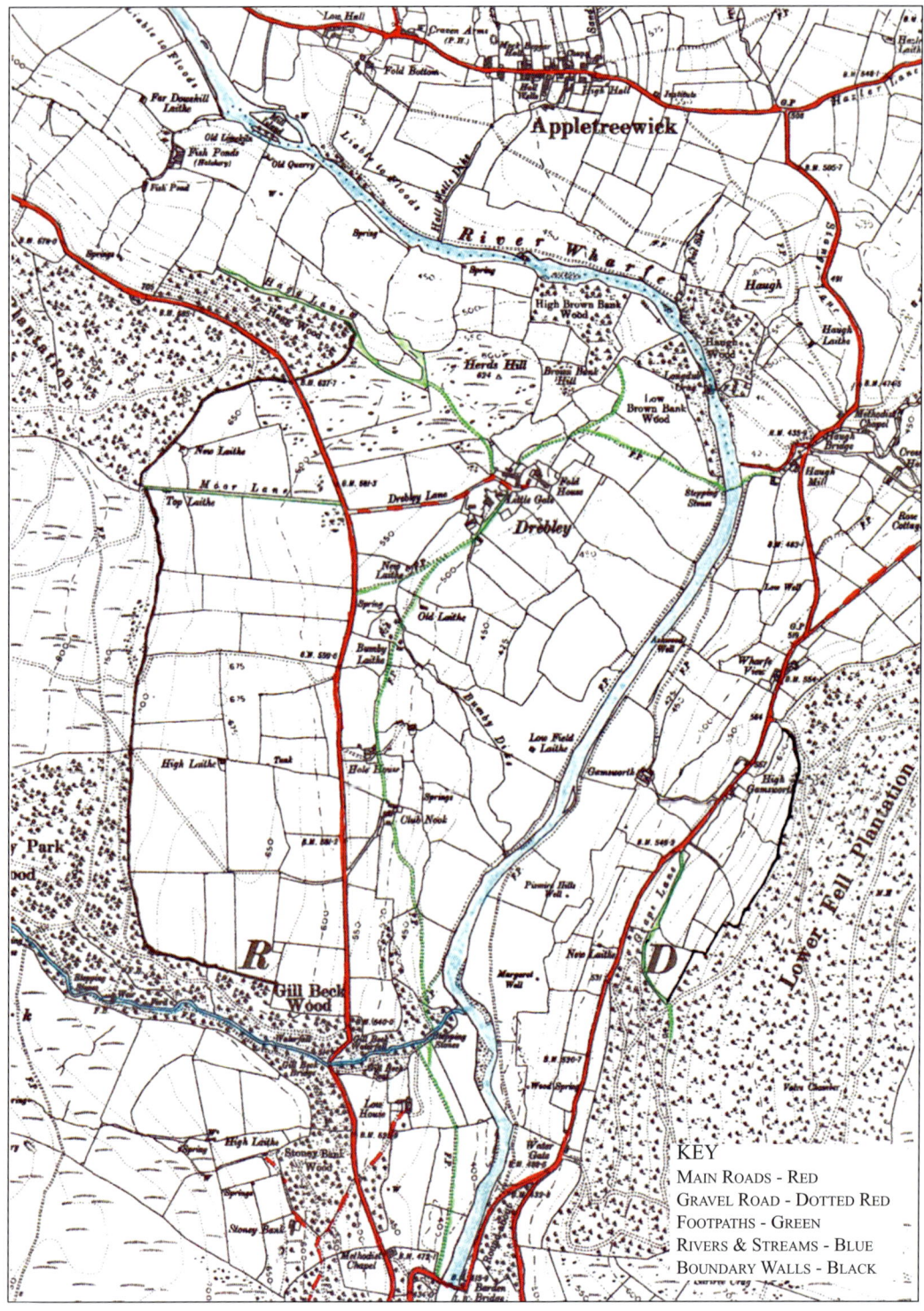

*Yorkshire (West Riding) Sheet 157 1896, Survey 1849-50, Revised 1899-90, pub. 1896.*

# Foreword

For the tens of thousands of visitors who enjoy the Wharfe valley in and around Barden and Drebley, the landscape appears completely unchanged and unchanging. It also appears 'natural' and the general assumption is that what you see today is what has been there more or less forever.

For those who live and work in the place change is much more obvious and it is constant. Farming practices change, woods are felled and re-planted, footpaths become wider and require fencing to keep the walkers and their dogs from the farmers and their stock. Houses are improved, telegraph poles are undergounded, Sky dishes appear. Old buildings find new uses or fall into disrepair and eventually collapse back into the ground. Change is continual and never ending. Most of this happens slowly, gradually and often unrecorded, certainly unrecorded as a whole history. Brontë Bedford-Payne has therefore written a book of immense value and interest. She and her colleagues have spent many years researching this work and every moment of this labour of love is immensely worthwhile.

This is real history, factual, in great detail and it is utterly compelling. I lived near Barden for over 20 years and I have spent time there on and off all my life. I have visited most of the buildings and walked nearly all the woods and fields as well as the river banks, many times. But, reading Brontë Bedford-Payne's words is a revelation, a fascinating historical survey of every aspect of this beautiful and ancient part of Yorkshire. The purposes of apparently random structures become clear, the historical layers are unpeeled and the reasons for why a building, a footpath or a wall is where it is become fascinatingly clear. To have this book in one's hands as you study the valley will make any visit infinitely more interesting. For all residents and for those responsible for the continuing management of the landscape, be they farmers, landowners or planners, this is essential reading.

We are all in her debt and I for one am in awe of her thoroughness, attention to detail and, above all, her deep understanding of the landscape and what it contains in this exceptional corner of England.

Stoker Devonshire
2015

# BARDEN IN WHARFEDALE, THE PLACE AND ITS PEOPLE

# 1
# Early Settlements in Barden

The Bolton Abbey estate stretches northward from Bolton Bridge to Barden through the beautiful wooded valley of the River Wharfe. The scenery might be described as linear, in that meadow land and pasture follow the course of the river which runs at a height of 50 feet OD. Both deciduous woodland and estate forestry plantations form a major part of the landscape, with the cultivated area rising to a height of rather less than 1,000 feet OD, after which open, heather-covered moorland stretches away to the watershed on both sides.

The northern boundary of Barden lies to the west of the river at Woodend Farm, and to the east, at Dalehead in the tributary valley of Howgill. Although there are several hamlets, such as the clusters of houses grouped around the green at Bolton Abbey, and those at Hazlewood, Drebley and Howgill, the estate is characterised by isolated or scattered farmsteads, cottages and barns, rather than by the classical village spaced around a manor house, a school and a church.

Remains of prehistoric villages and field systems are not a major feature of this part of Wharfedale, but the discovery of a spear-head dating from the late Bronze Age indicates a presence of prehistoric people in the area. Because of the absence of weapon hoards 'it is thought that the spear-head came into the district by peaceful penetration, by trading and not by conquest.'[1]

The presence of a carved stone head in the hamlet of Drebley is a possible indication of early occupation of the site, especially round the spring which bubbles up in a field adjoining the lane near the cruck barn. Although this feature has not been ascribed to a specific date, it is of considerable interest in relation to the Celtic origins of other stone heads, many of them having been found in association with springs. [2 & 3]

There is little evidence for Roman occupation, but Arthur Raistrick[4] recorded that sherds of Samian ware had been found in Appletreewick and Drebley, and, as described in Chapter 3 'Routeways Through Barden', Frances Villey postulated that a Roman road had passed through Barden, between Ilkley in Wharfedale and Bainbridge in Wensleydale. Further evidence for domestic settlement and cultivation in pre-conquest times has been shown by the discovery of two querns. One was recorded by Cowling as being of Celtic origin, with a flat grinding surface, and the other, found in the garden of Drebley House,[5] conforms to a beehive pattern, with holes for the hopper and two handles, suggesting that it dates from

---

1 Cowling, Eric T. (1946) *Rombalds Way*, Otley: William Walker and Sons (Otley) Ltd.
2 Jackson, Sidney, (1973) *Celtic and Other Stone Heads*, Lund Humphries, Bradford and London.
3 Billingsley, John, (1995) *Stone Heads,* Yorkshire History Magazine, pub. Mytholmroyd, West Yorkshire.
4 Raistrick, A. (1933) *Roman Road Down Wharfedale*, Yorkshire Archaeological Journal, xxxi.
5 Registered in Yorkshire Quern Survey: recorded 7/3/07 by John Cruse, Yorkshire Archaeological Society.

# BARDEN IN WHARFEDALE, THE PLACE AND ITS PEOPLE

the Romano-British period.

Arthur Raistrick, writing in his book *The Pennine Dales* (1968) described how,

> the pattern of (present-day) settlement was originated by Norse pastoral farmers, who, in the ninth century came from the West with their flocks of sheep, probably following the valleys of the rivers Lune and Ribble, and thence over the Pennine uplands. Many settlements became lodges and are named as such in the forest rentals. In Barden Chase, part of Skipton Forest, all nine 'lodges' are on the site of Norse settlements, some with names deriving from Old Norse such as Gamelwath and Holgill... In Barden the lodges remained as clusters of one or two farms, each with a small area of meadow ground, with pannage for swine, pasture for cattle and a small area to provide feeding of deer in winter.

## DOMESDAY

Thomas Whitaker[6] has described how,

> ...all the townships and manors belonging to the King's Thanes were acquired by the Romillies within little more than a century of the date of Domesday, and became part of the second Skipton fee. About the year 1140, on account of its vicinity to Barden, Drebley, though originally part of Burnsall, was excepted out of an endowment drawn up by Emma, who was the daughter of Bertram de Bulmer and her husband, Geoffrey de Neville, when the lands of Burnsall, with the advowson, were re-conveyed to Robert de Bulmer. In consequence of this, Drebley became a member of the demesnes of Skipton castle and of the castle parish.

The Domesday records tell us that,

> In the Manor and Berewic of Brinesal and Drebelaie, Dringel has two carucates and two oxgangs to be taxed, Osbern de Arches had these lands, but they are all waste, and now Count Alan has it.

Dringel was the mesne proprietor while Osbern de Arches was the overlord.[7]

> Gammalswath; 5 carucates taxable, 6 ploughs possible, Meadow 5 acre. The whole 5 leagues long, 1 league wide. Value before 1086 was 20s (At Domesday, Count Alan had it.)

---

6 Whitaker, T. D., 1875, *Craven*, p501
7 Faull, M and Stinson M., *Domesday Book*.

# EARLY SETTLEMENT IN BARDEN

**MEDIEVAL HISTORY AND OWNERSHIP TO THE PRESENT DAY**

After the death in 1087 of William the Conqueror, he was succeeded by William II who granted the Honour of Skipton to Robert de Romille. It was he who built the first castle. In 1310 Edward II granted the Honour to Robert 1st Lord Clifford in recognition of his military prowess and his support of the King. He was already a great landowner in the Welsh Marches. The blazon for the distinctive Clifford coat of arms is chequy Or and Azure, a fesse Gules.[8]

Within the Honour[9] was the royal Forest of Skipton, wherein was the hunting chase of Barden, where the deer ran free and the pleasures of the chase were indulged. There was a primary forest lodge, where the Court Leets took place on the site of the present Tower and it may have been known as Scabbitsyke.

The Soke Mill or manorial corn mill was at Hough Mill, near Howgill, the Lords of the Manor being the Earls of Cumberland. The earliest surviving lease for a mill on this site was granted to William Holmes of Barden by George Clifford 3rd Earl, dated 1604. Hough Mill is situated on a tributary, Firs Beck in Howgill; it is reached from Drebley by means of a trackway leading through the meadows towards the river, where there are now a set of stepping stones. It is not known when the stones were first set, but it is significant that the crossing lies on an ancient routeway between north-west and north-east of Craven.

MEDIEVAL INDUSTRIAL ACTIVITY AND SCORIA IN BARDEN

On the outer side of the wall built around the Bull Coppice, (formerly Henry Clifford's Little Park) Bailey Harker of Grassington, writing in 1869[10] claimed to have seen 'some ancient mounds of scoria (that is, slag or dross) from iron works in the area of Cinder Hill Gate.' He assumed the scoria to be derived 'very likely of the time of the Saxons,' but in fact, these mounds (in which there are also contemporary pottery sherds, dating from the thirteenth/fourteenth centuries) are the remains of a medieval iron smelting industry.[11] A similar site was noted by Arthur Raistrick as having been turned up during ploughing in Tower Field (by Cinder Hill) during the Second World War.

PLACE-NAMES IN BARDEN

By studying the landscape together with known facts concerning the historical development of a place, it is possible to interpret the meaning of place-names; in Barden the majority of them are either topographic or associated with personal names; they describe specific features in the landscape, the derivation of these names enabling us to recognise when changes in settlement had taken place, each group of settlers having either adopted pre-existing names or having introduced names deriving from their place of origin, using their own language to interpret the topographical meaning and the specific character of the place at the time it was settled.

---

8 Spence, Richard T. (2002), *Skipton Castle and its Builders,* p52, Otley, Smith Settle.
9 An Honour is a place of distinction OED. Origin of this word is ME from OFr.
10 Harker, Bailey 1869 *Rambles in Upper Wharfedale,* Skipton: Edmondson.
11 Stephen Moorhouse. Lecture note BB-P

# BARDEN IN WHARFEDALE, THE PLACE AND ITS PEOPLE

There are very few names of Celtic origin in Upper Wharfedale, but the name of the river Wharfe is believed to mean 'a winding, turning water course', and it is possibly derived from *Verbia* which is a personal name for a Celtic or Roman goddess.

The majority of place-names in Barden are of pre-conquest origin, many having their roots in the Old English or Anglo-Saxon period of history, e.g. *Barden, ley, den, croft, field, ridding,* and the colours *black, green* or *brown*. In other parts of the country these place-names are as early as the fifth to sixth centuries, but the earliest date for settlement in Barden is likely to have been in the seventh century, after the establishment of the Saxon kingdom of Elmet around Tadcaster.

Many names are of Old Norse derivation, e.g. *Thwaite, Scale* and *Intake*, dating from the Norse incursions around the west coast of Britain during the ninth and tenth centuries.

A few names derive from Old French OFr/Middle English ME following the Conquest and after the establishment of Skipton castle by Norman barons, who introduced the word *Forest*. These names were introduced as the need arose for enclosures associated with lodges in the hunting chase. e.g. Close, Hird Hill and Nook., and they have remained in use until the present day.

Later names, such as 'allotments' occur on nineteenth century maps, after enclosure and division of common lands such as Drebley Thwaite had taken place. As might be expected, names such as intake (OE and ON) have been re-used throughout centuries of change, so that it is important to differentiate between those that first appear on the earliest maps and relate to the earlier settlements, and the same names which have been re-used descriptively on later maps.

These place-names indicate not only that Barden was heavily wooded, but also, by the time of the conquest, there were fields, riddings and leys where woodland had been cleared from around such settlements as Gamsworth, Drebley and Howgill.

## The 'Shepherd Lord' in Barden

Much has been written about the 'exile' in Westmorland of Henry Clifford the 10th Lord Clifford, 1454-1523 (later known as 'The Shepherd Lord') during the Wars of the Roses between the Lancastrian and Yorkist claimants to the English throne. After the battle of Bosworth in 1485 when Richard III was killed, the victorious Lancastrians installed Henry Tudor as King Henry VII, together with his wife, Elizabeth of York. The 'Shepherd Lord', whose family had supported the Lancastrian cause throughout the conflict, then returned from exile to establish his court in Skipton castle. However, he preferred to live in Barden rather than in Skipton, and so he set about restoring and enlarging one of the old hunting lodges, possibly that known as Scabbitsyke, wherein the Court Leets were held, (see Chapter 2, 'Barden Tower' by Arnold Pacey). At the same time, the old hunting chase was empaled and subsequently walled in to form a Little Park around the tower itself, and to enclose the vast area of moorland which became The Great Park. Within these walls a parkland landscape was laid out, which included a deer-park, fishponds, and, on the east side of the river, opposite the tower, a coney warren and Warrener's house. The forest lodges remained on their original sites, where the officers lived and carried out their duties within the Chase.

# EARLY SETTLEMENT IN BARDEN

The Great Park[12] thus became separated from Drebley Field and the Thwaite[13] which formed the northern parts of the estate. Here, for the first time, husbanding and cultivation of crops could be carried out without fear of damage from the deer, or the danger of the Lord's Chase.

The terrace and footings of Henry Clifford's walls can still be seen as they follow the boundaries of his Parks, especially round the former Little Park (now known as Bull Coppice) surrounding the Tower precinct. Although largely rebuilt, especially by Lady Anne Clifford in 1654, distinctive features survive along the length of this wall, such as evidence of medieval stone quarrying, leaving no waste. The wall stands on a broad terrace with large boulders and orthostats forming its base, while massive tumbled boulders lie within the Park itself.

Pronounced ditches can be found along the lengths of many of the walls, where they would have served to prevent deer leaping out of the Great Park; these are shown on Matthew Oddie's map of 1778.

## FOREST LODGES IN BARDEN

Until recently it was understood that there were six lodges in the medieval forest of Barden,[14] and that they were named Ungayne, Laund, Gamsworth Howgill and Drebley, with the Tower as the principal Lodge. In 2003, Stephen Moorhouse published a Thematic Paper for the Yorkshire Archaeological Society[15] in which he identified a total of twelve Lodges in the Forest:

> There were twelve Lodges listed in the Forest of Barden, recorded in the manorial accounts for 1437/8. They are numbered in the sequence as given there, proceeding northwards on the eastern side of the valley from High Laund and then southwards down the western side of the valley finishing at Barden Scale.

Of these twelve:
i. Drebley, Gamsworth, Howgill and Eastwood Head are mentioned in medieval documents as vaccaries where cattle were agisted. Each can be identified as settlements from which the present-day farmsteads developed, the names of each one remaining unchanged.
ii. Gamsworth is referred to in the Bolton Compotus compiled by Prior Laund[16] where, in 1322/23 there are receipts for the hire of a vaccary.
iii. The sites of Tabcliffe, Over Fyshcrythe, Nether Fyshcrythe and le Mordgers are mentioned by Whitaker '...in the time of Thomas Lord Clifford AD1437, two other Lodges

---

\* see also *A Survey of Medieval Walls in Barden,* Alison Armstrong
12 Spence, Richard (1994), *The Shepherd Lord of Skipton Castle,* Otley: Smith Settle.
13 Thwaite ON for a clearing of woodland.
14 T. D. Witaker, 1878, *The History and Antiquities of the Deanery of Craven in the County of York*, 3rd Edn republished by Morton of Didsbury, Manchester, 1973.
15 Moorhouse, S., 2003, *The Archaeology of Yorkshire: The Anatomy of the Yorkshire Dales*, Yorkshire Archaeological Society Occasional Paper No 3.
16 Kershaw, I. B. P., 1973 *The Economy of a Northern Monastery*, Oxford University Press.

had been created in Barden – Over Fyshcrythe and Nether Fyshcrythe. These were probably on the banks of the Wharfe, and so called as containing some accustomed haunts or seats of the old fishermen.'

Moorhouse suggests Hole House as the site of Nether Fyshcrythe and Watergate as the site of Over Fyshcrythe, although he says 'no evidence has been found for their antiquity'.

I would suggest rather that the Warreners House may be on the site of Nether Fyshcrythe,[17] since it is in a topographically suitable location for a fisherman's lodge. Watergate does indeed stand in an equally suitable position, and may have originated as Over Fyshcrythe. These two ancient sites lie within a mile of each other, along the road to Storiths which branches from the highway between Hough Mill and Barden Bridge. They are favourably situated on a natural river terrace overlooking the river and meadows where flooding occurs frequently, the water draining away to leave small ponds in which fish could be naturally retained.

Moorhouse suggests that Le Modgers stood on the site of Wharfe View, but evidence has not yet been found for an early settlement around this nineteenth century cottage and farmyard. However, the present-day cottage at High Gamsworth lies alongside large walled enclosures extending southwards on the hillside above the former lodge and vaccary at Gamsworth itself. Many of the walls of these enclosures show features of early construction, especially along Grape Lane, which leads towards tracks in the direction of the medieval lodge at High Laund and the vaccary at Broadshaw. There are many huge boulders in the footings of these walls, and also some remarkable free-standing boulders, suggesting that they were early boundary markers. At one point, earthworks indicate the remains of a long-gone sheephouse. Inexplicably, this area is not included on the maps of either Ed. Beckwith 1731 or Matthew Oddie 1778, although the dwelling at High Gamsworth is shown and numbered 258.

The area is fully drawn and Grape Lane is marked as such on the 1st Edition Ordnance Survey map of 1853.

SUGGESTIONS FOR THE ORIGIN OF THE NAME LE MORDGER OR MOORGAIRE

| Old English | OE | *mor*: | moor, moorland, barren upland |
| | OE | *gaers*: | grass |
| | OE | *gach*: | steep, precipitous (for the hillside above Gamsworth) |
| Old Norse | ON | *garor*: | enclosure, yard |
| | ON | *gata*: | road, a cattle walk-up |
| | ON | *geat*: | gate or opening |

The site of Tabcliffe is lost and has not been identified. According to the system of numbering, it would have been in the area of Drebley Hagg, where Stephen Moorhouse has identified some relevant earthworks.

---

17 Holme House is on the site of the Warrener's house for the Coney Warren established by Henry Clifford for use during his residence at the Tower between 1485 and 1520.

# EARLY SETTLEMENT IN BARDEN

VACCARIES

After the death of 'the Shepherd Lord' in 1523 the life style of his Clifford descendants and subsequent Lords of Skipton Castle changed. As Arthur Raistrick has described:

> As the emphasis moved away from a hunting chase towards organised agriculture, so the need for forest lodges declined. Greater clearing of trees took place and the lodges developed into anything from a small farm to a hamlet set in a clearing in the forest, engaged mainly in the rearing of cattle and a few sheep.[18]

These clearings became vaccaries, where cattle were agisted.[19] Some are documented; for instance, in 1332/3 forest receipts from Barden Tower included those for vaccaries at Drebley, Holgill, Gamsworth, Launds and Eastwode, with agistments for plough cattle in the woods of Drebley and Eastwode,[20] and later, in the Bolton Compotus dated 1505 – 1510 the following record appears: 'Bolton hired a vaccary at Holgill in the Forest of Barden and agisted its cattle there'.[21]

To enclose the vaccaries, stones were cleared from the grazing areas, and walls were built on mounds, with large boulders in their foundations. Through careful study of the present walls surrounding the large enclosures attached to the former Lodges, it is possible to see these ancient footings, and thus to recognise the boundaries of the original vaccaries referred to in the Compotus. The former keepers or officers of the Forest became farmers whose dwellings developed into homesteads on the sites of the Lodges.

In the meantime the development of the landscape around Bolton Abbey was determined by the monastic influences of the Augustinian Canons to whom Alice de Romillie had granted the site for their new priory at Bolton in 1155. It was not until after the dissolution of the monastery in 1539 that the two estates, Barden and Bolton, were united under the hereditary founder and patron of the priory, Henry Clifford, first Earl of Cumberland.

---

18 Raistrick, A. (1991) Article: *Forests of the Dales* reprinted in *Arthur Raistrick's Yorkshire Dales,* Lancaster, Clapham: Dalesman Publishing Company.
19 Origin ME from O Fr: *agist* (lodging) or take in and feed for payment, OED
20 Victoria County History, Yorkshire, Vol I (London 1907, repr. 1974)
21 Kershaw, Ian, (1973), *Bolton Priory. The Economy of a Northern Monastery 1286-1325*, Oxford University Press

# 2
# Barden Tower

HISTORY AND ARCHITECTURE
Arnold Pacey

*Denis Flanders, 1947*

**Construction and reconstruction at the tower**

Barden Tower originated as one of several lodges within the medieval Forest of Barden, but while most lodges were vaccaries or livestock farms, this was a place where the Cliffords and their guests could stay when hunting in the forest. At the end of the fifteenth century, it was developed by Henry, 10th Lord Clifford, as a more ample residence that could be used all year, not just in the season when hunting was to be enjoyed, and he appears to have preferred to live here than in what was supposedly his main residence, Skipton Castle.

According to Stephen Moorhouse,[22] Henry Clifford began to develop Little Park around

---

22 S. Moorhouse, 'The medieval parks of Yorkshire: function, contents and chronology', in *The Medieval Park*, ed. Robert Liddiard, Windgather Press, 2007, pp.99, 119, 122-3.

the lodge in 1485.[23] At one time it was said that construction of Barden Tower itself came later, and was spread over a ten-year period between 1496 and 1506.[24] The chapel and 'priest's house' just to the south of the main building is quoted by the same authorities as having been built in 1515-17, but evidence will be cited below which implies a somewhat different view.

Barden Tower was attacked and ransacked during the rebellion known as the Pilgrimage of Grace in 1536, following which repairs were necessary. Seventy years later, in 1606-7, Earl Francis Clifford employed a team of twenty wallers and carpenters to make alterations.[25] The tower suffered serious damage during the Civil War following which extensive repairs were put in hand by Lady Anne Clifford in 1657-9. What remains of the building today therefore shows evidence of many repairs and alterations.

When scaffolding was erected around the building twenty years ago to allow conservation work to be carried out, a detailed record of all the evidence of alteration was made by archaeologists.[26] The report which follows does not repeat that analysis, but rather discusses some points to do with architecture that may cast new light on the history of the site.

## The late fifteenth century building and its affinities

Barden Tower is so called because Henry Clifford chose to build his residence in the form of a tower house. In some tower houses, such as Hellifield Peel, Bolling Hall (Bradford), or Yanwath Hall (in Westmorland but near Penrith), one wing was constructed as a defensible tower, other rooms being in a conventional one- or two- storey range. In other tower houses, such as Harewood Castle, a late fourteenth-century building further down the Wharfe valley, the whole residence took the form of a tower.[27]

Barden Tower may be said to belong with this second kind of tower house, although it has almost none of the military features of many of them, such as the corner turrets at Harewood. Instead, the structure erected for Henry Clifford was a house of three high storeys with the principal room on the first floor, large windows facing south, and a stair turret projecting on the north side. Lady Anne Clifford referred to the big first-floor room as the 'Great Chamber' (see Figure 1, which is a schematic plan, not to scale). Although the building is a ruin, considerable detail can be observed making it possible to mark the position of ceiling beams by noting the holes in walls where the ends of the timbers were supported.

In the centre of the south wall was a projection of which only foundations survive. This appears to have been a large bay window – some refer to it as an oriel – with lights on three sides. It would have commanded excellent views over part of Little Park. The moulded jamb of one of its windows survives attached to the south wall of the building. What is also of significance is that the opening from the Great Chamber took the form of a four-centred arch, and there was a similar arch below opening into the ground floor of the bay window.

---

23 S. Moorhouse, 'Anatomy of the Yorkshire dales: decoding the medieval landscape', in *Yorkshire Archaeological Society Occasional Paper No. 3*, 2003, pp.343-8.
24 Richard T. Spence, *The Shepherd Lord of Skipton Castle*, Smith, Settle, 1994, pp.35-40.
25 Richard T. Spence, *Skipton Castle and its Builders*, Skipton, 2002, pp.77, 90.
26 S. Moorhouse, 'Anatomy of the Yorkshire dales', as in note 2 above.
27 Peter Leach and Nikolaus Pevsner, *The Buildings of England, Yorkshire, the West Riding, Leeds, Bradford and the North*, Yale University Press, 2009, p.298 has floor plans for Harewood Castle.

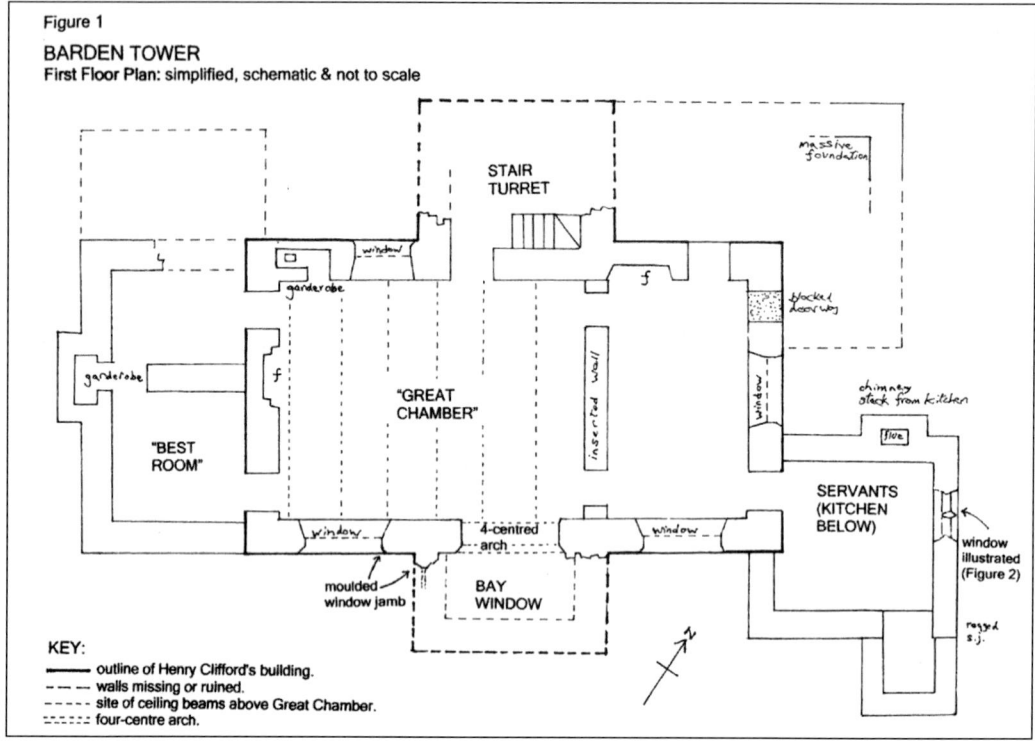

## Connections with church building projects

The detail of arches and the bay window jamb at Barden Tower suggests affinities with other building projects in which Henry Clifford was involved, including contemporary alterations to Addingham church. This has been explained in an unpublished history in the church's archives.[28] Because of the difficulty of consulting this, the relevant passage is quoted here in full:

> Inside St. Peter's Church in Addingham, on the north side of the nave, is a shield carved in wood at the foot of one of the wall-posts or brackets supporting the roof. It displays an unorthodox miscellany of heraldic devices... including the [Vipont] rings or 'annulets' from the Clifford [arms]...
>
> The member of the Clifford family who took an interest in Addingham church during this period was Henry, 10th Lord Clifford, often called the 'Shepherd Lord'. He is known for his generous gifts to many abbeys, priories and local churches, including Bolton Priory, but also Eshton Priory, Shap Abbey, Mount Grace Priory and Guisborough Priory. It is thought that he helped pay for building the tower of Carleton church on the other side of Skipton and it would have been typical of him to have paid for improvement of the church at Addingham also. Some architectural detail at Addingham church is closely similar to work that Henry Clifford had in hand at Barden Tower, six miles up the river, where building work was proceeding on the tower itself during the 1480s and '90s and until 1506, and where a chapel was built 1515-17.

28 *The church site at Addingham from the seventh century down to the Reformation* (with a history of the church building from its construction in the 1150s). Typescript dated 2010 in St. Peter's Church archives.

An example of similar workmanship at the two sites is the stonework for a late medieval window, complete with holes for glazing bars, which is re-used near the top of the tower at Addingham.[29] These jambs have the same mouldings as a former oriel or bay window at Barden Tower...

Within the church the three arches separating the nave from the north aisle are unusual by comparison with other local churches in being four-centred and lacking capitals. But four-centred arches of similar stripped-down appearance are to be seen in Barden Tower framing openings from the main body of the tower into [the former bay window]...

The passage continues by mentioning a rector of Addingham, Leonard Vavasour, in whose time the work on the church was done, and then resumes by saying that the similarities between arches and window mouldings at Addingham and Barden: "make it seem possible that Henry Clifford sent builders he had employed at Barden Tower to work on improvements that he and Leonard Vavasour had decided on for St. Peter's Church."

It also seems likely that Henry Clifford, at the very end of his life, joined with Richard Moone of Bolton Priory in a second phase of work at the church which comprised adding a north aisle to the church with the three plain four-centred arches previously mentioned.

## Lady Anne's work at Barden

Barden Tower had been in good order before the Civil War, but in 1644 soldiers stripped the lead roofs, leaving locals to think the building was abandoned and could be quarried for any building materials they needed.[30] This situation continued until a contract for repairs to Barden Tower was signed on 2 June 1657 by Lady Anne herself and two stone masons named as Thomas Day, father and son.[31] The work to be done included repair of the chapel as well as the main tower building and was supposed to be completed by the autumn.

The job proved to be more extensive than first envisaged, and was not completed until 1659. One reason was that, instead of merely repairing the building, Lady Anne decided on some extensions and improvements. This applies particularly to the small east wing which housed a kitchen and probably accommodation for servants. At the other end of the building, there was a first-floor room in the south-west corner that Lady Anne improved and then referred to as the 'Best Room' when she had guests to stay in 1660 and 1663.[32]

Architectural detail that tells us more is a window in the east wall of the kitchen wing, on the first floor. It has hollow chamfers and other mouldings that are similar to windows in the chapel which date from 1515-17, but is not in its original position and may have been moved here during the repairs. On the floor above is a window pieced together from stone salvaged from older windows so that its lintel does not match the hollow chamfer on its jambs. The moulding made to go above it has label stops at either end decorated with a scroll pattern that is unusual in Wharfedale but common in the Halifax area and in a few places further north (Figure 2). Other details at Barden suggest quite strongly that, before

---

29 I am indebted to Alison Armstrong for pointing out the similarity of mouldings in the two places and for recording the example at Addingham.
30 Richard T. Spence, *Lady Anne Clifford*, Alan Sutton Publishers, 1997, pp.130-1.
31 The contract was found by T. D. Whitaker among papers at Skipton Castle and a transcript was published in his *History and Antiquities of the Deanery of Craven*.
32 D. J. H. Clifford (ed.), *The Diaries of Lady Anne Clifford*, Stroud: Alan Sutton, 1990, pp.146-7, 162.

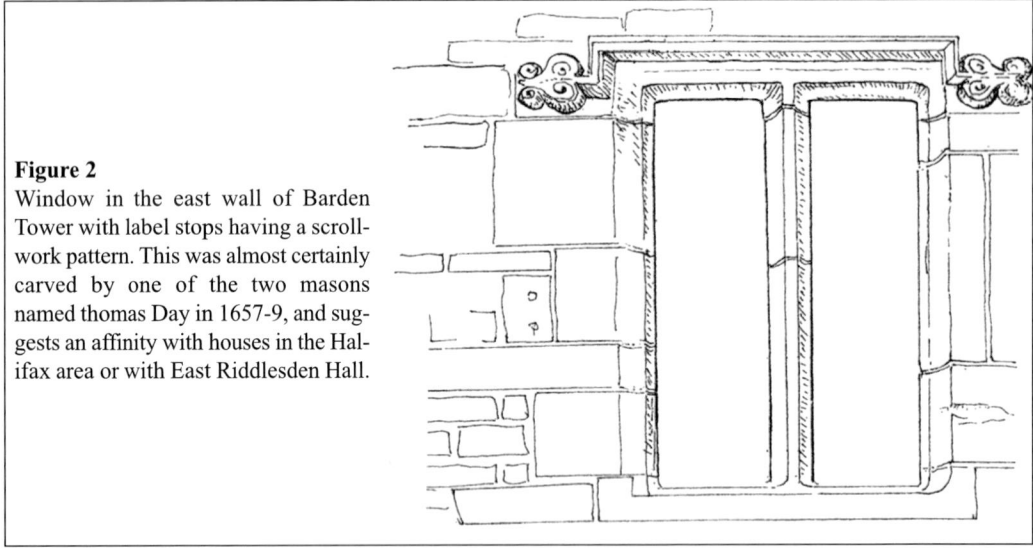

**Figure 2**
Window in the east wall of Barden Tower with label stops having a scroll-work pattern. This was almost certainly carved by one of the two masons named thomas Day in 1657-9, and suggests an affinity with houses in the Halifax area or with East Riddlesden Hall.

being employed by Lady Anne, the two masons named Day may have worked on East Riddlesden Hall near Keighley, which was rebuilt in the 1640s by James Murgatroyd, a Halifax clothier.

There are stories of a dispute about a nominal rent owed by Murgatroyd to Lady Anne. Both were forthright characters, and when Lady Anne decided to make up the quarrel by inviting Murgatroyd to dinner, they discovered they had a lot in common.[33] Both were enthusiastic builders, and it seems highly likely that they recommended stone masons and other craftsmen to one another. The two Thomas Days, and a certain Jonathan Gledhill,[34]

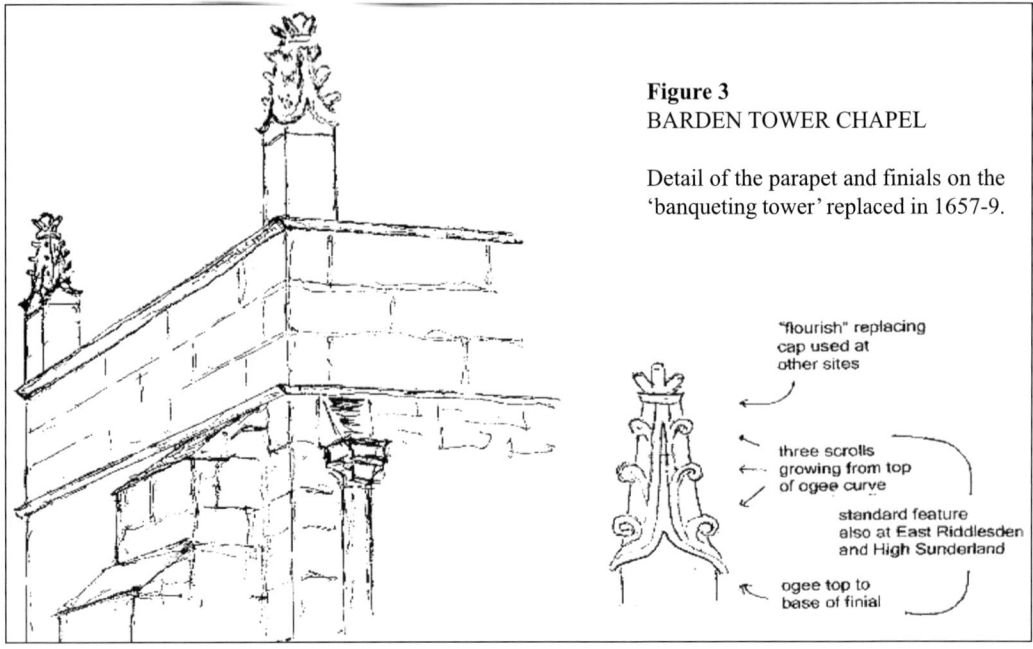

**Figure 3**
BARDEN TOWER CHAPEL

Detail of the parapet and finials on the 'banqueting tower' replaced in 1657-9.

"flourish" replacing cap used at other sites

three scrolls growing from top of ogee curve

standard feature also at East Riddlesden and High Sunderland

ogee top to base of finial

were probably among the craftsmen recommended to Lady Anne by Murgatroyd, and it seems likely that the Days had worked for Mugatroyd at Riddlesden.

Among other work done by the two Days at Barden, they made a new parapet and finials for the little tower attached to the chapel. The body of each finial shows close similarities with finials at East Riddlesden Hall, which may in turn be derived from finials on a house near Halifax named High Sunderland (now demolished). The main body of each finial at Barden, with three small projecting scrolls, is almost identical with examples at these two places, but the cap of the finial is different, and may be an invention of the Days (Figure 3).

## Barden Tower chapel

The chapel is located just to the south of Barden Tower as part of a block which also contains a 'priest's house' and a small tower that might be mistaken for a miniature church tower rising from above the chapel porch (Figure 4). There is a room with large windows on the top floor of the tower and a small kitchen with a bread oven on the floor below. The building seems to be designed to serve the sixteenth century fashion for dining in lofty rooms whose windows commanded good views.[35]

The kitchen storey in this 'banqueting tower or 'belvedere' is connected to the priest's house by a large room with a beamed ceiling known as the Oak Room. This is at first-floor level above a lobby at the west end of the chapel and seems once to have included (or given access to) a gallery looking down into the chapel.

The porch leading into the chapel, which occupies the ground floor of the banqueting tower, has very thick walls and a barrel-vaulted ceiling. The doorway from the porch into the chapel opens into the lobby below the Oak Room and there is a vestry opposite on the north side. The chapel itself has tall mullioned windows in the east and south walls and a low-pitched roof supported by transverse beams. Joists connecting the main beams support the boards which carry the lead roof covering, and divide the ceiling into square compartments. These give the roof the appearance of a Tudor panelled ceiling, but without the decoration common on such ceilings.[36]

The beamed ceiling of the Oak Room is a continuation of the chapel roof, but the roof beam above the partition between the room and the chapel has elaborate mouldings and nail-head decoration. The beam now appears merely as the head of the partition, but probably has this decoration because it originally served as a lintel above the opening made for the probable gallery. The purpose would have been to allow Henry Clifford and his family to hear Mass from the comfort of the Oak Room (with its fireplace) while his servants and farm labourers attended on floor level in the chapel. After this gallery opening was blocked by a partition, the west end of the chapel had a rather blank appearance (Figure 5), at one time relieved by two hatchments, one commemorating a Duke of Devonshire who had the

---

33 D. J. H. Clifford (ed.), as above, p.102. This editor assumes that the dinner was at Appleby Castle, but it was more probably held in Skipton Castle. Its date is not clear from the diary, but could be 1650.
34 Blake Tyson, 'Identifying... masons' marks', *Vernacular Architecture*, 25, 1994, p.12.
35 S. Moorhouse, 'The medieval parks of Yorkshire: function, contents and chronology', in *The Medieval Park*, ed. Robert Liddiard, Windgather Press, 2007, p.119.
36 Arnold Pacey, *Panelled ceilings and church roofs*, 2010, (now out of print).

chapel restored in the 1860s. Apart from the one beam with nailhead decoration, other ceiling beams in the Oak Room and chapel have simple chamfers, and joists have roll mouldings.

**The date and history of the 'banqueting tower'**

Stephen Moorhouse cites building accounts which show that the chapel at Barden was built in 1515-17, and it is usually assumed that the whole block, which includes the priest's house, is of that date.

However, further examination of the chapel porch and tower above reveals a more complicated history. The structure is of three storeys with windows whose lights have three-centred arched heads and hollow-chamfered mullions on the top floor.

On the floor below are smaller rectangular windows, two on the south elevation and one each facing east and west. Level with the lintels of these windows there is a change in the masonry of the walls, with roughly squared blocks of stone in the wall lower down, but more elongated blocks above. The latter are often roughly finished and with rubble introduced in places (e.g. on either side of the top window). At the top of the tower, the parapet is of much neater seventeenth century ashlar which (with the finials) can be attributed to the two masons named Thomas Day in 1657-59.

Apart from these three different qualities of walling (summarised in Figure 6), there are the differences in window mouldings. The top-floor windows with hollow-chamfered mullions match the windows of the chapel and are certainly of 1515-17. However, the jambs and lintels of the small windows have a more complex moulding which is similar to mould-

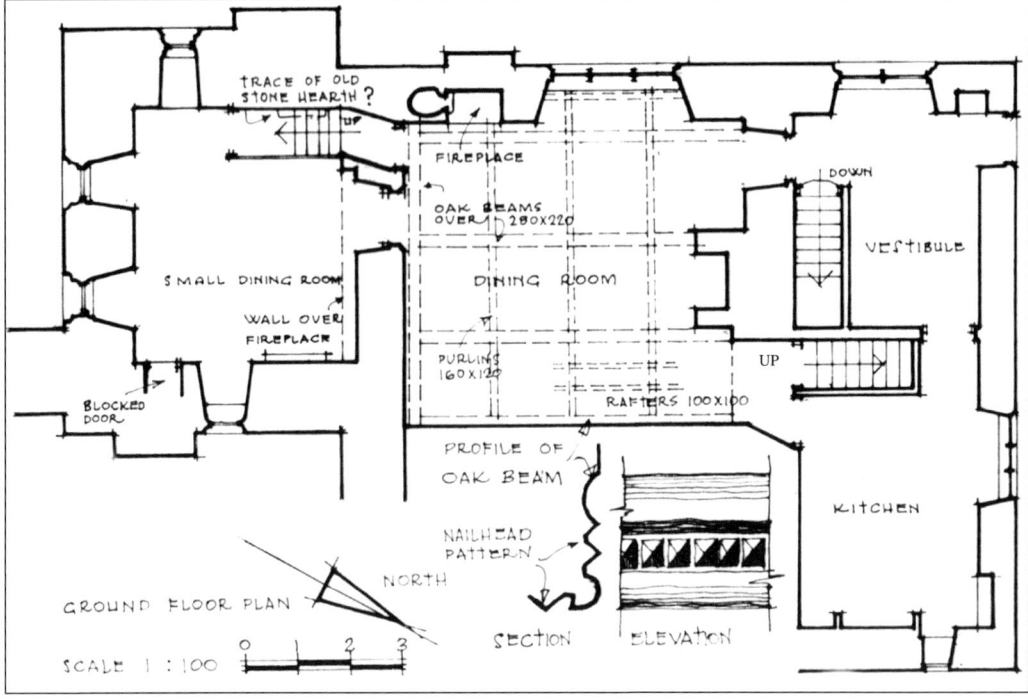

**Figure 4**
CHAPEL AT BARDEN TOWER and the Banqueting Tower or Belvedere, plan by Brian Moxham, UWFS.

ings on parts of the main building of Barden Tower (and on a fragment in Adddingham church presumed to be by Henry Clifford's masons). This suggests that the small rectangular windows, and the walls in which they are set, belong to an earlier phase of construction overlapping with the time when Barden Tower itself was being built, that is 1496-1506.

A more complicated picture emerges when the west side of the base of the tower is examined, particularly where it meets the west wall of the chapel (Figure 6).

Here are some joints in the masonry (marked on the plan, Figure 4) which are difficult to interpret. However, they could mean that parts of the west wall of the chapel were built before even the part of the banqueting tower with window mouldings that seems to date from 1496-1506. The question therefore arises as to whether there was an earlier building on the site of the chapel. Other indications of it are the small blocked window in between the two south windows of the chapel and the heavy plinth under the east window. Both details are marked on the plan in Figure 4. A more detailed survey and fabric analysis is needed to be sure, but it begins to look as though the chapel built in 1515-17 is on the site of an earlier building.

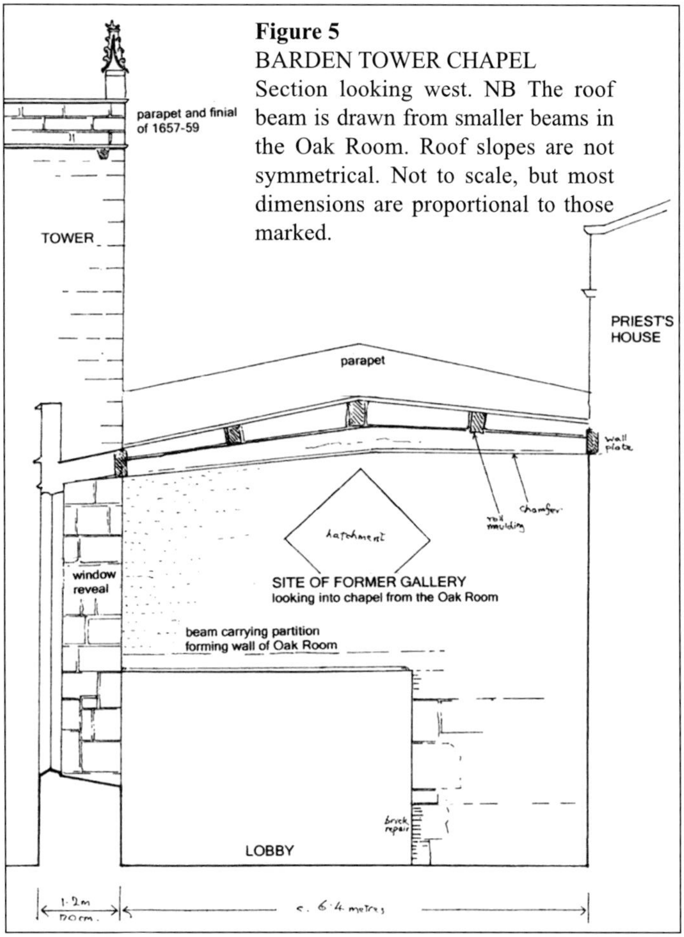

Returning to the porch which leads into the chapel and the tower above, there has been subsidence of the foundation at the south-east corner, and buttresses have been constructed at an unknown date to prevent the problem from developing further. The head of the arched doorway into the porch has been slightly distorted by the subsidence, making the arch flatter than intended, and there is a (repaired) crack rising from near ground level up to the left-hand jambs of both first and second floor windows.

What also needs to be noted is the exceptional thickness of walls at the base of the tower. At 1.85m (6 feet), the west wall of the porch is thickest, but the east wall measures 1.65m. The north and south walls, which are penetrated by doorways, are of the same thickness as the south wall of the chapel, 1.20m (just less than 4 feet). The thick east and west walls

**Figure 5**
BARDEN TOWER CHAPEL
Section looking west. NB The roof beam is drawn from smaller beams in the Oak Room. Roof slopes are not symmetrical. Not to scale, but most dimensions are proportional to those marked.

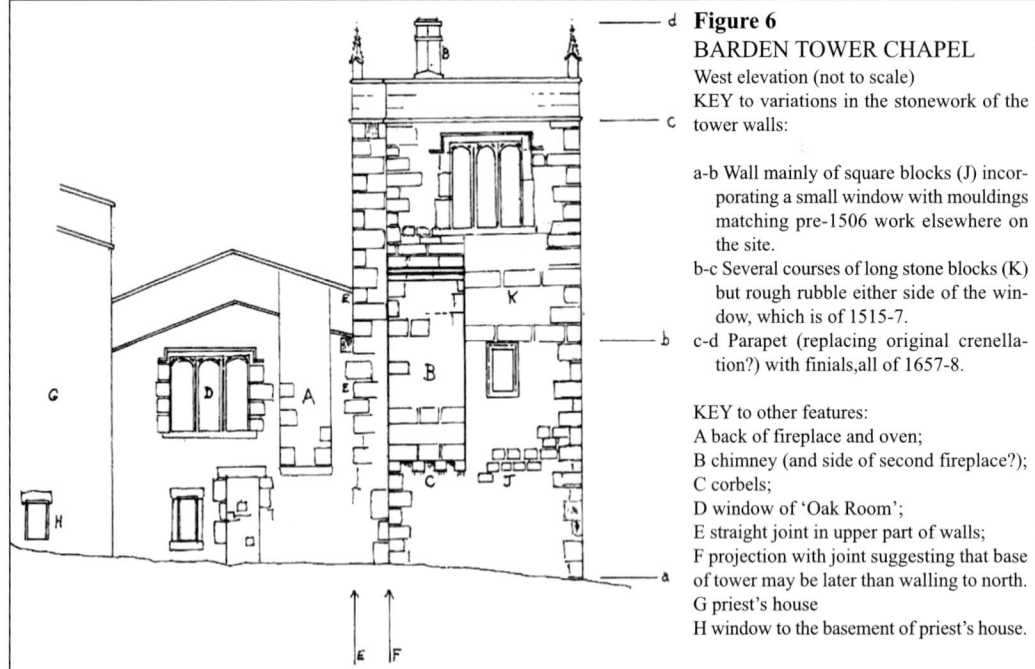

**Figure 6**
BARDEN TOWER CHAPEL
West elevation (not to scale)
KEY to variations in the stonework of the tower walls:

a-b Wall mainly of square blocks (J) incorporating a small window with mouldings matching pre-1506 work elsewhere on the site.
b-c Several courses of long stone blocks (K) but rough rubble either side of the window, which is of 1515-7.
c-d Parapet (replacing original crenellation?) with finials, all of 1657-8.

KEY to other features:
A back of fireplace and oven;
B chimney (and side of second fireplace?);
C corbels;
D window of 'Oak Room';
E straight joint in upper part of walls;
F projection with joint suggesting that base of tower may be later than walling to north.
G priest's house
H window to the basement of priest's house.

support the barrel vault which forms the ceiling of the porch, and the evidence of the external stonework is that the thick walls and barrel vault belong to the same phase in construction as the small rectangular windows with mouldings likely to date from 1496-1506.

## Possible explanations of early fabric on the chapel site

Although some church porches of the period had stone barrel vaults, e.g. at Featherstone and Kirkby Malham, the combination of this feature with the unusually thick walls suggests another affinity, namely with some of the smaller tower houses and bastles of northern England, at least one of which was well known to Henry Clifford.

Following the Wars of the Roses, the Clifford family estate at Skipton and Barden had been confiscated by the king (Edward IV) because the family had been on the wrong side in the war – the Lancastrian side. To avoid attracting the king's attention, Henry Clifford had lived as inconspicuously as possible, allegedly working as a shepherd in the East Riding, but at one stage he is also said to have 'gone into hiding' at Yanwath Hall in Westmorland.[37] The latter survives as a large farmhouse with a fifteenth century housebody, but incoporating an impressive fourteenth century pele tower with a barrel-vaulted ground floor room.[38]

One hypothesis might be that Clifford had this building in mind when he was planning the banqueting tower at Barden and wanted a tower with a similar vaulted ground floor. It could even be that, when Clifford started building at Barden, he did not at first envisage the very large tower house that he ultimately erected, but was thinking in terms of the smaller

---
37 Richard T. Spence, *The Shepherd Lord of Skipton Castle*, Smith Settle, 1994, p.14.
38 I have examined this building in person, but it is well described by Pevsner, *The Buildings of England, Cumberland and Westmorland*, Penguin, 1967, p.299.

# BARDEN TOWER

type represented by Yanwath Hall. Having made some progress in building that, Clifford may have changed his mind and decided to construct a tower house of the larger type represented by Harewood Castle, while adapting what he had already built as the chapel, priest's house and banqueting tower.

This, of course, is speculation, but explanation is needed for the irregularities and changes in masonry observed in the chapel block. It would also be helpful to know more about what buildings existed on the site before Clifford began his project. It seems that there was a large barn, of which one arch, presumably from a doorway, survives in isolation to the north of the tower. This was once attached to a small house which appears in a nineteenth century painting.

It is also thought that the wall running north from the east end of the chapel, incorporating a garderobe, may survive from the courtyard wall of an earlier building.[39] Nothing is definitely known as to whether there was a house adequate for Henry Clifford to stay when he first took over the site in 1485, and where he might have lived while his great tower house was under construction. If there was no such house, some kind of building, perhaps on the site of the priest's house and chapel may have been among the first things he had built.

## Summary and conclusions

The history of Barden Tower has been written mainly by historians, such as Richard Spence, or by archaeologists, for whom the surrounding park is of very special interest. The approach adopted in this report is instead based on architectural history and raises questions about what other buildings may be related to various aspects of Barden Tower in design, detail or workmanship, including other tower houses, churches to whose building Henry Clifford contributed, and gentry houses known to Lady Anne Clifford and her masons.

---

39 Oral information from Stephen Moorhouse, 27 June 1992.

Attention has also been given to differences in architectural detail which help identify different phases in construction. This has been used to develop an understanding of the chronology of the site that can summarized as follows:

In **1485**, with the death of Richard III, Henry Clifford regained possession of the site after it had been held by the Crown for some years, and soon began laying out Little Park. Evidence of stonework in the chapel complex suggests that he may have initiated some building there too, but a much more detailed survey and fabric analysis is needed to elucidate this.

**1496-1506** is usually accepted as the period when the great tower house was under construction. It was probably during or just after this period that masons who had worked here were sent to help with alterations at Addingham Church (with a second phase of work there following in the early 1520s).

**1515-17** is the period of construction usually cited for the chapel, priest's house and banqueting tower, but the building accounts do not seem to specify exactly what was built in those years. The larger and higher windows all have mullions with hollow chamfers and other detail consistent with this date, but several small windows low down in the structure seem to be earlier, as shown in the plan by Brian Moxham.

After Henry Clifford's time there were repairs to the buildings after 1536, alterations in 1606-7, and then Lady Anne's repairs and alterations in 1657-9.

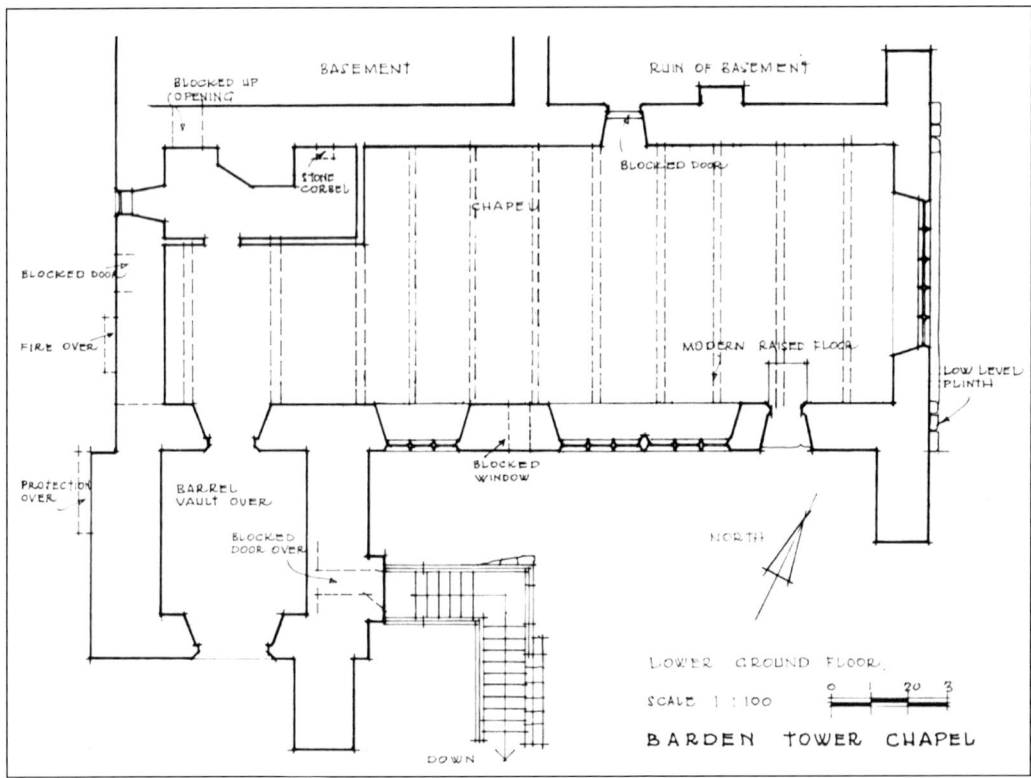

*The Chapel at Barden Tower and the Banqueting Tower or Belvedere. Ground Floor plan by Brian Moxham.*

# BARDEN TOWER

## Banqueting Tower and the Chapel by Brontë Bedford-Payne

Photographs show how the first floor entrance to this little tower was blocked at an unknown date for domestic convenience, and re-opened for access to the new restaurant in the Priest's House during the 1990s. The stone staircase is an addition to

*The entrance to Henry Clifford's chapel, through the original barrel-vaulted ground floor of the little tower, or belvedere.*

*The large, south facing window overlooks the medieval gardens laid out as part of the landscape associated with the banqueting tower.*

the medieval building: it is also of unknown date, possibly built by the Burlingtons in the eighteenth century, and may have been built at the same time as the two massive buttresses now shoring up the walls of the tower and the chapel. Many alterations and restorations took place in the 1860s when the 7th Duke of Devonshire was engaged in extensive improvements for the estate, and the rebuilding of many of his farmhouses and barnyards.

This photograph shows the bare, stripped interior of the chapel after it was abandoned as a place of worship in 1983. On the west wall can be seen one of two shadows showing where funeral hatchments were hung; these are now in the Boyle Room at Bolton Abbey.(a hatchment is a diamond shaped board on which the coat of arms of a deceased person is achieved).

33

BARDEN IN WHARFEDALE, THE PLACE AND ITS PEOPLE

**Heraldry depicted on the hatchments formerly hung in the chapel at Barden Tower.**
One hatchment is for William Spencer, the 6th Duke of Devonshire 1790-1858 who was a bachelor, therefore the whole the background is painted black.

The blazon is: Quarterly of 4
1 and 3 sable, *three bucks heads, caboshed argent* for Cavendish
2 *gules and argent a bend embattled* for Burlington
4 *checky or and azure, a fess gules* for Clifford.
The motto, *Cavendo Tutus* reads SAFE THROUGH CAUTION.
And the shield is set within the words HONI SOIT QUI MAL I PENSE.

The other hatchment, also quartering the arms of Cavendish and Burlington, but omitting Clifford, is for the 7th Duke of Devonshire 1808-91, and for his wife, Lady Blanche Howard who died prematurely in 1840. It was during the lifetime of the 7th Duke that major restorations of the chapel were undertaken and, in 1860, furnished to seat 100 people.[40]

The Cavendish crest is of a serpent nowed, fanged and resting on a wreath argent and sable, surmounted by a dexter-facing helmet (silver with gold bars), mantled. A ducal coronet surmounts the shield. The supporters are antlered stags, collared roses azure and argent.

---

40 Watkins, Peter (2005) *Beamsley Hall*, p63. Otley: Smith Settle.

## BARDEN TOWER

From the vestry at the west end of the chapel, a short tunnel leads into the cellar of the adjoining 'Priest House'. Folklore has it that Henry Clifford was an amateur astronomer, who spent many hours studying the stars from the roof of his belvedere, and that he learned from and shared his interest with the monks at Bolton Priory, several miles away down the valley… and that he travelled to the Priory by means of a secret tunnel… but was the reality that he simply disappeared down the stone steps still leading from what is now the kitchen of the Priest House into the cellar, and from there through the short tunnel into his chapel? From here, he could have reached the open air through the chapel's barrel-vaulted entrance and then have gained access to his belvedere by means of the outer doorway on the first floor, using a wooden ladder since there was no other means of access. There being no stone staircases within the tower, the further use of wooden ladders would have enabled him to gain access to the roof of the chapel or to the banqueting room with its large, south-facing window from which to study the stars (see plan on page 32).

This idea may seem very far-fetched but it is offered as an explanation of the folklore. Recording of the Chapel and Priest House by members of the Upper Wharfedale Field Society took place in 1989. The full report and all measured drawings are retained by the UWFS and also lodged with the YVBSG.

# 3
# Routeways

**Introduction to Routeways**

Feelings of anticipation, of curiosity and a sense of adventure can be aroused in the hearts and minds of travellers as they approach and then set foot upon ancient pathways or tracks, sunken green lanes and hollow ways. In the following chapter I hope to show how, through a period spanning maybe two thousand years, man has found a way to travel through Barden.

The very use of the word *through* implies that one is being led in a certain direction, and so it is, when looking at the map of Barden the roads can be seen to follow the flow of the river in a north-south direction. Walking along the river bank, or driving along the roads on either side of the river Wharfe between Burnsall and Barden Bridge, one is travelling established routeways through an area which has almost certainly been inhabited since the Bronze Age.

A network of roads is not a feature of Barden. It is only at the confluence with a major tributary stream from Howgill that the road on the east side of the river branches; this branch then follows the tributary towards its source and the watershed between Wharfedale and Nidderdale, while the main routeway continues on its way south towards the only bridge. At Watergate, the road is joined by a narrow lane from settlements around The Laund, Bolton Park and Storiths, while the road goes steeply down the hill to Barden Bridge where it crosses the river. It then climbs steeply through a deep hollow way which passes Barden Tower before joining the B6160 road from Burnsall. From here, the road continues up Cinder Hill before it divides, one branch leading over Black Park to Skipton and the other continuing down the valley to Bolton Priory and Ilkley. Old stonework, uncovered beneath the present modern walls and banks, indicate that this important junction was in use before the building of the hunting lodge at Barden Tower in the late fifteenth century.

**A Roman Road and a River Crossing**

The valley of the river Wharfe would have provided a natural routeway between the Roman forts at Ilkley (Olicana) and Bainbridge (Virosidum) and so it is not surprising that scattered evidence of Roman presence has been found in places along this route, such as the discovery of fragments of Samian ware near Drebley,[41] as mentioned in Chapter 1. In 1940, Francis Villey, writing in *The Bradford Antiquary,* Vol. VIII, postulated that a Roman road could be traced on its route through Wharfedale. It is still possible to walk along an old footpath passing through Drebley, and to speculate on its origin in relation to the supposed Roman road.

---

41 Raistrick, Arthur, *Green Roads in the Mid-Pennines,* 1978, Moorland Publishing Company.

## ROUTEWAYS

This footpath links the farms between Burnsall and Barden Bridge, and was used by local people until cars became common in the mid-twentieth century. Parts of the path have become walled green lanes, such as the one along the Hagg lane near Drebley, and while passing through the hamlet of Drebley its surface remains in the original state of un-metalled bedrock. Where the lanes peter out, the route can be traced by following a line of stiles in the present field walls built across the old track in the eighteenth century. The track is shown as a double-dotted line on the OS maps 1896/1909. It is unlikely that this old way through Barden could ever have been other than a footpath, for there are no signs of hollow ways having been worn by wheeled vehicles or trodden by the feet of ponies, flocks of sheep or herds of cattle passing through the valley.

On reaching the point where Barden Bridge now stands, the trackway may have divided, one branch crossing the river by means of a ford. There are only two places between Burnsall Bridge and Barden Tower where the river is shallow enough to be crossed, either on foot or horseback, one place being via the stepping stones between Hough Mill and Drebley, and the other at the point where Barden Bridge now stands. A ford here would have been a well-used vital link between communities living on either side of the river, and for travellers passing through the valley. It is conjectured that, having crossed the river by this means, the Roman way may have led south-east, up the side of the valley where there is now a footpath until it reached what is now a walled lane leading to the settlements of Storiths and Hazlewood. From here, it was but a short distance until it joined the Roman road which passed between Elslack and Ribchester in Lancashire and York in the East.

A clue towards the existence of a ford lies in the place-name of the nearby farm a mile or so north-east of the bridge. Here, the Domesday Book tells us that the pre-conquest Saxon Thane, Gamall, had a manor house with a meadow, and it is here that a settlement has survived as the farmstead of Gamsworth or 'Gamall's wath'. The place-name derives from the Old English name *Gamall* and *vao* or *wath* Old Norse for a ford.[42] The approach would have been by a trackway (now a footpath) leading directly from the ford to the settlement; it can be traced by walking a short way upstream along the present road on the north bank and then through a short stretch of woodland until open fields are reached. Faint but unmistakeable traces of this trackway can be seen in certain lights or under snow from the opposite side of the valley where it can be seen rising significantly through the fields above the flood plain of the river as it approaches Gamsworth. It is seen as a faint flattening of a river terrace, crossed now by walls and a gateway built centuries after the old track went out of use.

The other branch of the 'Roman road' may have continued on the west bank of the river

---

42 A. H. Smith, *The Place-names for the West Riding of Yorkshire,* English Place-Name Society, Vol. xxxvi, part seven, 1958-9, Cambridge University Press.

towards Olicana, crossing Barden Beck at the place where a hollow way, bounded on one side by an early wall featuring many large field boulders, leads directly to where stones on the bank of the beck may represent an early crossing. These features are now almost indistinguishable beneath the nineteenth century aqueduct carrying water from Nidderdale to Bradford. Further field work is needed to reveal evidence to show how this trackway continued in a southerly direction towards Bolton Abbey and Ilkley.

**Barden Bridge by Arnold Pacey**
There has been a crossing of the River Wharfe at Barden for centuries, but it is not clear what form it took in early times. The river may have been a little wider and shallower, making a ford possible except when the river was in flood. But it cannot have been very satisfactory, and there was probably a timber bridge of some kind from an early date. When the bridge was out of use for several years in the 1670s, a boat was provided as a ferry.

From soon after 1600, there are references to a bridge at Barden in the records of the West Riding Quarter Sessions Court (now in the care of the West Yorkshire Archive Service, Wakefield). This court was responsible for the oversight of bridges on public roads throughout the Riding. The court records indicate that the bridge was rebuilt in 1659, probably at the insistence of Lady Anne Clifford. But like most other bridges over the Wharfe, this relatively new bridge was severely damaged by the great flood of September 1673, and was not rebuilt until 1676. The delay was caused partly by arguments about who should pay for the rebuilding –

# ROUTEWAYS

local landowners (i.e. the Cliffords) or the West Riding ratepayers.

At a session of the Quarter Sessions Court held in January 1674/5 at Wetherby, the magistrates agreed to spend £10 on the boat used as a temporary ferry, but referred the question of who should pay for the bridge itself to a higher court, namely the York Assizes(file QS1/14/1/8/2 in the court records at Wakefield). It was not until April 1676 that the decision of the Assizes was reported to the Sessions Court, this time meeting at Pontefract (file QS1/15/4/8/5):

> ...at the Yorks Assizes it was found that the said Ryding ought to Repair the same [bridge], whereupon it was then ordered that the inhabitants of the said westryding should repair the said bridge before Christmas... the Court now taking into serious Consideration doe think fitt & accordingly order That the sum of three hundred and fifty pounts be forthwith assessed upon the said Ryding... and this Court do hereby nominate... Christopher Lawson and Thomas Atkinson surveyors...

Throughout the Riding, therefore, there was a levy on parish rates, and a plaque was built into the parapet of the bridge (now at the eastern end) which was inscribed with the date and the comment: 'This bridge was repaired at the charge of the whole West Riding.'

The bridge was built by some of the same masons who had just completed the reconstruction of Ilkley Bridge, including Thomas Cockshott and Michael Geldart. It is similar to Ilkley Bridge in having three arches of which the centre one has a span of about 50 feet. But the two smaller arches are higher and wider than at Ilkley, and the cutwaters are carried up to parapet level to form pedestrian refuges alongside the roadway. These tall cutwaters supporting high arches give the bridge a bolder, more impressive appearance than any of the others on the upper Wharfe. It seems from the irregular appearance of the eastern abutment that the abutment of the 1659 bridge may have been partially retained in the new work.

*Mason Marks on the underside of the eastern arch.*

After the bridge was complete, there was a dispute about money between the masons who built the bridge, and the surveyors, Christopher Lawson and Thomas Atkinson. The masons claimed that they had not been paid all that was due to them, whereas the surveyors said they had spent the sum owing on their own expenses, and there were also accusations that both parties had been engaged in 'collusive accounting'. Eventually the court found in favour of the masons and ordered the surveyors to pay the full amount due to them (see court files QS1/19/5/6/3 and QS1/20/5).

The bridge has been very little altered since completion, and has apparently withstood all subsequent floods without sustaining serious damage. However, new parapets, higher than the old ones, were provided in the 1850s, and the road approaches on both sides were altered at the same time to avoid the sharp bends in the approach road that previously existed and to modify gradients slightly. The records at Wakefield include a plan for this work initially by Bernard Hartley, the West Riding surveyor.

The other early drawings of the bridge in the Wakefield records, also appended to this report, is by John Carr, later famous as an architect based in York. This drawing shows the bridge before the parapets were built higher, and also before the slope of the approach roads on either side was altered.

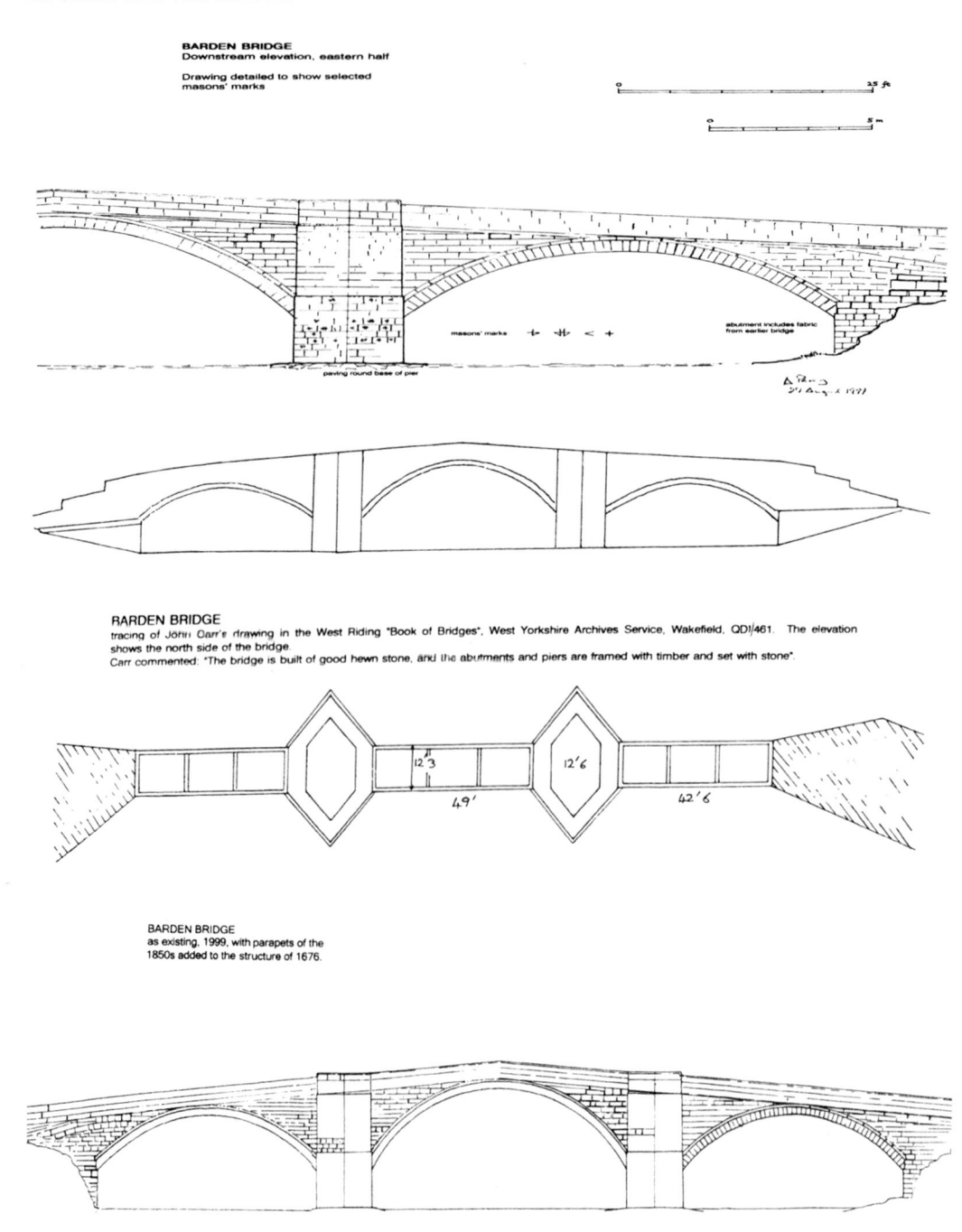

**BARDEN BRIDGE**
Downstream elevation, eastern half
Drawing detailed to show selected masons' marks

**BARDEN BRIDGE**
tracing of John Carr's drawing in the West Riding "Book of Bridges", West Yorkshire Archives Service, Wakefield, QD1/461. The elevation shows the north side of the bridge.
Carr commented: "The bridge is built of good hewn stone, and the abutments and piers are framed with timber and set with stone".

**BARDEN BRIDGE**
as existing, 1999, with parapets of the 1850s added to the structure of 1676.

# ROUTEWAYS

## A Packhorse way and the First Map[43]

Arthur Raistrick[3] has described how

> Packhorse ways differ from earlier patterns in their direct relation to the early economic and social life of the area they traverse, and in their intimate relation to the village pattern of the Dales. Packhorses and ponies were the prime form of transport for approximately five centuries; largely developed in monastic times they were only finally ousted from their important position by the transport revolution of the nineteenth century.

The packhorse or drovers' route through Barden was the 'Way unto Burnsall and Kettlewell and Buckden' marked on the estate map drawn in 1731 for the 3rd Earl of Burlington by Ed Beckwith and redrawn in 1778 by Mathew Oddie. The key to the map shows it as 'a horse-way or open road,' implying that it was not walled. It may still be traced in parts, starting from where the routeway came up the valley from Bolton through The Stank, and crossed Barden Beck by a ford which is now almost indistinguishable beneath a nineteenth century aqueduct carrying water from Nidderdale to Bradford. The presence of large field boulders in the base of the wall alongside this section of the track is an indication of the antiquity of the short hollow way which leads from the ford to a terrace, from which the present road (B6160) has been enclosed. The road then winds its way so closely between the houses and barns of Barden Scale that it is likely this small hamlet was an important 'stance' or stopping place for packhorse men,

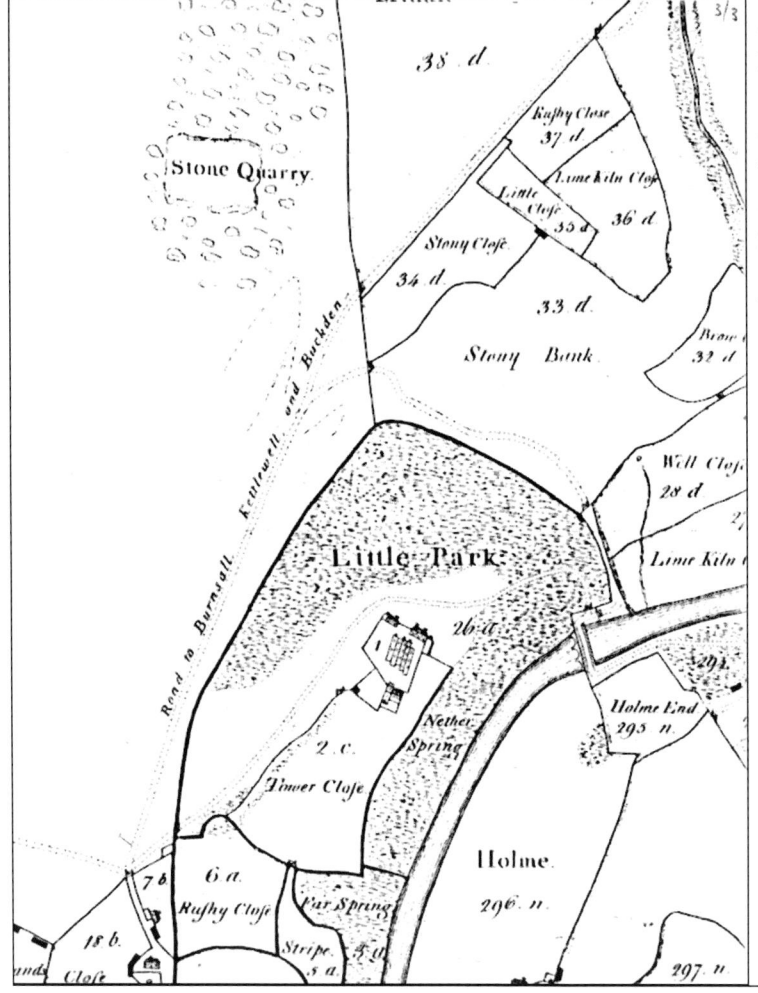

43 Section from the map of the Lordship of Barden in the West Riding of the County of York copied by Matthew Oddie in 1778, from a map drawn by Ed. Beckwith in 1731.

where their ponies could be loosed to graze overnight.

There is no documentary evidence for this supposition, and apart from mention in an estate survey of 1728 of 'a brewhouse occupied by Geo. D'Maine de Scale,' there are no other references to such in the leases held by successive generations of the Demaine family. They were the tenants who lived at The Scale when the horseway was in use. However, in 1665 George Demaine of Barden Scale in his will,[44] bequeathed 'to my son John Demaine all my instruments tools and instruments stencils wholefull belonging to my trade of Locksmith' and in 1696 this same John Demaine is listed in the estate lease book as having been a locksmith. Was he also a blacksmith and farrier? Whatever the truth, the fact remains that at no other point on the route are barns and houses so closely associated with the road as at Barden Scale.

Members of the North Yorkshire Vernacular Buildings Study Group (NYVBSG) surveyed the hamlet in 1997.[45] The report, published in their Bulletin the following year, indicates that the barns themselves may date from before 1750, and there appears to have been a major re-building around 1800. One member, Kate Mason, pointed out that there are many purpose built features in the barns, such as the use of stone setts or cobbles where horses were stabled and would have slipped if flags had been used. In the mid-nineteenth century the old farmhouse was extended, to include a yard and outhouses, rough dwelling accommodation, a wool store, a new cellar and brewery. At the same time a smithy was built onto the eastern side of the High Laithe, which was a thatched cruck barn.[46] Was this then, continuing a long tradition of wayside hospitality? The stone quarry from which the building stones for the Tower were hewn can be seen at the top left hand side of the map on page 41, while at the top right hand side, a section of the heavily wooded tributary stream of Gill Beck can be seen. Upon leaving The Scale, until a by-pass round the hamlet was built in the 1950s, the road followed the line of the old track, rising through a deep hollow way towards Broad Park, formerly The Great Park.

On reaching open moorland, traces of the packhorse track are now lost, although, according to Beckwith's map, it certainly skirted to the west of the Little Park surrounding Barden Tower. It would have been unthinkable to drive animals through the parkland around the old hunting lodge, the Lord's demesne, where they would have trampled and devoured crops belonging to him and his tenants; neither would travellers have passed through the private preserves of the Hunting Chase. It may have been for these reasons, concerned with the development of a Seigneurial[47] estate in Barden, that the old Roman road fell into disuse, while the new drove road opened high on the valley side. The wall enclosing the Little Park dictated the route followed by travellers between Barden Scale and the ford over the stream at Gillbeck.

Oddie's map shows that the packhorse way forked at the north-west corner of the Little Park, one section winding down towards Barden Bridge, and the other continuing

---

44 Borthwick Institute, York.
45 YVBSG Reports October 1997: 1547/ 1549/ 1552 Plans and drawings 1871 Chatsworth Estate Settlement
46 In 1952 This barn was dismantled and re-erected at Shibden Hall Museum , Halifax but was accidentally burned down shortly afterwards.
47 Seigneurial: land belonging to a feudal lord, or Lord of the Manor, OED.

northwards towards Burnsall. Apart from the presence of a gate still in its original position, field evidence does not support the map, and it is difficult to establish signs of the old track until a green lane is picked up in the region of the quarry at Stonybank, where a barn and a Keepers cottage were built in the early nineteenth century. Further on, an unmistakeable, broad terrace slopes down to ford the stream in Gillbeck. Here, on the north side of the beck, a large boulder lying across the hollow way may have been deliberately placed to discourage, or even to prevent the passage of packhorse traffic at a time when tolls were being introduced on newly constructed turnpikes, thereby enforcing their use. Indeed, such a road did exist as an alternative to the old packhorse road, for in 1801 John Dixon, a surveyor of roads, addressed a letter to Thomas Fentiman, Agent for the 5th Duke of Devonshire, in which he refers to 'the turnpike near Barden Tower'.[48]

*Club Nook, High Laithe in 2014.*

Beyond Gillbeck wood, it is again difficult to find any trace of the old road, partly due to afforestation which took place from 1815 onwards in the area marked Powson Park and partly due to the soft and, at times, boggy nature of the terrain; the track marked so clearly on the map has totally disappeared. Characteristically, this packhorse road, unlike a drove road passing through cultivated land, tended to follow a straight course, such as that shown crossing through Club Nook Bents at about 675 feet OD, where rough grazing would have been freely available, away from the enclosures at a lower level in the valley, with a line of water troughs along the same contour. The track is then shown hugging the walls between Peter Pasture and the High Closes (fields associated with the farms of Club Nook and Hole House) before reaching the gateway which opened into Drebley Thwaite. After this, until it reached the limit of the map, the track again followed a straight line, being joined at its furthest point, but still within the Thwaite, by a track from the hamlet of Drebley.

Clearly visible from a vantage across the valley above Hartlington, old packhorse tracks can be identified, descending from the high moorland, whence several hollow-ways lead steeply down the hillside towards Woodend Farm, Garrelgorm and Burnsall Fell. The abrupt, steep inclines of these hollow-ways are characteristic of many packhorse routes leaving or approaching villages, and on their way to and from watersheds.[49] Although the surface of these lanes is now characterised by an unusually heavy clutter of loose stones, indicating that they have been used as sled runs for extracting stone from the quarries on Barden or Burnsall Moors, they are deep, narrow and walled, and are likely to have originated as pony

---

[48] 'The Skipton to Pateley Bridge Trust' appears on the 1st Edn. Ordnance Survey Map for Barden, 1853, (see chapter 3).
[49] E.g. from Lofthouse in Nidderdale to Masham in Wensleydale, and from Kettlewell by Park Rash and Coverdale to Middleham.

tracks. At this point the routeway entered the parish of Burnsall, beyond the limits of Beckwith's map.

## New Road between Barden and Burnsall and the Moor Lanes

From surviving late eighteentth century correspondence concerning the re-routing of the way to Burnsall,[50] and from a map drawn for the Bolton Abbey estate dated 1806 it seems likely that, from this time onwards, new roads from Barden Tower to Burnsall on the west, and the Skipton to Pateley turnpike on the east side of the valley were in daily use. In the early decades of the nineteenth century, when the old packhorse road had probably gone out of use, four stone barns were built along the contour of this old route, namely, High Laithe, by Stonybank, belonging to Low Farm, High Laithe belonging to Club Nook, Top Laithe, belonging to Fold farm, Drebley, and New Laithe belonging to Drebley farm.

There is also an associated line of water troughs along the same contour as the barns. It may be significant that the only gate in the wall between that part of the Great Park labelled Powson Park, and Peter Pasture, which was part of Drebley Thwaite, lay directly on the route drawn for 'The Way Unto Burnsall and Kettlewell'. This gate no longer exists, for, in 1812 Drebley Thwaite was divided, new walls were built, and in 1823 Club Nook High Laithe was built on an older foundation, on the site of the former gateway.

Further evidence for the pressing need to divert traffic away from the old upland route are major changes which took place on the Bolton Abbey estate at the beginning of the nineteenth century: these changes were initiated by William Carr between 1789-1843, incumbent at Bolton Abbey and also agent for the 5th Duke of Devonshire. In 1812, at the time of enclosure and division of Powson Park and Drebley Thwaite, roughly 1,000 acres of woodland pasture were taken in hand as managed plantations of dense pine forest. Some acres were established in areas now known as Nelly Park and Hagg Wood Intake, through which the

---

50 Chatsworth Estate Settlement. Bolton MSS.

## ROUTEWAYS

packhorse route had passed. As already described all traces of the tracks have been lost.

It was not until the lifetime of the 6th Duke, William Spencer Cavendish, (1790-1858) that further major changes came over the Bolton Abbey estate, including the development of the roads and routeways in Barden. These survive today: they first appear on the 1st Edition of the Ordnance Survey map, which was surveyed in 1849-50.

It is likely that, over a period of maybe 150 years, between the death of Lady Anne Clifford in 1676, and the beginning of the nineteenth century, gradual infringements were made through the Little Park surrounding the increasingly deserted Tower. It must have been a slow, but steady process whereby several generations of local people and through travellers took short cuts, from Barden Scale down Cinder Hill to the bridge over the river, and hence, northwards towards the markets and fairs in Appletreewick and eastwards over the watershed to Pateley Bridge and Knaresborough in Nidderdale. Meanwhile, traders moving along the ancient upland route, to and from Burnsall and the north-west, through Threshfield and on towards Kirkby Lonsdale, continued as they always had done until a new road carried their traffic along a lower level in the valley, where they would begin to gain a nodding acquaintance with the people through whose land they passed.

Letters dating from between 1781 until 1801 have survived in the Chatsworth collection of manuscripts at Bolton expressing concern for the need to find and survey an appropriate route to replace Ed. Beckwith's old 'Way Unto Burnsall and Kettlewell'. Copies of these letters are shown below, together with a measured drawing of the proposed roads.

Sir,                                                                                                                  Barden, 23 June 1781
In order to give you a true estimate of the difference of the length of roads proposed thro' Broad Park we thought proper to measure them on Tuesday the 22nd inst, and we found it but very little. The length of that part going through the Hollow Car Hill is three hundred and one Roods one yard and the course of the upper part three hundred and one roods five yards. As the distance is so trivial we hope on consideration you'll find with respect to the length little remaining for a Dispute. As the Township seems to be divided with respect to the other particulars in favour of the upper...                   unsigned

                                                                                                                                 June 1781
Some of the Barden people have been to beg of me to represent to you that the whole township are unanimous about staking out the new road except two or three of the same troublesome persons who have raised all the former Opposition and Disturbance to this road. The road that the Township contends for is not the line that I had marked out, nor is it a Road which anybody had ever shewn me – but being shown, I do approve and adopt it in preference to my own line, both on account of ease and shortness, and consequently to be preferred *prima facie* both by the Duke, by his tenants and by the Traveller. But I understand that G. Demaine, G. Atkinson who determined never to think or act with their neighbours or like anybody else object to it on account of an inclosure of theirs that has been taken off the Park which this road will cut through without some satisfaction… This line that the old road (till this enclosure was made) always went – that it is not only shorter and easier, but that it will be made on account of the convenience of stones etc. far less by 2s a rood than any other way, and will be repaired at a less expense and require less repairs. That the situation for the Bridge is much more convenient and will render that too less expensive.

Will the Duke consent to thwart the wishes of the body of his own tenants, and the general public convenience by taking a more convenient line, or will he consent to a satisfaction; when more is due, the old road, having always gone that way, and the land of little value, while as I am told he has never permitted satisfaction to be taken in cases when the roads have been diverted through grounds of considerable value.

Dear Sir, it is for you to consider etc.    W. Baynes[51]

Sir,    Bolton, 4 July 1784

I've measured the intended road through Barden Park and find the difference in length to be 46 Roods. Viz. the low road is the shorter and will be made at considerably less expense. As to the bridge, I can't judge minutely, yet I think it will cost near 50 pounds. The higher road measures 374 Rood, the lower only 328 Roods and will be executed for far less money per Rood, which I think is a material object.

I am sir, your most obedient, humble servant,    Thos. Fentiman

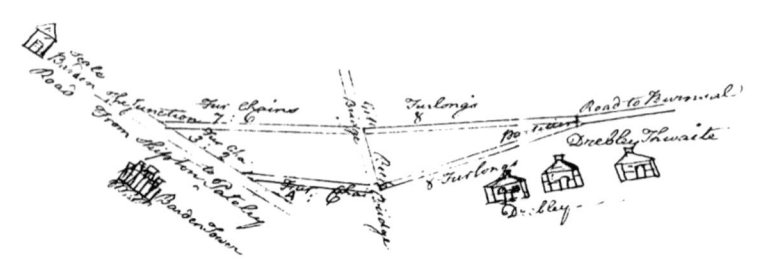

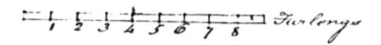

A Petition from the tenants of Barden to the Most Noble Duke of Devonshire to be relieved of the necessity of making the said private way into a public way for carts and carriages… it is almost impractible to form a road for carriages, and would probably cost a thousand pounds, which would greatly injure if not ruin many of your petitioners.

| | |
|---|---|
| A.Benson, …? | John Lister of Barden Tower Farm |
| Humphrey Ideson of Howgill | George Demaine of Barden Scale |
| John Holden of Eastwood Head | Henry Holme of Drebley |
| George Demaine of Littlegate Drebley | Joseph Wade of Applegarth, Drebley |
| George Demaine of Fold farm, Drebley | James Ward of Hough Mill or Holme farm |
| Francis Ward of Hough Mill (Miller) | |

The petition is not dated, but it must have been presented before 1793, when John Lister died.

Sir    Bolton, 24th 1801

At the request of James Ward, Geo Atkinson, Thos Atkinson, and George Demaine of Drebley, I write to inform you I have measured the road from Scale Lane Gate to Drebley Thwaite, where the new intended road will join it. I find the length of it to be 484 Roods. The new intended road

---

51 W. Baynes, the writer of the letter dated June 1781 had a 'vested interest' in the new roads, since he owned a corn mill in Embsay.

from the junction to the Turnpike near Barden Tower I find to be 389 Roods 5 yards, hence the difference is 94 Roods 2 yards. The above named farmers will undertake the new road to make at 3/6d per Rood, but the old road not under 5/-, so that the difference in making the roads will be £52.16s, valuing the bridge at Gillbeck on either thing equal. Besides, the new road will be more comfortable than the old, and of great service to the inhabitants of Drebley when they have occasion to go to the Mill or to Market.

I am sure, your obedient humble servant,                          John Dixon.

Thomas Fentiman was the Duke's Agent at Bolton Abbey, while John Dixon is presumed to have been the appointed surveyor.

The interest of these letters is compounded by the written views of those tenants whose lands would be affected when the proposed road was driven through their fields, and also by their anxieties over the cost of making such a road, especially where a bridge over Gillbeck was concerned. Hitherto a shallow stretch of the beck had been crossed by a ford, but if the new, more direct route was to be adopted for the growing needs of wheeled traffic, a stone bridge would be the only means of crossing over the steep sides of the gill.[52]

The new route being drawn up was to supersede the ancient way to Burnsall, and to pass from Barden Scale, down Cinder Hill past the Tower, and through the medieval apportionment of lands at Gillbeck, Club Nook, Hole House and Drebley Thwaite. The letters also indicate that there was a debate about the route of the road… should it have followed the line of the old packhorse road? It is interesting to consider the reasons for the eventual choice, based as it seems to have been on the shortest route and one that would be advantageous to farmers taking cart-loads from Drebley to and from Barden Bridge and thence to Hough Mill.

**Moor Lanes**

The farms of Low Farm, Club Nook and Drebley hamlet were then linked to the new road by means of specially constructed lanes. Where the settlement was on a steep hillside, as at Club Nook and Low Farm, (and at Gamsworth on the east side of the valley) the gradient on these lanes has been skilfully laid out to accommodate horse-drawn carts.

At Low House an un-walled lane winds diagonally up a sloping hillside between the farmstead and the Burnsall road. It connects with another, steeper lane, also un-walled, leading to high pastures adjacent to the remains of a medieval stone quarry at Stonybank, to a keeper's cottage and to a barn built in the vicinity of the old packhorse track.

At Club Nook, the lane is walled. In order to avoid a very steep incline, it takes a diagonal course, cutting through established enclosures, and crossing the foundation platform of an early barn. From its junction with the Burnsall road a walled green lane continues steeply up towards Club Nook High Side thus forming a funnel for driven sheep and cattle. These two lanes were probably constructed in 1823, at the same time as the tenant, Francis Atkinson, built a barn on his High Side with a shippon and provision for storing hay. His initials and the date are inscribed on a stone in the wall.

---

52 Over half a century later, in the spring of 1867 the bridge over Gillbeck was painted by the artist, Atkinson Grimshaw. The painting is entitled Ghyllbeck, and a copy of it can be seen in *The Yorkshire Dales, a view from the Millenium* compiled in 1999 by David Joy and Colin Speakman for Northern Books.

Because Hole House is situated relatively close to the new road to Burnsall, and on almost the same contour, there is no need for a lane. Access to the farmstead passes through a gateway in the wall of a small croft, and crosses over a length of level ground. At this farm there is no corresponding moor lane leading to high pastures, and there is no high barn.

Drebley Lane is long and walled. Unlike the lanes leading to other farms in Barden, it is relatively level, and leads to four dwellings in the hamlet. From its junction with the Burnsall road, but not exactly opposite, a walled green lane leads directly to the moor and to the high barns especially built for Fold Farm and Drebley Farm. These barns lie on the same contour as those for Club Nook and Low House Farm. This section of Drebley Lane was constructed parallel to the line of an earlier lane, shown on Oddie's map, which connected the hamlet with the old packhorse route. It would have been along here that carts were hauled when taking goods to market either up or down the dale, or to Barden Bridge on their way to Hough Mill. From 1812 onwards, after the division of Drebley Thwaite, the lane continued to serve its purpose as access to the allotments and the barns, and for driving flocks of sheep to and from their stinted grazing grounds on Barden moor, as it does today.

Until some time in the late nineteenth century the farm at Gamsworth was approached from the road between Howgill and Barden Bridge by means of a steeply inclined, walled lane which had been part of an important routeway to Hough Mill. This old lane still retains its grassy surface as it follows a sinuous line down the hillside from the cottage of High Gamsworth. The high, tapering walls stand on large boulders, themselves dating from medieval field clearances. The modern approach to Gamsworth rises from the farmstead and passes unwalled, at a gentler gradient through open fields, in the direction of Barden Bridge.

None of these access lanes are shown on Oddie's map of 1778 but they were established by the time the first edition OS map was published in 1853. The present-day approach to Gamsworth is not shown on the estate map of 1867 and I have not yet found the date when it first appears. These lanes are still in use; none have been surfaced with tarmac, and they require constant maintenance with gravel to repair the potholes which appear at intervals between outcrops of smooth bedrock.

Travelling north along the present road (B6160) as it winds its way up the valley between Barden Tower and Burnsall, it is possible to remain unaware of the bridge which crosses the deep ravine of Gill Beck. However, when peering over the parapet, water can be seen far below falling over a series of shallow cascades, the very steep sides of the gill being heavily wooded, with tangled blackberry bushes and ferns in the undergrowth. The road approaching the bridge curves round a bend at the boundary of Low House Farm, crosses over the gill and then ascends abruptly towards Club Nook Farm. As it does so, a massive stone revetment wall looms on the left, or the west side of the road, known to have been built at the same time as the bridge,[53] to prevent land slipping onto the highway from the edge of Nelly Park woodland. The remains of the approach to an old embankment can still be seen curving round on the east side of the road.

A postcard dated 14 September 1903[54] shows the old bridge as it was built at the beginning of the nineteenth century, when the proposed new road to Burnsall was surveyed by

---

53 Bolton Mss., Chatsworth Estate correspondence.
54 From the collection of Alan Stockdale, Burnsall.

*The bridge at Gill Beck, postcard dated 14 September 1903.*

John Dixon for the 5th Duke of Devonshire. It was this bridge which was painted by Atkinson Grimshaw in the spring of 1867. The postcard writer mentions that 'the photograph was taken about eight years ago' i.e. 1895.

By the end of the nineteenth century the bridge over Gill Beck no longer met the needs of a highway. It was narrow, having been constructed as an integral part of the road designed to replace the open 'horse way' on the edge of the moor, along which had passed trains of pack ponies and animals driven on the hoof. For the best part of a century, this new road and its bridge had met the growing needs of horse-drawn carts and others travelling along what was, at that time, a minor road of convenience, subsidiary to the turnpike on the opposite side of the valley. Meanwhile, the industrial revolution had taken place, bringing with it a demand for easier gradients and wider bridges.

Between 1903 and 1909 the surveyors for Skipton Rural District Council were corresponding with Alfred Downs, the Agent at Bolton Abbey for the 8th Duke of Devonshire,

*In the spring of 1857 the first bridge, with its lovely arched parapet in the style of a packhorse bridge, was painted by the Victorian artist Atkinson Grimshaw.
Reproduced in the 'Yorkshire Dales. A view from the Millennium', 1999.*

about plans for replacing the bridge. Specifications were drawn up, and by the 13 February 1906, it was proposed to 'pull down the present bridge and erect a new one a little lower down, so as to make the curve and gradient less dangerous.'

By the 18 May the same year it was proposed 'to use the old bridge below Barden Scale with additional masonry to make the arch higher.' (NB The new road bridge over Barden Beck had been built in 1897, in conjunction with the building of aqueducts for Bradford Corporation Waterworks. This note implies that dressed stone work, surplus from pulling

*The new bridge parapet can be seen at the top of the photograph behind the old bridge which is being demolished.*

*To the right this postcard, dated 1907, shows Ghyll Beck waterfall downstream from the bridge seen in the background.*

down the old bridge, had been kept in reserve and not destroyed as rubble.)

Another postcard[55] un-dated, shows the old bridge being dismantled, with the newly built bridge in the background 'a little lower down'. The correspondence and a plaque affixed to the side of the bridge confirm that it was built for Skipton Rural District Council in 1908.

---

55 From the collection of Alan Stockdale, Burnsall.

BARDEN IN WHARFEDALE, THE PLACE AND ITS PEOPLE

## A Turnpike: The Skipton to Pateley Bridge Trust, Watergate and Howgill as first shown on the 1st Edition Ordnance Survey map 1853

The main route up Wharfedale crossed Barden Bridge, and is shown on earlier maps such as that of 'Roads in the Craven Area', drawn by E. Bowen in 1756 and Thomas Jeffery's map of Yorkshire, drawn in 1775.

> Towards the end of the eighteenth century output from the lead mines around Appletreewick and Greenhow rose to levels of commercial significance; it was inevitable that a pressing need then arose for better routes for transporting the lead than had hitherto satisfied the old trains of packhorses. Ripples from the industrial revolution taking place in the great cities of the West Riding of Yorkshire and in Lancashire spread into remote valleys, causing landowners in small, rural communities, such as those in Barden, to reflect upon the opportunities which might become available to them, if only they could link their trade routes with those of great industrial entrepreneurs. No longer were their tenants to be dependant on the old feudal system and the social shelter of a great family, especially since the focus of their lives, and therefore the economy, had moved away from the medieval Forest on which they had hitherto depended for employment.
>
> It was in the landlords' interests to have roads capable of transporting goods to major routes and to the recently opened canal wharves in Skipton; they needed access to profitable markets where there was an increasing demand for coal, iron and lead as well as agricultural produce. Although the farmers' overriding concern appears to have concentrated on the cost to them of constructing the routeway, their need for better access to growing centres of population dependant on rural farm supplies was paramount, it was a time of more efficient and productive farming: the days of subsistence and local self-sufficiency were passing. Marketing their produce was vital and gave the farmers the means to buy goods such as flour, clothing, hardware, animal feeds and tools no longer produced locally.[56]

New links between Bolton Abbey Estate and the industrial north west were opened up after 1773, when the Leeds to Liverpool canal was cut through to Skipton. This major enterprise precipitated the creation of the 'Skipton and Pateley Bridge Trust', who established a turnpike to supersede the old ways. It went from the High Street in Skipton, past the Bailey[57], through Embsay and Eastby, and then over Black Park to the junction with the road from Bolton Abbey at Barden Scale. From here it turned north, down Cinder Hill and through the former Little Park passing the Tower to cross the river at Barden Bridge.

This turnpike is known to have been in existence by 1801, because, in a letter of that date a certain John Dixon, when surveying the route for the new road through Barden on the west side of the river, referred to it as 'the new intended road from the junction to the turnpike near Barden Tower.'[58] The turnpike is marked as The Skipton to Pateley Trust on the 1st Edition OS map for Barden, dated 1853. Near the bridge, lying hidden in the long

---

56 Ruth Camm, Upper Wharfedale Field Society.
57 Bailey: the outer wall of the castle, *Oxford English Dictionary*.
58 Letter written to Thomas Fentiman, the Duke of Devonshire's Agent; Chatsworth MSS at Bolton.

grass, there remains a round, wayside stone incised with a cross, which may be associated with the Trust, since others similar stones have been found near bridges along other turnpikes, for example at Bow Bridge, Threshfield.

Having crossed the bridge, the road climbs up a steep hill to a group of barns and the steading of Watergate. This smallholding lies at a junction with the minor road leading to The Laund, Storiths and Bolton Abbey. Watergate was a hostelry in the nineteenth century and from its name and place it is tempting to conclude that it was an important watering place for horses and cattle on their way to the market in Skipton and that the plain cottage still fronting the carriageway was built as a toll bar with a gate across the turnpike, the small opening in the wall adjacent to the entrance door having been for the purpose of collecting tolls.

The roadway between Watergate and Hough Mill has not been constructed in the manner of a turnpike; it is relatively narrow, with a sinuous line of walls pursuing their way between fields enclosed from the medieval vaccary of Gamsworth. During the mid-Victorian period, several substantial cottages were built along this roadside, some with small-holdings. Having passed the walled lane leading steeply down the hillside to Gamsworth farm, the turnpike passed the junction with an important bridleway leading to Howgill and eventually over the watershed to the markets of Knaresborough and Ripon.

After descending a steep hill the road reached the bridge over Firs Beck by Hough Mill, the manorial corn mill for Barden. The turnpike was, therefore, of prime importance not only to through traffic but also to local traders, including those Barden men, the Demaines, the Atkinsons, and the Holmes's from as far afield as Drebley, who needed to bring their carts of threshed corn from the west side of the valley to be dried in the kiln and ground in the mill. The only place where they could have crossed the river with wheeled vehicles would have been been by Barden Bridge. Although stepping stones over the Wharfe form the shortest route between Hough Mill and the hamlet of Drebley, it is unlikely that horses pulling carts could have crossed the rocky bed of the swiftly flowing river at this point, and there are no flat stones in the bed of the river or hollow ways to indicate where a crossing might have existed.

From Hough Mill, the turnpike continued along Stangs lane towards Appletreewick, and turned right to join Hasler lane in the direction of Skyreholme. Here, a New Road ascended by a series of very steep bends towards the lead mines of Appletreewick and hence to Fancarl where it joined another turnpike, established from 1759 onwards between Grassington and Pateley Bridge.

**Aqueducts and a road bridge near Barden Scale 1896/7**

The photographs[59] show stages in the construction of three bridges which opened over Barden Beck in 1896/7. Two of these are conduits, or aqueducts designed as part of the great enterprise for Bradford Waterworks Corporation which was engineered to carry water in pipes from the reservoirs in Upper Nidderdale to the city.[60] Water flows through the bridge over Barden Beck directly from the picturesque conduit bridge over the river Wharfe. In such a visible part of the landscape, this bridge was designed for the 8th Duke of Devonshire in a style appropriate to other buildings on his estate at Bolton Abbey. At the same time as these bridges were built, a new public road bridge was built over Barden Beck at Stank Gill, to replace the former crossing at the foot of a steep-sided ravine, now obscured by the new aqueduct. This road bridge was formally opened on the day of Queen Victoria's Diamond Jubilee in 1897 the ceremony being reported in the local newspaper, *The Craven Herald and Wensleydale Standard*.

The ancient trackway to the old crossing over the beck can still be trodden as a grassy hollow leading down the hillside towards the aqueduct. (see Chapter 3a, Routeways Through Barden 'A Roman Road?'

---

59 Bolt, Andrew C., *A Walk in the Past,* Mr Bolt Heritage Guides, 2007.
60 Bolt , A., Bradford Corporation Waterworks 1896/7

# ROUTEWAYS

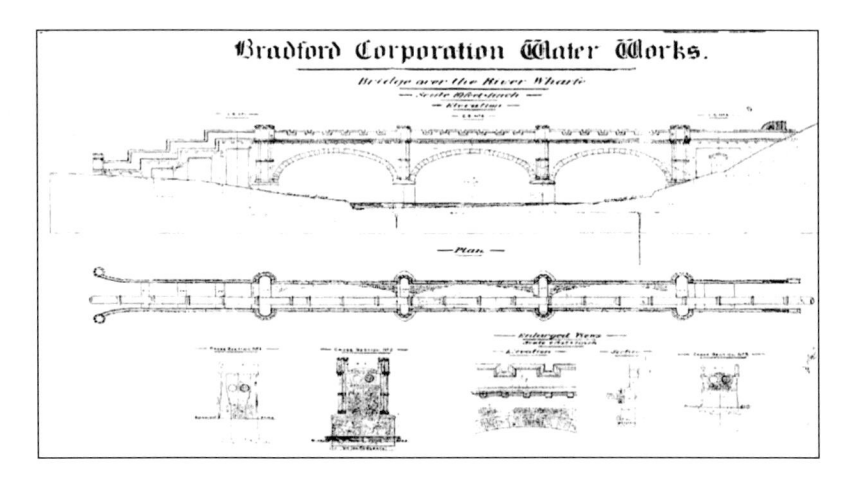

*Left, Bridge over Barden Beck, 4 May 1897 – photographs courtesy of Andrew C. Bolt, as note on page 54.*

**Craven Herald and Wensleydale Standard June 1897**
**Barden**
**Preliminary Opening of the Jubilee Bridge**

A strong, substantial bridge has at length been built by Messrs Mason and Morison contractors, to span the brook, Barden Beck, in the pretty but dangerous glen of Scale Gyle, on the road leading from Upper Wharfedale down to Bolton Abbey

*Public road bridge over Barden Beck, Bolton Abbey, 4 May 1897.*

and the railway station near to the Devonshire Arms. A preliminary opening took place on Tuesday (Jubilee day) principally for the neighbouring inhabitants and the workmen who have so well carved out the architectural features and plans of Messrs J. Varley and Son of Skipton. The bridge was opened as stated by Mr Demaine of Barden Scale and Mr. J. A. Bland of Burnsall. They drove to the centre of the bridge in a carriage neatly bedecked with banners appropriately bearing Her Majesty's Coat of Arms – this being an important matter in connection with the Queen's Highway and also on Her Majesty's Jubilee day.

Mr Demaine, in a short and appropriate speech, alluded to the long time that an agitation had existed for a bridge in that dangerous place, and also to the fatalities which had occurred, of which he had painful recollections. Now that a bridge had been built across the stream, with easier approach, such accidents could never occur again.

Mr Bland said he felt both pride and pleasure at being called upon to address them. It was altogether out of the question that they should have Royalty with them that day, or dukes, lords or knights, they being all engaged in higher and more important duties that Jubilee Day… and it was decided to invite the next best man to perform the duty. Two of the oldest names in that part of Wharfedale had met with their unanimous choice – names that had a place in the roll-call of William the Conqueror when he landed his forces at Hastings in 1066. They had met that day to perform a double duty – to celebrate Her Majesty's sixty years' reign and also to open to all her loyal subjects that useful, neat and substantial structure, Barden Dale Jubilee Bridge, so prettily situate in this picturesque woodland dell.

[Mr Bland followed this with 24 lines of his poetry specially written for the occasion, followed by a further short address]

In giving honour where it was due, he said that it was well known that the Duke of Devonshire had the greatest share in helping to raise the pretty structure over which they would ride and to which would shortly be admitted the general public (abridged version).

[Mr Bland then broke out in one of his usual poetic strains of which only about twelve lines have survived the ravages of time].

# ROUTEWAYS

**A newspaper article of unknown origin or date refers to a fatal accident which took place near this bridge**

The report describes how three stout ladies, namely Mrs Daykin, Miss Lee and Miss Pletts, had set off from Grassington at about six o'clock one Tuesday morning, to drive to Ilkley in a dog-cart loaned by Mr William Wrathall, and drawn by a spirited pony owned by Mrs Daykin. All the ladies were in their sixties, and they employed a youth aged sixteen to drive them. It appears that the pony lost control at a bend on the steep hill between Barden Scale and the crossing over Stank Gill, the cart overturned, and all three ladies lost their lives, while the boy lost an eye and was severely injured, with two broken legs. The inquest was held at the Red Lion Inn in Burnsall at which the following Barden men were amongst the thirteen who were sworn as jurymen: Sylvester Lister (foreman) Jonathan Birch, Joseph Constantine and Thomas Atkinson. Their opinion was that the dog-cart had been overloaded, thus causing undue pressure on the heels of the pony, and the verdict was 'Accidental Death.'

**Stepping Stones between Debley and Hough Mill**

Chris Lunnon of the Upper Wharfedale Heritage Group suggests that these stepping stones form part of an important routeway between Rylestone Fell and Greenhow. They lie between Drebley and Hough Mill.

# 4
# Buildings in Barden

**Buildings in Barden from cruck onwards through the 17th, 18th and 19th centuries\***

*Littlegate before 1886 when it was still thatched, with Christopher Demaine and his family.*

Early medieval houses were very simple, using the natural resources of stone and wood which were plentiful in the Dales, especially in Barden where oak was the dominant species. Many buildings were of cruck construction and several examples can still be seen. For instance, in the hamlet of Drebley, two complete crucks support the roof timbers in a formerly thatched barn, now protected with a corrugated iron roof, while at Littlegate an upper cruck can be seen within the present house, and a cruck survives in one of the barns. There is also one in a barn at Club Nook.

Other barns and dwellings in Barden either derive from these early buildings or are built on sites formerly occupied by them, and it is always worth looking out for cruck timbers re-used as lintels over barn doors, or supporting rebuilt barn roofs. At Watergate, for instance, the steep pitch of the barn gable indicates that crucks once supported the roof,

---

\* Illustrations are attached to the relevant sections for each named farmstead or barn.

although there are none now remaining. At Club Nook however, there is no evidence for a cruck having been incorporated into the tiny, stone-built single-cell cottage which stands on the hillside near the present house. From the gable end of this cottage (now in ruins) a massive stone chimney still rises to a height of several feet above the roof ridge.[61]

There is a marked difference between the styles of buildings on the Bolton Abbey estate and the houses which form a familiar part of the landscape in Upper Wharfedale. The difference is partly due to the geological nature of the Barden/Bolton Abbey area, in that all the buildings are of sandstone, whereas, from Burnsall northwards, limestone predominates. However, it was not only the quarries which influenced the builders; it was also the historical development of the estate from the time of the Dissolution onwards, whereby each of the tenements remained in the hands of the landowner. The rise of the freehold yeoman farmer, as described by Arthur Raistrick[62] could not have occurred in the same way amongst the leaseholders on the estate. Nevertheless, a few generations after the Dissolution, during the early part of the seventeenth century, it is evident that substantial houses were being built in Barden and it was the leaseholders who were building them in what has become known as 'the seventeenth century vernacular style of the Yorkshire Dales'[63]

Each has a fine stone fireplace, characteristic mullioned windows with dripstones, and simply carved entrance door-lintels. It is significant that these features are found only in those houses which stand on the sites of the original Forest Lodges, namely, Barden Scale and Barden Scale Cottage, Hole House, Drebley Littlegate and Drebley Fold Farm, Gamsworth, Howgill Lodge, Crossfield in Howgill, and at the back of the nineteenth century house at Eastwood Head.[64] Elaborately carved door heads, dates and initials did not appear on the lintels of any of these vernacular houses, despite the fact that they were the homes of different branches of families who had held leases in Barden since at least the time of George Clifford the Third Earl of Cumberland.[65] Generations of the same families then remained in these houses until the mid-twentieth century, farming the same land as had their forefathers.[66]

In the late eighteenth century a few new farms were established on land re-apportioned from old tenements or from marginal land reclaimed from intakes on the edge of the estate, and therefore not on the sites of former Forest Lodges where there had been a long history of human settlement. One of these was Club Nook. The farmhouse was built at a corner where the wall between Henry Clifford's Great Park and Drebley Thwaite turned and descended towards the river. Leases for this farm do not appear until after the mid-eighteenth century, suggesting that it did not form a separate holding until that time when a branch of the Atkinson family from Gillbeck Farm (now Low House) became tenants.[67] As might be

---

61 Walton, James, *Homesteads of the Yorkshire Dale*, 1947, Dalesman Publishing Company Ltd.
62 Raistrick, A., *Buildings in the Yorkshire Dale,* 1976, Dalesman Publishing Company Ltd.
63 ibid.
64 Only a datestone 1688 from the earlier building remains, moved from its original position and re-inserted into a wall at the back of the house newly built between 1860 and 1867.
65 Leases dating from 1602, Skipton Castle papers, YAS.
66 For example *Demaines at Barden Scale*, 1681, Will, Borthwick Institute, York.
67 Francis Atkinson, 1726-1804.

expected, the house is of eighteenth century style. The similar style of Low Farm house suggests that at the time when the farm at Club Nook was established and a new house was built, an opportunity was taken to rebuild the old home of the Atkinson family at Gillbeck. Again, the style of the farmhouse at Woodend is also of the eighteenth century because this small farm was not of medieval origin, having been carved out of birch and scrub woodland on the northern border of the estate, and then been sub-divided by afforestation in the early years of the nineteenth century.

Comments appearing in Estate Rentals for the late eighteenth and early nineteenth centuries imply that by this time most of the old cruck, thatched dwellings had fallen into disrepair and had become scarcely habitable. It was during the mid-nineteenth century, during the tenure of the seventh Duke of Devonshire that many barns and houses were altered or re-built to become the substantial stone dwellings we see today. At this time, thatched roofs were stripped off and, in some cases, replaced with thin blue slates, probably from the Burlington quarries in Cumberland. Transport would have been by means of horse and cart from the canal wharves in Skipton or Gargrave, and, later in the century, from Skipton or Bolton Abbey railway stations, travelling along the Skipton to Pateley Bridge turnpike,[68] and also along the Skipton to Cracoe turnpike, and thence towards lesser by-roads to individual farmsteads.

During the nineteenth century there was an extensive programme of building in a late Georgian style, the first being in 1806 in the tributary valley of Howgill, where the tenant of Howgill Lodge, Thomas Wilkinson had 'built at his own charge a dwelling house, slated and with sash windows.'[69] Likewise Dalehead, a farm not created until the end of the eighteenth century from the old lands of Lambert Ings and Arnegill Head, was inhabited in 1806 by George Sidgewick, and re-built in 1867 by his son John, who was evidently 'an intelligent improving tenant, building new walls at his own cost.'[70]

Meanwhile, at Drebley Farm, the house and cottage built by Henry Holmes in 1830 may have been as a result of improved prosperity in the hamlet following the division of Drebley Thwaite in 1812, and after the subsequent opening up of better communications for wheeled vehicles when the new road between Barden Tower and Burnsall (now the B6160) was constructed. The new house, like that at Dalehead and Howgill Farm is of Georgian style, and has very few architectural features linking it to an earlier house.

The major phase of building on the estate took place during the 1860s, when many new farmyards were laid out, each specifically designed with accommodation for a milk herd and its bull, calves, and pigs. The yards were spacious, walled enclosures with large troughs for running water, and above all, there were substantial barns for the storage of hay, the winter fodder for cattle and sheep. These great barns represented a northern hill farmer's reliance on shelter from Pennine weather conditions, for within them the farmer was able to move freely between his shippon, the fodder gang and the baulks. Here also he was able to store his summer machinery and his carts and maybe to thresh oats on the paving stones between the winnowing door and the big cart door.

---

68 See First edition OS map for Barden.
69 Estate Lease Book.
70 Ibid.

Horses were housed in comfortable stables, each with a 'paddy loft' above, for storage of fodder and even for sleeping accommodation for hired labour. The classic building of such a yard is at Drebley Farm, but many others can be seen in specially adapted forms on the Bolton Abbey Estate, such as at Hill Top, Storiths and The Laund, Howgill Farm, Gamsworth and Gamsworth Cottage, Wharfe View and Wood View, Low House, Barden Scale and The Holme.

Meanwhile, between 1860 and 1867, a distinctive new house was built by John Holden at Eastwood Head, on the site of an earlier dwelling. Although built in the mid-Victorian period, this house shows features which derive from the classic seventeenth century vernacular style of the Yorkshire Dales, and thus sits comfortably alongside its contemporary great barns and purpose-built outhouses.

After the building of the new Barden School in 1875 and the Methodist Chapel in 1885, the major building programme in Barden ceased. In 1891 the 7th Duke died, to be succeeded by the 8th Duke, Spencer Compton, who was a great politician having served parliament for half a century, 34 years in the House of Commons and sixteen in the House of Lords.[71] Spencer Compton's incumbency was relatively short, since he died in 1908, but during that time, two new cottages were erected at The Holme, and four new bridges were built. Two of these were water conduits constructed by Bradford Water Works Company in 1896/7, who then built a road bridge over Barden Beck. The fourth new bridge was over Gill Beck, where, in 1908/9 the old bridge was taken down and a new one re-built in a more favourable position, to plans drawn up by Skipton Rural District Council.

It was the end of an era, the former thatched, cruck-built steadings having been replaced by the well-built, slated stone barns and farmhouses we see today.

## 'The Picturesque' in a Romantic Landscape

Influences on a group of nineteenth century houses on the Bolton Abbey estate representing an architectural movement away from the vernacular:

> Towards the end of the nineteenth century there was noticeable in almost every sphere of human activity a growing craving for Romance. In architecture this nostalgia was particularly marked and took the form of a polite enthusiasm for the styles of faraway and long ago, Chinese, Indian, Egyptian and Gothic methods of building all in turn enjoyed a remarkable vogue among the cogniscenti, but it was the last style that proved most popular and the revival of which was to prove, though not at once, most disastrous for English Architecture. So long as the traditions and conventions governing the thought and manners of the eighteenth century remained in force, all was well. The patrons of architecture were enlightened and well-educated men who were perfectly well aware that a wholesale revival of Gothic methods of building would be intolerable, but regarded, quite rightly, the building of a cottage or two in what they hoped was a medieval but were quite certain was a picturesque style, as perfectly permissible. Thus the gazebos, the cottages ornés and the summer-houses which formed the principal output of the Gothic architects of the period, bore little relation to any known Gothic style; they remained, in fact, perfectly ordinary eighteenth century cottages on to which had been tacked a row of castellations and a couple of gargoyles. Ninety per cent of these productions had little connection with architecture at all, but

---

71 The Duchess of Devonshire, 1982, *The House, Portrait of Chatsworth.*

were simply works of smart interior decorators trying their hand at landscape gardening, or literary amateurs of exhibitionist tendencies creating a suitable background for their carefully cultivated personalities. Nevertheless, out of this innocuous and rather charming chrysalis would one day come blundering the dizzy great moth of Victorian revivalism.

Osbert Lancaster, *Pillar to Post,* 1938

Some of the most popular designs for this new style of architecture were drawn by the draughtsman P. F. Robinson 1776-1858. In 1832, Loudon, who in 1833 published an *Encyclopaedia of Cottage, Farm and Villa Architecture* wrote of it in *The Gardeners' Chronicle*:

…they present a perfect compendium of all the prettiest style of cottage architecture from the sturdy Norman to the sprightly Italian.

From the beginning of the nineteenth century many landowners throughout the country, including Lord William Cavendish, the sixth Duke of Devonshire at Chatsworth, were keen to encourage a variety of styles of building on their estates which included 'the cottage ornée,' 'the picturesque' and 'Gothic Revival'.

Between 1838 and 1842, the Duke worked at Chatsworth with his employee Joseph Paxton and his architectural colleague, John Robertson, to plan the rebuilding of the village of Edensor. Robertson had been influenced by his work from 1829 onwards, as an architectural draughtsman for Claudius Loudon and he accordingly created a village in a manner which gave full expression to the new style.

*Two cottages in the village of Edensor.*

In her book *The Estate* published in 1990, Deborah, Duchess of Devonshire, quotes Nicolaus Pevsner[72], in describing Edensor as:

---

[72] Pevsner Nikolaus, 1978, the Derbyshire volume of *Buildings of England*, Harmondsworth, Middlesex.

> ...an attempt at making the Blaise Castle type of picturesque and fanciful artificial village respectable by good solid stone masonry and a display of more serious architectural styles... one can see the hideously elongated, debased Italianate windows which Loudon liked so much in his 'Encyclopaedia' side by side with Jacobean gables, barge boarding, Norman window surrounds and Tudor chimneys.

The Duchess herself describes how:

> ...the sixth Duke and (Joseph) Paxton got to work in earnest on the building of Edensor. Out came the pattern books and John Robertson (who worked for Claudius Loudon) was given the enviable task of turning pictures into stone and creating a village which is positively theatrical in the exaggerated way architectural oddities are displayed in houses near one another. In spite of all this strange jumble they present a perfect compendium of all the prettiest style of cottage architecture from 'the sturdy Norman to the sprightly Italian' as Loudon wrote in *The Gardener's Chronicle* in 1832.[73]

Robertson took some of his patterns for Edensor from the books of P. F. Robinson (1776-1858), the draughtsman of the most popular designs of the 1830s, and some from Loudon's *Encyclopaedia of Cottage, Farm, and Villa Architecture* (1833). Amongst the notable features on these cottages, there is 'much wooden ornamentation of fancy finials and carved barge-boards on the gables.'

## Picturesque buildings on the Bolton Abbey Estate and the rise of 19th century Tourism

My collection of photographs show features on four cottages on the estate at Bolton Abbey which could have been influenced by and possibly derive from the distinctive style of architecture in Edensor. Hence, we find wooden barge-boards decorating steeply pitched porches, gables and dormer windows, bay windows with elongated mullions, and tall chimneys frequently set at an angle. Plans for two of these cottages were drawn up in 1848, and those for a third, some 22 years later, in 1870. It is significant that, in contrast to most of the farmsteads which stand on ancient sites first established as lodges in the medieval forest, each of these nineteenth century cottages was built on a virgin site which had no historical precedent for a dwelling. The sites were chosen as a result of social changes in management of the estate, associated with the rise in pursuit of game and with the increasing numbers of visitors who came to enjoy the 'picturesque' landscape around Bolton Abbey, of which the appearance of these cottages was an integral part.

## Strid Cottage

This large, somewhat ornate and prestigious cottage incorporating two parlours was built to plans drawn up in 1848 which, although they are un-signed, could well be attributed to Sir Joseph Paxton, who, in the 1840s had stayed several times with the 6th Duke at Bolton Hall. On these occasions, he and the duke went over every part of the premises, and he was given instructions to prepare a plan upon all matters here.[74] He stayed in August 1844, when

---

73 The Duchess of Devonshire, 1990, *The Estate*.
74 Markham, V. R., 1935, *Paxton and the Batchelor Duke*, Hodder and Stoughton Ltd., Edinburgh.

on the 27th of that month he wrote a letter from Bolton Abbey to his 'adorable fond wife', (Sarah, who had remained at home at Chatsworth) and he was there again in 1845.[75] Since the re-structuring and extension of Bolton Hall took place soon after Paxton's visits, it is thought that its plans were drawn up at that time,[76] together with plans for other buildings on the Bolton Abbey estate such as for alterations at Bolton Park which have survived[77] signed, but not dated, by Joseph Paxton.

Indeed, in 1869 Bailey Harker, of Grassington[78] wrote that 'Strid cottage had been built in 1848 for Mr Allen, the Wood Agent for the Duke of Devonshire, the architect being no less than the distinguished character Joseph Paxton, the architect of Crystal Palace.' Estate rent books and the census returns confirm that the Cottage at Strid was built to accommodate the Head Forester, Mr Allen. Provision was made for tree nurseries in the immediate surroundings of the house, while the presence of a large Ice House in the grounds to the north of the cottage combined with several smaller cottages accommodating estate workmen imply that this area has long been a centre for many of the other daily activities concerned with the maintenance of the estate. Strid Cottage remained the home of the Head Forester for the Bolton Abbey Estate until after the Second World War, (the name of the last incumbent being rather appropriately Cutmore) but it is now the home of Wharfedale Montessori School.

The Ice House, (date unknown, but likely to have been in use during the seventeenth century) might well have been built to store fish taken from the Wharfe and supplied to the great ducal houses at Londesborough or Chatsworth. For instance, Peter Watkins, writing in 1989 describes how in 1725, 'George Demaine (was) paid for salmon sent to Londesborough for Earl of Burlington by order of Mr Simpson, Agent.'[79] (George Demaine lived nearby at Barden Scale, and the Agent, John Simpson at Barden Tower).[80]

At the northern entrance to Strid Wood, the situation of Strid Cottage is one of great 'Romantic' appeal. From here visitors were encouraged to walk through a carefully laid out landscape,[81] passing awesome river scenery at the Strid itself on their way towards the southern entrance to the woods. At this point, another 'picturesque' cottage, the Wooden Bridge and the Chinese style Pavilion enhance the scene.

---

75 Markham, V. R.
76 Watkins, Peter, 1989, *Bolton Priory and its Church*, Watmough.
77 Bolton MSS, Chatsworth collection.
78 Harker, Bailey, 1869, *Rambles in Upper Wharfedale*.
79 Watkins, Peter, 1989, *Bolton Priory and its Church,* Watmough (Holdings) PLC.
80 Lease Books at Bolton, Chatsworth MSS.

## BUILDINGS IN BARDEN

**Pavilion Cottage**
Smaller but no less decorative than Strid Cottage, this cottage also displays features deriving from the Cottage Ornée and the Gothic Revival periods. It is likely the two were designed as a pair. As at Strid, the eye is attracted by steeply pitched gables, dormer windows with decorative bargeboards, elongated mullions and tall chimneys set at an angle. There are also two, distinctively large external chimney stacks.

These buildings were designed to impress and to welcome the ever increasing numbers of visitors, who throughout the nineteenth century came to enjoy the new pastime of experiencing not only the natural landscape, but also 'nature improved.'[82]

This cottage, the adjacent Pavilion, and the Wooden Bridge are a group of buildings strategically situated at the southern entrance to the woods, where they also form an important link between Bolton Abbey and the community on the other side of the river, who live in the former deer park, at the Laund, and in Storiths and Hazlewood. After 1888, when the railway between Skipton and Ilkley opened, most visitors arrived on the estate in pony-drawn carriages plying their trade between Bolton Abbey Station and the Pavilion. Provision was made for these ponies to stand and be watered while waiting for their passengers to make return journeys at the end of the day.

As the century progressed, many wives and daughters of estate workers living nearby gained employment in the large Pavilion, which had been built especially to provide shelter and refreshments for the visitors. The men also worked in the woods and as gardeners at Bolton Hall, and on summer days they occupied small booths at the entrances to the woods, where visitors were required to pay a fee. The woods were closed to the public on Sundays, and it was on those days that the Cavendish family and their friends could occasionally be glimpsed enjoying the beauty and freedom of their estates.[83] Sundays were also days on which tenants seized their opportunities to roam freely without paying the normally obligatory sixpence, and some, such as Dora Dunckley, the daughter of the school mistress in Barden, and Barbara Lister from Barden Tower, walked to church through the woods.

---

81 The 'Romantic' landscape was laid out by the Rev. William Carr, curate of the priory Church from 1789 to 1843, who was also steward of the estate. The poet Wordsworth, who stayed with Mr Carr at the rectory from time to time, said of him that he 'worked with an invisible hand in the very spirit of nature' in the planning of woodland walks and 'the siting of arbours and seats in outstandingly beautiful situations.' Wm Lemmon, 1972, *Bolton Abbey and the Wharfe*, Derby: English Life Publications Ltd.
82 Edwin Mullins, *Bolton Abbey: A Garden without Walls*, New Arcadians' Journal No. 13, Spring 1984.
83 Reg Harper, who lived at Waterfall Cottage, in the Deerpark, recalled seeing the Princess Royal and the Earl of Harewood sitting on rocks near the Strid, shortly before their engagement was announced.

## Watergate Cottage, and the 'Picturesque' in Barden

Watergate Cottage stands on the roadside, at the junction of the road between Barden Bridge and Howgill and the minor road from Storiths. It stands at the northern edge of the 'picturesque landscape', and would have formed a turning point on a circular carriage tour starting from The Pavilion. Having crossed the Wharfe by means of the Wooden Bridge, carriages would travel along the narrow country lane past The Laund to Watergate. From here, they would negotiate the steep hill down to Barden Bridge, and thence up Cinder Hill as they passed the Tower, until they reached Strid Cottage on the return journey to rejoin their ponies and traps by the Pavilion.

It is of interest to note that in 1867 the artist, Atkinson Grimshaw chose to paint a romantic scene incorporating the Tower from a vantage point at Holme Farm, on the lane between The Laund and Watergate, (see chapter 4, Storage Cellars for illustration). In the same year, Grimshaw also painted the waterfall in Gillbeck, which must at that time have been considered part of this 'picturesque' scenery, and a diversion northwards from the Tower, on the road to Burnsall, (see chapter 3, Routeways Through Barden for illustration).

Watergate cottage is the third of its type, the other two being Strid and Pavilion Cottages, although the plans, dated 1870, were drawn up for the 7th Duke of Devonshire, 22 years later than those for Strid Cottage.[84] Although generally less Ornće, the similarities with the first two cottages are striking. These features include elongated mullion windows, two dormer windows, one chimney set at an angle, another with a large external stack, and a mullioned bay window with a stepped, stone flagged roof. The rather plain bargeboards present a more severe façade than at the Strid and Pavilion cottages, while the diamond-headed windows are echoed further along the road at the even plainer Waterfall Cottage. The imposing stone doorcase repeats the design of a doorcase at Pavilion Cottage.

## Waterfall Cottage

This dwelling was built within the old deer park for a keeper to

---

[84] The 6th Duke had died in 1858 and Joseph Paxton in 1868.

control activities therein and also to monitor visitors on their way to enjoy the landscape in the Valley of Desolation and on the moors around Simon Seat. The design for this cottage is the least decorative of those already described, but its style can be seen to derive from the same source. All the features described at these four cottages, Strid, the Pavilion, Watergate and Waterfall can be seen on various cottages in Edensor.

The aqueduct bridge, downstream from Barden Bridge, was built by Bradford Water Works Corporation as part of the major late nineteenth century scheme to carry water from the reservoirs in Upper Nidderdale to the city of Bradford. It is said that the 8th Duke of Devonshire insisted that the bridge should be built in a style reflecting the picturesque landscape he was anxious to preserve. The bridge has castellated parapets and elaborate breakwaters.

Other less prestigious buildings dating from the late nineteenth century can be found in specific places around the estate, such as the small semicircular, stone-built shelters, each with a thatched roof, placed for visitors to enjoy particular view points in Strid Wood. They were given names, such as Pembroke Seat, which is on a promontory affording a splendid view of Barden Tower. The memory of another, described as Moss House, Valley of Desolation, is preserved only in a lithograph (above). It lay at the junction of Posforth Gill with the Wharfe.

## Brass Castle
Other buildings have been restored to form useful and attractive shelters for visitors walking in the woods. More functional are a pair of thatched stone huts known as Brass Castle. These beautifully crafted little buildings are situated on Barden Moor, between the Upper and Lower reservoirs. They were built to shelter sporting parties, and they contain strong rustic tables on which many initials have been carved.

## Nineteenth century non-vernacular buildings in Barden

Barden School was built in 1875 on a new site and from local materials. The style is of 'Dales School Vernacular', but echoes of the 'picturesque' can be seen in the steeply pitched roof and in the porch, with its decorated, fret-work bargeboards, and also in a tall chimney, characteristically set at an angle.[85]

The Wesleyan Methodist Chapel, opened in 1885, was also built of local sandstone. It stands on the roadside in Barden, adjacent to the site of the old school-room, and it was the last building to be erected in Barden in the nineteenth century.

Holme Cottages are a pair of semi-detached cottages which were erected at the beginning of the twentieth century, to provide accommodation for estate workers. They are situated on the edge of the former rabbit warren, directly on the side of the road to Storiths.

## Storage Cellars in Barden and Howgill

In many of the farmyards in Barden a single, very small, low stone building can be seen,[86] driven into the rising hillside. None is attached to any other building, each has a slated, gritstone roof, a gable-end entrance doorway, and a small opening on the opposing gable, so that, although placed below the eaves within, it is at ground level outside. This suggests that the opening was used for ventilation and/or for shovelling in loose storage items without having to lift them. The interior of each building has a domed roof, which is either smoothly whitewashed, or, (as under the cruck barn at Drebley) composed of narrowly stepped, corbelled stones. A stone shelf is a standard fitment, accompanied in some cases, but not all, by stone alcoves in the wall, and there may be a drain in the floor.

These skilfully constructed little buildings, each with slight differences, appear to have had the same set style or plan which was functional, and they are so similar it is tempting to identify a single purpose for the group, i.e. storage of root crops and in particular potatoes, followed in more recent years by dairy produce. Each is free-standing, usually in an area away from the farmhouse which is not even part of the farmyard complex itself. Two, at least, have been built beneath a cruck barn, as at Club Nook and below the barn in Drebley Lane, while the building at Littlegate, Drebley is a hybrid, having two chambers, one being subterranean, with a couple of stone steps between the two.

It is obvious that great care was taken to ensure protection of whatever was stored in these small buildings from changes in the weather and rodents. Their purpose is not known for certain, although it is likely that they were originally designed for storage of root crops in a cool, dark, and well ventilated environment. Turnips and potatoes were certainly grown in Barden, which was known as a great potato-growing district. This fact came to the notice of Ella Pontefract and Marie Hartley, who, in their book on Wharfedale recalled how

…every winter the farmers would take a cart-load of potatoes to sell at Skipton market.[87]

---

85 Bedford-Payne, B. and Beaumont, H., 1997, *The Story of Barden School: its patrons, pupils and teachers*, Prontaprint, Durham.
86 E.g. Drebley, Littlegate, Howgill, Eastwood Head.
87 Pontefract, E. and Hartley, M., *Wharfedale,* 1938, J. M. Dent and Sons, London.

## BUILDINGS IN BARDEN

Potatoes were also mentioned by Harwood Long in his survey of Yorkshire 1969:

> At the end of the eighteenth century... Skipton still relied on dales farms for its potatoes. And some barns still have cellars under them where the crop was stored until a pack horse or the farm carts took it to town on market day. The arrival of the railway killed this trade in the middle of the nineteenth century and farmers from the Vale of York thenceforward supplied Skipton with potatoes.[88]

Because there is evidence of shelving and of whitewash on the ceilings and the walls of these little buildings, it has been suggested that milk, butter and cheese were stored here, together with a churn, (see photograph). It is likely that, once the market for potatoes dwindled, some of the little buildings were indeed used as convenient storage places for dairy produce. Betsy Inman (b.1920s) of Keepers Cottage, Drebley, certainly remembers some of them being used in this way. It should be remembered, however, that each farmhouse had a cool, stone-floored dairy at the back of the living kitchen, and there would have been no need for a special dairy or cool store in the yard. It is also worth mentioning that whereas root crops played a major part in the economy of Barden, the marketing of cheese and other dairy produce was not as significant as it was in other dales, such as Swaledale and Wensleydale.

Pig killing should be excluded, because there is no evidence for slaughter-tables, such as survives in a different type of building at The Fold farm in Drebley. However, although hooks do not appear to have been standard fixtures in the ceilings, a few have been found, and the existence of a floor drain suggests that newly killed and freshly salted haunches of pork, beef or mutton could have been hung from the ceilings of these small buildings.

Peat is less likely to have been the item, because a shelf and stone alcoves are not associated with a peat stack, while other buildings adjacent to the back doors of farmhouses were labelled as 'peat houses'.

### Three Storage Cellars in Howgill:

### Howgill Farm
The roof of this little building is ridged and slated with local sandstone. Shown on the photograph is the unusual stepped gable composed of individual blocks of sandstone.

---

88 Long, W. H., *A survey of the Agriculture of Yorkshire: County Agriculture Surveys No.6 for the Royal Agricultural Society of England 1969*, RACSE, 35 Belgrave Square, London, p.52.

The first photograph, supplied by Bernard Foster of Howgill Lodge, shows the churn in use (previous page). The photograph to the left shows the gable end of the storage building, and how it was indeed likely to have been used as a dairy, and as a storage place for the churn.

**Old House in Howgill**
On the side of a steep hillside in Howgill stands a tall, free-standing building, stone-built and slated. The upper storey, has an open-fronted cart-house facing towards a trackway leading to the barnyard, with a storage cellar at the lower level. Again, this is driven into the earth-bank, and is entered through a doorway facing the farmhouse. Within, there are stone shelves and small stone alcoves on which cheeses might have been stored. There are four ventilation holes on the front wall of the cellar.

*Store at Old House, Howgill.*

## BUILDINGS IN BARDEN

**Eastwood Head**
This building is small and square, bearing some resemblance in size and shape to the one at the nearby Howgill Farm, although the gable wall is without the stepped slates, and is entirely of smooth coursed sandstone. There is a ridged, slated roof. By 1941, 'a quarter of an acre of potatoes, main crop and second earlies, together with a quarter of turnips and swedes for fodder'

*Store at Eastwood Head.*

were still being grown at Eastwood Head, when Marion Holden was the leaseholder. The continued production of these staple crops may well have been imposed by food shortages experienced during the Second World War.[89]

**Storage cellars in Drebley**

At Drebley House the situation of the storage cellar is unusual in that it is adjacent to a large stone barn in a small yard immediately opposite the back door of the 1830 house. Its roof is skilfully slated, with a neat stone ridge. Note how the eaves sweep down to earth level on one side, but not on the other, where that part of the side wall above earth level is composed of huge, un-coursed boulders. It is not clear whether the other wall is similarly built, since it is below earth level. The small, gable-end window (at earth level from the outside) is glazed and has a protruding lintel. The ceiling is domed and has been whitewashed.

---
89 Ministry of Agriculture and Fisheries Agricultural Return, 4 June 1941.

## Littlegate

At Littlegate, the building is at first misleading, in that entry is into a small, stone building which might have been a small calf-house. However, the anti-chamber leads via a couple of steps into another, domed-roof chamber, with its side walls and roof driven into rising ground. Both chambers have been whitewashed, and the height of the inner chamber is considerably greater than that in other similar buildings. An indication of alternative methods of short-term storage of dairy products is the fact that, in the 1920-50 era, the gamekeeper's wife at Keeper's Cottage made butter commercially, albeit on a small scale, and stored it in an alcove above the adjacent spring-fed trough, whereas the farmer's wife at Littlegate stored her butter in this small building.

*The storage chamber at Littlegate, Drebley.*

## The cellar below the cruck barn in Drebley lane

There is no ground-level doorway or window into this cellar. Instead, a short flight of stone steps leads down from the interior of the barn into total darkness, with very little daylight on the steps. The domed roof of the cellar is of narrow, dressed stonework, similar to that on the dividing wall in the barn, and unlike any other seen locally. However this cellar presents a problem as regards the handling of loose root crops: it is very difficult to understand how they could have been stored in here, even in sacks or baskets… how would they have been brought up the short flight of steep stairs into the barn, other than in very small quantities, and could a horse-drawn cart have been 'backed' into the area for loading? Perhaps they were loaded only onto packhorses, as suggested by Howard Long in his survey.[90] Could the workers have avoided damaging the vegetables with their tools? Perhaps they used wooden spades, as can be seen in local Folk museums. There is no local tradition for growing willow for the making of baskets, and none have survived.

It would certainly not have been feasible to use the cellar as a dairy.

## Club Nook

The cellar here has been driven into the hillside from the west gable of the house. It is unlit, and approached by a flight of stone steps leading directly from the kitchen, and as at Drebley, it would not have been feasible to use it as a dairy. There is a ventilation opening at ground level along the northern side-wall. Above, is a small cruck barn, indicating that the cellar and the barn at Club Nook date from an earlier period than the present house and farm buildings.

---

90 Long, H., 1969

## Low Farm

At Low Farm it is also likely that the cellar was initially part of an earlier dwelling than the present house. An estate plan drawn in the 1860s shows how it is entered by a flight of stone steps from the gable end of the dwelling house and is driven into the rising hillside. This is very similar to the position of the cellar at Club Nook, from which it differs in that it has not been built below a cruck barn. The front wall here is above ground, and is of two storeys, with a window on each level. The upper storey was designed in the 1860s to be a wool store above the cellar, lit by its own window and approached by an outside flight of stairs.

Note: Where sectional stone jambs occur, they indicate a construction date for as early as the seventeenth century. Straight stone jambs indicate a construction date from the eighteenth century onwards.

The roofing slates are all composed of local sandstone (i.e. no blue Westmorland slates, as appear on many nineteenth century buildings in Barden).

# 5
# Farms

*The new Fordson Major tractor at Drebley in the late 1940s, driven by Helmut, ex-prisoner of war, with Matti, a visiting student from Finland.*

**Woodend Farm**

This farm lies at the northern end of Barden directly on the route of the 'old way to Burnsall', between the deep ravine of Garrelgum on the north and Drebley Hagg in the south, with a short steep lane leading to the roadway which has become the B6160. It is somewhat isolated from other settlements nearer to the Tower and was, like Drebley, a part of Burnsall at the time of Domesday.[91] It did not originate as a Forest Lodge, nor did it become a vaccary in the medieval period.

The earliest enclosures, being near the house, are named West Leys, Leyr, and Calf Garth. They are likely to date from the time of pre-Conquest settlement, while those names deriving from the Anglo-French, such as 'close' suggest that these enclosures took place some time after the Norman Conquest. Those place-names High and Low Birk Close indicate that the area was always wooded, and specifically with birch.

The Burnsall registers record the marriage in January 1612 of Mary Inman, (a member of a very long established Barden/Howgill/Appletreewick family) to John Moorhouse of

---
91 Whitaker, *Craven*, p.501.

## FARMS AND OTHERS

*Woodend Farm.*

Woodend, and on 12 November 1613 the baptism of their son was recorded. Throughout the nineteenth century the tenants at Woodend were named Thompson. They also held a Laithe and 27 acres of meadow land named High and Low Dowsgill, situated at almost river level, below the Closes. This land was part of the ancient manor of Woodhouse, on the west side of the river, between Hartlington and Appletreewick, and not part of the Bolton Abbey Estate. Both the Grassington local historian, The Rev. Bailey Harker, writing in 1869 and the late Victorian author Edmund Bogg writing in 1904 describe how this came about:

> The Doxhill's estate in Appletreewick and Burnsall yields about £80 a year in rent… after the Dissolution this ancient manor was granted to Henry Earl of Cumberland 1542, and sold or given by Francis, Fourth Earl to John Waters who built a substantial house at Woodhouse, his initials appearing on the old fireplace thus: IW 1635. Tradition has it that this John Waters, or his son, having fallen into disgrace, fled and ultimately settled in the West Indies, where he died having bequeathed Doxhill to the Society for the Conversion of the Negroes in the West Indies.

The total acreage of the holding at Woodend was reduced in 1806 from 190 acres to 70 acres, while by 1867 an estate map shows that it had been reduced to 52 acres. As Heather Beaumont has shown in her study 'Settlement and Land Use in Upland Barden',[92] land was taken in hand from the early years of the nineteenth century for a new estate policy of afforestation: the map shows that by 1867 the plantations adjoining Woodend Farm at Garrelgum and Hagg Wood were well established.

It is interesting to note that in 1806/7 Thomas Thompson of Woodend was employed as a gamekeeper. No doubt this dual occupation was necessitated by the small acreage of his holding, after so much of it was taken in hand for the new plantations. His work in controlling vermin, and in particular rabbits, would have assumed great importance in order to

---

92 Beaumont, Heather, *The Local Historian*: Volume 26, no 2. *Tracing the Evolution of an Estate Township: Barden in Upper Wharfedale*, Cambridge University Press, 1996.

# BARDEN IN WHARFEDALE, THE PLACE AND ITS PEOPLE

*Woodend Farm, looking across the valley to Simon's Seat and Howgill, a painting by Rosemary Lodge of Burnsall.*

protect the newly planted seedlings.

On the western boundary of the farm, eleven acres of rough moorland named Bracken Haw[93] lie on the hillside, while next to this is a small enclosure of two acres, known as Kirk Close. (Burnsall church is a mile away in the valley below, the bells being clearly heard on

*These two photographs[94] show members of the Thompson family haymaking during the first part of the twentieth century.*

---

93 *Haw har* OE associated with a boundary, or *ha(r)* ON for high (A. H. Smith).
94 Photographs supplied by Bernard Foster of Howgill, farming at Woodend early 20th century.

# FARMS AND OTHERS

occasions.) A small enclosure named Bombey Close lies near the Hagg plantation. This name is associated with a family who, for several hundred years held a small holding situated between the hamlet of Drebley and Hole House.

The present house and the barn with its large cart entrance, are of the late eighteenth to early nineteenth centuries, with stone slated roofs and Yorkshire sash windows. As at Club Nook and Low House, a storage chamber adjoins the western gable, being driven into the rising land of the hillside. There has been no attempt to form a fold yard of buildings as can be seen at many of the other farmsteads on the estate e.g. Drebley. This reflects the scale of farming at Woodend, where relatively small numbers of cattle and sheep could be supported on the reduced acreage of pasture and meadowland available.

# 6
# Drebley

# DREBLEY

## The Topography of Drebley
*Report from Upper Wharfedale Field Society field visit 1990, Drs. David and Beryl Turner*
Drebley consists of a cluster of three farmhouses, and a keeper's cottage. It lies on the west side of the valley, 450 feet OD above the flood plain of the River Wharfe and sheltered on a south-westerly slope below Herd Hill. It is situated about a quarter of a mile to the east of the road between Burnsall and Barden Tower (B6160) from which it is almost invisible.

The hamlet is built on an outcrop of millstone grit, which runs nearly east-west, forming the boulder strewn ridge of Herd Hill and continuing across the river to Haugh Hill. Several of the farm houses are built almost directly onto solid rock. Below the hamlet, south of this rocky outcrop, a line of small, steep-sided hills runs from the stepping stones south-westwards. In a field nearest the stepping stones, known as The Hippings, the hill has a very flat top. These hills are all composed of rounded pebbles and boulders, mainly of limestone with a few of sandstone and shale, being the eroded remains of a river terrace with very thick deposits of river gravels. These may have been deposited in the immediate post-glacial period, when the river was over 20 metres above its present level. The flat fields in the valley bottom beyond are underlain by finer and younger river-deposited gravels and have very thin soil.

*Herd Hill and Thwaite.*

## Report from the Botany Group, Upper Wharfedale Field Society
We visited Drebley on 7 July and 22 August 1993. A full list of the plants we recorded was filed with the records of the Local History Group.

A wide variety of plants, characteristic of well-drained meadow and pasture land, was noted. An interesting feature was a possibly artificial water-course connecting several troughs which yielded a number of moisture-loving plants, including Bog Stitchwort, Marsh

Bird's Foot Trefoil (*Lotus uliginosus*) and the comparatively rare Marsh Foxtail Grass (*Alopecurus geniculatus*)

Plants on the small hills near the river included characteristic lime-loving species e.g. Purging Flax (*linum catharticum*), Eyebright, Self Heal, Lady's Mantle, and Mouse-ear Hawkweed. The presence of these plants indicates that the hills are composed of post-glacial material containing limestone from further up the dale.

On the gravel bank a striking feature was the great increase in creeping yellow-cress (*Rorippa sylvestris*) since our last visit in 1991.

*Creeping yellow-cress.*

### Early Settlement in the hamlet of Drebley

The presence of a carved stone head in the hamlet of Drebley is a possible indication of early occupation of the site, especially round the spring which bubbles up in a field adjoining the lane near the cruck barn. This carving is now fixed to the wall of an outshut from a barn built in Littlegate farmyard in 1840. Although it is impossible to date this feature, it is of considerable interest in relation to the Celtic origins of other stone heads, many of them having been found in association with springs.

Some evidence for domestic settlement and cultivation in pre-conquest times has been shown by the discovery of two querns. One is recorded by Eric Cowling[95] as being of Celtic origin, with a flat grinding surface, and the other, found in the garden of Drebley House, has a curved grinding surface.[96] Composed of millstone grit, it is formed from the bedrock on which the hamlet stands, and conforms to a beehive pattern, with holes for the hopper and two handles, suggesting that it dates from the Romano-British period.

The Drebley Quern (pictured opposite) has been deliberated damaged in antiquity, in such a way that it was rendered useless. Arthur Raistrick, writing in the 1940s[97] offers an explanation for this:

> Following the Norman Conquest, a feudal and manorial system enabled the Lord of the Manor to exert a monopoly over the building and working of his water-powered corn mills. His peasantry were obliged to grind all their corn at the manorial corn mill, and to pay to the miller all

---

95 Cowling, Eric T.
96 Registered in the Yorkshire Quern Survey: recorded 7/3/07 by John Cruse, Yorkshire Archaeological Society.
97 Raistrick, Arthur, 1940s, *Arthur Raistrick's Yorkshire Dales,* p77, compiled by David Joy, Dalesman Publishing Co, Clapham, Lancaster.

# DREBLEY

mulcture fees. It was an offence against the manor for a peasant to make or own a hand-mill or quern; any querns discovered were confiscated by the Lord of the Manor and broken up by the manor steward or disposed of in some other way, sometimes to mend a path or sometimes built into a wall. Its owner would have been severely fined.

The damaged Drebley Quern may have been found built into one of the stone walls, or it may have lain in a pasture, un-noticed for centuries, until the late 1930s when the enterprising Drebley farmer, Herbert Chester started ploughing his meadowland and re-seeding it with grass; his plough-share may have struck the stone as he turned it up in a furrow and carried it home as a garden ornament.

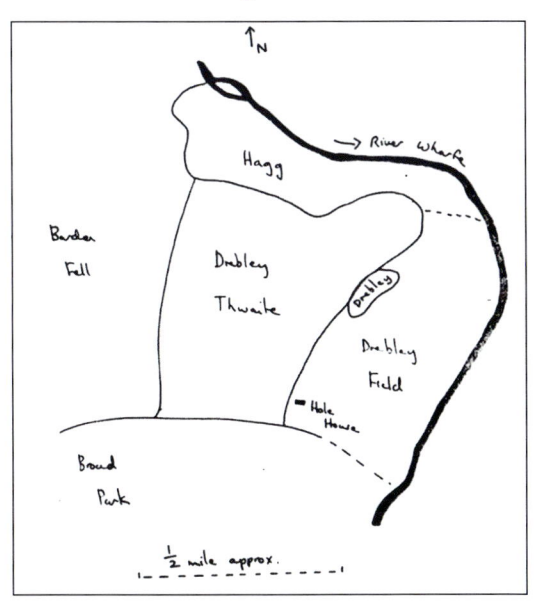

*A sketch plan by Heather M Beaumont, showing the areas from which land was allocated to each of the three farms at Drebley.*

## Medieval Walls around Drebley Thwaite
(with photographs by Alison Payne)

Walls dividing the former Drebley Thwaite, Drebley Field and Brown Bank are drawn on Ed. Beckwith's map of 1731, showing that they were in place at least 70 years before the walls built to divide the Thwaite in 1812; these early walls are of considerable significance, since the names of the fields they enclose suggest that they follow the boundaries of the first medieval divisions of land, when the Drebley vaccary was in use.

The photograph on the next page shows the irregular, sinuous line of the wall which divides the area of Brown Bank from the former Drebley Field. However, it differs from

# BARDEN IN WHARFEDALE, THE PLACE AND ITS PEOPLE

other early walls closer to Drebley hamlet, in that it is not built on a bank and there are no large boulders or orthostats in the base. In the photographs below, note that the loosely placed top-stones are flat and overhanging, which may have been for the purpose of discouraging sheep from jumping out, or predators such as wolves from leaping into the enclosure. The wall's composition of coarsely juxtaposed stones suggests that it has been rebuilt many times, and the sturdy wall-end shows how it tapers from a broad base to a narrower top.

# DREBLEY

*Large field boulders form the base of the wall between the Long Garth and Intake.*

The Long Garth at Drebley is an enclosure through which a section of the prehistoric footpath still in use today, passed through Drebley on its way between Burnsall and the ford over the river at the point where Barden Bridge was built.

Here, as in the wall dividing Drebley Field from Brown Bank, there is an absence of uniformly dressed top-stones, and the upper courses of the wall have been rebuilt in a random fashion. There are several tall, narrow sheep creeps along its sinuous length.

Through the recent opening in the wall between the Long Garth and Intake, another wall incorporating large boulders can be seen on the far side, forming a boundary round the former Thwaite (now the Herd Hill). Here, the names of the enclosures and the large field boulders in the base of the walls indicate that they were built at an early date, when incursions were being made into the Thwaite to form valuable grazing assarts to the Drebley vaccary, walled off from the rocky outcrops seen on the horizon.

From prehistoric times the track through the Long Garth also formed part of a well-used route passing through Drebley to and from a place where the river was fordable, (whether on foot or horseback would have depended on the state of the river). At some date, so far unknown, the Hipping Stones were put in place to enable people to cross over, but for many centuries the crossing must have been used by horse and cart plying between Drebley and the manorial corn-mill, situated on the Firs Beck at its confluence with the Wharfe. As such, and as shown in the photographs, it is not surprising that the boundary wall dividing the Long Garth from the Intakes into what was Drebley Thwaite shows evidence of antiquity.[98]

Because this ancient trackway lies on bedrock, a distinct hollow has not formed, despite at least a millennium or more of use, although some grass covered channels through the bedrock show where wheeled vehicles have eroded the surface over such a long period of time.

*The cart track through bedrock in the Long Garth at Drebley, with walled intakes into the Thwaite in the background.*

## The boundary wall between Drebley Thwaite (now the Herd Hill and its Intakes) and Simm Bottom, on Barden Fell

It is generally accepted that in 1654 Lady Anne Clifford repaired rather than built this wall which had been in existence since Henry Clifford enclosed his Great Park at the end of the fifteenth century.

The photograph shows a section of the boundary wall or head-dyke between the Thwaite and Barden Moor at Simm Bottom. The massive boulders lying on the hillside beyond the wall, together with customary clearance of field boulders, would have been a ready source of supply for those seen forming the base of the wall (photograph by David Johnson).

The classical position of the wall, lying as it does at a point where the land rises, would have been favourable for enclosing deer, and encouraging others to leap in, but not out of the Park. Field evidence and hassuring marked on parts of Mathew Oddie's map of 1778 indicate that there was a ditch. Chris Lunnon (Upper Wharfedale Heritage Group) when walking the length of this wall, suggested that the flat platform on which the wall is built

---

98 i.e. the wall stands on a bank following a sinuous line, and is characterised by the large field boulders and orthostats which make up its base.

# DREBLEY

between the Intakes and the steeply rising moorland, was maintained as an important feature in the management of the Thwaite and the deer in the park, combined as it is with the so far enigmatic purpose of the unique square openings at shoulder height along the entire length of the wall. I would suggest the holes date from the time of Lady Anne Clifford's repairs, when fodder grown in the Thwaite was stuffed through for the deer, as 'they descended to lower ground and allowed themselves to be fed.'

> In 1654, by agreement made between the Countess Dowager of Pembroke and Elizabeth Countess of Cork, a herd (of deer) then wild was driven into the Parke of Barden, which was lately walled in by this said Countess of Pembroke, there to remain until such time as there shall be a parke walled in and made staunch at Bolton or Stedhouse by the Countess of Cork.
>
> The herd now numbers about forty head and in the summer, the animals are very shy and seek the most sequestered spots on the moors but in winter when food is scarce they descend to the lower ground and allow themselves to be fed…
>
> *The History, Antiquities and Scenery of Upper Wharfedale,* Harry Speight, 1900

## Drebley House and Yard: A Planned Victorian Farmstead

Drebley farmhouse was built on the site of an earlier dwelling of which very little remains. The initials HH and the date 1830 over the front door are those of Henry Holmes, who was the tenant at the time of the new building. The farmyard itself was built later in the century, soon after plans drawn up in 1862 during the time of William Cavendish, the Seventh Duke of Devonshire.

> … he had inherited Chatsworth in 1858, together with formidable debts which he set about redressing by planning and financing new hotels and shops in the seaside resort of Eastbourne in Sussex. His work as a town planner in the 1870s stands as memorial to him today.[99]

The Duke's endeavours to improve his estates at Bolton Abbey are reflected in the rebuilding of the homes in which his tenants lived. Many properties were described in the estate lease books as 'old, thatched and in poor repair or cruck-built'.[100] As a result of so much re-building there are many architecturally similar houses and farmyards on the Bolton Abbey estate, of which Drebley is one of the most complete. Despite the fact that dated drawings and plans exist, they have not been attributed to a named architect, and so it is possible that in common with other great landowners of that period,[101] the Duke's own steward or agent drew up the plans using established pattern books for guidance. The names of two agents for the Duke of Devonshire have been associated by hearsay with these plans: Joseph Petyt of Stank House, Bolton Abbey, a local man who died in 1883, and Gilson Martin who by 1881 was the Duke's agent at Chatsworth.

Although these new estate buildings date from the second half of the nineteenth century, it is possible that the designers were influenced by the earlier work of Daniel Garrett, who

---

99 The Duchess of Devonshire, 1982, *The House,* Macmillan, London.
100 Chatsworth/Bolton MSS.
101 Wade Martins, Susanna, 2002, *The English Model Farm: Building the Agricultural Ideal 1700-1914*, Windgather Press, Lancaster.

had north-country associations:

> Some of the earliest examples of planned and model farmsteads are to be found in the north of England… In 1747 the first book of farm designs was published by the London trained architect Daniel Garrett. From 1720 he had worked as a clerk of works for Lord Burlington… 'they were neat, symmetrical and utilitarian designs … built in as regular, cheap and convenient a manner as possible'.[102]

It is also possible that the Duke's agents may have been influenced by the work of John Carr, the York-based architect who was employed at Harewood from 1805. Examples of these late nineteenth century buildings in Barden itself can be seen as follows:

- In 1862, three new cottages were built on land adjoining Gamsworth, on the east side of the valley. Of these, Wood View and Wharfe View were built to support smallholdings for estate workmen, especially woodmen to tend the maturing forestry plantations. Each had a full complement of buildings arranged around a small, classically designed fold yard. The third cottage was built to accommodate the gamekeeper. Here, there was no fold yard, but provision was made for dog-kennels. Also built during this period was a new fold yard at High Gamsworth Cottage.
- Plans dated 1871 show that additions and improvements were made to the house and barns for William Demaine at Barden Scale. A yard and outbuildings were added to the west side of the house, while the housebody and parlour were re-arranged to create a dairy within the space of the parlour and a new staircase.
- In 1873, at Low Farm, Gillbeck, a huge barn complex was built for John Atkinson, and in 1887 a wool chamber was added to the house for his son, George Atkinson.

Although such bold re-ordering of the buildings on the estate must have reflected an increase in the demand for wool, and better means of transport to centres of trade such as Bradford and Halifax it is unlikely that very high returns could have been sought on the Duke's capital outlay in accordance with an expected rise in prosperity. It may be that the building programme was forced upon him by the dereliction of the existing houses and barns as described in the rent books. However, the mark left on the estate by the seventh duke reflects not only a spirit of mid-Victorian confidence and optimism for the future of farming, but also a determination to improve the living and working conditions of his tenants, their lives having been considerably enhanced by the sturdy stone buildings which replaced their former thatched and cruck-built homesteads.

Drebley farmyard is an exemplary model for this period, providing all the buildings needed to manage 114 acres of a mid-nineteenth century hill-farm where sheep and cattle were the mainstay of the economy. The acreage of the farm increased only slightly during the century, when the small farm of Applegarth, held until 1860 by the Wade family, was apportioned between the three larger farms in the hamlet and Parker Inman of Gamekeeper's Cottage.

---

102 Wade Martins, Susanna, 2004, *Farmers, Landlords and Landscapes: Rural Britain, 1720-1870*, Windgather Press, Lancaster.

## DREBLEY

The plans drawn up for Drebley in 1862 show that, instead of a traditional fold-yard, where the farmhouse formed a strategic, commanding position on one of four sides, the buildings are arranged in the shape of a Z, and set apart from the house. Was this because of the lie of the land, or mainly because of a constraint caused by older buildings that were demolished to make way for the new?

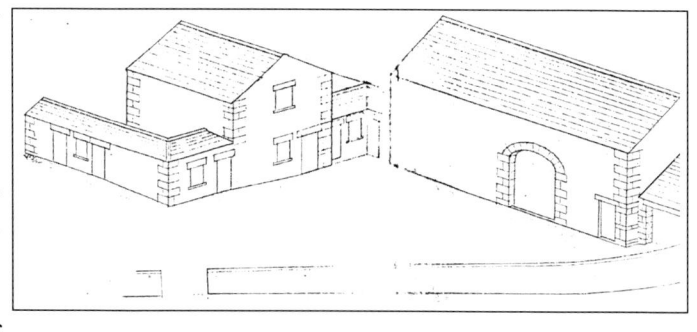

Two of the plans show traces of another building lying across the yard – was this drawing for an alternative plan, or was it the 'ghost' of an earlier building? It is likely that the form taken by the new yard and buildings was dictated by the fact that the house built in 1830 was already in situ, with a good barn in the kitchen courtyard dated 1831. This barn is also shown on another plan together with outlines of buildings in the croft on the north side of the house, reached by a short flight of steps. None of these exist today, although there is a large, level area on which some stone 'footings' can be seen.

Drebley yard is unusual in that, apart from the boundary wall, the south side of the yard remains open, and none of the older buildings were restored, as was the case in the other two farmyards in the hamlet. There are no remains of old buildings to indicate where they might have been, apart from the root store opposite the back door on the north side of the house.

*Drebley yard as it is today.*

### Farmyard buildings

The pig sty was nearest to the orchard and garth, and also to the kitchen door of the farmhouse. Swill was thrown into the feeding trough through an ingeniously designed opening in the wall of the sty. From the adjoining orchard, a ladder led through a small pop-hole into the hennery with a slatted floor above the pig sty. A loosebox for young calves or bottle-fed lambs came next, followed, along the south-facing long arm of the Z, by a larger loosebox for 'stirks' or non-suckler calves.

Midway along was the stable, partitioned for a maximum of four horses. Built for the convenience of man and beast, the stable had a loft, reached by a narrow, vertical 'Jacob's ladder' fitted, not with rungs but with spaces to accommodate the shape of a man's boot.

The 'paddy loft' above the horses had a window and was intended not only for hay , but also as rough accommodation for a farm man, or for itinerant labourers who came every summer for haytime. Hay was pushed through a floor opening into wooden wall racks placed at an angle above the horse-troughs, while corn was stored in rat-proof metal or wooden bins on the ground floor. It was here, in the hayloft, that the farm cats often had their kittens, and where they were fed with warm milk from the nearby shippon.

Between the stable and a shippon (dialect of Germanic origin for cattle-shed, from OE *scypen*) for ten or twelve cows was the loose box for the bull, with its large mucking out hole into the midden adjoining the orchard. Hay was stored in the great barn, in which there was another smaller shippon. Here there were foddering gangways, with wooden *baulks* for the hay-mows above, while each cow in the milking herd stood in its individual *boose* tethered to a *stang*. Wooden *boskins* separated each pair of cows.[103] This arrangement was common to all the barns in the Dales.

Drebley barn itself was probably used for threshing small quantities of corn with a flail: the space between the cart doors and the opposite small doorway, now a window (see photo above) having been used for winnowing in the wind as it blew through. At other times, this space housed carts and sheep-shearing benches, haytime machinery, turnip-chopper, wheelbarrows and such like. A small horse-drawn trap or 'float' would have been housed in the single-story building adjoining the lane: by the mid-twentieth century this building had become a garage for motor vehicles. In the yard a large drinking trough was always kept full of clean running water, supplied from a tank in the croft which also supplied the house. Abundant water for these purposes came from springs on the edge of Barden Moor: it was frequently stained brown, from its passage through peat beds.

The yard and the front garden are enclosed on the south by their original stone walls, with uniformly made coping stones and stone gateposts, while a straight flagged path leads through the garden to a stout, semi-circular front doorstep which matches the stone step between the lane and the path.

In the kitchen yard the well-built barn bearing a datestone for 1831 is identified as a 'turf house'. It is likely that the datestone was inserted when the roof was raised to make provision for an upper floor, the re-used roof timbers indicating that an earlier building stood on this site.

Across the yard is a very small low building driven into the hillside. It has a barrel-

---

103 The names for all these features have been handed down through the Dales dialect, which in itself derives from the Old Norse and Old English words of pre-conquest Yorkshire.

# DREBLEY

vaulted roof, on which enormous flagstones rest, and a small opening at roof level opposite the entrance door. It is now used to store coal and paraffin, but was probably built as a storage chamber for root vegetables, see Chapter 4, Buildings in Barden.

Attached to all farmsteads was an earth closet or privy. The one at Drebley (now demolished) was approached by a flight of stone steps, leading up from the small backyard past a series of ornamental troughs which appear to have been constructed from stonework removed from the older house. As shown in the photograph the clean overflow water from these troughs runs through the yard in an open paved gully, with the pig sty in the background.

The relatively large size of Drebley farmhouse, with its attic bedrooms approached by a wooden staircase from within the 'polite' quarters of the house, is itself a rare if not unique feature on the estate. In 1886, payments appear in the estate cash book for 'building a new kitchen, glazing new windows, repairs to floors and priming and painting of doors.' Jacob Holmes was the tenant at this time and to him befell 'the cost of cartage of all materials.' These improvements were followed in 1905 by substantial additions to the east end of the Georgian house. At this time, a new scullery was added with a wool store above, reached by an external stone staircase. 'The steps leading to the chamber to be best description weather proof stone, square dressed and broached ,bedded in mortar.'[104]

It is evident that from 1830 until the beginning of the twentieth century, a great deal of care went into the functional as well as the aesthetic design of this house and garden and its farm buildings.

**Comments on the Estate Expenditure and Rentals for Drebley**
The enclosure and division of Drebley Thwaite, followed by the subsequent allotment of rough pastures had taken place from 1812 onwards, when one might have expected a marked change in rental values, but this is not reflected in the rent books. The building of the new house at Drebley in 1830 attracted only a modest rise in rent from £40 to £45 per annum,

---
104 Bolton MSS, Barden rentals.

although an abrupt rise to £80 took place in 1845. This is difficult to explain, since the acreage of the farm did not increase until after 1861, when land, formerly part of the small farm of Applegarth, was re-allocated to the three remaining farms in the hamlet. The substantial re-building of the farmyard took place in the 1860s and accordingly, the rent rose, this time by £10 per annum from £85 to £95, and remained at that level for 20 years. From 1870 onwards agricultural markets became generally depressed throughout the country, but it was not until 1887 that the Duke reduced rents to ease the hardship. Reductions were again introduced in 1894 and inexplicably do not appear to have been raised again after the new kitchen and the new wool store with its outside stone staircase were added in 1905.

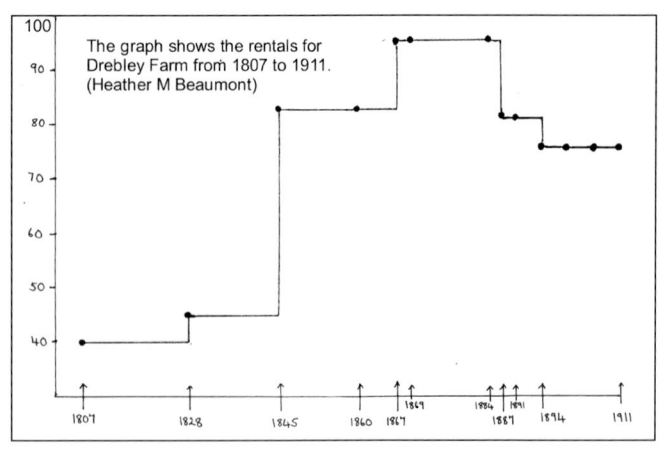

The graph shows the rentals for Drebley Farm from 1807 to 1911. (Heather M Beaumont)

After 1957, when Herbert Chester retired, the pattern of farming at Drebley changed. The empty buildings have remained intact, but concrete now obscures most of the old yard surface, the raised pavement and the kerb stones. The water troughs are dry while the great barn, the pig sty, loose boxes, stable, shippons and bull box, have echoed hollowly for half a century and more with sounds of the animals which had occupied them for nearly a hundred years. The rustle of hay in the farmer's arms as he moved along the fodder gang, the hiss of milk as it hit the sides of the buckets and the clatter of clogs, together with the smell of fresh, warm manure, are but a memory for a dwindling few.

## Other Farmsteads in Drebley: Fold Farm and Littlegate

At the same time as Drebley farm yard was undergoing such radical changes, one of the other three houses in the hamlet was almost doubled in size for the tenant, George Demaine. This was Fold Farm, where in 1862 plans were drawn up for an extension to the rear of the existing seventeenth century dwelling to form a substantial double-pile house.

During this period the farmhouse at Littlegate also underwent major changes, whereby the old thatched roof was removed, an upper storey was constructed, square sash windows similar to those at Drebley Farm were inserted, and the roof raised to support new 'blue' slates, similar to those on the roof of the great barn in Drebley yard. Meanwhile, the cruck barn in Little Gate yard had been restored, while, in 1841 a new barn was built in the style of others in the hamlet. As at Fold farm, the arrangement of the new and old buildings at Little Gate is informal, and in no way resemble the planned, model yard at Drebley farm.

Although the majority of buildings in the hamlet are roofed with local gritstone flags, there are 'blue' Lancashire (Burlington) slates on the roofs of the nineteenth century great barn in Drebley farmyard, the extension to Fold Farmhouse, and the former thatched, seventeenth century house at Littlegate. Because of their weight and the difficulties of transport, the use of roofing slates to replace thatch in even the most remote communities, such as that of Drebley, was an innovation that could only have been brought about by the advent of the canal, and later the railway, to Gargrave and Skipton. Could these slates have come from the Burlington quarries near Holker Hall, the home of the seventh Duke?

**Drebley Farmhouse** (surveyed in 1991 by R. A. Bedford-Payne, B. Bedford-Payne, John Ball, Colin Fullard and Brian Moxham)

SITUATION: The house is situated at the west end of the hamlet, on the north side of the lane. It faces south, with a small walled garden to the front. The east side faces a farmyard in which the buildings date from the 1860s.

GENERAL DESCRIPTION: A double pile, three storey building, with a two storey extension on the east gable. The building is of random local stone with gritstone slates on the roof, and dressed stone quoins, sills, jambs, and lintels. The third storey is in the roof space. There are three chimneys, one at each gable end and one at the gable end of the extension. Each chimney has a simple moulding round its upper edge.

FRONT OR SOUTH ELEVATION: This is asymmetrical, with the front door and the window above offset to the west. There are five sash windows with two lights per sash, each with dressed stone jambs, lintels and sills. The front door has no wooden frame, but closes onto stone jambs. The date stone above the door is inscribed H. H. 1830 for Henry Holmes. On the east gable, set back from the building line, is a two storey single cell extension to the house. It has two four-light sash windows, one set above the other, each with stone sills and lintels, and sectional jambs with centre quoins. The garden is enclosed by a stone wall with uniform coping stones and stone gateposts, while a flagged path leads straight to a stout, semi-circular doorstep.

EAST ELEVATION: Plain gable with small attic window at second floor level. Two-storey extension to the house. In 1890 a specification was drawn up for substantial additions to the east end of the Georgian house. At this time, a new scullery was added with a wool store above, reached by an external stone staircase. 'The steps leading to the chamber to be best description weather proof stone, square dressed and broached, bedded in mortar.'[105]

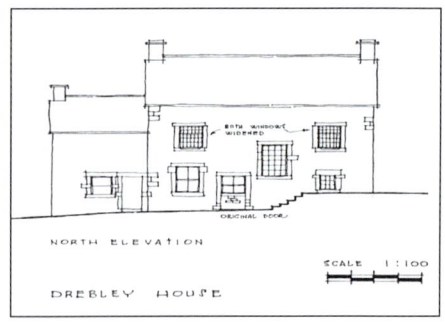

NORTH ELEVATION: It can be seen from the plan that the original back door has been walled up, and a window inserted into the upper half of the opening. To the left of this blocked doorway is a two light sash window, two lights per sash. The jambs are sectional, with quoins to the top. Two first floor windows are multi-paned, with upper opening lights; both have been widened, with jambs offset on their inner sides by about 15mms. To the right of the blocked doorway is a small multi-paned single light window, also using sectional jambs, but with quoins at the top. The multi-paned staircase window is offset to the west of centre line, in line with the front door. It has one sectional jamb, with centre quoin and one plain jamb. As with the front door, the back door to the extension has no wooden frame, and closes directly onto the stone jambs. Juxtaposed to this door is a two light sash window. Both door and window have sectional jambs and centre quoins.

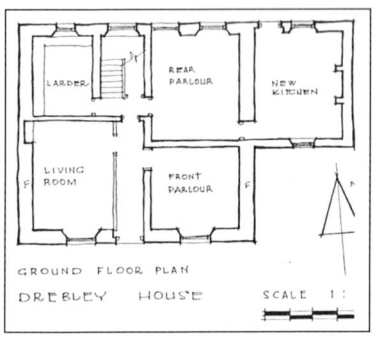

INTERIOR, GROUND FLOOR: All the rooms in this Georgian-style house are unusually 'lofty', each having a ceiling height of 2.8 metres. The original house consisted of a heated living room or housebody into which the front door opened. The heated front parlour led off this room The thin partition wall creating a front hall is a later alteration to the original plan, later removed)

The larder, staircase and a rear service room are in their original positions, with original stone-flagged floors, and in the larder, stone shelving. During the alterations carried out in 1886, when the back door was walled up, the rear service room became the living kitchen, with a cooking range and fireplace. Set into the wall of this room, to the left of a modern fireplace, is a small wall cupboard of late seventeenth century style.

---

105 Chatsworth/Bolton Mss, 1890.

# DREBLEY

The door of the cupboard has a raised, fielded panel, pegged framing, a brass keyhole and knob, and nailed butterfly hinges. From this room a doorway leads into the scullery extension, where there is a fireplace and the back door.

UPPER FLOOR: There are four rooms corresponding to those on the ground floor, and a large woolstore in the extension. This connects through a doorway into the house via an outside stone staircase.

THE ATTIC FLOOR: is approached from the first floor landing by a wooden staircase. A wooden partition and door enclose two rooms with a central hallway. The roof timbers are not under drawn, and appear to have been re-used from an earlier building. The relatively large size of Drebley farmhouse, with its attic bedrooms approached by a staircase from within the 'polite' quarters of the house, is itself a rare if not unique feature on the estate.

HISTORICAL DEVELOPMENT: A dwelling house is shown on this site on a map dated 1730. The house and its named occupants are mentioned in an estate rent book dated 1806, but from the present building there is little evidence to show where this house might have been; it is unusual for all the features of a stone house dating from the seventeenth to eighteenth century to disappear altogether, as these seem to have done. For instance, the tall facade of the house and the associated height of the rooms are unexpected, and there is little suggestion of any earlier stonework which might have been associated with mullioned window openings or dripstones, as can be seen at the other two farmhouses in the hamlet. Despite this, it is thought that the following features have survived from the earlier house which pre-dated the one built in 1830:

- ❏ The pantry window on the north west elevation, and the stone flagged floor and shelving within.
- ❏ One or two stone steps in the lower part of the staircase, the rest of which is wooden.
- ❏ The wall cupboard in the rear living kitchen.
- ❏ Quoins in the footing at the south west corner of the present house.
- ❏ Re-use of sectional window jambs and other stone work in ornamental troughs in the small back yard (now dismantled).
- The unusual lack of symmetry might suggest that the off centre positions of the front door and upper window were dictated by walls surviving from the earlier house.

Drebley conforms to a style which developed from about 1700 onwards, and was common in the north and south Dales, and in the Craven area.[106] These houses were two-cell, direct entry, end-stack plan. They consisted of a large housebody into which the front door opened, with a smaller parlour leading off it. The stairs led up from the rear of the housestead in a projecting turret or an outshut which included a dairy and service room. At a later date, some direct entry houses were altered to partition off an entrance passage, thus keeping the housebody free from draughts. At Drebley however, although there is a thin partition

---

[106] Harrison, Barry, and Hutton, Barbara, *Vernacular Houses in North Yorkshire and Cleveland*, Edinburgh, 1984, John Donald Publishers Ltd.

forming a passageway through the original housebody, the ceilings have been raised and there is no indication of any original beams or of the firehood.

When the new house was built in 1830 the rear service room became incorporated into living/cooking quarters, with a back door opening directly into it. It is suggested that the original firehood with its cooking range was removed from the old housebody at this stage, and re-positioned in the new living kitchen while the old housebody became extra living and sleeping accommodation.

In 1886 the back door was partly walled up, a window inserted in the opening and a new kitchen and back door added at the east end of the house. Payments appeared in the estate cash book for 'building a new kitchen, glazing new windows, repairs to floors and priming and painting of doors.'[107]

In 1890, a scullery with a wool store above, approached by an outside staircase were built, thus completing the house which stands today:

> October 3rd 1890, the specification of the several works required to be done in the building of a new kitchen and wool chamber over, at Mr Jacob Holmes, Barden, for His Grace the Duke of Devonshire, agreeable to the drawings here finished. Estimates to be sent in detail as to qualities and to prices.
>
> All cartage of materials to be done by the tenant.
>
> Take down the walls of the old scullery and coal place and take up gateposts into backyard and draw wall for doorway into present kitchen.
>
> Excavate the ground for foundations, drains and receive concrete floor.
>
> The sound and approved old stone from old buildings to be used for the new walling – any extra wall stone stones required will be provided. The whole of the walls to be built in a manner to correspond with the present walls having similar main quoins.
>
> Remove and securely fix slop-stone on brick piers, also fix lead pipes, (which will be provided) to discharge onto dish-stone.
>
> Set furnace in brickwork and set kitchen range.
>
> The steps leading to the chamber to be best description weather proof stone, square dressed and broached, bedded in mortar.[108]

Many other dwellings mentioned in early nineteenth century Barden rent books were described as being 'thatched and in very poor repair'; it is possible that Drebley was one that was beyond repair. It is evident that the alterations were to be at the expense of the landlord, although cartage was to be the responsibility of the tenant. This is the only house in Barden, (and possibly on the Bolton Abbey estate?) to show dated initials on the lintel above the front door.

*Henry Holmes, 1830.*

---

107 Jacob Holmes and his wife, Ann, were the tenants at this time.
108 Barden Township rentals: 1890, Bolton MSS., Chatsworth Estate.

# DREBLEY

## Some of those who lived at Drebley Farm 1627-1957

1627 – Francis Atkinson

1641 – Humfrey Holmes of Barden, husbandman, held a lease for a messuage, closes, lands, etc. 'sometime parcel of the ancient messuage late of Christopher Ellis of Drebley, deceased' north half part of the Netherfield Close called Hagg, also close called Winter Gap Yeats.

1650 – George Atkinson

1720-1805 Henry Holmes. In 1795 he had pew no 24 in Bolton Abbey and in 1774 paid tithes on 26 lambs and 60 sheep

1740 – Gershom Holmes, born 1726, son of Ingram Holmes of Drebley in Barden: Farmers and Shoemakers: he married Jane Iveson of Hartlington, (Burnsall Parish Register). A letter conveys a request to be admitted as tenant to Thos. Atkinson's farm at Drebley

1750 Rent paid £8-15-0 increased to £11-11-0

1754 Rent paid £12-5-0

1804 Gershom Holmes admitted into the church (i.e. baptised), son of Henry Holmes and Rebecca Demaine. Henry Holmes, born 1777, married Margaret Demaine aged 26 in 1803 at Bolton Abbey. Son Jacob born 1814.

Jacob Holmes, 1814-93, married Ann 1828-1901. Headstone in Bolton Abbey churchyard. Farmed at Drebley 1851 census. Rentals 1860, 1867, 1881 census 114 acres.

The last member of the Holmes family left in 1929, when Hebert Chester took up the tenancy. He farmed there until 1957. Some years later the lands were re-distributed between Littlegate and Fold farms.

## Fold Farmhouse, Drebley

(surveyed by Upper Wharfedale Field Society, 6 November 1991)

### SITUATION

Fold Farm lies at the end of the lane. The house faces south, with a small walled garden adjoining a paved yard to the front.

### GENERAL DESCRIPTION AND VERNACULAR BUILDING SURVEY[109]

The front section of the house dates from the late seventeenth century. In the mid-nineteenth century major alterations and an addition to the rear of the house took place. It is a three bay two storey house, double pile, under a double roof with a valley gutter. Built of rather thin coursed sandstone it has a central chimney stack and another chimney at each gable. The roof is blue slate.

### SOUTH ELEVATION

The entrance door is at the west end, with a large monolithic, roughly shaped lintel similar to the lintel over the entrance door to Littlegate Farmhouse (Arnold Pacey). There are two

---

[109] Survey Team: Upper Wharfedale Field Society, Report No. 33 and Yorkshire Vernacular Buildings Study Group, Report No. 1252, B. Moxham, Ian Goldthorpe, Kate Mason, Richard and Bronte Bedford-Payne, Beth Fullard, John Ball.

windows on the ground floor, each under a dripstone with dropped and returned ends. The western window is four-light, and the eastern window is three-light, with chamfered mullions.

The upper storey has three two-light mullioned windows with double recessed surrounds, each with a central mullion. There are traces of former openings in the stonework.

# DREBLEY

*Gable end of Fold Farm, Drebley.*

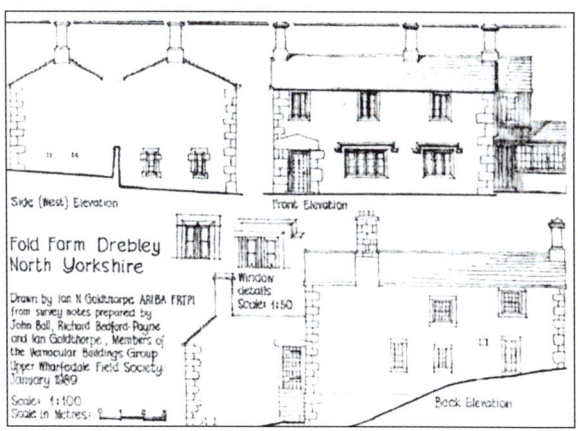

*Drawn by Ian Goldthorpe, ARIBA, FRIPA, from survey notes prepared by members of the Vernacular Buildings Survey Group of the Upper Wharfedale Field Society, January 1989.*

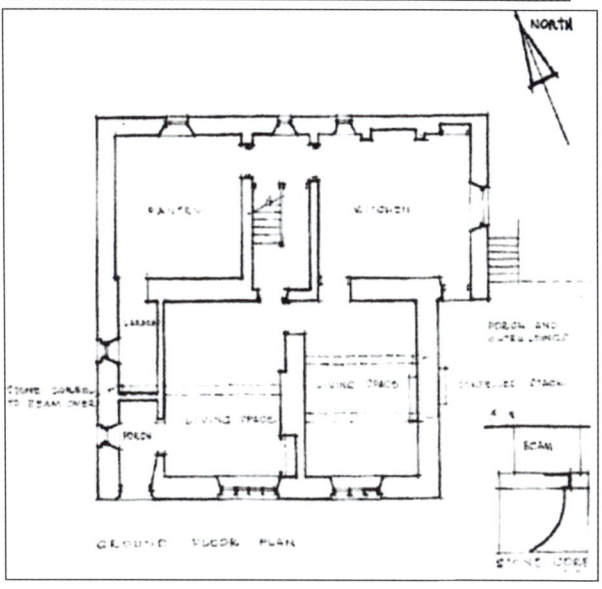

## NORTH ELEVATION

There is an indication of there having been a 'cat-slide' roof on the north wall, now replaced by a two-storey extension to the rear of the original house. This is built on a massive plinth of bedrock, rising from ground which falls rapidly away. The bedroom and service room windows are mid-nineteenth century with flat stone frames.

# BARDEN IN WHARFEDALE, THE PLACE AND ITS PEOPLE

## East and West Elevations

On the east gable the chimney stack is corbelled out at first floor level. Attached to the gable end of the house is a single storey outhouse where a stone centre table still in situ would probably have been used for pig killing. On the west, there is a plain double gable.

## Interior

This house has been much altered. It is probable that a single storey rear out-shot was raised to two storeys, thus making a double pile house with two extra bedrooms. It is not clear where the original staircase was situated. The parlour fireplace has been altered and the ceiling beams boxed in so that earlier features are hidden. It was not possible to see the roof trusses.

## Nineteenth century Barnyard

The farm is mentioned in the Barden rentals 1806 and 1828 and 1860: 94 acres at £84 rent per annum. In 1860 the acreage was increased by the addition of Hagg Closes, formerly farmed by the Wades of Applegarth, Drebley.

The large barn bears an initialled datestone, WD 1840 for William Demaine. The roof is slated with gritstone flags, as would have been normal at this date, before blue slates were brought to Barden.

A short flight of steps leading to an adjoining small barn are very heavily worn by the passage of iron shod, clogged feet.

## The Demaines at Fold Farm

The earliest surviving leases for this farm date from 1602. The Demaine family name recurs throughout the centuries as tenants of farms on the west side of Barden. In Drebley, they lived at both Littlegate and Fold Farm, but it is not always possible to identify which branch lived at which farm, or even to establish a sketchy family tree. The Demaines (besides farming in Bolton Abbey) were also at Barden Scale and at Hole House, but not at Woodend, Drebley House, Club Nook or Low House (Gillbeck) neither did they farm on the east side of the valley. The recurring, principle Christian names of the male members of the family at Fold Farm were William or George.

There is a headstone in the churchyard of Bolton Priory for

> Mary, wife of George Demaine of Drebley, Nov. 26th 1818
> George Demaine, 2nd September 1821, Aged 71 years.

Another generation later William Demaine died 27 April 1844. In his will dated 1842,[110] he bequeathed to his son George, born 1805, his lands in Appletrcewick and Burnsall, money, the whole stock of cattle with ploughs, carts, and instruments of husbandry, and one half of his furniture; the whole of the goods and chattels did not exceed £2,000. He also willed that 'if agreeable to His Grace the Duke of Devonshire and his agents that my son George may become the tenant of the farm which I hold under His Grace the Duke.'

He also bequeathed to another son, Benjamin, born 1811, lands and buildings situated at Embsay, two thirds of his money 'lent on note and one half of his furniture'

Later on in the century George Demaine and his wife Mary had seven children.[111] After George's death in 1888, Joseph Constantine, born 1833 in Appletreewick, and his wife Mary

---

110 Borthwick Institute, York.
111 1851 census.

née Demaine, farmed the Fold while George's grandson, Mary's nephew Hubert Demaine born in 1877 was a minor. Hubert lived with them, was a pupil at Barden School, and then took the lease of the farm in 1912.

**Twentieth century farming at Fold Farm**
In the 1920s an outbreak of Johne's disease afflicted the farm, during which time, to discover the cause of this wasting disease, and the means to prevent its recurrence Hubert Demaine consulted the agent at Bolton Abbey, Mr Downs, and local veterinary surgeons. Surviving correspondence reveals that difficulties in daily cleansing of the old shippons were partly to blame, and as a result, the Estate was obliged to modernise them. In addition, Hubert was advised to change his herd of cattle from beef to dairy, since he could no longer sell his diseased beasts to the butchers, and it must have been assumed that the milk would be free of infection.

His daughter Joan won a County Minor scholarship from Barden School, and was a pupil at Skipton Girls High School. She was one of the first to travel daily from the station at Bolton Abbey because by the time she went to school in Skipton, her father had a motor car and was taking milk in kits for transport by train to a dairy in Ilkley. And so Joan went to the station with the full kits each morning, and returned with the empties in the afternoon. She later married Harry Riley, and their son Robert was the last member of the Demaine family to farm the Fold.

**Billy Mason's memories of farming at Fold farm, Drebley in the 1920s**
(From a tape recording circa 1992, transcribed by Heather Beaumont):

> I went to Hubert Demaine's farm in 1925, when I were fifteen years old, and I left in about 1929, just before Chesters came to Drebley. My father took me in a taxi from Addingham Moorside, where we had our farm. Taxis were just coming in then. They dropped me at t'lane end, and I were left to mysen. I had tuppence in m'pocket. All my father said were 'Do plenty of work for thy master.' He were one of eleven children and I were one of eight, and so by that time I had to leave home and fend for mysen.
>
> Mr Demaine behaved exceptionally well to me, and so did t'wife, but she were a funny person, rather. (It was well known that whenever his wife had a 'funny turn', Hubert would go and sit on the back steps of the farmhouse and play his trumpet. The sound could be heard all round the valley and particularly in Drebley hamlet).
>
> They looked after me manfully. T'women did all the washing, everything. We had candles, and there were all blooming chores to do, you know, fetching tatties, filling t'coal buckets, and Tilley lamps to trim.
>
> But in all the years that I were there, I had nowt but good luck because I came wi' nowt, and I picked her up (his wife, Mary Ideson of High Gamsworth). Trade at that time were pretty flat, and there were nowt much doing, but we got plenty to eat and I was always well treated, so I did not grumble. I got ten bob a week and me keep. I liked me job and money never entered into it, really speaking. I think you're a lot happier if it doesn't.
>
> My first duties on getting up, for a start, not very early, not in them days, in winter about half past seven. Mr Demaine lit the fire while I went and gave t'cows some hay and when I came

## DREBLEY

back he had a cup o'tea ready for me. Then I went round those barns, foddering t'cattle. I went to Haggs first, then to our high barn, then back home for breakfast. It took me about an hour. After that we did all t'chores, cleaned out cattle foddered again and went round t'barns again. We had it all to walk, three times a day and now, when they have tractors, they only go once. Milking came on after we'd done t'barns, but there were no milking when I first went there. When he started again, Mr Demaine took it in his car to Hindle's dairy in Ilkley or got it taken to Bolton Abbey station for the Creamery. In a bad winter, snow could block the road.

I once walled a gap just across from John Hustwick's place (at either The Scale, or The Holme farm) I were about sixteen, and I were really proud o'me work because t'boss had sent me to do it on me own. Hustwick were across t'field doing some draining, so I shouts across, 'I've finished walling this gap, Mr Hustwick; will ye come and 'ave a look at it, and tell us what ye think.' So he walks across to me and lit his pipe with about a yard of twist while walking round and round and back again and then he said, 'Well if tha really wants to know, it looked better down.' Talk about being deflated…!

There were bits of arable land left after t'First World War. Harry Holmes had four acres at Drebley, but we had a few turnips, a few mangolds and a few potatoes, just a few acres to plough, which they made 'em do during t'war. Then it went back to grass, but they made 'em plough it up again during t'Second World War. But it wern't in same way, because by then they 'ad better tackle, tractors and such-like. They all kept their sheep of course, like they do now, with a flock on Barden moor. Harry Holmes had 200-300 Swaledales on that bit of ground. It aint just good enough for Dalesbred sheep. At that time, we dipped at Fold farm, but then Chester's made a new one, just by t'back door, and they all made it among 'em.

They were still breeding a few horses and breaking 'em in themselves. Cecil Demaine did that at Littlegate. You can do with one horse in winter, but in haytime you need more, and we had two at Fold farm when I went to work there.

We mostly grew what hay we needed but there were a bit to buy sometimes. Believe me, they wern't that well-off and it could be bit of a disaster if there were hay to buy.

In haytime, Mr Demaine hired Irishmen off Skipton High Street. He would give them so much 'fastening money' to make sure they followed him home, but even then some of them would bolt and get more from another farmer. The trick was to take the man's bag home with you. When I were at Demaine's, the same two came every year. They came to Skipton railway station where t'boss met them wi t'hoss and trap.

They came for a month, but if t'weather had been too bad for haymaking, it were all to do after they had gone home. At Drebley, they slept in t'room at the top of the outside stone steps, while with us they slept in the Little Croft, below t'stairs. They preferred to sleep out, and then when they went drinking in t'evening, they could come in when they liked. They used the wooden footbridge to get to the New Inn in Appletreewick.

I didn't often get to Skipton. We used to go at Whitsuntide, and make an Outing of it.

T' first time I went to market were in t'back o' t' Trap. They yoked up t'hoss, and then while t'boss, wi' wife and daughter sat in front, I sat in t'Dicky seat in t'back. It didn't seem a long way, and time seemed to go pleasantly enough. We used to walk it if it were t'only way we could get. A carrier from Appletreewick would bring the things home in his cart, while we walked back. A horse and cart brought coal from Bolton Abbey station. In 1925 the first motor cars were just beginning to come up t'dale.

Every autumn there was a sheep sale in a field by Barden Tower. A man called Abraham Banks used to come to t sale from Malham Moor (Capon Hall) and stay with his nephew, Herbert Chester at Drebley. Every year he bought Miss Demaine's draught ewes from Barden Scale and

# BARDEN IN WHARFEDALE, THE PLACE AND ITS PEOPLE

then walked 'em home by Skyrethorns and Mastiles Lane. The lands up there were a bit better going, and he would breed another crop or two of lambs before they went to market.

Rabbits were a terrible pest. Cecil Demaine used to say that when he went off rabbiting he had to lift a few out of the burrow, before he could put t'ferret in.

Stephen Birch were t'head keeper when I first went to Drebley. There were about nine of 'em in his family and they all won scholarships. There is a whole list of them on t'Honours Board in t'school. Beautiful little school. You could have envied them when they went to school. They used to go on nature walks, and we'd tek 'em bird-nesting. It were a great time. Duchess used to come and present prizes, while t'kids curtsied, and all t'rest of it.

Some nights, us lads went to t'Reading Room at Watergate. We went up some little steps round t'back There was just one room where t'locals played billiards or darts. Quite frankly, I thowt there were nowhere like Drebley, although I sacked mysen once when we fell out over summat! And when it got round to t'weekend, I says to t'boss 'do yer want me to go?' and he says, 'please yersen.' And so, I stayed.

*Photographs taken in the 1930s show Hubert Demaine with some of his prized Swaledale sheep at Fold Farm.*

Recommended reading from the *Dalesman,* vol. 41, July 1979, No.4, *Some Haytimes of Long Ago* by W. R. Mitchell, based on personal recollections from the 1920s and conversations with Billy Mason of Low Hall, Appletreewick.

# DREBLEY

## Littlegate Farm, Drebley

### The Farmhouse

In 1806, the buildings of Littlegate Farm were described in the estate rent books as a dwelling house, barn and cowhouse. The cowhouse was said to be thatched, and it is evident from other documents and a later photograph that the farmhouse was thatched as well. However, in 1886 the house was re-roofed with blue Lancashire slate. At the same time the front wall was raised just over a foot higher to give more headroom in the upstairs rooms, and to allow the small upstairs windows to be replaced by taller and wider ones, framed with stone jambs and lintels.

These alterations left many older features intact and, to investigate these, a survey of the house was made by members of the Upper Wharfedale Field Society in 1989.[112] Later, when the house was unoccupied in 2010, a second survey lead by Alison Armstrong recorded details that had not previously been clear (report appended at the end of this article.)

### Description: Exterior

The house faces south and has walls of evenly coursed gritstone which rise from a well defined plinth. It has a rectangular plan with three rooms on the ground floor and an outshut at the back. Access to the upstairs rooms was originally via a stair in the outshut which also functioned as a dairy.

Windows to the ground floor rooms were less altered in 1886 than those upstairs. Mullions of two of them were replaced, but the window at the west end of the frontage retains its original form with mullions and jambs double chamfered, partly with a form of hollow 'cavetto' moulding. Mullions with this profile suggest a construction date before 1650, and probably before the Civil War. Between two somewhat altered windows further east is the

---

[112] Including Molly Chisholm, Robert Chisholm, Brontë Bedford-Payne, Jean Reinsch, and Colin Fullard, with help from two other local historians, Kate Mason and Arnold Pacey.

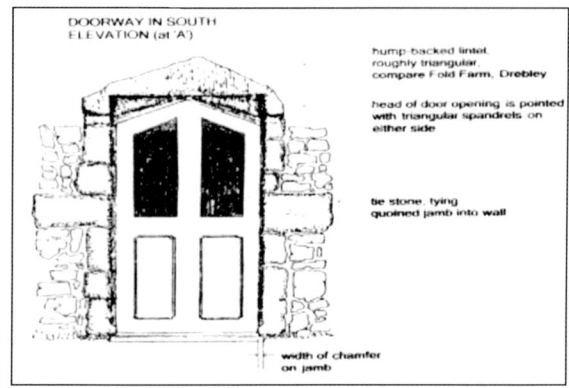

main doorway, which has a pointed doorhead under a 'hump-back' lintel that is almost triangular in elevation. This detail is likely to date from the seventeenth century, the hump-backed shape of the lintel is unusual. Its date is partially confirmed by the house at Fold Farm (Drebley) which has a door lintel that is similarly humped, though in a more regular triangular manner. This is thought to be have been a style preferred by a particular local mason at the time.

INTERIOR
The three-room plan of the house with outshut at the back is illustrated by a drawing of the ground plan, where the middle room is labelled as the 'housebody'. This was the main living room and was the location of the principal hearth or fireplace where most of the cooking was done (now replaced by a plain nineteenth century fireplace with a gritstone surround). The end rooms were both probably parlours (though one is now the kitchen), whereas the outshut at the back accommodated the original staircase and was equipped with the stone shelves that would be required in a dairy.

Looking at the windows from inside, one sees how the west parlour (kitchen) window has its original chamfered and moulded mullions whereas the other windows have been altered. The housebody and east parlour have heavy ceiling beams with wide chamfers that end with curved, hollow stops. This detail, like that of the west parlour window, is consistent with an early seventeenth century date.

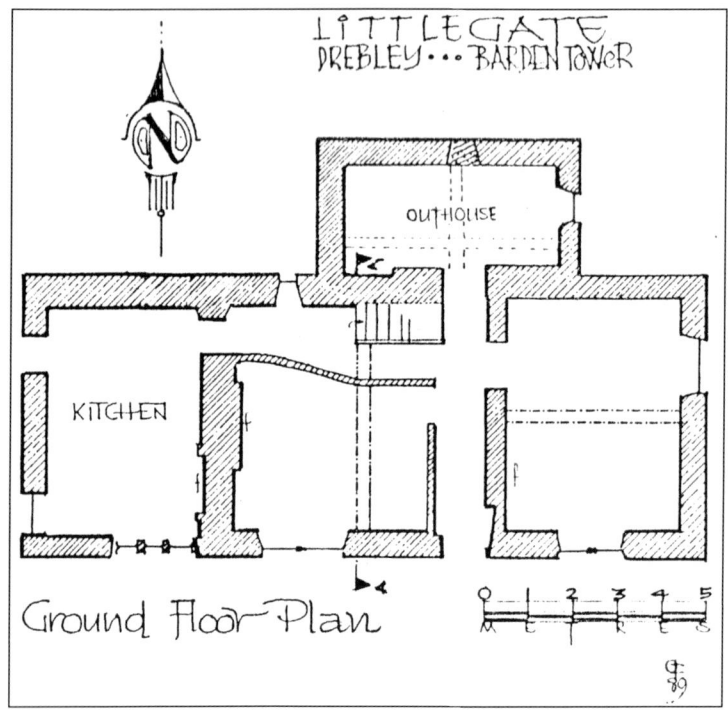

The modern stairs are parallel with the back wall, and at the top of them there is a pair of steeply-inclined roof timbers forming the 'upper cruck' truss which is illustrated. The feet of the inclined cruck timbers are tenoned into the main transverse beam supporting the first floor, which is also the ceiling beam seen from within the housebody. Both timbers are curved and each has a distinct knee, as shown in the illustration.

The truss is symmetrical, two crucks having been cut from a single tree trunk, so their shapes match. The tree was a massive oak, and the timber is rather knotted and waney, as is characteristic of trees grown in the open rather than in dense woodland. The timbers are linked by a collar-beam (labeled in the illustration) which is well made and is joined to the main timbers with 'half-lap joints' in the cruck tradition.

There is also an upper collar above the ceiling in

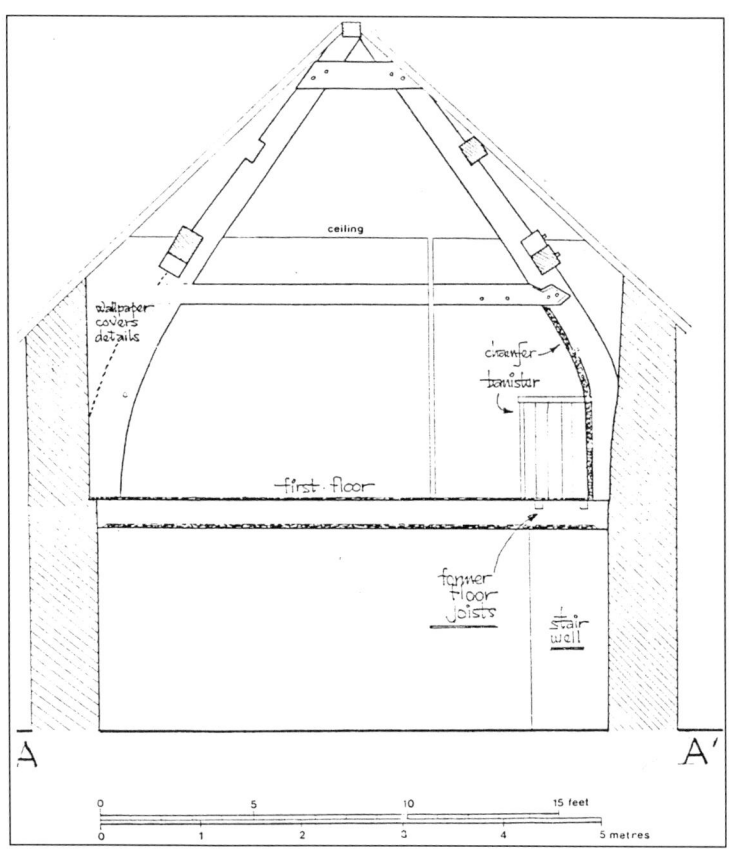

*The upper cruck truss of Littlegate Farmhouse, drawn by Arnold Pacey, January 1989.*

the attic space. It was possible to examine this during the 1989 survey but it was not accessible in 2010. The collar has a redundant joint and peg-holes where a ladder stair may once have been fixed for access to the attic rooms which were obviously much used, since they retain thick layers of limewash up to the ridge.

THE EARLY HOUSE IN SUMMARY AND ITS LATER DEVELOPMENT

The above description includes most of what can be deduced by examination of the building. While the house may be on an old site, and the plinth perhaps survives from an earlier building, the present structure has many features of early seventeenth century appearance, including the mullions of the oldest window and the chamfered ceiling beams. In their book on Yorkshire vernacular houses, Harrison and Hutton pointed out that houses like this with three rooms arranged along the length of a rectangular plan mostly date from before 1650 and a number have upper crucks. Littlegate is typical of its period in its plan and structure as well as in architectural detail.

As to the history of the house in the nineteenth century, there are estate rent books that provide more information, including one which mentions the cowhouse and barns in 1806 as well as the house itself. Another reference in 1867 described the 'dwelling house' at

# BARDEN IN WHARFEDALE, THE PLACE AND ITS PEOPLE

*Willie Demaine.*

Littlegate Farm as 'thatched and in bad repair'. It added that the farm buildings were mostly good, apart from a barn that needed re-thatching. Another barn was rebuilt in stone in 1841 and has a datestone with the initials WD for William Demaine. Other barns associated with Littlegate include two of the cruck barns that still survive in Drebley.

Rent books tell us that in 1886, 'Christopher Demaine of Littlegate repaired a thatched house at his own expense.' It was probably at this date that the alterations noted earlier were made, when the old thatched roof was replaced by a slightly higher roof of blue slate, most windows were altered, and a partition was inserted in the housebody to create a passage containing the stairs at the back of the house.

Addition to Yorkshire Vernacular Buildings Study Group Report No 1249 (1989); Little Gate Farm, Drebley, Barden.[113]

## Exterior

The plan is of three cells with a central housebody, east and west parlours and a stair/service outshut. There is direct entry into the housebody. It is of full two storeys. The linear three cell house is of one build with a large axial stack which has been rebuilt in nineteenth century. There is a large plinth all around the house. At the front (south) it is very flat and may have been the base of an older linear building of timber-framed construction. The rear outshut is added and has a rougher plinth. Inside the outshut, the plinth of the linear house is hidden below the floor level but is probably there. (Fold Farm at Kettlewell, has a large boulder plinth to a linear former timber framed building of six bays and tree-ring dated to 1450-60).

The house is known to have been thatched as seen in an old photograph. Thatch was very common in mid/upper Wharfedale as there is no roofing stone. Barden Tower (built circa 1485) had a lead and turf roof. Steep rooflines remain in many local barns and houses as well as re-used cruck timbers. The timber-framed Great Barn at Bolton Abbey (circa 1518) however had a sandstone

*Cecil Demaine with Dalesbred lambs.*

---

[113] Following a visit on 29 April 2010, Alison Armstrong, Brontë Bedford-Payne, Jo Drake, Sonia Wilkinson.

# DREBLEY

*Cecil with Hubert Demaine's prize Swaledale tup.*

roof, possibly of Bradley flags from stone mines on the Clifford's land at High Bradley.

The roofing of Littlegate is now of graded Lancashire slates put on in 1886. The raised roof line from thatch to slate can be seen as a ledge in the stonework on the frontage some 40cm below the eaves. At the rear, the line is seen as a change in stonework. The outshut was originally continuous with the thatched roof but is now below the slated eaves line. The changes resulting from the raised roofline are also well seen in the internal roof space over the west chamber, but because the exterior gables are rendered no roofline can be seen. The upper cruck roof truss was sufficient to hold up a steep thatched roof but new replacement sawn rafters now support the raised roofline and the slates.

*William (Willie) Demaine was born in 1883, the son of Christopher (1832-1906) and Ellen (born 1851) Demaine of Littlegate, Drebley. Willie and his sister Elizabeth (Lizzie) were pupils at Barden School and both are mentioned in the school's log book. Lizzie was the mother of Cecil Mossman Demaine (1900-93) who later farmed at Hole House.*

At the same time as re-roofing, new windows were inserted. The mullioned windows of the housebody and east parlour were removed and the jambs hacked away to allow for small sash or casement windows in the openings. The hollow-chamfered, early seventeenth century, three-light mullions of the west parlour (now the kitchen) were retained. Four extra sash windows replaced the two small first floor windows tucked under the eaves. (This report was written by Alison Armstrong)

*Cecil Demaine ploughing in Low Meadow in the 1940s.*

*Cecil Demaine setting off to fodder the outbarns in the 1930s.*

## Keeper's Cottage, Drebley

Although this house has earlier stonework in its walls, it is not mentioned in any rent books until 1806 when the entry reads as follows: '...the dwelling house was occupied by Henry Holmes's father, but was built by the son.'

Later, Henry Holmes lived and farmed at Drebley House, where his initialled date stone HH 1830 is inscribed on the lintel over the front door.

The later rent book entries for the Cottage read as follows:

In 1828, the peat-house attached to the western gable was replaced by a barn.

In 1860 'the dwelling house was newly repaired', and transferred to Parkinson Inman, gamekeeper who came from Howgill.[114]

In 1867 Thomas Birch, gamekeeper, was living in the cottage when it was described as 'nearly new and very complete'.

In 1868 'addition to Parker Inman's cottage at Drebley.'

*Parkinson Inman.*

This cottage was one of many others in Barden which underwent major improvements during the 1860s. The attached notes and photographs indicate what changes were made, and how from being a single cell, thatched cottage, it became a substantial, although small two storey house, with a slated gritstone roof.

## Observations about the structure of the cottage by Arnold Pacey

A straight joint, composed of large, irregular quoins, can be seen to the left of the present front door. These quoins show the extent of the earlier building, and are an indication that the present entrance doorway is not in its original position. The outline of a blocked doorway can clearly be seen to the left of the present entrance, while irregularities in the stone work show that the present doorway, together with its lintel and jambs, has been moved from its original position in the single cell cottage to its present position.

The stonework around this doorway and the three new windows with dressed jambs, lintels and sills may have been the work of an estate mason perhaps dating from the 1860s.

---

114 Photograph of Parkinson Inman courtesy of The Craven Museum, Skipton.

# DREBLEY

Differences can also be seen between the two earlier windows on the frontage.

Evidence for an even earlier phase in the history of the building lies in the stonework towards the end of the building, low down below the sill of the parlour window. A large vertical stone here may be the jamb of what was once a fire window, set low to illuminate the hearth and allow anybody cooking to see what they were doing. An alternative interpretation is that the large stones low down in the wall here were the base on which a cruck or the support for a bressumer once stood, but they are really too near the end of the building for either of these possibilities to seem likely.

Changes in the quoins at the west corner indicate that the roof has been raised and the first floor window inserted. Similarly, changes in the stonework around the ground floor window suggest that it was modernised at the same time, the right hand jamb showing how the original window opening here was somewhat lower. This may be the building referred to in 1806 as having been built by Henry Holmes' son but lived in by the father.

The slated roof with one chimney is probably part of the 1868 building, when a staircase was installed, leading straight up from the entrance door and small lobby. The kitchen and the two 'new' bedrooms are unheated. The stone-built garage and entrance drive were added in the late twentieth century

## Social History

The domestic water supply was from a trough in the lane supplied from springs in the adjacent field, and carried in buckets up a short, steep hill through the garth in which the cottage stands. At some time, a hand pump was fixed in the scullery to supply water collected from the roof. Despite the convenience of the pump, it is presumed that drinking water continued to be collected directly from the springs. This water supply would have been of prime significance to the entire Drebley settlement from its earliest days onwards. Standing across the lane, the trough for the nearby cruck barn is also supplied with running water from the same source.

In the mid-nineteenth century, when gamekeepers were first appointed on the Bolton Abbey estate, it was necessary also to provide them with opportunities for subsistence, their wages being very low. In the hamlet of Drebley, the land surrounding Keeper's Cottage had formed part of Littlegate farm and Applegarth, a small farm occupied by the Wade family until abandoned in 1860; after this date, two pastures in Drebley Field were apportioned to the keeper, Parkinson Inman, who was then able to graze a few sheep and a cow with a

*Fred and Laura Inman with the family.*

calf, and to take an annual hay crop.[115] At the same time, a vegetable garden by the cottage and a separate croft were walled in; here, a small poultry flock were kept, while pheasant chicks for the estate shoots were hatched under broody hens, confined in coops with wire runs. The keeper paid £15 annual rent for his cottage and garth, the meadowland and cruck barn, where he kept a couple of pigs, raised calves and milked his cow in the shippon. A horse was not needed, and could not, in any case have been afforded.[116]

## DREBLEY CRUCK BARNS
### The Cruck barn at Littlegate, Drebley, visited October 1979
This is probably the barn mentioned by James Walton in his paper for the Yorkshire Archaeological Society Journal, Vol. 37. 1948-51, p.65,
This barn stands well back from Drebley Lane, in a walled field, and is built of rubble gritstone. It was originally thatched but now has a corrugated iron roof.

It is of three pairs of crucks, which makes four bays, one couple being set in a cross wall that divides the barn into two halves. The eastern end has a porch and cart entrance with a blocked winnowing doorway opposite. This barn was probably intended for threshing and storage of grain, although there is little space east of the threshing floor. (We could not visit the west end because it was closed and in total darkness).

The crucks are not as tall as those in the corn barn and have no windbraces. Their sectional dimension is about the same, circa 25 x 60 at wall top height and they are split trees, with one fair and one waney face. There are halvings for spur ties and (missing) tiebeams, two pairs of purlins and a ridgepiece but no windbraces. All the original roof covering has gone, but was probably the same as in the corn barn, i.e. closely set, riven laths, with thatch tied onto them. The present use is as a cattle shelter in the open end.

(Report by Barbara Hutton, member of The North Yorkshire and Cleveland Vernacular Buildings Study Group, 1979).

### Drebley Cruck Barn, visited 20 May 1991
The larger of the two barns is situated in a field opposite Keeper's Cottage, at the side of the lane running through the hamlet of Drebley. Approximately seventeen feet long, it is in two sections; the first section, to the left of the main cart entrance, is the smaller of the two, with a barrel vaulted, underground root crop store, approached by a flight of stone steps within the store. One full cruck frame is placed centrally between the outer wall and the internal dividing wall. The entrance is in the front elevation, with a blocked winnowing door opposite. The dividing wall is of small uniformly sized sandstone blocks, and goes up to the ridge.

The larger section has a cart entrance with porch in the front elevation, and a doorway opposite. There are two full cruck beams and an end wall of mixed rubble. In this section all the cruck frames, which are of oak, are complete with tie beams and collars. The roof

---

115 Michael Ogden, farm lad at Drebley during the 1940s, recalls how, after the main load had been carted away, every wisp of hay was gathered from the wall bottoms, by nag-raking across the fields. A nag-rake was A framed, with attachments enabling a farm worker to drag it over the grass.
116 In order to collect his weekly pay, the keeper cycled down to the estate office at Bolton Abbey.

structure is also complete, with rafters, purlins and roof tree, and traces of the original ling thatch. There are also several braces, all the timbers being joined by wooden pegs, although some are missing.

It is assumed that the oak came originally from the ancient forest of Barden, which was famous for its oak trees. It is difficult to date the building more accurately than from the late sixteenth to early seventeenth century and there is no mention of the date of origin in estate records.

The roof is covered by corrugated iron to preserve the timbers, which are in a very good state of preservation, as are the tie pieces and remaining collars.

Surveyed and report written May 1991 by Brian Moxham, John Wright, Richard and Brontë Bedford-Payne, members of The Yorkshire Vernacular Buildings Study Group and The Upper Wharfedale Field Society.

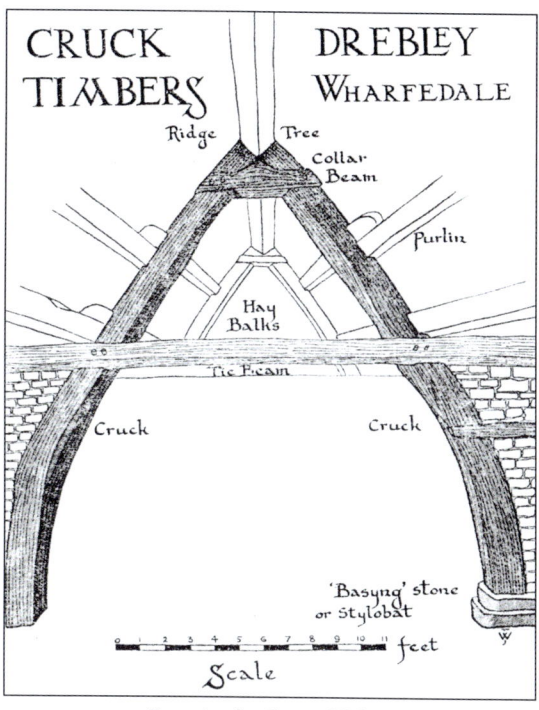

*Drawing by James Walton,*
*'Homesteads of the Yorkshire Dales', 1947.*

# 7
# Twentieth Century Life and Farming in the hamlet of Drebley

Information issued by the technical development sub-committee of the West Riding for the war Agricultural Executive Committee, October 1943, Volume Two, Number Five.

### FARMING TODAY
*One of a series of articles by practical men describing how they are overcoming the difficulties of war-time farming.*

by Mr. H. Chester, Drebley, Bolton Abbey, Skipton.

# FARMING IN DREBLEY

As I look out over my farm lands I see one of the most beautiful valleys in the whole of the Yorkshire Dales.

Beneath me flows the bonnie brown Wharfe and along its banks are the fertile meadow lands, light sharp gravelly land, which in good hands can produce a bumper crop of hay and fog. But the contour rises sharply and the high pastures of millstone grit are brown and bare where they reach up to the dark pine woods and the moor just now ablaze with purple heather.

In the early thirties, when the slump came to the Craven farmers, we were breeding sheep and cattle and, seeking an avenue of escape, started selling milk. I soon found there was no milk to be had from those brown pastures so I set out to improve them with lime and slag. It was a heartbreaking job and I soon realised my labour was all in vain. I even began to doubt the old saying 'that there is nothing as honest as land' until my friends from the University of Leeds came along with the key and said 'Why don't you plough and reseed'? My answer was a simple one, that I was a sheep man not a plough man for I had never handled one in my life. But with their help in 1937, we started on a worthless field of six acres which was covered with moor mat grass and bent, and six weeks after ploughing and re-seeding I had the joy of seeing 25 young heifers grazing in the rich lush grass putting on a bloom that even my best meadow lands could not produce. In the autumn this field *fattened* my hill lambs, actually fattened them where formerly only store condition could be attained.

Since then the plough has steadily advanced every year until it has been round the farm and this year we are back where we started in 1937. Last year the field first ploughed in 1937 was mown for hay for the first time and we got 26 good loads off six acres. To-day, it stands in stook with six different varieties of oats, one of the best crops I have ever seen and it is undersown to grass again. Thus we have started the second round. This time, with the increased fertility, it will be one of the best grazing fields in the district. Under the stress of war-time conditions my farm is immensely more productive than it was ten years ago with 17½ acres oats, 10½ wheat, 1½ potatoes, 16½ maiden seeds, 18½ reseeded. And in 1937 we regarded the plough as an unwanted alien in our dale!

Let us turn to my livestock. Ten years ago I was very proud of my typical dales herd of shorthorn cattle, but it opened my eyes when I joined the Yorkshire Milk Recording Society and some of these 'grand' animals finished their lactation with only 140 gallons of milk to their credit. I took a very big plunge from Dales custom when I went to Captain Skipwith of Doncaster and purchased a pure-bred Friesian Bull. The improvement in my herd was as spectacular as the change in the grassland by reseeding. He left me sixteen daughters and I was fool enough to sell him before I realised his true value purchasing under the Ministry's Livestock Improvement Scheme a dual-purpose Shorthorn at a cost of 85 guineas. He landed me back into the same hole I was in ten years previously. One of his daughters a 'grand animal' has just finished her lactation in 144 days having given 116 gallons of milk! Fortunately I realised my mistake two years ago and went back to the same breeder of consistently good milking Friesians and purchased another bull off a 1,290 gallon heifer. I have my good foundation cows and in the near future I hope to have a black and white herd of really good milking cows. They are all attested and I am hoping to sell TT milk in ever increasing quantities.

The flock of Swaledale breeding ewes heathed on the moor is half the size. I remember with some bitterness my best hill lambs being bid by public auction to 8 shillings a head in 1938. Last year all but four were graded at the Skipton Centre and the average weight was just over 29 lbs. giving a net return of over £2 a head. Re-seeded land can do sheep better than any crop I have ever tried. The first week in August this year I graded two single lambs off half-bred ewes crossed with a Suffolk at 65 lbs. each, a net return of £8 16s.

Having once set my hand to the plough I do not intend to turn back. It is true the old leisurely days have gone – for me, for ever – but ley farming has brought new heart to my land, a new interest in life and although in this peaceful Dale we are far removed from the scene of conflict we know that we are playing our part in the food production campaign.

BARDEN IN WHARFEDALE, THE PLACE AND ITS PEOPLE

**Farming at Drebley 1929-1956**

The farming hamlet of Drebley lies to the north of Barden Tower, between the river Wharfe and the road to Burnsall. It is mentioned in the Domesday Book and is situated on the line of what is probably a pre-historic track-way running through the valley. It has developed on the site of one of the medieval hunting lodges in the Forest of Barden, owned first by the Romillies and then by the Cliffords of Skipton Castle, until it passed through marriage to the Burlingtons, and finally the Cavendish family, the Dukes of Devonshire.

Herbert Chester arrived at Drebley in 1929, having sold all his livestock of sheep and cattle before leaving Low Trenhouse. A neighbouring farm lad, Billie Mason of Fold farm, has recounted how he saw the new tenants arrive, bringing with them a wooden, horse drawn cart on the sides of which were painted the name of its maker, John Chester, Low Trenhouse. In the cart he saw bundles of wood-working tools and farm implements, such as hay rakes and forks, spades and shovels, for John Chester (Herbert's father) had been a carpenter as well as a farmer. Neighbours in the hamlet were the families of Hubert Demaine at Fold farm, William Demaine at Littlegate, and Fred Inman at the Keeper's Cottage. Forebears of the Demaines had lived on four of the same farms in Barden for at least 350 years, and so the Chesters were considered to be 'off come'd uns'. That is, although they were dales folk, they came from 'off the estate'.

Early setbacks arose, because the previous tenant at Drebley had been a sick man, who had not tended the farm carefully. This meant that many hazards befell the newly bought-in stock. For instance, a valuable young heifer was lost when it drank from a trough in which poisonous sheep dip had been carelessly thrown, and the milking herd were affected by a severe wasting disease, (Johne's disease) transmitted via the dung from the previous tenant's cattle which had contaminated the grazing.

Farming has always been hard on this upland terrain, with its high rainfall, and his holding was described by Herbert as follows:

> Along the banks of the Wharfe there are fertile meadow lands which, in good hands, can produce a bumper crop of hay and fog. But the contour rises sharply, and the high pastures of the millstone grit are brown and bare. Between the river and the unenclosed moorland the land rises from a height of about 450 feet to 900 feet above sea level.

The rearing of sheep and cattle has long dominated the agricultural scene in the dales; thus, when he took over his 200 acre holding Herbert Chester followed many of the traditional patterns. However, the slump of the 1930s brought much hardship, prompting him to seek expert advice and to pioneer farming methods that were new to Wharfedale.

At that time, farms in the Craven area were almost exclusively devoted to stock rearing;

most of the milk produced locally was made into butter and little, if any, was transported in liquid form, the 'milk kit' being practically unknown. In an effort to increase the production on his farm, Herbert first sought to improve the quality of those brown pastures at Drebley:

> Initially I set out to improve them with lime and slag, but it was a heart breaking job, and I soon realised that my labour was in vain. However, in 1937, with advice and assistance from the University of Leeds, (most notably, Dr Ian Moore, one of the foremost grassland authorities in the country, who was later attached to the West Riding War Agricultural Committee) I started, for the first time in my life, ploughing and reseeding. I started on a worthless field of matt grass and bents, and eight weeks later I had the joy of seeing 25 young heifers grazing in the rich lush grass. They put on a bloom that even my best meadow lands had hitherto failed to produce. In the autumn, this field fattened my hill lambs where formerly only store condition could be attained. Since then, the plough has steadily advanced every year until in 1942 we got 26 good loads of hay from six acres, mown for the first time off the first field ploughed in 1937. The following year that field stood in stook with six different varieties of oats (part of Ian Moore's experiments). This was one of the best crops I have ever seen at Drebley, and I have under sown it with grass again.

In later years, he became a firm believer in silage, and every year he devoted a few meadows of his 60 acres of fertile land to growing good grass for the pit. The need to maximise food production during World War II also posed new challenges, including the cultivation of arable crops, although arable farming, particularly the ripening of cereal crops was always a difficult struggle in the wet Pennine climate. Thus once the war was over, the unequal struggle was abandoned. However, the technique of ploughing and reseeding on marginal land, pioneered at Drebley and Club Nook, has stood the test of time. The management of ley grassland became an established practice which now forms the basis for grass cropping for silage and provides fodder for the 'black and white' milk herds, and for flocks of Swaledale, Dalesbred, crossbred and many other breeds of sheep now such a familiar sight throughout the Yorkshire Dales.

In the mid-1930s the milk herd at Drebley consisted of Ayrshire and Shorthorn cattle, each yielding an average of 500 gallons per lactation. At that time, the milk was taken twice daily in kits on the back seat of the car to Bolton Abbey station, from where the carriage was paid to a dairy in Leeds; milk fetched one shilling a gallon with no certainty of prompt payment. The eventual formation of the Milk Marketing Board brought with it, for the first time in farmers' lives, a guaranteed regular income. From that time onwards, the three farmers in Drebley hamlet took it in turns to take all the kits up the lane by horse and cart, for collection by lorry from the milk stand built on the Burnsall roadside. One of the farm lads has described loading a rubber wheeled, flat tail cart round the three farms each morning, having first struggled to harness up the horse. He dreaded one highly strung horse called Jock, who would rear and bolt at the slightest unexpected noise, such as the twang of a wire along the tops of some of the walls, but the lad said it was so quiet along Drebley lane in those days that it was a rare event for Jock to do anything but plod his way to and from the roadside. It was not until 1946 that a tractor arrived, and this was not purchased, but on trial from the Ford Motor Company, in Dagenham.

Herbert kept at least two horses until he retired, and only then did the stables fall empty. Now, in the twenty-first century, it may be hard to understand the relationship which existed between a man and his horses until the age of farm mechanisation displaced them in the mid-twentieth century.

The horses, like the collie dogs, were an integral part of everyday life on the farm, and especially so for Herbert. As a young man at Low Trenhouse he had bred and 'broken in' his own foals, using manuals he obtained by post from America. Indeed, his sister Mary used to say that, when her brother had a newly harnessed, 'fresh' young colt between the shafts, she was terrified to ride over the roads on Malham Moor in a pony and trap driven by him.

To improve his dairy herd, Herbert Chester made an application to the Ministry of Agriculture Livestock Improvement Scheme to purchase a 'Premium Bull', and he joined the Bull Breeding Club in Cambridge. He went with an agricultural advisor, and returned with a Shorthorn bull named Townend Squire. However, bad luck overtook this enterprise, for it became apparent that an illicit exchange of pedigrees had taken place, and the animal which came to Drebley was not the one to whom registration papers had applied. Valuable time in breeding terms was lost as a result of this confidence trick, until the setback was noticed and remedied by replacement with another bull. By this time, however, comparison between the poor yield of the Shorthorn and the higher yielding Friesian breeds had influenced Herbert to buy a Friesian bull from an accredited breeder, Captain Skipwith, who farmed near Doncaster. He was accompanied to the sale by one of his nieces, aged twelve years at that time, and in a letter to her parents she explained how…

…the calf is not registered as a pedigree bull because it has a small black spot on one foot, whereas a pure Friesian would not have any black below the knee. It would have otherwise been worth about 150 guineas, but as it is, Uncle paid 30 guineas for him. We bagged him up, and he rode home to Drebley in the back of the car with me. He slept most of the way…

From this new venture a herd of 22 Friesian milking cows was built up, the yield steadily increasing to 1,000 gallons per lactation by 1954. By 1938 the herd was attested Tuberculin free, the price of such milk attracting a worthwhile premium; but as Herbert stressed, it would have been impossible to support this number of cattle on the acreage and original quality of the 'brown pastures' at Drebley before they had been improved.

*Herbert Chester with Friesians, 1940s.*

### Sheep

When he first came to Drebley, Herbert had bought his flock of sheep on the open market. These sheep were not bred on the farm, and it was not long before he realised that it was an almost impossible task to shepherd these 'unheathed' animals on Barden Moor, where he had his allotted 'gates' of pasture.

> Sheep born on farms around the moor have a tremendous homing instinct. One generation after another they teach where home is, and if sold they will climb many a wall in an attempt to get back home.

However, he soon gained experience in

*Gathering sheep and shepherds at High Dock, 1929.*

'gathering the moor' with all the other farmers in the area; men who came from the hamlets and villages situated on the fringe of the moor, such as Barden, Eastby, Embsay, Crookrise, Rylstone, Cracoe, Thorpe and Burnsall. On a prearranged date, each man would take his dogs, and spend the day gathering sheep from the nearest part of the moor to his own farm.

The sheep were then driven to the holding pens at the High Dock, by the Upper Reservoir, where they would eventually be separated by recognised markings on their fleeces and horns into groups depending from which area they came.

The men and dogs then set off home in the direction of their own villages, driving streams of sheep that could be seen moving off the moor in radial directions, following the same channels formed when the melt water drained from the ice cap some thousands of years before. Women folk at home in Drebley yard have spoken of how in winter, they could hear the sheep coming down Drebley lane in the dusk, icicles on their fleeces jingling as they walked.

In summer, there might occasionally be a young lamb slung around a man's neck as he strode along, his clog irons striking like flints on the rocky surfaces. A lamb born late in the season was too young to walk at the pace of the flock. On arrival in Drebley yard, while the dogs flung themselves into the water troughs, the three Drebley farmers, Herbert Chester, William and Cecil Demaine from Littlegate, and Hubert Demaine from the Fold, with his son-in-law Harry Riley shed their flocks from the others, and drove them the extra few yards to

*Sheep dip being built, 1930s.*

## FARMING IN DREBLEY

their own fields.

The next few days were occupied in shearing, clipping, and dosing or in dipping the flocks in concrete troughs specially built for the purpose between the Long Garth and Drebley yard. Dipping was a communal activity shared by each of the farmers in turn, which meant that there was a continuous movement of bleating sheep through the yards around the house, combined with the pungent smell pervading their fleeces as they emerged from the dip.

At another time in the year, when the lambs were speaned, or separated from their dams, the yards were also full of sheep and the air again resounded with plaintive bleating which continued endlessly through the light summer nights as the lambs and ewes sought to find each other. Meanwhile, the market had 'looked up'. Whereas in 1932 at Barden sheep sale, wether hoggs had been bid at eight shillings (40p), in 1942 Swaledale lambs were fetching over £2 per head, while a small flock of Masham ewes, kept on lower improved land and crossed with a Suffolk ram, produced lambs which sold for more than £4 apiece. The annual sheep sale took place on the same weekend as Harvest Festival, in a field by Barden Tower, where hurdles were specially erected for the occasion.

As part of wartime government policy to encourage an increase in food production, Herbert was twice invited to broadcast from Manchester for the BBC Home Service in a fortnightly series *Country Magazine*, and once he came to Broadcasting House in London. The well known broadcaster Ralph Wightman was the commentator. These were memorable occasions, when his homely Yorkshire voice came over the air, full of confidence and honest pride in his achievements on the two hill farms in Wharfedale. He became a Founder Member and Chairman of the Yorkshire Adventurers' Club, which is a group of men and women who are pioneers in farming methods, who are not only willing to show a spirit of enterprise in meeting agricultural problems but also to assist young people and students. He was also a member of the British Grassland Society and of the Cambridge Animal Breeders' Club. Locally he was a representative on Skipton Rural District Council and the Craven Executive Committee. He was a governor of Ermysted's Grammar school and of Upper Wharfedale Secondary School.

Eventually, ill health forced him to retire, and so in November 1956 he held his farm sale, and left Drebley to live in the East Riding of Yorkshire. Here, he and Gladys established a small poultry business attached to the farm of Herbert's niece and her husband. Herbert died in 1969 at the age of 73. He was greatly missed by his family and his many friends, having been a very fair man of equable temperament, a well informed naturalist, and a valued raconteur of Dales' farming memorabilia.

**Sale Day at Drebley, November 1956**

FARMING IN DREBLEY

IMPORTANT TOTAL DISPERSAL SALE OF A HIGH BRED STOCK

# DREBLEY, Nr. BOLTON ABBEY
## Thursday, November 22nd, 1956

**T. H. TAYLOR & SON** in conjunction with **F. M. LISTER & SON**
favoured with instructions from MR. HERBERT CHESTER
(who is leaving the farm)
WILL SELL BY AUCTION AS ABOVE, HIS

### 76 VALUABLE PEDIGREE and NON-PEDIGREE FRIESIANS
(details overleaf)

### UNCROSSED SWALEDALE EWES and 14 HALF-BRED EWES

| | |
|---|---|
| 131 Ewes 1 to 4 shear | 14 Half Bred Ewes |
| 50 Gimmer hoggs | 1 Suffolk 4 shear Tup |
| 35 Wedder hoggs | |
| 2 Swaledale 2 shear tups | |
| 2 Ditto tup hoggs | also 6 Young Geese |

### HAY AND EATAGE
Winter eatage to March 25th, 1957

### DREBLEY FARM

1. Long Garth ; Square Garth; Home Meadow Hippings and Far Meadow 22 acres of over eaten fog.
2. Herd Hill Croft ; Intake ; Brown Bank ; Camp Field and Back Fields 36 acres of pasture.
3. Inmans Meadows 8 acres.  *High Meadow 7½ acres.*
4. Low Meadow 11 acres.  *Pastures 12*
5. Hagg Pasture 8 acres.

### CLUB NOOK FARM

6. Low and Middle Bumby Pastures 10¼ acres.
7. High Bumby Pasture 5 acres and 1 acre of Kale.
8. Pastures below the Road 23 acres.
9. Pastures and Meadow above the Road 58¼ acres.

### HAY WITH ACCOMMODATION UNTIL MARCH 25th, 1957

1. Drebley Home Barn Mow 190 yds. with lying for 22 cows.
2. Low Barn Mow 152 yds. Baulks 48 yds. with lying for 10 cows.
3. High Barn Mow 38 yds. 2 Baulks 80 yds. with lying for 12 cows.
4. Club Nook Home Barn Mow, 56 yds. 2 Baulks 166 yds. with lying for 21 cows.
5. High Barn Mow 78 yds. Baulks 29 yds. with lying for 11 cows.
6. Approx. 100 tons of silage in concrete pit made June.

## AN EXCELLENT COLLECTION OF IMPLEMENTS
### INCLUDING

Fordson Major Tractor with power lift, pulley, power take-off; Fordson Major Tractor with high road gear; Bamford mid-mounted grass cutter; New hydraulic hay sweep; Patterson buck rake; International green crop loader; Nicholson's Tractor strawing machine (as new); Denning Tractor side rake (as new); Atkinson's Universal manure spreader, recently overhauled and in good condition; Bamford swathe turner; Jarmain s.d. rake; Horse rake; 2 Tractor trailers; Hearson electric incubator; Cambridge roller; Root cutter; New electric de-horner; Cattle clippers; Ladders; "Klim" refrigerator cooler; Sterilizing chest; Washing trough; Boiler; Provender bins and buckets; Tattoo set earmarkers; Joiner's bench; 4 Gascoigne milking units; 1 h.p. Petter engine; Electric motor; The usual collection of small tools. 4 12' x 8' Hen Huts; 6 Night Arks.

## 76 CHOICE ATTESTED CATTLE.   Herd No. Y804

| Lot No. | Description | born | Tattoo Mark |
|---|---|---|---|
| 1. | Heifer calf | 20/10/56. | 64 |
| 2. | ditto | 29/5/56 | 63 |
| 3. | ditto | 16/8/56 | 62 |
| 4. | ditto | 12/8/56 | 61 |
| 5. | ditto | 11/8/56 | 60 |
| 6. | ditto | 1/8/56 | 59 |
| 7. | ditto | 21/7/56 | 58 |
| 8. | ditto | 17/7/56 | 57 |
| 9. | ditto | 11/7/56 | 56 |
| 10. | ditto | 9/7/56 | 55 |
| 11. | Bullock | 9/5/56 | 54 |
| 12. | Heifer | 6/5/56 | 53 |
| 13. | Bullock | 26/2/56 | 52 |
| 14. | Heifer | 27/2/56 | 50 |
| 15. | Bullock | 12/12/55 | 48 |
| 16. | Heifer | 19/12/55 | 47 |
| 17. | Ditto | 27/12/55 | 46 |
| 18. | Ditto | 29/12/55 | 45 |
| 19. | Bullock | 4/12/55 | 44 |
| 20. | C.S.R. Heifer | 15/11/55 | 43 |
| 21. | Ditto | 31/10/55 | 42 |
| 22. | Bullock | 12/11/55 | 41 |
| 23. | Heifer | 10/10/55 | 39 |
| 24. | Ditto | 27/8/55 | 36 |
| 25. | Ditto | 14/8/55 | 37 |
| 26. | Ped. Ditto | 23/8/55 | 38 |
| 27. | Ditto | 29/7/55 | 35 |
| 28. | Bullock | 17 months old | 34 |
| 29. | Ditto | 23 months old | 31 |
| 30. | Ditto | 2 years old | 28 |

# FARMING IN DREBLEY

| Lot No. | Description | Born | Tattoo Mark |
|---|---|---|---|
| 31. | Bullock | 2 years old | 27 |
| 32. | Ditto | 2 years old | 26 |
| 33. | Ditto | 2 years old | 22 |
| 34. | Ped. Heifer | Recently served | 33 |
| 35. | B.S.R. Ditto | Fit for service | 30 |
| 36. | Heifer | Recently served | 29 |
| 37. | Ditto | Fit for service | 25 |
| 38. | Ditto | Recently served | 24 |
| 39. | Ditto | Recently served | 23 |
| 40. | C.S.R. Ditto | Fit for service | 21 |
| 41. | Ditto | Fit for service | 20 |
| 42. | Ditto | Fit for service | 19 |
| 43. | Ditto | Fit for service | 18 |
| 44. | Ditto | Fit for service | 17 |
| 45. | Ditto | Fit for service | 16 |
| 46. | Ditto | Fit for service | 15 |
| 47. | Ditto | Fit for service | 14 |
| 48. | Ped. Ditto | Fit for service | 13 |
| 49. | Ped. Ditto | Fit for service | 12 |
| 50. | Ditto | Geld in full milk | 10 |
| 51. | Ditto | Geld in full milk | 7 |
| 52. | Ditto | Geld in full milk | 5 |
| 53. | Ditto | Geld — forward in condition | 3 |
| 54. | Ditto | Geld in full milk | 1 |
| 55. | Ditto | Geld in milk | EF/7596 |
| 56. | B.S.R. Cow | Springing | EF/7506 |
| 57. | Ditto | Calved September | EF/6053 |
| 58. | Ditto | Calved September | H2C/1 |
| 59. | Ditto | Calved August | EF/5301 |
| 60. | Ditto | Recently calved | EF/1583 |
| 61. | B.S.R. Ditto | due March 6th. | NB/46102 |
| 62. | Ditto | Springing | NB/39176 |
| 63. | Ditto | Geld — forward in condition | NB/39175 |
| 64. | Ped. Ditto | Geld | NB/25676 |
| 65. | Ditto | Springing | EF/5300 |
| 66. | Ditto | due March 1st | NB/25681 |
| 67. | Ditto | Geld in milk | NB/25680 |
| 68. | Ditto | due December 19th. | N/92816 |
| 69. | Ditto | Geld in milk | NB/53536 |
| 70. | Ditto | due December 19th | NB/39076 |
| 71. | Ditto | Geld — forward in condition | NB/39077 |
| 72. | Ped. Ditto | Geld in milk | NB/39080 |
| 73. | Ped. Ditto | Geld in milk | NB/39075 |

# FARMING IN DREBLEY

## BULLS

74. Pedigree Bull "Winyates Toby" (25149)         PF/300
    Dairy licence No. 560418. Born 19/9/55.
    Sire : Terling Tempest R.M.
    Dam : Terling Baby 55th.
    Pedigree supplied or given at time of sale.
    This bull was the top price at Otley Sale, Sept. 1956.

75. Drebley Dainty's Tempest                      Y804/49
    Born 4/2/56. Sire : Terling Tempest R.M.
    Dam : Varges Dainty R.M.
    Pedigree supplied or given at time of sale.

76. Drebley's Lilac's Tempest                     Y804/28
    Born 14/12/55.

Note :   The Drebley Herd was started in 1929 and became Attested in 1938. There has never been a re-acter in the Herd, and the last test was April. Every animal with the exception of Lot 74 has been bred on this sound high district farm, some of the pastures running to nearly 1,000 ft. and they can be recommended with every confidence, and will prove themselves well wherever they go.

All the in-calf cows and heifers have been selected matings to A.I. service to Terling bulls.

The sheep are a noted high gone flock of uncrossed Swaledales, the Moor running to 1,500 ft.

The implements are a very good lot and have been well maintained and cared for.

---

SALE TO COMMENCE PROMPTLY AT 11 a.m.
(Order of sale : Implements, Hay and Eatage, Sheep and Cattle)

---

Refreshments by Messrs. Pickards of Skipton.

Auctioneers' Offices :-

Swadford Chambers,                                Manor Square,
Skipton-in-Craven.                                Otley.
Telephone : Skipton 2226.                         Telephone : Otley 2265

## BARDEN IN WHARFEDALE, THE PLACE AND ITS PEOPLE

**Gladys Chester (née Inman) her early life at Keeper's Cottage from 1915 to 1939**

Gladys was born in Skyreholme, where her father Frederick Inman and her mother Laura lived in one of the mill cottages nearly opposite Tom Lumb's paper mill. Fred was employed in the mill during the First World War. Many generations of Inmans had lived in and around Howgill and Burnsall, but Laura came from further afield, near Spofforth. Gladys grew up with her three sisters, Emmie, Winnie and Betsy, and her brother, Clifford. The family then lived in Appletreewick for a time, before settling for the rest of her father's working life in the Keeper's Cottage at Drebley.

All Barden children went to the school which had opened in 1876 on a new site near the Tower. Fred Inman had been a pupil there when Miss Jane C. Matty was the schoolmistress. In 1895, the report from His Majesty's Inspectors shows that she had proved to be a painstaking and intelligent teacher, despite the limitations imposed on the small school by its isolation and the large number of pupils of varying ages who attended. By this time, the infamous 'payment of teachers by results' had long ceased, as had the obligation to pay 'school pence' but Fred remembered with some rancour that the children were obliged to buy their own books.

When she started school, Gladys's father took her on the cross-bar of his bicycle, but it was not long before she walked, often in the company of a neighbour's son, Cecil Demaine, who lived at Littlegate farm. She described how they would play along the way, with Cecil wielding a little stick, pretending that she was a pony or small horse. From the yard between their homes, they walked along a grassy track, which led across a field towards Hole House, and thence to the dusty road which led to Barden Tower and the school. Before descending to the bridge over Ghyllbeck, the old road can still be seen on the east side, curving over a mound. In the early days she wore laced clogs, and buttoned leggings, which were difficult to put on, especially when wet and muddy; eventually, rubber Wellington boots became available for those who could afford them. Gladys longed for a pair, but when she got them, she found that although they kept her feet dry, they were 'oh so cold'. It was not long before their thick woollen socks were brought out and worn inside the boots, much as they had been worn with clogs. Not only were the boots cold, but they were uneconomical, for they wore out much faster than clogs on the rough stony surfaces, and they could not be repaired on the shoe-last in the home workshop.

There seems to have been an aura of envy around those who wore shoes, for it was cause for comment when a photograph of the schoolchildren appeared in *The Dalesman* magazine in the 1990s, and it was noticed that 'even Dora Dunckley (the daughter of the schoolmistress) wore clogs'.

A keeper's pay was small, and life was hard in the cottage, where there was no electricity, no piped water to the house, and no indoor sanitation. Gladys's parents were hardworking and thrifty, and very little food would actually be bought. As with all the tenants on the estate they held turbary rights for supplies of peat for their fires, and although labour intensive, this form of fuel was a considerable saving on bills for coal. On their small-holding, which included Drebley cruck barn with its potato cellar, they grew all their own vegetables and fruit. They kept two pigs, and some poultry. The hens were necessary, not only for their eggs, but also as broody birds. When pheasant chicks were being raised there were always several wooden coops dotted around the grassy croft in front of the cottage.

They also had sufficient meadow land to get a crop of hay each year, which provided fodder in the winter for two milk cows, which were crucial to their economy. Not only did the cows provide daily supplies of milk to the family, but by careful management, Mrs Inman was able to make and sell surplus butter, and sometimes, cream cheese. The butter was hand-turned in a heavy wooden churn which stood all the year round in the small kitchen, and she had a regular sales arrangement with a man from Appleyards in Addingham, who came on a motorbike with sidecar to collect her produce. The butter was stored on a scrupulously clean shelf above a trough of running water by the cottage gate in the lane. The water, flowing as it did from a nearby spring, was icy cold, and crystal clear, while the trough, built snugly into the stone wall of the lane, was surrounded by moss and ferns.

When Gladys left school she attended some classes for dairy skills, provided by the University of Leeds and held at the Tower for local farmers' wives and daughters. She received a certificate of proficiency at the end of the course, but she wasn't sure whether her mother felt that it improved her skills. Decorating the chapels for harvest festivals and for Christmas was a job Gladys thoroughly enjoyed. She loved to gather armfuls of autumn fruits, leaves and bracken from the lanes and woodlands she knew so well. Her father helped her to find the best hips and haws and branches on which rowan berries glowed, and together they would either load them into the van from Drebley Farm, or onto their bicycles in order to get them down to the chapels.

Fred Inman taught his children an intimate knowledge of the lanes and moorland where he spent his days as a gamekeeper, and so they grew up knowing exactly where to harvest wild fruits as they came into season throughout the year. Garrelgorm, for instance, on the steep hillside between Woodend Farm and Burnsall, was a place where the best blackberries grew, while raspberries and wild strawberries grew in profusion on roadside banks near Ghyllbeck. Dora Dunckley recalled how, each summer, Betsy would make a little pocket money by supplying the schoolmistress with welcome cans of raspberries. Bilberries from the moors were prized as a special treat for pies in August, and in the autumn, although mushrooms were gathered from their own fields around Drebley it was forbidden to trespass on a neighbour's field, whether he gathered his crop or not.

There was no question of being able to afford a horse, and so the family were dependant on the distances they were prepared to walk or cycle in order to go about their business and to see friends. A tall, 'bony' man, Fred cycled to work each day, as far as the Barden Scale entrance to the Great Park, and then along rough gravelled tracks which led past Brass Castle to the grouse butts and eventually to the shooting box on Thorpe Fell and often he walked over his rough terrain followed by his dogs. Inevitably there would be a Jack Russell, or a fox terrier, sometimes a spaniel, and rarely a black Labrador. He also cycled to collect his weekly wage from the agent's office in Bolton Abbey village. His wife and the children walked everywhere, until the girls were old enough to ride bicycles of their own. If there was an urgent need to visit Skipton, their nearest market town, their neighbour, Willie Demaine of Littlegate, took them in his horse drawn trap.

Gladys has clear memories of riding with him to buy an overcoat, and on another occasion, of going to the dentist, to have some teeth taken out. (Most young people had a complete set of 'false teeth' by the time they reached adulthood.) On the rare occasions when Mrs Inman's homemade remedies failed to cure an ailment the doctor came from Addingham or from Grassington. Betsy had vivid memories of being given an anaesthetic for the removal of her tonsils whilst lying on the living room table. She also recalled how a district nurse called regularly to check her progress in walking, since she had severe rickets, and was unable to walk to school until she was at least eight years of age. When she heard the nurse recommending iron splints for her legs, she fled and hid, rather than be measured for them.

*Fred and Laura Inman, 1950.*

The social lives of the Inmans revolved not only around Barden, but also around Appletreewick and Howgill, where they had lived during Gladys's youth. In order to reach these places, which lay on the opposite side of the river to Drebley, they walked down through the fields to a wooden footbridge which spanned the Wharfe, just upstream from the stepping stones, or hippings, at Haugh Mill. There was a village institute in Appletreewick, where dances and whist drives were held, and where members of the Burnsall, Appletreewick, Thorpe and Skyreholme Club socialised and arranged outings. Although there were two inns in the village, the Inmans, who were staunch Methodist teetotallers, refrained from patronising either of them. A great friend named Nellie Atkinson farmed by herself at Crossfield in Howgill. An unmarried lady, she was descended from the ancient family of Atkinsons of Low Farm in Barden, and such was her pleasure in receiving visits from the Inmans that, having received a letter in the post warning her of a forthcoming visit, she always had tea ready for them when they called.

In 1935 the footbridge was washed away, during an exceptionally high flood, when a large tree trunk demolished the central stanchion, and carried the timber downstream as far as Gamsworth fields. Some of these timbers were later hauled back by a team of estate horses, but despite all good intentions the bridge was never restored. Betsy Inman the gamekeeper's youngest daughter has described the long walk through the fields between Drebley and Barden Bridge, and then the long walk back past Gamsworth to Howgill in order to visit their old friend. She recalled the tasty smell of the sponge cakes she knew Nellie would be taking out of her oven as she approached along the narrow lane and how she would wait in the warm kitchen while Nellie finished her milking before coming indoors to settle down for a chat.

Then there was the long walk home to Drebley … and Betsy suffered so severely from rickets that she had been unable to go to school until she was seven. Gladys spoke regretfully of the inevitability with which their old friendships withered after the bridge disappeared, and of how the once familiar track from Drebley, down through the Long Garth and the Hippings meadow, became overgrown through lack of use. There were not many women of Mrs Inman's age and figure who would cross the stepping stones with confidence, especially when the height and force of water in the Wharfe was so unpredictable.

The family observed the Sabbath. They did not indulge in any games, nor did they knit or continue with any other handicrafts such as making peg-rugs, or dressmaking, but they certainly went to church. Although Fred Inman attended the Anglican service in the chapel at the Tower, his wife attended the Wesleyan Methodist Chapel. Their children attended both, for it would have been unthinkable not to do so, and as Gladys said, there was nothing else to do. She recalled how a typical Sunday would include teaching Sunday School at the Tower from 1.30pm to 2.30pm before attending the service from 3pm until 4pm. She would then walk or cycle home to Drebley for tea, and return to the Methodist Chapel for the evening service at 6.30pm. She often played the organ for the hymns, but having found the music for psalms and canticles incomprehensible, she was glad when her friend, Frank Almack from Club Nook, played for that part of the service. It was from him that Gladys had learnt to play the piano and the organ when she was a young woman. If for any reason, Frank was prevented from attending one of the services, he would send a message to his friend John Gill, who lived at Gamsworth, directly across the river from Club Nook. There were no telephones, and so, if on a Sunday morning a white tea towel was hung out of the tiny window on the gable-end of Club Nook house, the Gills would understand that John was required to get himself ready to 'stand in' and play for the services that day.

Gladys recalled how, as soon as their summer holidays started she and her sisters helped to prepare for the season by accompanying their father onto Barden Moor as far as Thorpe Fell shooting box. They would set off for a four mile walk through Sim Bottom, carrying with them their cleaning supplies for the day, a can of hot sweet tea and some sandwiches; these were always made from a 'treat' such as

*Fred Inman.*

a tin of salmon, specially saved for the occasion. Once the tea can was empty, they rinsed it out in one of the many small becks running down the hillside towards the upper reservoir, and then filled it with bilberries which were taken home for their mother to put into pies.

Having arrived, they swept and scrubbed the barn-like building until it was considered to be clean enough, and then they scrubbed the wooden tables and the benches on which 'the gentry' would sit. They took these outside to dry, and, when they were small children, they played see-saw and slid down them. On other days, their father cut huge bundles of bilberry bushes, which they then helped to fit into the stone seats in the butts, and also onto the top shelves where the men would rest their arms and guns.

The most important day of the year for the family in Keeper's Cottage was 12 August when the Duke and his guests opened the grouse shooting season. The fact that King George V was a regular guest added especial interest, not only to the estate workers, but also to their wives and children, who were aware of the excitement as the day approached. Fred wore his best tweed suit, provided by the Estate and tailored by Simpsons of Swadford Street in Skipton, while special 'brushed wool' stockings and garters with tassels were brought out of the cupboard, and his heavy leather boots would be polished more than usual.

*King George V on the white pony from Sandringham.*[117]

When he returned in the evening, hot and tired from the long day's toil on the open moor, he was almost speechless with exhaustion from the endeavour to serve and not to fail his employer the Duke, and his King. He would tuck into a good hot meal, and light his pipe as he stretched out his long limbs on the great oak settle placed alongside the fire in their living room. Donald Wood, writing in 1996, in his book *Bolton Abbey. The*

---

[117] Photographs by kind permission of Kate Mason.

## FARMING IN DREBLEY

*Time of my Life* describes him as being 'one of the nicest men I have ever met ... almost crippled with rheumatism and arthritis he never complained or grumbled, and he taught me how to walk on rough going'

The King stayed with the Duke at Bolton Hall, and Gladys remembers seeing him astride his well known white pony from Sandringham, which he rode while out on the moors. Each year the schoolchildren had an opportunity to see him with the Duke and members of his family, and many other illustrious guests, for Mrs Dunckley, their schoolmistress, took them from school to the moor gate by Barden Scale to see the royal party leave the moor after a day's sport. People on the estate were also familiar with the Rolls Royce in which Queen Mary rode when she was driven to lunch at Parcevall Hall with her godson, Sir William Milner. Gladys remembers standing on the roadside on many occasions, and seeing her wave a gloved hand as she drove past. There was a strong sense of 'family pride' amongst the estate tenants, who shared their reminiscences with one another at the end of these special days.

### 1939 to 1993

In the spring of 1939, when Gladys was 24 years old, she married Herbert Chester and became the farmer's wife at Drebley. The Second World War broke out in September of that year, and changed forever the quiet and often lonely life she had led. Her housekeeping skills were immediately challenged by the imposition of rationing for food, clothes, and petrol. Uncertain markets for their farm produce, and the arrival of different members of Herbert's family as refugees stretched her purse, so that she was plunged into a world far removed from the one she had known for so long, down the lane in Keeper's Cottage.

She and Herbert then decided to befriend one of the young Jewish refugees from Nazi persecution who had arrived in Ilkley with others under the care of the Quaker Society of Friends. These youngsters needed to find a place to live where they could also earn their living, and so it was that Philip Pfeffer came from Vienna to Drebley, to live 'as family' and to work on the farm with his employer and host. All the other accommodation in the house being occupied, Gladys made one of the two attic rooms available to Philip, and he spent his evenings with them, reading or listening to the radio by the lamplit fireside. She washed and mended his clothes, cooked all his meals and cared for him, while respecting his need to practice his Jewish faith. However, no concessions were made; he worked alongside them on Saturdays and he obligingly ate bacon, pork, ham and pastry made with lard when it was put before him. Times were hard, and the pig formed a staple part of a farmer's diet in wartime Britain. Philip was fourteen when he came to Drebley, and he stayed until the war was over in 1945, after which he joined his twin brother in London. His account of life at Drebley during those years follows this chapter.

Farming at Drebley has been described in the section An Agricultural Pioneer. Like all farmers, Gladys and Herbert worked extremely hard. The large, unheated house was cold

131

and damp, and difficult to look after, especially since money was short. There was no electricity until shortly before they retired in 1956. Wash days involved heating a copper in the outhouse across the kitchen yard, turning by hand a heavy mangle and then carrying huge baskets up a flight of stone steps to reach the croft, where long clothes lines awaited the pegs and props. Sheets were coarse and heavy, likewise the clothes, and took a long time to dry.

Strong winds were a mixed blessing, as Gladys struggled to peg out the washing on a wild day, in the unpredictable weather of the Yorkshire Dales. At times, there would be two or three farm lads 'living in', with all their washing to do and mouths to feed, and, during haytime one or two Irishmen were accommodated in the second attic, where beds were reserved for their use, the bedding being washed separately after they left. Baking days were formidable, and it was not until the mid-1940s that a Rayburn stove was installed in the scullery to replace the range in the living-kitchen. The pantry, with its stone floor and shelves, was a long walk from the scullery, through the kitchen, a small hall and three doorways. All the flagged floors were scrubbed by Gladys on her hands and knees.

*Gladys and Herbert in 1939.*

*Herbert Chester in breeches and gaiters at the autumn sheep sale at Barden Tower.*

Then there were the visitors – she and Herbert had many friends, for as he embarked on his farming enterprises and became well known, people came to see the farm and to share his enthusiasms. Members of Herbert's family frequently came to stay, and Gladys made them all welcome.

The annual sheep sale took place on the same weekend as harvest festival, in a field by Barden Tower, where hurdles were specially erected for the occasion. One of the greatest attractions at the sale were Miss Sarah Demaine's draught Swaledale

## FARMING IN DREBLEY

ewes from Barden Scale; they could always be relied on to fetch a good price, even during 'the slump' in the 1930s when prices were so low that farmers were obliged to butcher and eat their own sheep rather than sell them at a loss.

At this time of year Gladys was especially busy because many of Herbert's old friends came from Settle and Malham, and she quite naturally gave them lunch beforehand and tea afterwards. Traditionally, she also provided a bed for Herbert's uncle, old Abraham Banks, who had walked over from Capon Hall on Malham Moor especially for the sale.

It was hard work, looking after these visitors, preparing and putting lunch on the table and clearing it away before Herbert drove down to the Tower with his Uncle and their dogs in the van, together with as much of the stuff for decorating the chapels as they could get into it. Gladys herself cycled down, and 'set to' in whichever chapel she was decorating. She then cycled back home and put tea on the table in readiness for the return of Herbert and their friends.

*Abraham Banks.*

There was always a freshly starched cloth, which she had embroidered herself, and all the food was home-made, including the bread, teacakes and pastries, the jam, butter and sponge cakes. There might even have been home-cured ham, cut from the flitch hanging in a muslin bag in the cold, stone-floored pantry.

They were not blessed with children of their own, but they were a much loved uncle and aunt. Eventually, ill health forced them to retire, and so in November 1956 they held their farm sale, and left Drebley to live in the East Riding. Here they established a small poultry business attached to the farm of Herbert's niece and her husband, the niece who had spent much of her childhood and school holidays working with him around the farm at Drebley. On the fertile soil around their new home Gladys was able to devote time to her garden, her love of flowers, and her bountiful crop of soft fruit, especially strawberries, thus earning considerable respect amongst members of her family. She was a true countrywoman, born and bred.

*Gladys, centre, with two of her neighbours, Willie Demaine of Littlegate and Joan Riley of Fold Farm, 1950.*

### Nostalgia

My sense of nostalgia springs from memories evoked from the age of ten years whilst staying at Drebley as an 'evacuee' from the Essex edge of London, at the beginning of the Second World War. From the time of our birth, my sister and I had spent all our holidays with my mother's family at Drebley, but this time it was different; it was not to be a holiday. We were to walk to school in Burnsall each day while our parents remained in Essex, living under the unknown threats of wartime Britain.

When I was a small child, before the Second World War, Drebley was a very quiet place… 'off the beaten track' you might say, where there were few visitors calling, unless on business. Ella Pontefract, writing in the book *Wharfedale*, which she and Marie Hartley published in 1937 described Drebley as '… a peaceful forgotten place, straggling down grassy lanes with little form or plan …'

The long lane which leads to the hamlet from the road between Barden Tower and Burnsall has a sandy colour, with outcrops of white bedrock. It is dry and stony on hot summer days, with large potholes and puddles after heavy rain. I used to think that the only link with the outside world was a line of wooden poles, along which was strung a single telephone wire through which I could hear the wind singing as I trudged along.

At that time, my uncle's house was the only one in Barden to have a telephone, and it was only used for urgent messages that could not be relayed quickly by post. Surprisingly, the neighbours did not share the telephone, maybe because the receiver was situated on the staircase half-landing, where for instance, farmers in boots would not have been welcome. Neither would they have felt comfortable, for this was a private part of the house. I remember how my parents would dial from our home in Essex for a 'long-distance call', and how the operators would ask us to confirm the names of the exchanges at frequent intervals as they passed our call northwards along the length of England before we reached Burnsall 214. In later years, during my August holidays some of my matriculation and professional examination results reached me by these means.

As one walked up and down the lane the constant sounds were the bleating of sheep and the calls of birds, especially in springtime, when lapwing and curlew returned to breed on the upland pastures. Otherwise, I particularly remember long periods of profound silence, so often interrupted by loud shouts and threats as the farmers swore at their dogs barking and rattling their chains as they slunk around their kennels, and the sounds of iron shod, clogged feet in the yards, the clanging of buckets being dragged over stone flagged floors, and the slamming of a gate with an iron hasp. By the rumbling of wheels everyone knew when horses and carts set off for a day's work, and so we timed the phases of each day and the seasons of the year. These impressions were gained not only from our own farmyard, but also from the other two yards in Drebley hamlet, and even from across the valley, where activities at Gamsworth went on in much the same manner. For instance, although we could see when they started hay time at Gamsworth, we could also hear when they started work

## FARMING IN DREBLEY

in the mornings, and when they moved their flocks of sheep or herds of cattle.

What we could not hear was the red bus, or the postman's van as each one travelled up and down the valley at regular times each day, but we could see them, and set our watches by them. Neither do I remember hearing the river when it was in spate, roaring down the valley between the flooded fields.[118] Its silence had a menacing quality about it. But I do remember the wind as it howled around the chimney pots and whistled through gaps as it rattled the ill-fitting wooden window frames of our houses at Drebley and Club Nook. Sometimes it was a warm wind, but mostly it brought rain or snow, and then it would be an elemental force to be reckoned with as we huddled into our feather beds, or gathered closely round the coal fire, rubbing our chilblains and sipping hot, sweet cocoa.

*Elisabeth and Gladys, 1932.*

Drebley House was modernised in 1929, when my grandmother and my uncle and aunt arrived from their previous home at Low Trenhouse on Malham Moor. It was the first house in Barden to have indoor sanitation and a bath installed, and we loved the warm spacious bathroom, which was partitioned with white painted wood panelling from a larger room. The space beyond the panelling was dark, its only window being in the partition, and so it became a box-room, in which large mahogany chests of drawers held spare clothing, bed linen and towels. The hot water cylinder warmed the bathroom and from it we filled our baths with soft, peat stained water in which we might, for a rare treat sprinkle Lux soap flakes. I remember how my aunt would take the blue box from inside the cylinder cupboard and shake it carefully while the hot tap was running, while my sister and I sat in the big white bath with our noses protruding above the froth, our faces red from the fresh air of days spent out of doors on the farm. When there had been a lot of rain, the water became very brown, since it drained from Barden Moor.

The soft water made wonderful tea, especially when it had been boiled in a kettle hung on a reckan over a coal fire. No matter if it had black flecks in it, and tasted smoky. The water made even better ginger beer, which in summer was taken to the hay meadows for 'drinking time'. This was the mid-morning break. The beer was taken in stone bottles, in large baskets lined with snowy white teacloths, along with ginger biscuits and buttered teacakes spread with glistening butter from the cool, dark pantry. The baskets could be quite

---

118 Roaring in this context means 'to happen fast and stormily as in the roaring forties,' Oxford English Dictionary.

*Haytime at Drebley.*

heavy, and so, when possible, the women would watch for an empty hay cart leaving the barn, and let the horse do the work for them. In the afternoon, cans of hot tea were another matter, and I well remember how they could burn our bare legs as we carried them and toiled down the lane to the meadow. However, we knew that the men, labouring away with their rakes and forks from dawn to dusk when the weather was fine, or racing to get the hay in before the rain came, were always pleased to see their laden women folk coming through the gate with the horse and cart.

**Reminiscences of Philip Pfeffer, Jewish refugee from Vienna, 1939-46**
Recorded in February 1992, at Philip's home in Wembley, North London:

I arrived in England in December 1938, together with my twin brother Harry, via the Kinder Transport which rescued Jewish children from the persecution being carried out in Austria and other European countries by Adolph Hitler and the Nazi regime. Through the Quaker Religious Society of Friends I arrived in Ilkley where a hostel had been established for receiving us, and where we and a few others remained for a few months. During this time we were taught to understand some English, and to speak enough to make ourselves understood. Clothes were found for us, and enquiries made in the surrounding area for the possibility of obtaining somewhere to live while at the same time earning a living. My mother had not been able to accompany us, and my father had died before I left Vienna. In June 1939 I was welcomed into the household of Herbert and Gladys Chester of Drebley farm, near Barden Tower, and I stayed with them until

## FARMING IN DREBLEY

after the end of the war, which broke out in the September of that year.

For the first year I earned only my keep, since I was completely ignorant of all farming practices, and especially those peculiar to the Yorkshire Dales, with all its changing weather conditions. I was aged 14, and had lived in Vienna all my life. I simply had to learn to improve my English in order to communicate at all, and of course I was very lonely. I felt scared, but the Chesters were a very nice, kind couple with whom I felt able to spend this unexpected stage of my life. Eventually, I discovered that Harry Riley, the neighbouring farmer at The Fold Farm, was looking for a lad 'to live in', and so I persuaded him to arrange for my twin brother to come over from a farm near Helmsley, where he had gone from Ilkley. So, we did have each other's company for a little while, but unfortunately, his arrangement was not as successful as mine with the Chesters, and he did not stay for as long as I did.

Through the Quakers, particularly a lady named Miss Borman, we managed to get our mother away from Vienna. By obtaining a work permit for her to be a domestic helper in the house of a widow of a retired General in the British army in India, then living in Ilkley, my mother gained entry to this country in July 1939, just six weeks before war was declared. I was able to see her from time to time, because Herbert Chester was careful to take me in his car, when he had sufficient petrol to do so. Otherwise, I walked to Barden Tower (about two miles) and went on the bus which called there each morning and afternoon, on its way between Grassington and Ilkley.

However, by the following year, the British government became concerned about the number of alien nationals living in the British Isles during this critical war-time period, and they rounded them all up. Much to her consternation, my mother spent ten days in Holloway women's prison before being moved to one of the internment camps in the Isle of Man. She was released during 1941, and then went to distant relations in London. And so, I remained on my own as regards family at Drebley throughout the duration of the war.

Herbert Chester although a man with no formal education after the age of 14, had a great interest in and was very curious about almost everything that came his way. I myself therefore learnt a great deal as we shared our conversations throughout those years. He would ask me questions about Vienna and our lives there, about Austria and the school system, and innumerable other subjects. In turn, I would listen to him as he spoke about his business of rearing animals, of the auction market in Skipton, the planting of root crops, and his sales of milk to the Milk Marketing Board which ensured a monthly cheque for economic survival. He was a pioneer for new Dales farming methods, and he became host to the Agricultural Department of Leeds University when they decided to plant experimental crops of wheat, barley and oats on hill farms. This was of paramount importance to the country, in response to the need to increase food production during those difficult war-time days.

I became very interested in these experiments, especially when Dr Ian Moore, the principal of the Agricultural College, came to see the results on the farm. Of course, when the seedlings germinated in the strips we had planted out in certain fields, I could see for myself that some grains did better than others. Until then, root crops had been a major part of the staple diet for man and beast alike. These crops, together with animal husbandry, had formed the basis for what was almost subsistence farming at Drebley at that time. Under war-time conditions, it was decreed that we were to grow oats, wheat and barley, but because of the climate, and the relatively early onset of the rainy season, the crops did not ripen and it was impossible to harvest these grains. I remember how land-girls were hired, as were tractors, ploughs, and any other machinery not normally owned by hill farmers.

Another of the developments concerned the production of milk. Mr Chester gradually built up a herd of pedigree Friesian cows, all of them attested free of tuberculosis. This was very unusual

# BARDEN IN WHARFEDALE, THE PLACE AND ITS PEOPLE

in the late 1930s, and he was considered to be very advanced in his farming practice.

At Drebley, we lived in the inner kitchen, round the fire in those long, dark winters. As there was no electricity, Mrs Chester lit paraffin lamps, with wicks which had to be kept trimmed, and the glass chimneys free of smoke. Later, Tilley lamps gave a better light and were a great improvement. During winter evenings we did not go out socially, for there was no transport other than by bicycle, or in Mr Chester's car, for which the ration of coupons for petrol was very limited. My memory of that wet climate is vivid. I never seemed to be dry when working outside, and it was certainly very difficult to get our heavy woollen overcoats dry in between times. Mrs Chester hung them on ceiling racks or on clothes horses round the fire whenever she could. I wore clogs with iron shod wooden soles, which kept my feet warm, but when the work was particularly wet, I wore wellington boots. These were the coldest things I have ever known, and could freeze my feet. I repaired my clogs myself, by going up the outside stone steps to the workshop above the kitchen where there was a vice and a bench. You could buy nails and an iron rim in Skipton for 3/6d. They did not wear out very often because apart from the yard and the lane, I only walked on grassy paths.

My grasp of the English language really came to me through reading a collection of Victorian novels which were kept in a mahogany bookcase in the living kitchen. The Chesters had collected them over a lifetime, and I read them avidly. (Victor Hugo's *Les Miserables* was a particular favourite, but Dickens and Trollope came high on the list). As an exercise, while Mr Chester's sister, Mrs Mary Foster was away in hospital, I wrote letters to her, and she replied. My style drew much comment from her elder brother, Dr Richard Chester who was a doctor in Bradford. He recognised the sources from which I had learned to express myself, and I caused some amusement with these letters. My speech, too, was a mixture of Viennese, the broad vowels of the Yorkshire dialect, and the delicacy of Jane Austin's literary style, combined with the indescribably old-fashioned quaintness of Charles Dickens

Dr Chester and his family visited the farm most Sundays. He brought with him a copy of the weekly journal *The Spectator*, which I then read from cover to cover, in order to keep in touch with current affairs and opinion. There was also the wireless, which ran off battery accumulators, which were re-charged regularly in Burnsall. We all listened to the radio as we sat round the fire, evening after evening until bed-time.

I slept in my own room on the second floor of the house; in fact, it was the attic, where the ceilings were not underdrawn and there were thin wooden partitions between my room and the next.

Although the house walls were very thick, it was through the windows that the wind and then the snow blew into my room. During the worst of the winter months, I remember taking to bed with me a candle in one hand and a brush and shovel in the other, in order to sweep the snow off my counterpane before getting into bed. Once in the iron-framed bed, I kept warm rolled in a thick feather duvet and wool blankets, although the mattress was probably made of straw, and the pillows were certainly filled with hens feathers.

Occasionally there were too many boys working at the farm for everyone to have their own room, and there came a busy time when I had a boy in with me. He was not very bright – he didn't need to be for his job! – and he noticed how I always read to myself in bed. One evening, when I was comfortably settled he suddenly asked, 'whatever are you doing, up there, muttering away like that?'

I was reading the Bible, which I had brought upstairs with me, from the bookcase in the living room, and when I offered to read it to him he seemed very pleased. We carried on like that for quite a while…

## FARMING IN DREBLEY

We, that is the Chesters and I, always looked forward to the school holidays when Herbert's brothers, Richard and Abram Chester and their sister Mrs Griffiths brought their children, and left them to stay for several weeks at a time. There was Peter from Mansfield, who stayed at Drebley, sometimes camping with his mother in the Intake, while Betty and Eileen from Bradford, and Brontë and Elisabeth from Hornchurch in Essex stayed with Mrs Foster at Club Nook.

One day there was a tragedy at Club Nook. Jim Foster was found dead in one of the fields, with his dog, Roger beside him. We all helped to carry him on a wooden gate, down the lane to the house, and I will never forget the struggle we had. He was an exceptionally tall man, and his weight, combined with the gate was something we had not bargained for. After his death, Mrs Foster stayed in the house, but the lease for the farm was taken by Mr Chester. We then found that we had to walk between the two farms in order to fodder the animals in the barns, and walking on the road caused more wear and tear not only on my clogs, but also on the horse's shoes. Mostly however, I was able to walk over the fields, on a path connecting the line of stiles between Demaine's at Littlegate, Hole House and Club Nook. I carried a daily supply of milk for the house in a back-can.

After the first year I earned £2/10s a week, plus keep, which was the top wage for a farm labourer. I could have an evening out in Skipton by cycling there, paying 3d at the cinema and 2d for a bag of chips.

Social life in Barden revolved around the same people as you might meet during the day's work on the farm, and one did not make the effort to cycle on one's own to the nearest village of Burnsall, or to the Institute in the old school by Barden Tower. Whist drives and beetle drives were held here in winter. The Chesters were teetotal and never ever went to a public house, and rarely to the chapel by Barden Tower.

Library books were left at the Institute by the county library service, so I used to go there regularly and get the key from Miss Pullen, who was the caretaker at the nearby Methodist Chapel. There was never anybody else in the old schoolroom, and nobody checked what became of the books.

I could not judge the standard of living at that time although Mr Chester often spoke of the Depression which took place during the 1930s. I learnt that the price of lambs had been so low that he would fail to sell them in the market at Skipton. Indeed, on one occasion, when their butcher had driven into the yard, and quoted his prices, Herbert had told him to move off, for he was forced to slaughter and eat his own lambs, and would continue to do so until he began to look like a sheep himself. They had been lean years until wartime, when the Ministry of Agriculture was formed and guaranteed prices, after which there was more prosperity. When I was at Drebley, the Minister was a man named Hudson. I remember him coming to see the results of experimental ploughing, re-seeding and fertilising, and to see the herd of cattle from which the milk yield had improved so dramatically following grassland improvement and selective breeding.

During the best days of summer we worked all the daylight hours to get in the hay. An Irishman named Danny was hired for a couple of weeks every summer for many years, and I liked him. He occupied the attic room adjacent to mine. He taught me a few country tricks, like how to set rabbit snares, for instance.

When I first went to Drebley we had three horses: Bonny, Captain and Jock. This last named horse was very highly strung, and when in harness would bolt as soon as he heard any unusual sound, taking me and the cart with him. As the horses grew too old to work, they were replaced with a tractor, but that did not happen in my time. After milking in the mornings, every third week I used to harness up a small, flat-tailed cart with rubber wheels and take the milk kits up the lane to the main Burnsall road, where they were collected by a lorry and taken to Leeds. We took it in turns with the other two farmers in the hamlet, Demaines at Littlegate and Harry Riley at The Fold.

There were seven to eight kits per load, each weighing about a hundred-weight, and each bearing a metal tag on which the owner's name was indented. These were all man-handled onto the milk-stand, and thence onto the lorry, since it was not driven down the lane to individual farms. We got one pence a gallon more for our milk because it was TT attested: i.e. from a tuberculin free herd. Before being put into the kits, the milk was strained and cooled in the dairy, and the utensils were sterilised by means of boiling water. This meant that a special boiler house had to be built, which I remember being put up under the scullery window, in place of the dog kennels. Eventually, the electricity generator was also kept in here, for powering the milking machines, and supplying light to one room in the house.

Talking of dog kennels, no, I did not have my own dog, but after Jim Foster died at Club Nook, I took his dog to Drebley, and gradually we got used to each other. He was called Roger, and he had a cast in one eye. I was able to do a certain amount of work with him, such as fetching in the cows at milking time, but on the days when Mr Chester gathered sheep from the moor, he took his own dog with him. I do not think I could have got a dog to work for me who had worked for someone else.

Skipton was the market town. For private cars there was only a small petrol allowance for essential business, and so I remember how, one day, I rode one of the horses over The Park to the blacksmith in Skipton. I was short, and that horse was no hunter! My legs stuck out rather than fit into the stirrups as we made steady progress at two miles per hour. As we approached the top of Eastby Brow, where there was a camp for German prisoners of war, the British soldiers on guard looked at me critically and shouted, 'Here comes Gordon Richards'. I could only share the joke (Gordon Richards being a foremost jockey at that time).

The first prisoners of war to come here were Italians, and there seemed to be thousands of them. Then there were the Germans, who worked on the land, doing all the worst, back-breaking jobs. In the mornings they were dropped off from lorries, without guards, and collected in the evenings, at the end of a day's work on appropriate farms. I understood what they were saying to each other, but I kept my distance, and I never spoke to any of them. On one occasion, the Germans were sorting potatoes, but putting ripe and green ones into the same basket, despite being told to keep them separate. I could see that Mr Chester was getting frustrated, and we wondered whether they had misunderstood their instructions. I then offered to tell them in German, but he would not hear of me revealing my nationality.

Mr Chester protected me from any risky contacts, which again strengthened the relationship between us, and enhanced my trust in him.

Living as we did on the estate of the Duke of Devonshire, I soon became aware that 12 August was when the grouse shooting season opened. In 1939, the King (George VI) was expected as usual, and as I was a newcomer in the country, I was hoping I might have a chance to see him, but he didn't come. However, the Duke's party were on the moors and so, in order to earn a little pocket money, I asked if I could join the beaters. At that time, a week's wage was 10 shillings and that was what I earned for a day's beating. It was terribly hard work in amongst the heather, on very rough ground, trying to drive a straight line for the birds and the men in the butts, and I never did it again.

The estate was managed by the Duke's agent, a man who was treated with great respect; he visited at intervals to check on the state of the property and to make any necessary decisions such as when to repaint woodwork and when to carry out general maintenance. (They used to

## FARMING IN DREBLEY

say it was a task rather like painting the Forth Bridge). It was to him that farmers made complaints about the number of pheasants encroaching on the fields alongside woodland. These birds were not being controlled by managed estate shoots, as they had been in pre-war days, and although they tended to feed on painstakingly produced crops, woe betided any of the tenants who shot or snared one of them. It was more difficult to keeper the estate when most of the men had been 'called up', and I remember how tempted some of the local men were to go out rabbiting with a gun and then come home with a pheasant hidden inside a jacket sleeve. You could sell anything edible in those days, especially to The Fell Hotel in Burnsall. A man used to come on a bicycle to collect any surplus thing we could sell him, and he would have a job sometimes to wheel it back along that very hilly road, all hung with small animals and poultry.

At the nearby farm of Hole House lived a very old man whose surname was Emmott. As the years went by, he simply withdrew into his farmhouse, from which he continued to pay rent, using only those fields and a barn nearest to his house. All his stock dwindled away, but he would not leave the place. Eventually the War Agricultural Committee brought an action against him, on the grounds that the farm was needed to provide food towards the war effort, and he was evicted. I could not recall a similar situation, and I have never forgotten seeing the abandoned land. Cecil Demaine took the lease after that and with his Uncle Willie Demaine farmed it along with Littlegate.

During one stage of the war, German night bombers used to fly over the east coast and across Wharfedale on their way to attack the Merseyside cities of Liverpool and Manchester. A line of searchlights were installed across the country, and one of these points was near the wood by the Herd Hill, alongside the Burnsall road. When these were in action I could read a newspaper in Drebley yard, which is quite some distance away. We were always worried that these searchlights would be attacked, and Drebley with them, but it didn't happen.

I did not contemplate what might happen if the war went against us; I simply got on with the very hard life, in atrocious weather conditions, where one accepted the fact that at least half the day would be spent in wet clothes. After that, a hot bath, and one would be warm and dry again. Yes, it was a harsh existence, but there was no class distinction between farmer and boy, and we all shared the hardship and all the jobs.

When the war was over, I left Drebley to join my mother and my brother Harry in Wembley. He and I embarked successfully on a market gardening business, from which we financed ourselves to train and qualify as chartered accountants. I married Barbara, and we have three daughters. It was many years before I returned to Drebley with my family, but when I did, the Chesters had retired. The first things I noticed were the electricity supply lines and poles. Then I saw what a change had come over the farmland, for Drebley was no longer a 'working farm', the new tenant being more of a dealer in animals, with a wagon parked on the concrete now covering the old yard surface. The shippons, stable and loose boxes were empty, and grassland in the fields showing no signs of all that we had done in the 1940s. The only person whom I met who remembered me was Harry Riley. He appeared in the lane and recognised me at once, especially as I relapsed into me old way of speaking. My family were astounded ... they could not understand a word I said!

## Day by day at Drebley, February-December 1946

Michael Ogden worked for Herbert Chester as a farm boy at Drebley from 1946 until 1948. At the same time, Clifford Inman ( Gladys's brother,) and Billy Howe, a pre-veterinary student were employed on the farm. Both Michael and Billy lived 'as family' at Drebley, while

Clifford lived with his parents in Keeper's Cottage. During that time Michael kept a diary of events as he saw them. Excerpts from his diary follow:

**1946, February**

Mon 4th – Started work at Chester's. He keeps Friesian/Shorthorn crosses and has a Fordson major tractor. Just milked.

5-6th – Clipped cows with machine: dressed with lice powder. Set the grinding machine going to grind corn; in afternoon, went muck spreading

16-17th – A heifer (Whitesocks) calved a bull calf which took a lot of pulling. Nightshade calved a heifer. Saw a skylark and some peewits.

19-20th – Boss took bull calf to auction I stayed at home and went muck-spreading in Club Nook high meadow with Clifford. I am learning to drive the tractor; it is good to know all about it.

21st – Went muck spreading all day in Club Nook low meadow, from Low Barn.

**March**

4-5th – Delivery of Mangolds, 5tons 5cwts. Went to Skipton to see *Laddie Son of Lassie* at the pictures.

6th – Lead hay with tractor from the stack in Low Meadow to our High Barn and to Club Nook.

8th – Billy gone to Mansfield for weekend, to stay with Mr Chester's brother Abram, which makes it hard work for us. Spread muck in Club Nook high meadow.

19th – Brought sheep down from the Moor.

20th – We got our first lambs (twins) doing fine, but mother no milk.

21-22nd – Spread slag (i.e. basic slag, a by-product of steel manufacture) at Low Barn

26th – Milk recorder came. We gelded the sheep while Clifford spread the slag. There are a lot of lice on the sheep this time. We are covered.

27th – Billy and Mr Chester dipped sheep for lice while Billy and me carted hay to Home Barn and High Barn

28th – Billy and I weighed up corn: 56 pounds of seed oats to 12 pounds of beans and two and three quarter ounces of Arogasan.

29th – Sowed oats in High meadow, 12 stone oats to 2 stones of beans to the acre, straight into furrows and then disced in disc harrow.

**April**

2nd – Clifford slagged in potato field (last year) five hundred weights to th eacre we put in oats and then he disced it. Bulled Lilac.

5th – Led hay. Cliford disced Low Meadow and the field down at the edge of the river; also harrowed them. I saw my first sand-martin today.

6-9th – Led hay (daily) I shall be glad when it is finished,

10th – Led hay to the high barn. Rolled Low Meadow, Bumby Low Field, our High Meadow and field below road at Club Nook. Clifford put artificial fertiliser on Bumby Little Meadow and on the top patch of kale.

11th – Led hay to High Barn and then ground corn. Clifford disced on Brown Bank. I went to watch him in evening, as soon as we had finished milking, to see what gears he was using for certain jobs. Yesterday I bumped into a gate post but did not do any damage to the tractor.

15th – Sowed kale in Bumby Little Meadow, four and a half pounds per acre.

16th – Led hay to Home and High Barn. Billy and Mr Chester direct reseeded little field next to Club Nook, bottom side of the road.

17-18th – Set potatoes all day, and put artificial on the ridges before we set them.

**May**

1st – Direct reseeded Low Meadow; harrowed with tractor.

2nd – Led all decent hay to Home Barn and finished the stack.

3rd – Laid the cows out day and night. Clifford harrowed and put one bag nitro-chalk and two bags of ammonium phosphate to the square yard of Low Meadow. Lit fire to burn remains of stack.

6th – Billy and Herbert marked the lambs and took them up onto the moor.

8-10th – Muck leading in first meadow. Stone picking in Wheat Close and in Jim's field. Same in High meadows.

12th – Picked stones, Far and First meadow, and creosoted henhouses in both Herd Hill and Intake.

13th – Cleaned out Bull Box and dumped stuff in First Meadow.

14-15th – Stonewalling in Club Nook Little meadow, putting up odd gaps. Built foundation in big gap in First Meadow. Clifford ploughed High Meadow for kale; sowed kale in our High Meadow.

16th – Sowed turnips, carrots and beet (sheepmeat) in Low Meadow i.e. part not done for potatoes. Clifford put slag on. I creosoted some hen-huts. Billy rolled kale. It rained. Two thunderstorms.

17th – Clifford harrowed potatoes in Low Meadow. We stubbed thistles.

18th – Mr Chester stayed up two nights to watch Bonny. She foaled this morning at 7 o'-clock. Rang up Mr Holland (vet) at night to say she had not cleansed and he was here in 25 minutes from Keighley to remove the afterbirth.

20-23rd – Put nitro-chalk on bit of re-seeding at Club Nook High Meadow also on Home meadow: two bags to the acre. Went to Burnsall for fish and chips. Clifford put super-phosphate on Jim's field.

24th – Treated five first-year heifers for ring-worm

28-29th – Put phosphate on Hagg. Billy and I took all the dock leaves out of Bumby Little Meadow and Clifford ploughed it again because it was very weedy and poor.

30-31st – Took first year yearlings to Club Nook High Side. Picked Hippings. Put 4cwt nitro-chalk on Bumby Little meadow.

**June**

3-4th – Five tons of hydrated lime came, so we put part on the sheep-feed. Clifford got lime in his eyes which became very swollen.

7th Clifford ploughed Bumby Low Meadow and we put sheep-feed on and 3cwts nitro-chalk.

12-13th – Clifford ploughed and disced Bumby Low Meadow; walled gap in the Fold. Mr Chester put limestone grit, 22 bags of nitro-chalk and one phosphate on the sheep-meat in Bumby meadow.

14th – Clifford and I took Captain to Burnsall and got him shod.

17th – Whitewashed both shippons. A big killer dog has been seen on the moor; it has killed 118 sheep.

18th – Stubbed thistles and painted cart.

20th – Ninety six folk came from the East Riding to see stock and farm, (three bus loads).

21st – Scuffed kale in our High Meadow. Started clipping sheep.

24th – Singled kale all day. Not finished.

25-26th – Gathered sheep on moor. Clipping all day.

28th – Thinning kale. Took ewes and lambs back to the moor after marking and castrating them.

**July**

1st – Singled kale all day.

3-13th – Haymaking: half Inman's, half Jim's Field, Wheat Close, all High Meadow, part of First Meadow, then it rained.

14-26th – Messed about waiting for some good weather; mended tools; started cutting Hippings with tractor mower until tractor steering box broke. Started mowing Mr Inman's Bottom Piece with horses; led some hay, piked the rest.

**August**

3-5th – Finished haymaking in Hippings field and led hay from Inman's to our Low Barn.

6-7th – Rained; mowed thistles and rushes next to Club Nook High Side for Dr Moore's experiments in killing rushes.

11-12th – Gathered sheep off moor; dipped and separated sheep from lambs.

26th – Back after week's holiday; six cows had calved.

28-29th – Weather terrible and haytime drags on, the worst for a long time. The corn is ready and it is a wonder the wind does not lay it. Ditched part of Bumby Dike because floods are lifting the potatoes.

30th – Black eyed Susan made £46 at Giggleswick market. Peony made £40 at Otley market.

**September**

3-4th – Put slag, half ton to the acre on Jim's field also on two plots on the rush field (next but one to the top of Jim's field) for an experiment, (one ton to the acre).

6-8th – Haymaking. It's all muck.

10-12th – Binder came; cut high meadow; stoking.

13th – The heifer Thistle and a good Guernsey heifer made very poor prices at Otley market.

16th – Led a load of hay … very wet but as good as it ever would be. Binder and two tractors came, and we completed Club Nook. Got two rabbits.

17-26th – Put up stooks in High Meadow, lead corn and made two stacks.

27th – Another fine day. Stacked the last of the corn at Club Nook, and we now wait the thresher. Moved two of the henhouses to two of the cornfields. Potato spinner has come.

28th – Marton farm sale. Very bad prices because of shortage of hay in all areas. Mr Chester bought a potato shovel (a bit worse for wear) and good pick for 1/6 pence.

## October

1st – Picked ten large rows of potatoes. Clifford went on the round-up for Barden sale to sort out the shearlings and sell all the small poor ones.

2-3rd – Picked potatoes all day and got about 3cwts. Four German prisoners of war came to pick with us.

8-10th – Picked potatoes all morning. Thresher came and threshed at Club Nook (two stacks) and at Cecil Demaine's then threshed our High Meadow and put straw into barn … fifteen of us there. So it soon got done. Germans riddled potatoes.

16th – Finished riddling potatoes: started sacking potatoes (Woodheads) for seed. Mary, (Mr Chester's sister from Club Nook) helped with sewing and sealing the sacks.

19-20th – Harrowed potato field and picked up potatoes.

23rd – Dr Moore and his followers came from Leeds University.

24-25th – Hogs gone to Pateley Bridge sale. Put two tons of lime on Jim's field, drill broke down so had to spread it with shovel.

28th – Took the Suffolk tup to the half-bred ewes. Viola calved a bull. Led muck at Club Nook.

30-31st – Sorted 20 lambs for Skipton auction; they made 28 shillings and the half-bred ones 44. Gathered moor for winter dipping and to loose the tups into them. Finished leading muck at Club Nook.

## November

8th – Started laying in the cows at night.

11th – Brought the best of the carrots, beet and turnips up from Bumby and turned 71 lambs onto sheep-meat in it.

26th – Clifford got married. Mended boskin in Club Nook little shippon.

27th – Raining. Got some kale.

## December

4th – Mended puncture in tractor tyre and fenced off the stack in Stack Field.

6th – Put all the young beasts in all the outbarns.

11th – Ground some oats and mixed pea meal with some oats but some would not eat it. Drenched Violet with some good stuff called Sulphonamide (M&B ed.) because she has fallen in a back tit. Crud (Yorkshire way of describing it ed.) is white stringy stuff which comes out – if it gets worse it will be yellow. To tell whether a cow is alright or not, look at its nose … it should have dew-drops on it, if not, it may have a fever. Feel the base of its horns … they should be warm.

13th – Rushed off to take Captain to the blacksmith, as there is always a long queue if I am late.

## The Winter of 1947
### January

Sunday 5th – Very cold south/east wind; could hardly keep warm ploughing on tractor.

6th – Very cold, started to snow very fine stuff all day; still snowing tonight.

7th – Snowing all day; stopped at night, about two inches deep but drifted a lot deeper. Morning went round barns.

8th – Snow melting fast. Milk lorry had a job to get out of the lane.

9th – Frozen hard. Roads all icy. Got a batch of kale while it rained heavily.

10th – Did barns. Got a load of kale in the morning; afternoon another load with horse and cart.

23rd – Went ploughing but did not get much done. Started snowing.

24th – Went in the snow for some kale … Very cold stuff.

25th – Snowing about two inches, also freezing.

26th – Lovely day sunshine until Noon.

27th – Still snowing and freezing.

28th – Snowed, freezing hard.

**February**

2nd – Nightshade calved a heifer at 2.45am. I went home in the morning. At night it was drifting and blowing a blzzard, and it was very hard coming back over the Tops [over Black Park] some deep drifts.

3rd – Snowing heavily and drifting. Milk wagon did not come so we dumped milk at the top of the lane. Lorry came in the afternoon. Postman did not come. We just did the barns and I cleaned the mowing machine. Put six of our lambing ewes in our High meadow, out of the Bottom. Cecil Demaine has two died. One of ours also died; they are like rabbits. I ran a rabbit down in a drift.

4th – Snowed up to ten foot drifts all over the place. Milk wagon missed and snow wall-top to wall-top by the Stack Field opposite Bull Field.

5th – Milk man missed again. Bowdin and his wife brought groceries on horse and sledge. Just ground some provender and oats.

6th – Still snowing and freezing – milk man missed again. Put the separator together to start tomorrow as we have 90 gallons of milk in the dairy and all the milk kits are full.

7th – Snowing still. Drifts very deep. Separating milk all day, three days milk. Fed the sheep. Very boring day, slogging about everywhere in the snow. Can't go home at the weekend because of snow on the roads. They say it is two feet deep in Eastby.

8th/9th – Went home for the weekend and walked all the way, eight miles. And a very nice walk too.

10th – came back today; had five helpings of trifle and cleared out the dish. Foxglove calved a bull.

11th – Nothing doing. Still snowing.

14th – Went up the moors to gather sheep because they are hungering and need some hay.

17th – Up on the moor again to find some sheep, there were a lot dead and dying, and all as thin as the rabbits are at present. Took them to our High meadow and fed them with hay. Put the boiler on to warm some blue milk for the calves. The roads are still not open and we are starting to store milk again

18th – Went looking for sheep in Hagg Wood; got about 40 or so.

19th – Did the barns and then cut a way out of our yard into the lane. Road cutter has got through to our lane end from Burnsall.

20th – More snow.

24th – Did three barns and then took milk to the lane end to be picked up by the road-

## FARMING IN DREBLEY

waggon which brought us eleven extra kits.

25th – Roadmen got the road open to the Tower with the help of a bulldozer; it is snowing again tonight. Proctors came with some provin and got stuck at the lane end. Postman got through with his van… first time for three weeks.

27th – Grassington, Hebden and Burnsall isolated by snow.

28th – Men with bulldozer bribed to come down Drebley lane for dinner of ham and eggs – so they came, and cleared the lane.

**March**

5th – We dosed some sheep which were ill after eating the little yew tree on Club Nook lawn. We gave them some strong coffee and it soon brought them round. Then we destroyed the yew tree and also some rhododendron bushes as they also poison sheep. Hay position getting serious.

6th – Did the barns and then fed sheep. Went for 25 bales of hay that Proctors put at the end of the lane.

7th – After dinner, cleared the bull box into the midden. Weather still as bad as ever, middens getting higher and fuller and still snowing and blowing a blizzard … seven inches this morning and snowing tonight. It is five weeks today since the storm started.

10th – Snowed and blowed in the night but a widespread thaw is forecast, with fog and drizzle.

11th – Took four bales of hay to our High barn. The hay at Club Nook Home barn is finished, also at Low barn, and at our High barn. The sheep are fast dwindling the hay at Club Nook High Laithe. The thaw expected today was a freak, or so it says in the paper; there is a north wind and it is very cold.

12th – Proctors only let us have 25 cwts of hay; they brought it today with this month's provender. In the afternoon we took four bales to the Low barn and four to Club Nook High barn for the sheep. The weather is worse than ever tonight; it is blowing a northeast wind, snowing, drifting, freezing.

[Michael has described how his boss, Herbert Chester with Glen, his black and white sheepdog, and himself in front to lead the way, drove a herd of cows along snow-bound roads from Drebley to the railway station at Bolton Abbey. On the way, he particularly remembers how the wall top railings at the corner by The Riddings Farm were submerged in snowdrifts. After the cows had been loaded onto the train, they were taken to a lowland farm where fodder was still in good supply, while man and boy struggled back home to Drebley with a very tired dog.]

13th – Snow blocked the roads again and more is forecast.

15th – Willie Demaine has got a lamb but cannot find its mother. It can stand in the snow, but is covered with ice.

16th – The thaw has set in – it is raining hard. Moved the clocks back one hour.

## BARDEN IN WHARFEDALE, THE PLACE AND ITS PEOPLE

**The Camp Field at Drebley**

On the 13 July 1929 an agreement was drawn up between the Governors of the Bradford Grammar School and Herbert Chester, farmer, whereby a field known as Low Wood Piece, part of Drebley Farm, was let annually for the purpose of camping. Permission was granted to level a site on which a wooden hut was then erected. From this date onwards, until some time after the Second World War, masters and boys, scoutmasters and scouts came to camp in the field during the Easter, Whitsun, and August holidays. Initially, the campers came by train to Bolton Abbey station, and then walked six miles or so to Drebley, carrying all their supplies in rucksacks on their backs, but eventually lorries were hired to bring large tents, marquees and latrines, as well as bulk food supplies, while the campers travelled by coach. The regular influx of a large number of youngsters from Bradford was always a source of considerable anticipation and excitement at Drebley. From the farmyard, everything was then carried through the Long Garth and the meadow to Brown Bank, where a very steep hill descended down towards the river. The camp field was bordered by woodland on two sides, and, on the third, by the swiftly flowing River Wharfe.

Having erected their tents, the boys came to the farmyard daily to collect milk and drinking water, which they carried back to their camp in metal cans. Two boys could carry one can between them. Although there was no spring in the camp field, there was one amongst the rocks on the other side of the river. It was not long before a pulley device was rigged up, where, by an enterprising system of ropes, the boys conveyed food such as meat and butter to be stored in a naturally water-cooled larder. The boys found the river a great challenge, for there were huge boulders, deep pools and rapids alongside the camp field, and, only a short distance away the wooden footbridge afforded a diving board from which they could, with care, spring into a deep pool below.

The future politician, Dennis Healy, was one of those boys who came to Drebley in his

## FARMING IN DREBLEY

youth. In his autobiography *The Time of My Life*, published in 1989, he quoted Dylan Thomas, (Fern Hill) in describing how:

> Every Whitsun we had our school camp in a field by the Wharfe near Appletreewick. As we walked to church in Burnsall 'the Sabbath rang slowly in the pebbles of the Holy streams…' One day we always set aside for a walk down the river through Bolton Woods to the ruined abbey, then up the Valley of Desolation and over the moors to Simon Seat, before dropping back into the valley to the camp. This part of Wharfedale is to me what a Shropshire was for Houseman, 'the land of lost content'.

## The Log Bridge

A small footbridge once existed between Brown Bank Wood, Drebley and Hough Wood, Howgill. It had handrails and was constructed from a single log of wood which, according to local knowledge, came from Canada. The plans for this bridge remain in the Chatsworth manuscripts stored at Bolton Abbey, where the date of its construction can be found. The photograph on the next page shows how the bridge spanned a rocky, turbulent stretch of the Wharfe, situated between Drebley camp field upstream and the stepping stones by the Hippings meadow downstream.

In 1937 a great storm caused the river to flood, and to bring down so much debris that some tree trunks were caught on the central stanchion supporting the bridge, thus causing it to collapse.

The remains of the bridge were later found about half a mile downstream, in one of the riverside fields below Gamsworth; a photograph shows the timber being hauled back to Howgill, using heavy carthorses and chains. Although the estate maintained a supply of carthorses for general use in the forests, these horses and men with their heavy equipment were probably supplied by the well known haulage merchant, Arthur Green of Silsden. The remains of the log bridge were later sawn into lengths and stored for 50 years or more on the roadside opposite Hough Mill. The boulder which supported the stanchion remains in the centre of the river, whilst on each side, almost buried beneath the annual fall of beech leaves and decades of leaf mould, are the metal structures from which the bridge sprang.

The loss of the bridge caused major social changes between the hamlets of Drebley and Howgill and the village of Appletreewick, where the two public houses or hostelries immediately lost custom from the three farmhouses and the keeper's cottage. It was said that the Irishmen, who were hired for a month's hay-time each summer were then at a loss to know whether to drag out the old farm bicycles or whether to walk a couple of miles to and from Burnsall to seek a pint after a day's work in the fields.

At that time a thriving social club met regularly in Appletreewick village hall which had been an easy and popular venue for the younger Drebley folk to reach on foot. It was called the BATS Club (Burnsall, Appletreewick, Thorpe and Skyreholme). After the loss of the bridge, they met in Burnsall Village Hall, but it was much further to go, and they were then dependant on bicycles, or occasionally Herbert Chester's motorcar. Other memories of the footbridge include those from the boy scouts who recklessly used it as a diving board when camping in Brown Bank field upstream from the wood. Family friendships too were severed by the loss of the footbridge, for the stepping stones were by no means an adequate substitute, especially for older people who never regained the easy means of exchanging visits they had known when the footbridge had linked the two sides of the river.

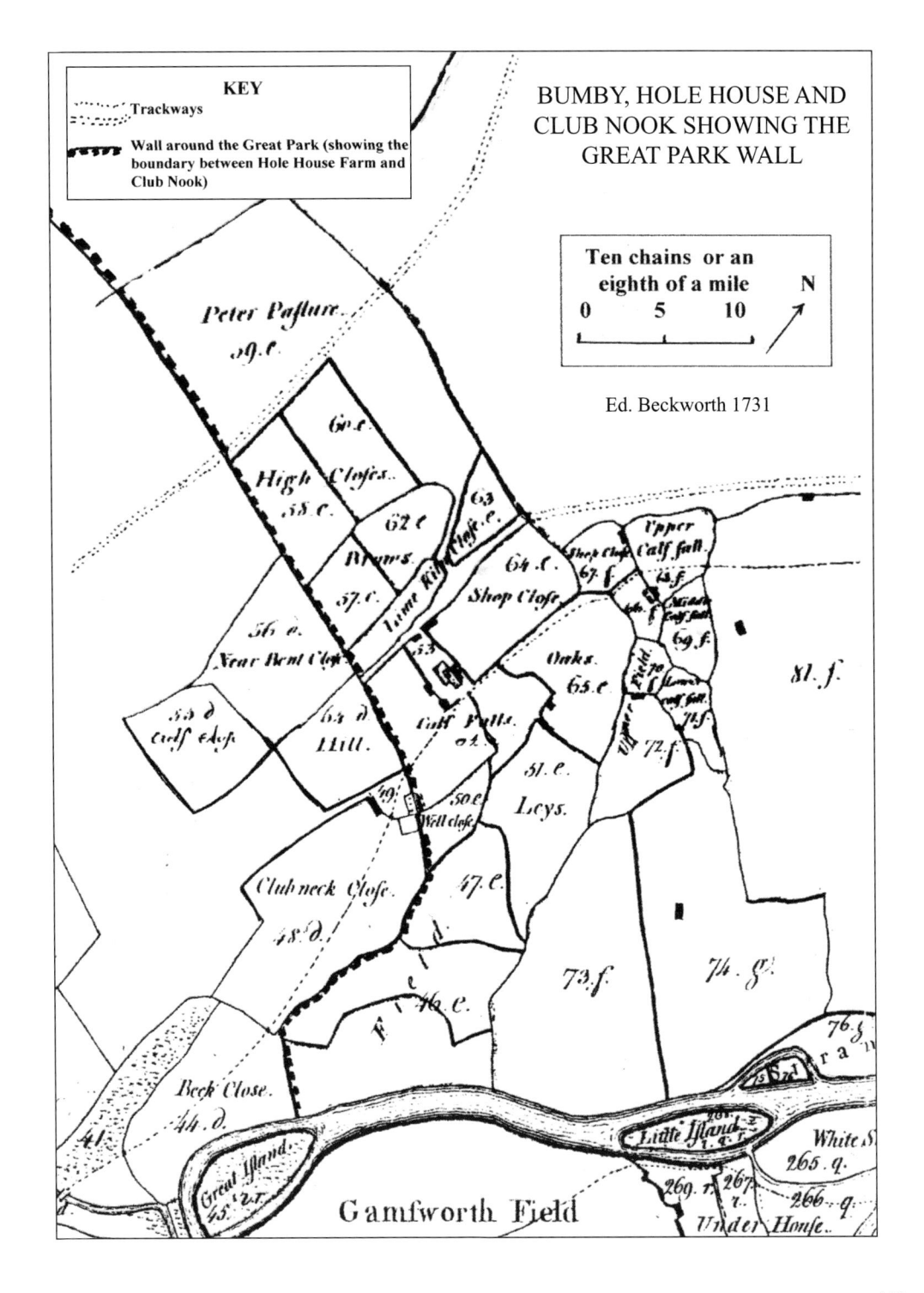

# BUMBY, HOLE HOUSE AND CLUB NOOK

**KEY**
- ...... Trackways
- ▬▬ Wall around the Great Park (showing the boundary between Hole House Farm and Club Nook)

**BUMBY, HOLE HOUSE AND CLUB NOOK SHOWING THE GREAT PARK WALL**

Ten chains or an eighth of a mile
0   5   10

N ↗

Ed. Beckworth 1731

**Bumby Barn (Bombey Barn), Barden**[120]     (map reference: SE 05065882)

Bumby Barn is a ruin in fields between the Burnsall-Barden road (B6160) and stands beside the small beck known as Bumby Sike. Only the north wall of the building stands to its full height and this now forms part of a field wall. Stone has been robbed out of most of the other walls leaving some foundation courses showing through the grass. However, at the northeast corner of the building a stub of wall with a window opening was still standing in 2009. In addition, fallen masonry near the south-east corner includes a massive door lintel shaped for a doorway with a pointed head, and with a broad chamfer to the former opening. Combining site measurements of these details with information from a book by James Walton,[121] it has been possible partly to reconstruct the east elevation of the former barn as a scale drawing (Figure 1). Whereas the door lintel could be sixteenth century, the window opening and surrounding stonework are more likely to be nineteenth century, and look like the work of estate stone masons. The lintel over the window opening seems to have been re-used, perhaps from the footings of a boskin.

### Descriptions of the building by earlier authors

The significance of this site would probably have been overlooked except that the illustrations in Walton's book, including a perspective sketch by his wife, show the barn as having a steep thatched roof. The thatch was so much decayed at the time when the sketch was made that rafters were exposed in places. Walton's interest was in the plan of the building, and he notes that it was built on sloping ground with a 'mistal' or shippon for cattle at the lower end. There were two steps up from this to the upper part of the barn which was entered from the field via a wide cart entrance and had ample storage space for hay. A door in the back wall opposite the cart entrance would have allowed the space between the two doorways to be used as a threshing floor.

The shippon (mistal) in Bumby Barn was wider than the main body of the building, and Walton saw this as due to an extension of the original building 'affording increased accommodation for cattle'. Such an extension would have involved repositioning the sixteenth century door lintel, but from what little can be gathered about the walls of the extension, they again look like nineteenth century estate masonry.

Walton rather strangely omitted to describe the structure of the building, but Hartley and Ingilby stated that 'Bombey Barn had one pair of crucks in the 1930s',[122] although when they revisited the site in the 1980s, the crucks had gone and the building had already become a ruin, for which they provided a simplified plan. The plan in Figure 2 attempts to incorporate all the information provided by Walton and Hartley and Ingilby combined with our own observations and measurements.

---

120 Report written by Arnold Pacey on the basis of information collected on site during visits with Brontë Bedford-Payne in 2000, and with Alison Armstrong on 17 March 2009.
121 James Walton, *Homesteads of the Yorkshire Dales*, Dalesman Publishing, 1947 and 1979, pp. 36, 37.
122 Marie Hartley and Joan Ingilby, *Dales Memories*, Dalesman Books, 1986, p. 55.

**BUMBY BARN**
Figure 1
East Gable Elevation

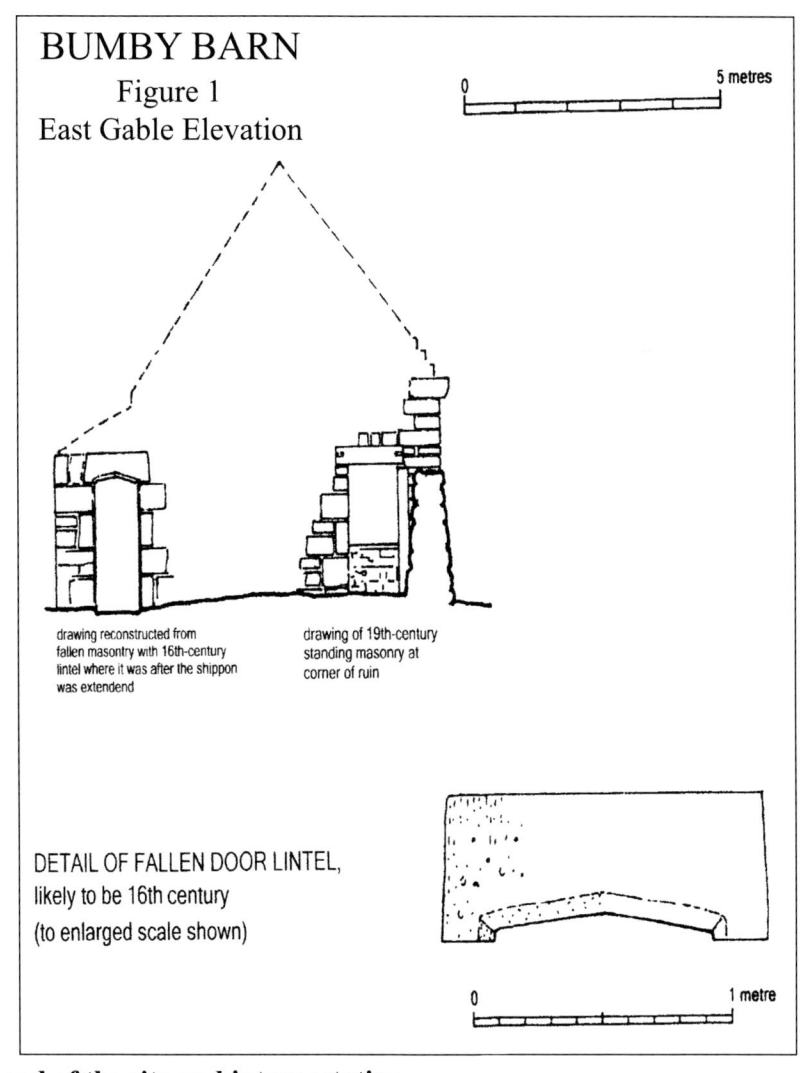

0 — 5 metres

drawing reconstructed from fallen masonry with 16th-century lintel where it was after the shippon was extendend

drawing of 19th-century standing masonry at corner of ruin

DETAIL OF FALLEN DOOR LINTEL,
likely to be 16th century
(to enlarged scale shown)

0 — 1 metre

### The east end of the site and interpretation

An unusual feature of the site is that two metres beyond the east end wall is the edge of a conspicuously level area that extends another five metres and is demarcated by prominent kerb stones.

The surface of this space appears to have been deliberately cobbled or paved, although grass now grows over most of it. Beyond this level area is a rectangular stone-lined pit (or sunken trough) about 2.25 metres long and over 60 cm (or two feet) wide. The top of pit is closed by four large slabs of stone, but one had partly fallen in, revealing that the pit was at least 50 cm deep with an unknown depth of silt and debris in the bottom.

Initial interpretations of the site were based on the assumption that the barn was built as a field barn, with a shippon or mistal at the lower end, and had functioned as such throughout its working life. The stone-lined pit was downslope from the shippon and would inevitably be affected by drainage from the shippon. Experts consulted at the time, including the late

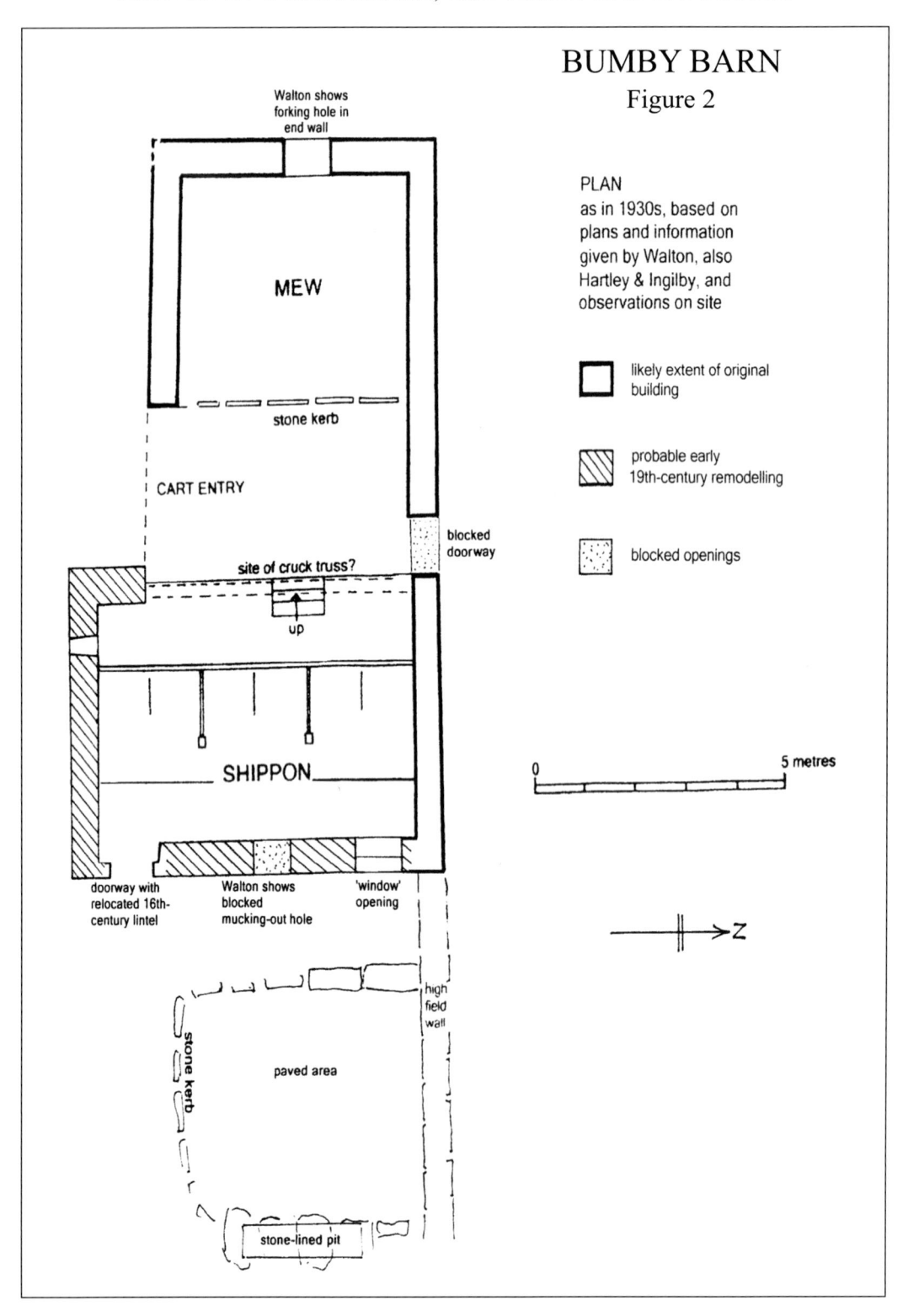

# BUMBY BARN
## Figure 2

Walton shows forking hole in end wall

MEW

stone kerb

CART ENTRY

site of cruck truss?

blocked doorway

up

SHIPPON

doorway with relocated 16th-century lintel

Walton shows blocked mucking-out hole

'window' opening

high field wall

stone kerb

paved area

stone-lined pit

PLAN
as in 1930s, based on plans and information given by Walton, also Hartley & Ingilby, and observations on site

☐ likely extent of original building

▨ probable early 19th-century remodelling

▦ blocked openings

0 — 5 metres

→ Z

## BUMBY BARN AND HOLE HOUSE

Kate Mason, suggested that the pit had been designed to collect liquid manure. Similar examples of pits associated with shippons were noted. At Jack's Cottage, Feizor, near Austwick, there is one where dung was shovelled from the shippon into a roofed midden with a floor of slate slabs, with gaps left for drainage into a tank hole under the floor. Comparison with that site suggested that the paved area with a kerb at Bumby Barn could be the site of a midden, and the stone-lined pit could be the tank hole. However, there was no obvious drainage channel leading from the paved area into the hole, and in its present state, the pit is not water-tight. Gaps in the stone lining may once have been plugged with clay.

The false assumption underlying this argument was evident when it was realised that an estate map of 1731 showed the building as a house, not a barn. In addition, the Hearth Tax returns of 1672 indicate that the first inhabited house south of Drebley was occupied by William Bumby, and had one hearth.[123]

Bumby's house can probably be identified with Bumby Barn, but that does not preclude the existence of a small shippon on the site, since most families would keep a cow or two if they could, and the house could have taken the form of a small longhouse. Whatever the detail, this building probably had a single pair of crucks, and must have been remodelled after the map was drawn to create the field barn that Walton recorded, which had accommodation for six cows in its extended shippon. Judging by the nineteenth century stonework in the eastern part of the building, this may have been after 1800.

The stone-lined pit seems likely to date from the period when the building was in use as a house, and may have been related to some kind of cottage industry practised by the occupants of the house. Among the most widespread domestic industries in the seventeenth and eighteenth centuries were those connected with textiles, which might need tanks or troughs for such processes as retting flax, scouring wool or fulling woollen cloth.

### Postscript

Subsequent to our examination of the ruin in 2000 and 2009, there has been an archaeological investigation of several features in the field where Bumby Barn stood. This was led by Dr. David Johnson, with an associated study of the barn site and associated field walls by Alison Armstrong. The archaeological work led to discovery of the remains of two small potash kilns not far from the the barn. Since potash could be used with water to produce 'lye' for wool scouring, and could also be used to produce the soap needed in fulling or cleaning textiles, the case for thinking of this as a textile working site is greatly strengthened. This would probably be during the seventeenth and early eighteenth centuries.

### Hole House: Interpretation
Arnold Pacey

Hole House either originated as a single cell, possibly timber-framed or cruck built dwelling, now represented by the seventeenth century stone walls on the south-west. or, if it were a two cell stone house, all but the south-west corner was demolished, to be replaced by the present building in the late eighteenth or early nineteenth century.

---

[123] The Hearth Tax list for Staincliffe and Ewcross Wapentakes, 1672, Ripon Historical Society, 1992, p. 11.

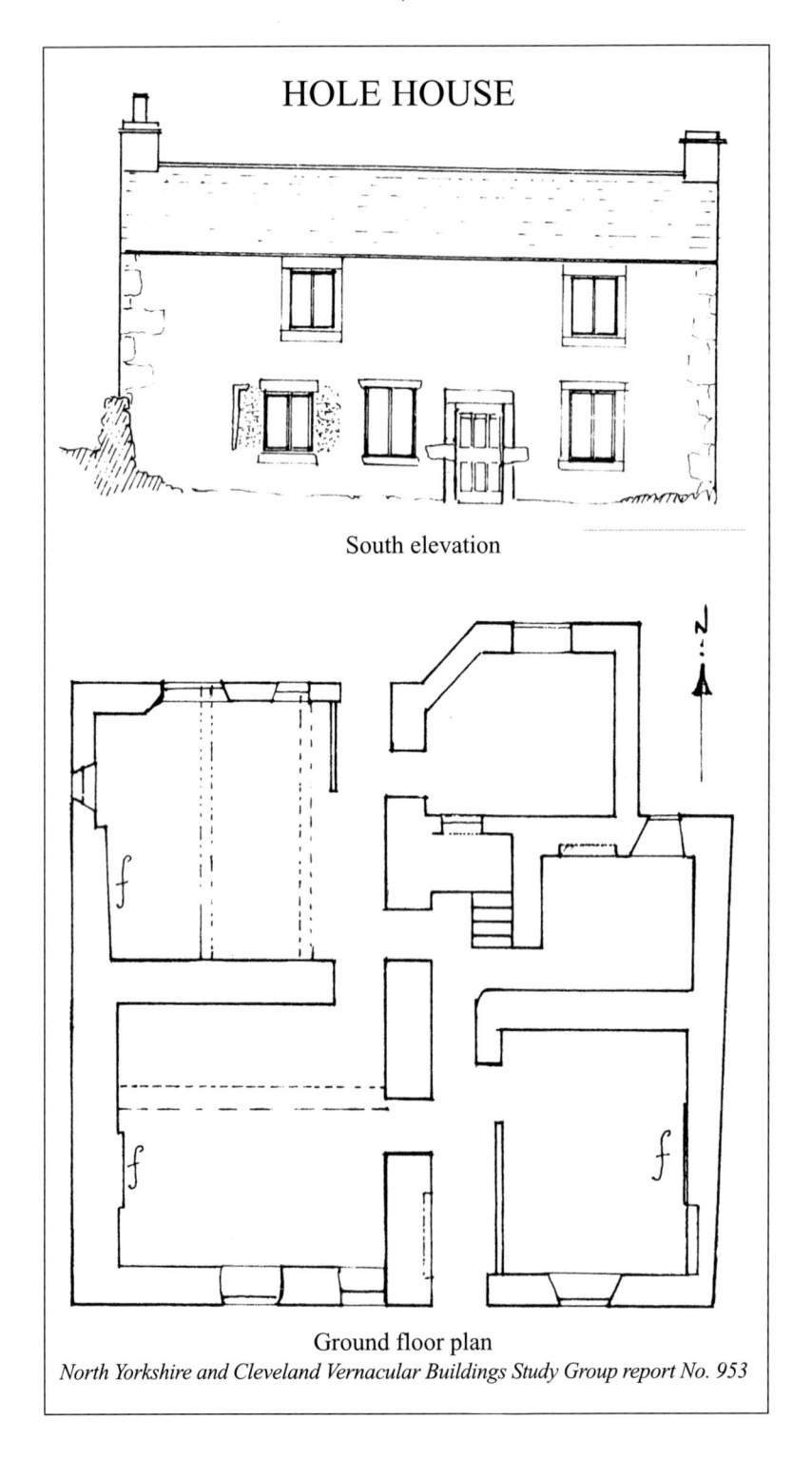

## HOLE HOUSE

South elevation

Ground floor plan
*North Yorkshire and Cleveland Vernacular Buildings Study Group report No. 953*

## HOLE HOUSE

This is a plausible interpretation in view of the historical evidence that Hole House was one of the lodges *le Holhog* listed in the manorial accounts for the Forest of Barden 1437/8.[124] there would therefore have been a dwelling to house the lodge-keeper on this site from medieval times onwards.

The earliest part of the house standing today dates from the seventeenth century. Our survey shows, by the thickness of the walls, that the early part consisted of a house-body on the south-west corner, with kitchen to the rear. The parlour on the south east corner, with pantry and staircase behind, were probably built at the same time that the entrance door was moved from its central position, and new windows inserted in the front, south facing and west walls. The blocked front window has the shape of a three light mullion window, while the upper west wall retains evidence of a former drip-mould in the wall around the present window. Changes in the masonry of the front wall, with the insertion of a window in the former position of the entrance door indicate how it would have opened directly into the house. These changes would have been to accommodate the thinly walled passage shown on the plan, which ensures a degree of privacy and warmth in the house-body.

There are no original fireplaces or roof timbers to help with dating, therefore the survey of the house and its site is not complete.

**General Description**
Brontë Bedford-Payne

Hole House lies between Bumby Barn and Club Nook, alongside the footpath which follows the line of the ancient track between Drebley and Barden Bridge. The place name indicates that it was settled in pre-conquest times, in that it is derived from Old English *hol* or Old Norse *hoir* for 'hole' or 'sunken, lying in a hollow', but topographically there is no hollow in the area of the settlement. Historical evidence dates from 1437/8, when it was listed in the manorial accounts as one of the Forest Lodges, and identified as *le holhog*.[125]

The house itself, its late medieval closes, and a large enclosure of seven acres named Peter Pasture is shown on both Ed. Beckwith's map of 1731 and Matthew Oddie's map of 1778. Other fields associated with this farm, including Peter Pasture, lie outside the Great Park, between Powson Park and Drebley Thwaite. The 'house with fold and garde' is numbered 53 on the 1778 map and is shown facing south, with four barns around the perimeter of the garth. Passing the entrance is a walled lane, lying in a hollow way ending to the north in a gate leading into Drebley Thwaite. From this point, the unwalled trackway, marked by Oddie as a horseway or open road, continues until it reaches the entrance to the hamlet of Drebley. This relatively deep, walled section survives today as part of the B6160, while the horseway has become a definable but disused footpath which passes through fields on its way to Drebley lane and the entrance to Littlegate Farm.

The southern end of the hollow way was blocked by the Great Park wall continuing down from Powson Park towards the river, thus separating the enclosures around Hole

---

124 Moorhouse, Stephen, 2003: *The Archaeology of Yorkshire*, Yorkshire Archaeology Society, Occasional Paper, No 3.
125 Moorhouse, Stephen, *The Archaeology of Yorkshire*, Thematic Paper No 3, *Anatomy of the Yorkshire Dales: decoding the landscape*, p343.

House from those of Club Nook. The absence of an opening at this point is further evidence to show that there was no 'through way' between Drebley Thwaite and the Tower, other than by the packhorse track crossing through Peter Pasture and Powson Park, high on the valley side; a reminder that the old footpath through the fields between Drebley and Barden Bridge was in daily use when Beckwith's map of 1731 was drawn. The poorly drained enclosure situated in the hillside opposite Hole House is named Lime Kiln Close but the remains of the kiln have not survived apart from stones now built into nineteenth century field walls. It is likely that the lane and hollow way were associated with this kiln and its connections with the farms in Drebley hamlet, and also with a well-defined track which leads steeply up the hillside to join the packhorse road at a point where there is now only a fallen stone gatepost to mark the location of this trackway.

A narrow, grass covered terrace lying north/south across the hillside now covers a pipe line laid in 1861 by Bradford Water Works Corporation during construction of the High and Low reservoirs on Barden Moor.

Although listed as one of the Forest Lodges, Hole House did not develop into a traditional vaccary as happened at Drebley. It is likely that it long remained as a tenement Lodge, where forest workers were housed. In 1867 the estate rent books show that the acreage for Hole House farm was 53 acres 3 furlongs, which was considerably smaller than for neighbouring farms of Club Nook (99 acres 1 furlong) and Littlegate (65 acres 2 furlongs). The four barns in the yard west of the house (shown on Beckwith's map) have not survived; this remarkably level area is now occupied by several large sycamore trees. In other words, there is no fold yard adjoining the house, with a classical arrangement of outbuildings such as would be needed for the rearing and shelter of animals and storage of hay. However, a large barn, dating in style from the late eighteenth or early nineteenth century, stands in a detached position within its own small fold yard in a field on the hillside to the west of the house, and it was from here that the tenant at Hole House farmed. No information has been discovered to date to explain the reasons for this unusual arrangement.

**Who lived at Hole House?**
Records show that since at least 1605, both Hole House and Littlegate were farmed by successive generations of the Demaine family who were more closely related to those at Littlegate than to the Demaines farming at The Fold Farm, or to those at Barden Scale.

In 1665 George Demaine of Hole House, who was a locksmith, drew up his will in favour of his son John to whom he bequeathed 'all my instruments stencils wholeful belongings to my trade of locksmith'.[126] In 1692 another George and his son Peter, also a locksmith, appear on the Tithe List, while in 1693, William Demaine of Hole House, who died in 1718, drew up an inventory of his belongings, and bequeathed to his wife Mary all his messuage and house. He willed that his body be buried in the chapel at Bolton, the document being witnessed by John Demaine and others.[127] He had a son named George.

Three nineteenth century headstones in the churchyard at Bolton Abbey relate to the Demaines of Hole House:

---

126 Borthwick Institute of Historical Research, York.
127 ibid

## HOLE HOUSE AND CLUB NOOK

George Demaine, 1750-1821 and Mary his wife, who died in 1818.
Christopher Demaine, 1781-1861 and Anne Demaine 1791-1808.
Jane, daughter of Christopher and Anne Demaine, 1814-31

For a century or so, between the 1850s and 1940, the lessees were members of a family named Emmott, who came from Beamsley. They are reputed to have possessed 'some fine specimens of furniture carved in old forest oak'.[128]

As the twentieth century progressed it became increasingly difficult to prosper on this small farm, where the land included very little meadowland or good pasture, and so it was hardly surprising when in 1940, at the beginning of the Second World War, the then elderly and infirm farmer was evicted for failure to conform to the demands of the War Agricultural Executive Committee to improve his land and increase his output. After this unusual event occurred the tenancy went to William Demaine of Littlegate. He and his nephew Cecil Demaine then farmed the two properties as one entity, until Cecil married and brought up his own family at Hole House; he eventually retired to Skipton. There is a headstone in the churchyard at Bolton Abbey, bearing the inscription: 'Elizabeth Ann Demaine, Littlegate Farm, Drebley, died 15 February 1955 aged 76 years. Cecil Mossman Demaine, died 17 February 1993, aged 85 years, Husband, Dad and Grandad.'

The house then became a separately tenanted property while the land remained part of Littlegate Farm, with Ralph Stott as the lessee. The house was first surveyed by members of the North Yorkshire Vernacular Building Survey Group, and again in 1983 by the Upper Wharfedale Field Society, when evidence for a seventeenth century house was found incorporated into the present eighteenth century building.[129] The report written by Arnold Pacey is attached to this account.

**Club Nook**

The place name nook derives from Middle English or Old French *nok* meaning a corner. There are five places so named in Barden, four of them associated with corners in the walls enclosing Henry Clifford's Great Park, constructed at the end of the fifteenth century, while the fifth is associated with the former vaccary at Howgill.

Club Nook (SD051585) was an important corner in the park, where a clubbed oak tree grew. It was here that the medieval trackway between Drebley and Barden Bridge crossed through the Great Park wall to enter Drebley Field from Drebley Thwaite and to continue thence on its way to the river crossing (see Oddie's map). This footpath is still shown on the first edition Ordnance Survey map, although it now passes through a series of blocked stiles in field walls built since the division of Drebley Thwaite in around 1812. The presence in Club Nook yard of a cruck barn and the tiny one cell cottage with its massive external chimney are reminders that a small settlement existed here before the present farmhouse and its nineteenth century barns were built. From this point, forming a corner or Nook, where it might be assumed a clubbed oak stood, the wall of the Great Park turns sharply south in the direction of the Tower, and continues towards the river at Great Island.

---

128 Speight, Harry, 1900, *Upper Wharfedale,* London: Eliot Stock.
129 North Yorkshire and Cleveland Vernacular Buildings Study Group, Report No. 953

*The gnarled (clubbed) oak tree surviving in Tower Close from the ancient forest of Barden, drawn by Rob Keep of Grassington.*

*Park Nook* (SD040579) occurs at the north west corner of walls dividing the present Barden Broad Park from Barden Moor and Mucky Park; this was where the corner of the medieval wall which divided the Great Park from Drebley Thwaite met the greater area of open moorland known as Black Park. At this point the wall turns sharply in an eastward direction towards the Little Park surrounding the Tower, and so to the river.

*Smithyman Nook* (SD085574) occurs on the east side of the river, south east of the medieval rabbit warren. It lies in a corner formed by walls enclosing the former Lodge within Laund Pastures and the former vaccary at Broadshaw.

*Dicken Nook* (SD083570) is situated at the furthest point in the boundary wall enclosing the rabbit warren. The place name Dicken derives from: *dic* Old English, *dick* Old Norse for dike or ditch and *diggen* Modern English.[130]

Topographically, the watercourse which lies at the head of Posforth Gill, now the Valley of Desolation, forms the dike or ditch from which this Nook gets its name. The wall between Dicken Nook and Smithyman Nook formed the boundary between the medieval vaccary at Broadshaw and the Forest Lodge at Laund.

*Stockdale Nook* (SD060587) lies at the point where the packhorse way coming north from Barden Tower branched to skirt round the vaccary in Howgill, on its way to Eastwood Head and thus to the eastern watershed at Greenhow.

---

130 Old English (Anglo-Saxon), Old Norse (Old West Scandinavian).

# CLUB NOOK

**Club Nook Farmhouse**[132]　　　　　　　　　　　　　(map reference SE05055845)

Arnold Pacey

Club Nook Farm is centred on a farmhouse with attached barn aligned east-west, with an eighteenth century barn to its south. The farm was not one of the lodges in the medieval Forest of Barden, but originated later. The farmhouse itself has a three-room plan with rear outshut.

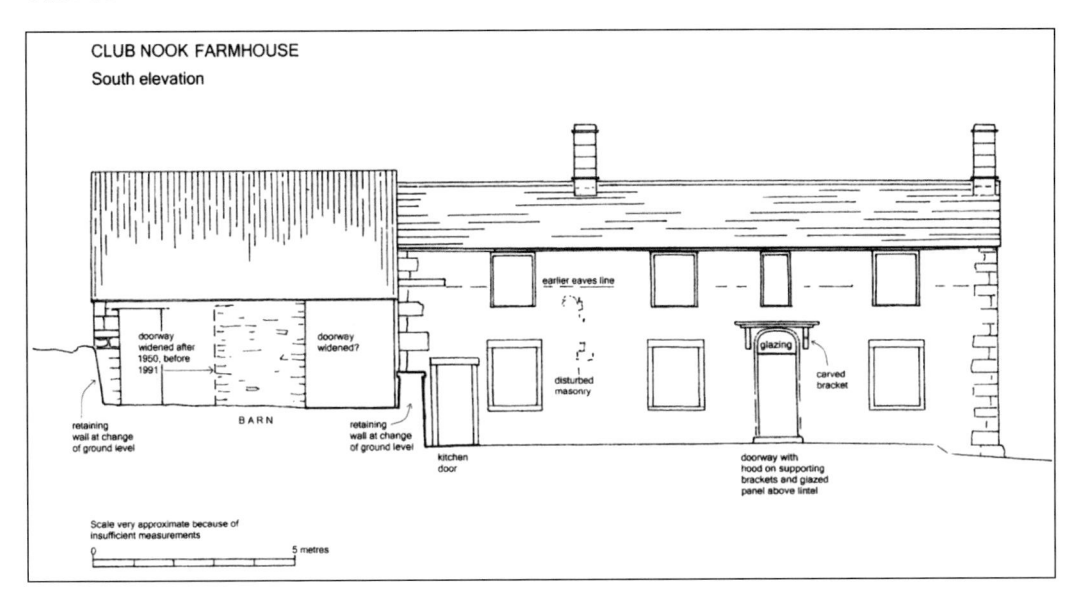

*CLUB NOOK FARMHOUSE — South elevation*

The main house doorway has a projecting stone hood supported by carved brackets of Victorian design. This entrance is placed centrally between the housebody and the parlour. To the west of the housebody is the kitchen, which has its own doorway adjacent to quoins that mark the west corner of the house front. Butting against this corner is a wide doorway into the barn. The kitchen doorway has a lower lintel than the main entrance and plain monolithic jambs. The barn stands on slightly higher ground with a retaining wall outside the kitchen door marking the change in level. There is a cellar under the eastern part of the barn which is entered from inside the kitchen.

Examination of the south elevation reveals a slight change in stonework some two feet (60cm) below the eaves, with smaller quoins at both ends. This demonstrates that the front wall of the house has been built up to accommodate a roof with higher eaves, probably when the house was reroofed with sandstone flags. The original eaves level was only slightly higher than the existing eaves of the barn, and it seems likely that the whole building originally had a steep roof with the same profile as survives on the barn. It was probably thatched throughout.

Windows on the ground floor have monolithic jambs and heavy lintels that could well be early nineteenth century. Irregularities in the front wall of the kitchen could be due to

---

131 Report written by Arnold Pacey on the basis of measurements made on site during visits with Brontë Bedford-Payne in 2000 and photographs taken at various dates over 50 years down to 2012.

the removal of earlier windows but may be because the front wall of the two principal rooms of the house was entirely rebuilt in the nineteenth century while leaving some older masonry in the walls of the kitchen.

The first-floor windows were inserted at the same time as the eaves were raised and are slightly narrower than those on the ground floor. They also have monolithic stone jambs with a slight splay such as was favoured by estate stone masons later in the nineteenth century. The first-floor windows, therefore, could be of the same date as the Victorian door hood.

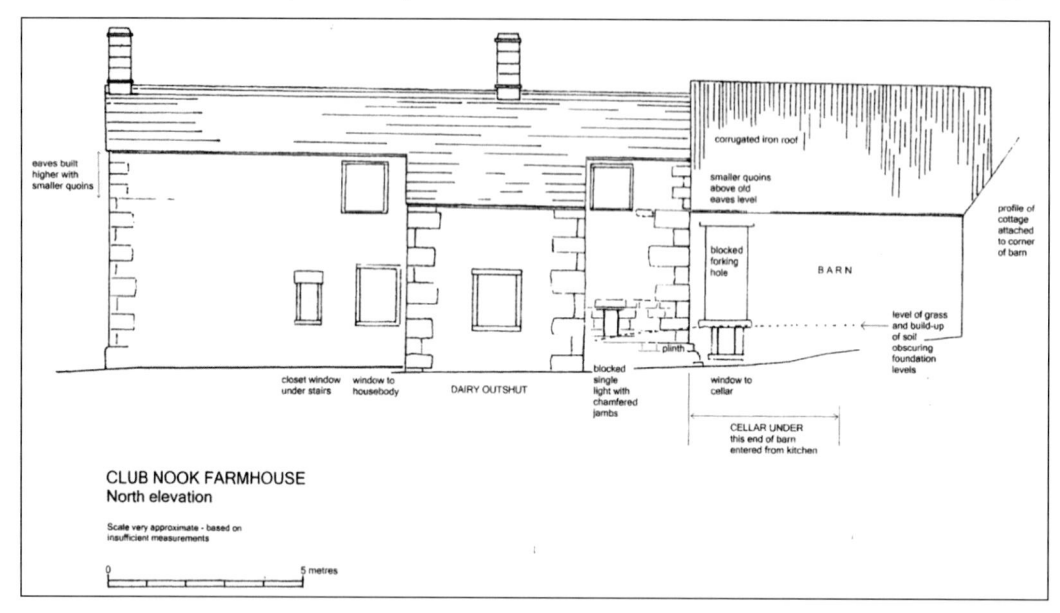

**CLUB NOOK FARMHOUSE**
North elevation

Scale very approximate - based on insufficient measurements

0    5 metres

At the back, on the north side, the linear form of the house is interrupted by a small outshut extension behind the kitchen, said to have been a dairy, and by a ruin attached to the far western corner of the barn. Windows at the back of the house are of the same pattern as those at the front, except that there is a small closet window opposite the front door, presumably to light a space below the stairs.

There is a straight masonry joint where the attached barn butts against quoins belonging to the original fabric of the house. It shows clearly that the barn is a later addition. Between the straight joint and the outshut, the house has a window at first-floor level, and below it, a small single-light window low down in the wall. The latter is blocked, but the stones on each side which form its jambs may have been slightly chamfered in a seventeenth century manner (though the chamfer is largely obscured).

Somewhat lower than this window, on the west side of the straight joint, there is another blocked window set low down in the wall of the barn. This lights the cellar below the barn. When examined in the year 2000, the window was seen to have monolithic jambs and a lintel with slightly rusticated masonry tooling. Above the lintel was a blocked doorway, interpreted as a forking hole for loading hay into the barn.

Between 2000 and 2012 there may have been some earth dumped at the back of the barn, and there has certainly been a considerable growth of grass which obscures much of the de-

## CLUB NOOK

tail that was measured and drawn earlier. A dotted line on the drawing shows the limit of what can now be seen as compared with the full line representing the measured ground level in 2000.

A further point about the straight joint is that the higher-level quoins are smaller than those lower down, and have the same slightly rusticated tooling as the lintel of the cellar window. Lower down are larger quoins with much plainer tooling. The smaller quoins with the distinctive tooling appear to be part of the nineteenth century alterations of the house. Before this alteration, the eaves at the back of the house were at the same level as the existing eaves of the barn.

Hence, there appear to be at least two phases in the masonry of this part of the building, one probably seventeenth century, comprising the single-light window and some of the lower quoins, and the other comprising the nineteenth century cellar window in the barn together with the upper part of the house walls (after the eaves were raised).

The main entrance door opens into a small, square hall from which the staircase rises

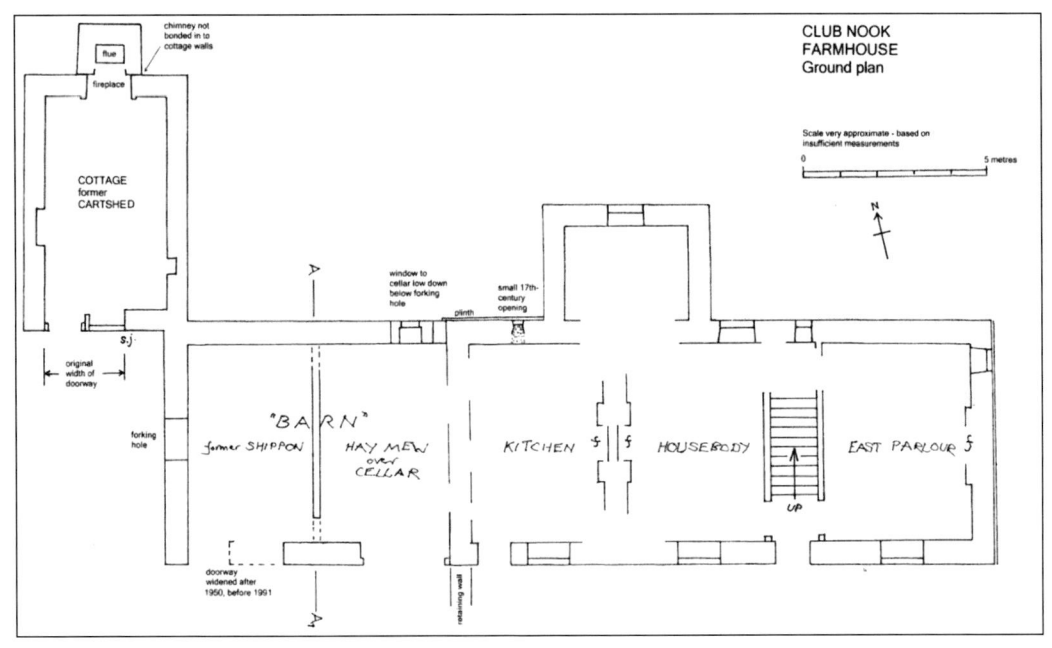

between the walls of the adjoining walls. The staircase is lit by the glazed panel over the door. The kitchen is at the west end of the house with a fireplace that shares the same stack as the fireplace in the next room (the housebody). To the rear is the outshut, latterly a dairy. This could have been the site of the original staircase, but it has to be borne in mind that the outshut is clearly an extension, perhaps built after 1800. Before that, access to the attics may have been by ladder. Before the roof was raised to its present level, space available upstairs was probably very limited.

In the kitchen, a doorway through the west wall opens onto a flight of six steps descending into the cellar under the eastern half of the barn. This is roofed with a stone barrel vault and was originally lit by a small window on the north side.

## The barn

The interior of the barn is outstanding for its roof truss which takes the form of an upper-cruck (which should not be confused with full crucks, such as those in barns at Drebley). The cruck principals are supported by a tie beam which spans the width of the building, and their workmanship, including chamfers, pegged joints and form of the apex, strongly suggest they originate from the seventeenth century. However, this upper-cruck truss is not in its original position, and a lease of 1850 describes the barn as 'newly crucked'. What may have happened is that, when the house was reroofed with higher eaves and a low-pitch flagged roof, an upper-cruck roof truss from the old house was salvaged for re-use in the barn. The barn roof was then thatched and when the thatch was replaced by corrugated metal, various blocking pieces had to be added to raise the roof covering to a level that would take it over the barn walls.

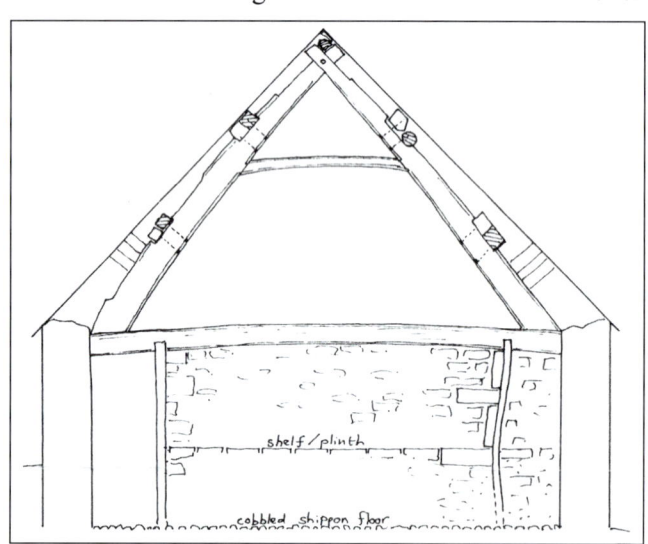

Under the roof truss in the barn is a thin dividing wall. To the west of this was originally a shippon, whose cobbled floor partly survives. To the east was probably a hay loft above the vault of the cellar. The two parts of the barn have their own doorways, and photographs show that the western, doorway has been widened so replacing a relatively narrow shippon doorway with one more appropriate for a garage.

## The cottage

An unusual feature of the site is the ruins of a cottage built onto the north-west corner of the barn. The cottage is quite narrow with the only window placed alongside the doorway in the south gable. The window is set in a thin section of wall which is not bonded into the thicker, structural wall of the gable, and it appears that the window and door replace a wider doorway, about seven feet (2.1m) wide, which may have been sufficient to admit a small cart or trap.

# CLUB NOOK

The large chimney raises further questions. The flue within the chimney is set back much further than usual behind the front of the fireplace which it serves. A first thought was that this may have been done to accommodate a bacon-smoking chamber within the massive thickness of the chimney, but closer inspection suggests that the apparent size of the chimney arises from the way it was built against an existing, earlier gable wall rather than being incorporated into it.

In other words, the cottage as first constructed did not have a fireplace or chimney, probably because it was a farm building of some kind, possibly a cart shed.

### Interpretation

Although Club Nook Farmhouse is of nineteenth century appearance, and there are documentary references to repairs or improvements in 1806, as well as evidence of alterations about 1850, the kitchen walls appear to contain older masonry (which is especially evident at the back), and the upper-cruck truss in the barn is of seventeenth century, though not in its original position.

The house has significant similarities with Littlegate farmhouse at Drebley where there is an upper-cruck truss still in its original position. Both houses have the typical three-room plan of the period and in both there is a major chimney stack located between the house-body (or west parlour) and the kitchen, serving fireplaces in both rooms. In addition both houses are of the same width (6.3m measured externally), and both have parlours of about the same size.

Club Nook differs in the position of the later, inserted staircase and in having the fireplace for the east parlour in the end gable wall. A more significant difference is in the kitchens of the two houses. Club Nook has a smaller kitchen than Littlegate, but with access to the cellar (whose date is uncertain).

### The Birch family of Broad Park and Club Nook

Thomas Birch was born in Burnsall in about 1816.[132] For at least 60 years he was the gamekeeper for Barden Great Park on the Bolton Abbey Estate. He was appointed head gamekeeper in 1859, and, after the upper and lower reservoirs were constructed in the 1880s for Bradford Water Works Corporation, his home was at Park House, by the Low Reservoir. When he became too old to work, his son Stephen continued as head keeper. Stephen and his wife Hannah, née Worsley, had seven children, all of whom walked daily from Park House to Barden School, where each child obtained a Boyle and Petyt or a County Minor scholarship. These remarkable achievements enabled them to continue in secondary education at either Ermysted's Boys' Grammar School or Skipton Girls' High School. Their names are recorded on the Honours Board still hanging in the porch at Barden School: 1907 Dorothy Birch; 1908 Tom Birch; 1910 Edna Birch; 1913 Edgar Birch; 1916 Alec Birch; 1917 Hubert Birch; 1920 John Birch.

*Left, the farmyard at Park House and, right, a headstone in Bolton Abbey Churchyard.*

---

132 Thomas appears on the 1841 census living as a lodger at Barden Park, with the head of household, Richard Croft. His age was 25, and his occupation that of gamekeeper. A photograph was taken at Barden Tower of his marriage to Ellen Lister of Fleensop, Coverdale. It was published in the *Craven Herald* (date unknown) but their first child, John, was born in 1843.

# CLUB NOOK

## Birch at Club Nook
In 1926 Stephen retired, which meant that he had to leave Park House, since none of his sons wished to apply for the job of gamekeeper. In order to maintain himself and those of his large family still living at home, he applied successfully for the lease of Club Nook when the former tenant, Frank Almack, retired and the farm fell vacant. After this, aided at intervals by his sons, he farmed Club Nook until his death in 1934, by which time none of his boys wished to remain as tenants on this small hill farm. All the children went to college or to university, but it was John, the youngest son, who went to Leeds University to study Agriculture. He obtained his BSc, and then found employment as Chief Agriculturalist, Levington Research Station, Fison's Limited (manufacturers of fertilisers).

## Links with Herbert and Mary Chester of Drebley Farm
After Stephen's death, the lease for Club Nook Farm was taken by their neighbour Herbert Chester, who seized the opportunity to augment the acreage of his small farm at Drebley. It was then that John Birch came forward with a vision to carry out experimental ploughing of the land, followed by re-seeding of grassland, augmented with fertilisers. Advice was sought from Dr Ian Moore at the University of Leeds, who was at that time the foremost authority on grassland improvement, and he soon became a frequent and respected visitor

*Club Nook, 1940.*

167

to the farms. During the 1940s experimental planting of cereal crops was encouraged by the West Riding War Agricultural Committee, who were engaged in a programme of increased food production in war-time Britain; thus it was that John Birch and Herbert Chester developed their experiments, advised by Ian Moor, and backed to a certain degree by Fison's who had an interest in promoting their fertilisers.

Although Herbert Chester leased the farmland at Club Nook it had been convenient for Stephen Birch's widow, Hannah, to remain in the house while Herbert and his sister Mary continued to live at Drebley Farm. However, in 1938 Mary Chester married a farmer named Jim Foster. They became joint tenants of the land at Club Nook and so, two years later, Mrs Birch vacated the house for them and the family left Barden for ever. Drebley and Club Nook were then separate farms, albeit working in unison for a few years, until Jim Foster unexpectedly died.[133] After this, Mary remained in the house while Herbert again farmed Drebley and Club Nook as one unit until he retired in 1956. Since that date, firstly Edwin Thwaite and then his daughter Hilary, with David Pighill, have held the lease.

**Nostalgia**
Down the lane to Drebley and Club Nook, as to all the farms in the dale came the daily postman. Because of the distance from his sorting office in Skipton, he travelled in his red GPO van, and it was this cheery little vehicle which we looked for at his appointed times. After the last delivery of his round at Woodend Farm on the way to Burnsall, he would retire to a wooden hut in the corner of a field at the top of Drebley lane, and spend several hours sleeping and cooking his lunch before setting off back to Skipton. On his return journey, he collected out-going mail from the little red boxes fixed to various points along the way. This was a recognised routine, which was repeated up and down the dale. During this period in our lives, my sister and I lived at Club Nook with our widowed Aunt Mary who kept up a copious correspondence with old friends and relatives; so much so that her life was regulated by the arrival of the post van. She would drop all housework until she had read her mail and replied to quite a proportion of it, so that she could walk up the lane each afternoon at about 2.45pm and catch the afternoon collection as the postman went by. My mother used to say that because of this habit, her sister was a terrible housewife!

There was a weekly rota of three postmen, with whom we became quite friendly. One was Tom Parker, who had a reputation for being morose, but when Aunt Mary discovered that he suffered from migraines she felt that was sufficient explanation! I suffered from the same complaint but it was hardly a means of communication between us… What we did like about Mr Parker, however, was his ability and willingness to mend our bicycle punctures and to adjust the troublesome Sturmey-Archer three speed gears on my brand new Sunbeam bicycle. This iron steed gave wings to my feet at an isolated and lonely stage in my life when I was evacuated from home in Essex. I had no means of going anywhere further than where I could walk, apart from the bus journeys to school and occasional shopping trips to Skipton or Ilkley. Such trips involved walking to Barden Tower, where we caught the twice daily Grassington to Ilkley bus, and returned after tea. However, we had little pocket money

---

133 He suffered a thrombosis whilst out hoeing crops in one of his fields.

and such trips were usually combined with visits to the dentist or for serious shopping.

Whatever the reason for our journeys, the timetable was inexorable and there was rarely time to browse in a bookshop for instance, or go to the cinema. In addition the difficulties in wartime of getting on the overcrowded bus for its return journey up the dale were of daunting proportions, and there was always the fear of being left behind in a queue. In order to avoid this we resorted to a variety of tactics; on one occasion Aunt Mary expressed her outrage by walking round to the bus station with her laden basket and challenging the driver to let her get aboard before all the people waiting in the queue. On arrival at the proper bus stop she stood up by her seat and explained to all and sundry what she had done, for she felt that whereas she was struggling to shop for essential household supplies, many of the other passengers were having a 'day out'. This was acutely embarrassing for a teenager, and it maybe explains the peculiar freedom I felt about possessing a bicycle.

*My sister and I fishing.*

In wartime Britain it was a privilege for my father to have obtained a bicycle for me, and I certainly appreciated Mr Parker's expertise in keeping it roadworthy. Motor cars were not common and, although a few tractors were around, horses were still in use on all the farms. It was almost impossible to purchase a new car, even if such a thing could be afforded. At Drebley, my uncle (Herbert Chester) bought his cars from his brother, who, as a doctor in Bradford needing to maintain a serviceable vehicle, could afford to buy a new one every few years. The bodywork was usually rusty as a result of all the salt used on the roads in Bradford throughout those long snowy winters of the 1940s, and I well remember one car in particular where so many holes appeared in the floor of the car that my uncle had difficulty in finding anywhere solid to put his feet. We could see the road beneath as he drove along, avoiding puddles and potholes where possible.

In 1940 my uncle became the Barden representative on the Rural District Council, which met in Skipton on one Saturday morning each month. For these meetings he had a petrol allowance which meant that he could take his wife Gladys, and maybe two other passengers into Skipton to shop. Very occasionally, I was one of the lucky ones. There was a tremendous sense of freedom on those outings, but it was combined with a rather miserable sense of urgency which was instilled in me by Aunt Gladys, who rushed around with an over-long shopping list. She carried a huge basket, which banged into less pressured housewives as she jockeyed for position at the various shop counters. She was always anxious 'not to keep Herbert waiting' as she coped with queues, rationing and coupons. There was no time for frivolous purchases!

There were one or two memorable occasions when we snatched a hot drink at the Carla

Beck milk bar, or we slipped into the Middle Row teashop for a toasted teacake and an elegantly served cup of coffee. Nevertheless, she kept one eye on her wristwatch, and never overstayed. At that time, the shops were mostly owned by family businesses, each with its own particular smell and ambience. Manby's, the ironmonger's smelling of oil and paraffin, was indisputably the most frequented by both farmers and their wives. It was dark inside the shop, with very little room in which to move between the implements and tackle which occupied almost all the floor space, and hung from the walls and ceilings.

Whitaker's Confectionary was the shop with the most appetising smell, for not only did they supply top quality chocolates, but also bread, teacakes and biscuits. Although Aunt Gladys bought yeast and did all her own baking, she could not resist the luxury of buying some of Whitaker's delicious food. We always gazed enviously at the display of luxury chocolates arranged behind the glass counter, but neither coupons nor housekeeping were sufficient for us to purchase such delicacies. Inevitably there was a butcher whose sausages were irresistible, and a change from those delivered with the weekly order from the Grassington butcher. We looked forward to lunch after these Saturday shopping expeditions.

I particularly remember sneaking off to Waterfall's Bookshop in Sheep Street, where I would look at the books and maps of Wharfedale, but I could rarely afford to buy anything. However, it was here that I bought my first Ordnance Survey map for Wharfedale and Malham Moor, and where I spent my first book token. This was a school prize, to mark my matriculation, and I chose *Wharfedale* by Ella Pontefract and Marie Hartley. I still have my book, and that first map.

Washing day was always on Mondays, and what a wearisome toil it was, for there was no electricity and all the water had to be heated in the copper boiler in the wash house, itself unheated and in a separate building from the house. The clothes were boiled and possed before being rinsed and passed through a wooden roller-mangle and then carried in baskets to the croft. At Drebley, this was up a flight of stone steps outside the pantry window, but at Club Nook, the clothes line crossed a steeply inclined lawn outside the wash house. Pegging out was difficult in the windy climate, but there were no short cuts to drying the heavy cotton sheets and table cloths, and thick woollen clothes. In winter, these were hung to dry on the old 'bread flake' suspended from the kitchen ceiling in front of the fire, but later in the year, when the sun shone, we would see the garden lawn and soft fruit bushes draped with white teacloths, bleaching as they dried in the sweet breeze of a summer's day.

Then there was the ironing. I remember the warmth and thump of the flat-iron, heated on the open fire, and pressed down on the folded sheets as they lay on a blanket on the scullery table, and how my aunt would sprinkle the embroidered cloths and handkerchiefs with cold water to 'dampen them down'. Later, in the evenings, there was the mending and darning to do, by the soft light of a Tilley lamp at Drebley, or by a brighter light at Club Nook, where bottled calor gas had been installed. This feature was held in very high regard for it meant that in each of the three downstairs rooms we had a central ceiling light which could be lit by simply applying a match to the wick; this was a significant labour-saving device which relieved us of the daily tyranny of cleaning and trimming lamps.

At Club Nook there was also a two burner stove with a grill which stood on an oil cloth covered table, quite away from any convenient work surface, or the sink. It was not used a great deal, partly because of the cost of the gas but really because Aunt Mary always lit the range in order to heat the kitchen, to bake and heat the water. However, the stove could be used in the rare bleak emergency when the fire had gone out or had not been lit.

The last time I saw it in use was the day before my sister's and my wedding in September 1952, when, in order to press our organdie wedding dresses and those of two of the six bridesmaids, the gas iron was lit. My mother's friend, Mrs Coates painstakingly pressed the dresses while she groaned with apprehension (if not terror) in case the dresses caught fire.

Meanwhile Aunt Mary agonised over the dwindling supply of gas left in her cylinder, which she kept under the stairs. We all needed the gas for lighting and there was no means of replenishing the supply until the next routine date of delivery. Without a car or a telephone or electricity, living in the dales was a matter for thrifty housekeeping.

**References to leases for Atkinsons who lived at Club Nook**
from lease books, Bolton Abbey Parish Register and census returns:

1728 George Atkinson formerly of Drebley
1750 Thomas Atkinson of Gillbeck born. Later leaseholder of Club Nook, he died in 1809 aged 59 years.
1774 Thomas Atkinson paid tithes on his flock of 22 lambs and 90 sheep
1791 Francis Atkinson born
1804 Headstone* 1726-1804 Francis Atkinson of Club Nook aged 78 years
1806 Lease Book entry: Dwelling house, newly repaired with fold and two thatched barns in indifferent repair.
Thomas and Ellen Atkinson held pew no. 31 in Bolton Abbey church.
1823 Francis Atkinson's initials appear on the datestone on the barn built in High Bent Close across the track of the then discontinued packhorse way between Barden Scale and Burnsall.
1843 Frances Atkinson's initials, together with those of his wife, Ann, FAA appear on the datestone on the barn in Club Nook fold yard.
Their headstone in the churchyard* at Bolton Abbey is inscribed as follows:-
Francis Atkinson of Club Nook, born 1791.
Ann Atkinson, born 1789, died 1857, aged 68 years, (née Young of Appletreewick)
George Atkinson, born 1823, died 1851, aged 28 years
1850 Thomas Atkinson 1810-75* was the leaseholder.

**Almack of Club Nook**
1876 After the death of Thomas Atkinson, Club Nook was leased to John Ward Almack (married Ellen Ward of Holme House Farm). At this time the farm consisted of 99 acres.
1881 census: John Almack from Kirkby Malzeard.
1897 George Almack took the lease from Lady Day, followed by his son Frank Almack born in 1866, whose name is on Barden Roll of Honour 1914-18. He retired to Cowling in 1926.

# BARDEN IN WHARFEDALE, THE PLACE AND ITS PEOPLE

**Twentieth century tenants**

1926 Stephen Birch, 1863-1934, (head gamekeeper for Barden Moor, and living at Park House, by the Low Reservoir) retired and moved to Club Nook. Stephen's wife was Hannah née Worsely, 1873-1964. They had seven children, whose names appear on the Honours Board at Barden School. Birch family headstone*

1934 Herbert Chester of Drebley Farm.

1939 Mary (née Chester) and Jim Foster.

1942-56 Herbert Chester.

1956 Edwin and Suzanne Thwaite, followed by their younger daughter, Hilary Thwaite and David Pighill.

## Low House Farm (Gillbeck Farm)

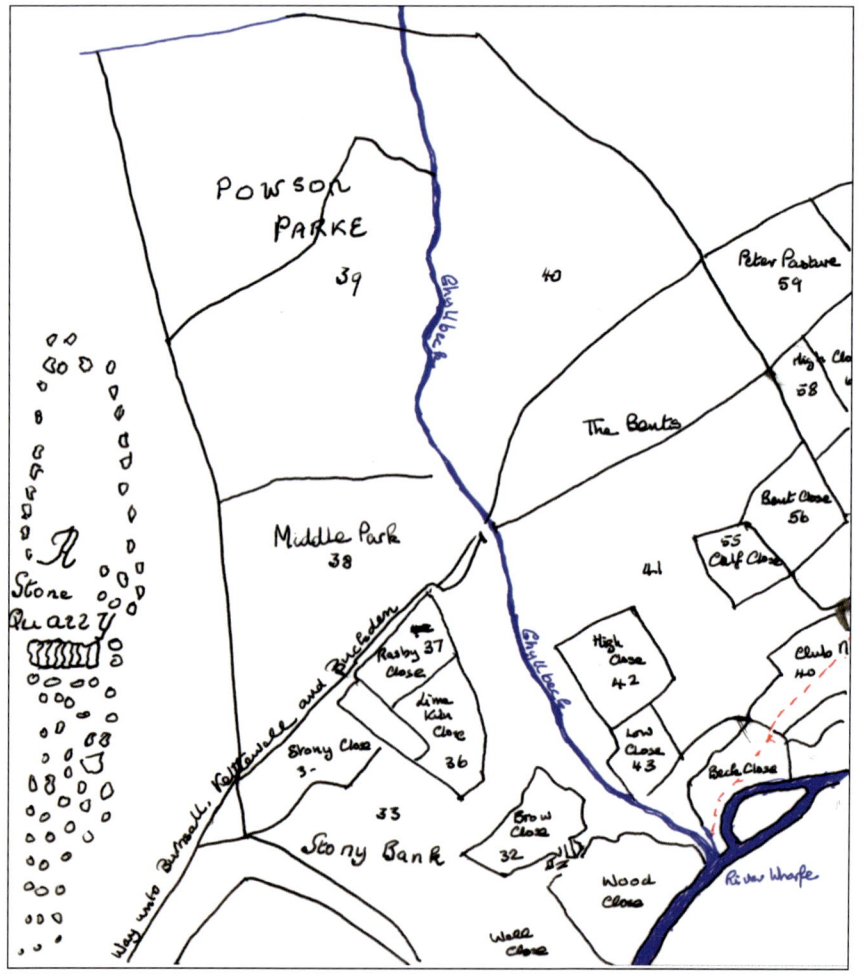

Low House Farm was the home of the Atkinson family. In the early leases the holding was referred to as Barden Farm. It then became Gillbeck Farm, (sometimes spelled Ghyllbeck) and finally Low House Farm.

## LOW HOUSE FARM

An excerpt from *The Cattle Herds and Sheep Flocks of the Earls of Cumberland in the 1560s* by Professor R W Hoyle (Reading University), Yorkshire Archaeological Journal, 2001, Volume 73, page 82:

> Following the death of Henry the 10th Lord Clifford in 1523, his successor the 1st Earl of Cumberland, (died 1542) used the parks at Skipton for the reception of his cattle and their breeding stations.
>
> By 1543 the herbage of the Great Park at Barden was farmed to Humphrey Polson, the forester of Barden and Palliser of the Great Park there, for £10 probably because it had become surplus after the transfer of the cattle and sheep operation to Bolton.
>
> In the fifth and sixth year of the reign of Elizabeth 1563/4, Henry Atkinson was the deputy receiver at Bolton who was charged with the collection of rents for the 2nd Earl of Cumberland's house at Barden.

Clifford Leases,[134] dating from 1602 to 1604 refer to a Barden yeoman named William Atkinson who paid rent 'for a messuage and an ancient tenement, late Thomas Polson's, and for the third part of the great parke.' His wife was named Ellen, and his sons were William and Thomas.

From 1620-50 leases refer to enclosed ground in Powson Park, summering and pasturage in Barden Great Park, Atkinson's Parke, and common of pasture, turbary, etc. Powson Park is shown on the estate maps dated 1731 and 1778, which confirm that it was part of Gillbeck Farm, bounded by the watercourse of Gillbeck and the walls of the Great and the Little Park.

During the Civil War, in 1643, when the Royalist forces were garrisoned at Skipton castle, the comptroller purchased ten oxen from Thomas Atkinson of Barden.[135]

In 1657 'On July 4th, 11th and 18th, upon these three market days notice was given at ye cross of Skipton that Thomas Johnson of Storres and Alice the daughter of Thomas Atkinson of Barden, both within the parish of Skipton aforesaid, did intend marriage and no let appeared to hinder their proceedings.'[136] In 1664 the marriage is recorded between Mary Atkinson of Barden and William Inman of Burnsall.[137]

In September 1670, at Appleby Castle, the household accounts for Lady Anne Clifford show that '…Thomas Atkinson of Barden supplied for her own use eight ready-made fox skins at 2s-5d each.'[138]

In August 1675 when Barden Bridge was still unrepaired after floods had carried it away nearly two years earlier, Lady Anne financed her tenant Thomas Atkinson the younger to solicit the West Riding Quarter Sessions at Pontefract and also York assizes, his costs and those of counsel and witnesses amounting to £17-10s. This lobbying succeeded, the work being marked by an inscription: THIS BRIDGE WAS REPAIRED AT THE CHARGE OF THE WHOLE WEST RIDING, 1676.[139]

---

134 Formerly stored in Skipton Castle, and now with the Yorkshire Archaeological Society in Leeds.
135 Spence, Richard, 1991, *Skipton Castle in the Great Civil War 1642-45*, Otley Smith, Settle.
136 Bolton Abbey Parish Register.
137 ibid.
138 Spence, Richard, 1997 *Lady Anne Clifford*. NB At the age of 80 was the Countess feeling the cold?
139 ibid.

```
August, 1686. THOMAS ATKINSON, Barden, Yeoman, Will-very bad
                                                  signature.
Purse and apparel                                 2   0   0

4 oxen and 2 stears                              23   0   0
9 kine                                           27   0   0
6 heifers and 4 stirks                           20   0   0
4 calves                                          2   0   0
4 horses                                          4   0   0
97 sheep and 37 lambs                            34   0   0
                                              Continued/

IN LOW PARLOUR 1 bedstead and feather bed         1  10   0
and bolster, a rugg and curtains and vallans

1 table, 2 forms, 1 long settle                   2  10   0

IN THE UPPER PARLOUR 2 bedsteadsand 2 feather
beds, 2 coverletts, 1 pr. blankets and4 bolsters, 2
chests, 2 chairs and 1 stool                      2   0   0

IN LOW CHAMBER 2 (?) old bedsteads, 2 feather
beds, 6 bolsters, 2 ruggs, 2 coverlets, 2
pannell chists, one chist and gimlin              2   0   0

IN THE CHAMBER over the house 2 arkes             1   0   0

IN THE FOREHOUSE 2 tables, 2 cuppboards,
1 long settle, 2 forms and 2 chairs               2   0   0
2 pewter dishes, 1 chamber pott, flaggons
candlesticks                                      1   0   0
2 great pans, 4 pots, 4 panns                     1   0   0
Iron baxyton, reckon and tongs                       10   0
Wood vessell and other huslements of the HOUSE       10   0
7 linnen sheets, 1 table cloth 11 napkins
1 millow board                                    1  10   0

IN THE LAITH 1 old ark 3 pairs wheels, harrow,
1 waind (?) maine (?) body, 6 yoks, 5 teames
othes (oats ?)                                    2   0   0
For wood                                          4   0   0
                             Total   £          133  10   0
```

In 1686 four oxen and two *stears* are mentioned in the inventory for the probate of Thomas Atkinson of Barden.[140]

Two years later in 1688 'February 26th Christening of Thomas, ye son of Richard Jenkinson of Skipton, begotten in fornication upon ye body of Ellen Atkinson of Bardin.'[141]

Members of the Atkinson family were also at Drebley in 1650, and at Club Nook during the eighteenth and early nineteenth centuries.

In 1867 Low House Farm (tenant George Atkinson) comprised 363 acres 2 furlongs and 21 chains. The rent was £80 per annum.[142] The area of the farm included Mucky Park and one fourth of Broad Park (see first edition Ordnance Survey map) formerly part of the medieval Great Park and Powlson's Park.

---

140 Borthwick Institute for Historical Research, York.
141 Bolton Abbey Parish Register.
142 Item contained in Lists of tenants, farm holdings and field names prepared by Heather Beaumont for the Yorkshire Dales National Park, 199?

## LOW HOUSE FARM

At some time during this decade, at the same time as other buildings were being designed for Barden, plans were drawn up for a large stone barn on the site of the old, decayed farm buildings. Within this barn, provision was made for storage of hay, with unusually tall, brick built archways giving access to 'fothering gangs' alongside two shippons, each accommodating six milking cows in paired bays or 'booses'. Single storey additions were made to the outer walls of this barn, comprising a stable and a cart house, and several loose boxes in which to rear calves. Although vernacular in its use of local sandstone, the size and design of this barn, and the use of brick for internal walling are unique in Craven. The influence may have derived from Thomas Coke's Great Barn at Holkham in Norfolk, designed by Samuel Wyatt in 1790.

The Atkinson family continued to farm at Gillbeck until the mid-twentieth century. Their names appeared in all the census returns, they had a large family, and the children attended Barden School. For instance, in 1885 they had seven children, the names of Margaret aged fourteen, Grace aged twelve and George aged eight appearing on the school register. However, in 1872 their father was one of those mentioned in a letter to the Duke of Devonshire from one of the school managers, William Demaine of Barden Scale, who complained that several of the parents had refused to pay the obligatory school pence towards the master's salary. At that time, John Atkinson was a Trustee for Barden Wesleyan Chapel, and as a non-conformist it may be that he objected to the religious affiliation of the school, whereby the Rector at Bolton Abbey was a manager, and would have overseen the teaching of the catechism to all the children irrespective of their faith.

Inscription on headstone in the churchyard at Bolton Abbey:
    George Atkinson, 1839-1915, his wife Mary 1843-1923,
    Elizabeth Ellen Atkinson 1882-1955 (of Crossfield, Howgill.)

*Low House Farm.*

Low House is an eighteenth century building with an end entry plan, a central stack and heated parlour. Stairs, dairy and service room lie to the rear.

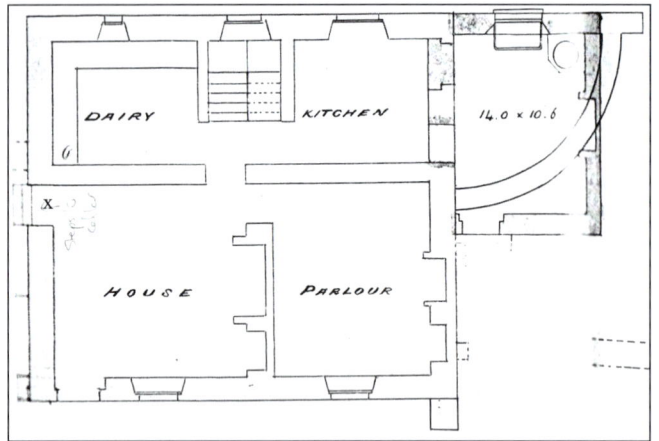

This plan shows at x where steps lead from the gable end of the house into the storage cellar. This is driven into rising ground, as at Club Nook. The addition of a scullery with corner boiler is shown at the east end of the house, but a connecting doorway into the kitchen has not been shown. There is no explanation for the curved line, which forms no part of the present building.

The photograph of the house after removal of the central chimney stack shows features which are similar to other houses in Barden, such as the garden wall with stone posts and dressed top stones (Drebley House) and casement windows (Woodend Farm). The addition of a wool store over the cellar took place on the west gable. The roof of the house is tiled with gritstone slates, but the nineteenth century extension is roofed with thinner blue slates (c/f Drebley houses and barns). These slates were supplied to George Atkinson on 30 September 1875, when a similar load was also delivered to the schoolhouse being newly built by Barden Tower. The sum of £16 8s 4d was paid to T. Johnson.[143]

*The present farmhouse after removal of the central chimney stack.*

It was not possible to see the door lintel in order to compare it with those over the front doors at Fold Farm and Littlegate, as referred to by Arnold Pacey in his article describing these houses.

---

143 Cash Book entry, Bolton MSS.

# LOW HOUSE FARM

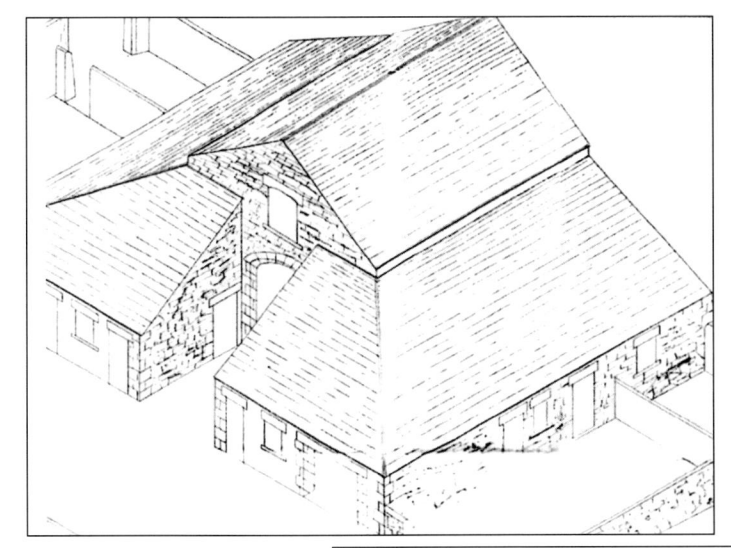

*Left, plans drawn for the great barn at Low House Farm in the 1860s, when the tenant was George Atkinson 1839-1915.*

Do the plans with dotted outlines show the footings of old buildings, or were they alternative buildings plans for the new buildings?

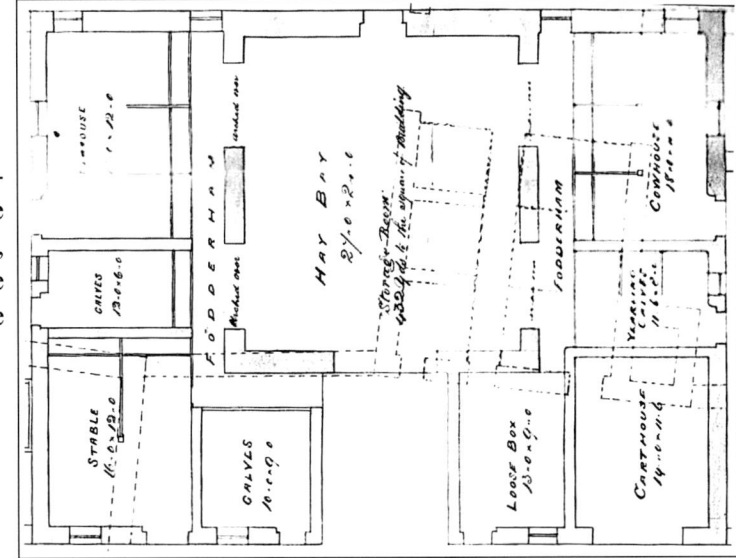

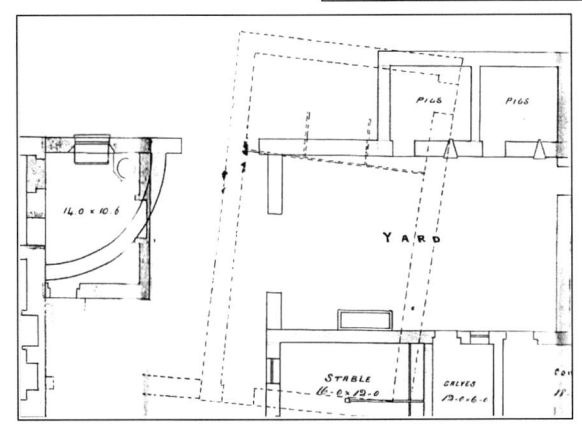

177

## The Methodist Chapel: A Dilemma for Duke and Parson

The first Wesleyan Methodists had no chapel in Barden. Instead they occupied the building originally used for the Park School which in 1875 had moved to its present site nearer Barden Tower. From a surviving letter[144], it is apparent that by 1881 they had begun negotiations with the 8th Duke of Devonshire to obtain a suitable piece of land on which to build their own chapel. The tone of the letter reveals that the site chosen by the Duke for Wesleyan worship had been a matter of contention, and that the Minister presiding over the Grassington Circuit had been placed in what he referred to as 'an embarrassing position' over the dispute.

> To Gilson Martin,
> Agent at Chatsworth for Spencer-Compton, 8th Duke of Devonshire, 19 October 1881
> Sir,
> Sometime ago I wrote to you respecting the piece of land which his Grace the Duke of Devonshire had selected for a Methodist Chapel at Barden. I pointed out the inconvenience of the situation, and on your declining to recommend a better site, according to promise, I communicated with His Grace in August last, asking him to reconsider the matter, and if there was no very strong objection against it, that he would grant us the site of the schoolroom we occupy, which in the judgement of all who know the case, is the best for our purpose. Doubtless his Grace has intimated to you his decision, and I should esteem it a great favour, if you could help us in the matter by throwing some light on the subject. I am sorry to be obliged to trouble you so much, but I am placed in the most embarrassing position. I cannot positively decline the offer of His Grace, and I am equally bound not to accept the proposed site. Our people at Barden and in the Grassington Circuit decline to erect a chapel across the river and more than this, these gentlemen think they are not fairly dealt with. They loyally supported the interests of His Grace during the last Election, and they may be asked to do so again, and now they are refused the small favour they ask. If they are not soon in possession of what they seek, I know how some of them will dispose of their voting power at a future date. I hope, therefore, Sir, you may have the power to return a satisfactory reply to our request.
> With Great Respect, I am, Sir, Yours Very Truly,
> William Jones, Wesleyan Minister.

The 8th Duke was an active politician and leader of the Liberal party who, in 1880, had been asked by the Queen to form a government.[145] He would, perhaps, have been expected to take the request of his erstwhile voters seriously. The letter reflects a growing awareness of independence by the tenants on the Bolton Abbey estate, who realised the potential power of withholding political support for a candidate who they felt had treated them unfairly.

It is not known what site the Duke had in mind. The 1853 Ordnance Survey map shows a building named The Park School on School Brow, near to where the present chapel now stands.[146] The school is shown occupying a flat piece of land tucked into the corner wall of a field which, since the time of Lord Henry Clifford in the late fifteenth century, was part of The Little Park. This platform of land on which the building stood can still be seen, and

---

144 Bolton MSS, Chatsworth Collection; Barden Township.
145 The Duchess of Devonshire (1982) *The House. A Portrait of Chatsworth*, London, Macmillan, p3.
146 First edition Ordnance Survey map, 1853.

## CHAPEL AND SCHOOL

so can the track trodden by the feet of pupils who trudged from Barden Bridge through the wicket gate and up the hill to school. This must surely be the site of the schoolroom mentioned in William Jones' letter. However, it seems that the site for the chapel, favoured by 'our people at Barden and in the Grassington Circuit' was not granted, nor did they move across the river as the Duke suggested, the reasoning behind the final choice of site remaining a mystery.

The chapel has been built on an extremely steep slope, above living accommodation, and a room known in the twentieth century as 'the schoolroom'. A flight of stone steps, hazardous and icy in winter, are located on the outside of the building, connecting the lower rooms with the chapel and the road. A similar example occurs at Hough Mill, where the Primitive Methodist Chapel is also squeezed between the road and a steeply rising hill, and in neither case was provision made for carriages to wait during services; it is almost as if the only land granted for the chapel was of no profitable use for the landlord and that very few concessions were made towards the needs of nonconformist worshippers.

Agreement having been achieved, the land was then leased for 99 years at a rent of five shillings per year and the chapel was built; one can still see within the porch a stone plaque commemorating its opening in 1885. The first trustees included the tenants of nearby farms, John Ward Almack of Club Nook, John Atkinson of Low House Farm by Ghyll Beck, William Croft, a farmer and joiner from across the bridge at Holme Cottage and James

Johnson, the reservoir keeper living at High Dock in Barden Great Park.

In 1892, a letter requesting assistance with the purchase of a harmonium was sent to the Duke of Devonshire for: 'we have a good choir who are wishful to obtain an instrument to help with the better rendering of the musical portions of the service'.[147] The Duke, responded with a contribution of £2, and 24 other subscribers gave between half a crown and £1 each, eleven being residents of Barden, and the others living at Beamsley, Bolton Abbey, Burnsall and Appletreewick. Services continued to be held in the chapel until the late 1960s, and the schoolroom was much in demand for social occasions such as Sunday School teas, harvest suppers and shepherds' meetings.

When the river was not roaring down the valley in spate, families walking towards the chapel from their scattered homes on both sides of the valley could hear the shouts and songs of their neighbours and the sound of their boots ringing out on the hard surface of the road, while on dark winter evenings familiar clusters of lantern lights could be seen bobbing along the lanes leading from each of the farmhouses; during services these lanterns were extinguished and left in the chapel porch before being relit for the return home. During the Second World War, when oil and paraffin for the lamps were in short supply, and when blackout restrictions were strictly imposed, evening services and functions were often arranged to coincide with the full moon, so that people could find their way without the use of lamps.

Eventually, support for the chapel dwindled as Barden families found more freedom from the old Sunday conventions, and many were increasingly drawn to worship with a larger Wesleyan community, such as in the neighbouring village of Burnsall. The chapel became a private residence in 1969, with an art and craft shop selling goods made in Yorkshire.

**Chapel in Barden Tower**

Anglicans attended services in the medieval chapel adjoining Barden Tower. This chapel was built in 1515 by Henry Clifford, known as 'the Shepherd Lord', to commemorate the victory of the battle of Flodden Field. It was then 'a chapelry of Skipton parish and its priest was appointed by Lord Henry'[148] who, as the 10th Lord Clifford of Skipton, already controlled the parish. After the Dissolution of Bolton Priory in 1539 the monastic estates passed into Clifford hands,[149] after which time Barden Chapel was served by the priest in charge of the Priory Church at Bolton.

From 1917-54, services were conducted by the Reverend Cecil Tomlinson, Rector of Bolton Abbey, a well respected pastor who often cycled round his far flung parish to visit his flock. During his long incumbency he became an authority on local wildlife, being a keen and knowledgeable birdwatcher and possessing a notable collection of butterflies. Barden youngsters were encouraged to join the Bolton Abbey Choir, which meant long journeys down the dale after school in a horse drawn trap, packed tightly together under a weather-

---

147 Bolton MSS.
148 Spence, Richard, *The Shepherd Lord of Skipton Castle*, Otley, 1994, Smith Settle.
149 Hamilton Thompson, A., *Bolton Priory History and Architecture*, 1928, Thoresby Society Vol XXX, Leeds, J. Whitehead and Son Ltd.

## CHAPEL AND SCHOOL

proof blanket.

Childhood friendships formed here lasted a lifetime and former choristers, when they got together in later years told many tales of the happenings on choir outings in years gone by. They also recalled how decorating both chapels for festivals provided opportunities for socialising, when the gamekeeper's daughters from Drebley always brought large contributions of berried branches, mosses and primroses, found in remote places by their father. Ruth Lister who lived at Barden Tower enjoyed decorating the pulpit with holly for Christmas mornings: she said its prickles would keep the sermon short! For Easter, the girls gathered violets and wild daffodils from Springs Wood and took them round to housebound neighbours.

Many headstones in the graveyard at Bolton Abbey are inscribed with familiar names associated with the farms in Barden: Demaine of Drebley and Barden Scale, Atkinson of Low House and Club Nook, Holmes and Holme of Drebley, Gamsworth and Hough Mill, Ward of Hough Mill and Holme Farm, Birch of Barden Low Reservoir and Club Nook, Ideson of Howgill and Gamsworth, Inman of Howgill and Drebley, Lister of Barden Tower and Watergate. From the Clifford papers formerly held in Skipton Castle, and now in the library of the Yorkshire Archaeological Society in Leeds, and from estate rentals held for the Trustees of the Chatsworth Estate at Bolton Abbey, it is known that generations of these families have leased the same farms since at least the early seventeenth century, when, in 1603 George Clifford, 3rd Earl of Cumberland issued them with leases. Now in the twenty-first century few of these family names survive, farm leases being less frequently passed down from one generation to another.

Services continued to be held at the ancient chapel attached to the Tower until the 1970s. It was closed in 1983, and has since become an echoing shell, stripped of its polished pews and ornaments of faith. Bolton Priory, five miles down the valley, now attracts a congregation which includes those from Barden whose forebears although baptised, married and buried there, could not have imagined regular church attendance at such a distance from their homes.[150]

### Barden School[151]

> Barden School stands at what is perhaps the most beautiful highway corner in all England ... backed by a friendly belt of woodland, rising to the moors and fronting the grey Tower ... while ... below Tower and school, the road winds down to the bridge ... takes Wharfe in its stride, and climbs to the pine forest and moors beyond. Forest and heath and river are part of the children's lives as they go to school and home again.[152]

A building named Park School appears on the first edition Ordnance Survey map published in 1853. It is shown lying adjacent to the road to Burnsall, in a corner of a field in the Little

---

[150] Sources: Personal reminiscences of Dora Dunkley daughter of Barden's schoolmistress, Betsy Inman and Gladys Chester (née Inman) gamekeeper's daughters, Ruth Lister farmer's daughter, and Sidney Binns, whose father was an estate woodman.
[151] Brontë Bedford-Payne and Heather Beaumont, *Barden School: its patrons, Pupils and Teachers*, 1997, Durham.
[152] Hallewell Sutcliffe, *The Striding Dales,* 1929, illustrator A. Reginald Smith, Frederick Warne and Co Ltd, London.

*Barden School lies close to the Tower.*

Park named School Brow.[153] From Barden Bridge it was reached by means of a wicket gate leading to a steeply inclined path across the hillside on which the Methodist Chapel now stands. This path can still be seen from a viewpoint across the river. It is evident from estate records that this building did not fulfil the requirements of the 1870 Education Act, and so, in 1875 a new school building was erected on a level site nearer the Tower. Although the architect's plans included designs for a cottage for a teacher, it was never built, and rented accommodation was found for her throughout the 56 years' life of the school.

The style of the new school departs from the vernacular tradition of Upper Wharfedale. With its steeply pitched roof, porch bell-cote, chimneys and decorative barge-boarding it has features in common with a large number of schools built all over the country in the 1870s. In particular, it also has features in common with the cottages at Waterfall, Watergate, the Pavilion and Strid, as described in the chapter concerning 'The Picturesque in a Romantic Landscape'.

After the school closed in 1931 the building was used as the village institute. However, in 1993 it re-opened to accommodate some of the pupils attending the Montessori school, based at nearby Strid cottage. (For more information about the school, see separate section at the end of the book.)

---

153 The field in which the Methodist chapel was built in 1885.

# CHAPEL AND SCHOOL

**Equality for Women in Barden 1931** – The school teacher's wheel of signatures

By 1931, there were so few children on the register for Barden School that the decision was taken to close it at the end of the summer term, after which, the few remaining children who needed primary education were taken daily by taxi to the Boyle and Petyt school in Beamsley. At the same time, Mrs Dunckley, the schoolmistress who had held her post since September 1914, retired. These events caused a profound change in the life of the Barden community, who had hitherto looked no further than their own school and its headmistress for social interchange. Mrs Dunckley rose to the challenges by heading a petition from the women to the Duke, supporting the men's request for the use of the old schoolroom as a centre for community activities. Signatures on the petition, including her own, were arranged radially, to ensure that no one woman took precedence over another.

Until then, a Men's Reading Room with a small billiard table had been open adjacent to the site of the old house at Watergate, where, earlier in the nineteenth century, The New Inn had sold 'Free ale tomorrow for nothing', but after the closure of the school and the successful outcome of the petition, whist drives, beetle drives, dances, and meetings of the Women's Institute were held regularly in the former School Room. The Public Lending Library was stored here, in a cupboard, while Miss Sarah Pullan, housekeeper to Mr Ideson and caretaker of the Wesleyan Methodist Chapel, was appointed the cleaner/caretaker and key-holder of the Old School. She lit the fires and boiled the tea kettles before each of the winter events.

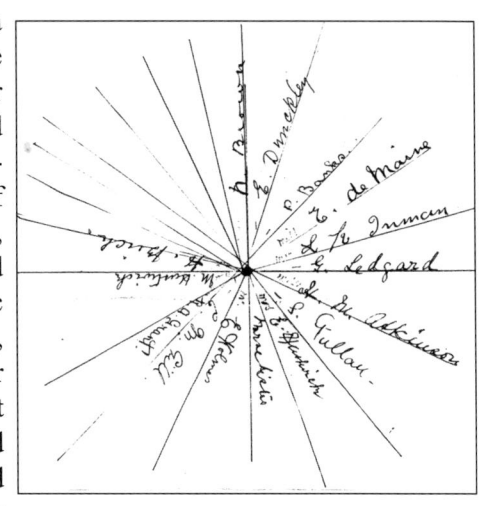

**Stoneybank Cottage**

Mrs Dunckley, the Barden schoolmistress 1914-30 and her daughter Dora 1909-2002 lived in this cottage. Dora Dunckley wrote:

> In summer it was lovely place to live, especially when the windows could be opened wide. On such days, when the piano was played, it could be heard across the valley at Watergate. Swallows returned to nest in the tall shed year after year, and used our clothes line as a perch from which their young were fledged. We could look across the trees to the rocks of Simon's Seat high above the river on the other side of the Wharfe, but on dull days, when the rocks were wreathed in mist, we would say 'Simon's got his hat on, and it is going to rain.' The wind made a great sound at Stoneybank, sighing and soughing in the branches of the trees which surrounded us on both sides, for the cottage had been built between the woods of Gillbeck and the Bull Copy.

Stoneybank Cottage is small and stone-built. It lies high on the west side of the valley, above the farm of Low House. It is reached by a track which ascends steeply from the Burnsall road, alongside a wall bordering the forestry plantation associated with Ghyllbeck and Nelly

# BARDEN IN WHARFEDALE, THE PLACE AND ITS PEOPLE

Park. The old packhorse way to Burnsall and Kettlewell passed close by the cottage before it was superseded by the new road to Burnsall at the beginning of the nineteenth century, but a nearby barn has ensured that a section of this old trackway has remained in use for farm carts and tractors. Also nearby is the remains of the medieval stone quarry, from which Barden Tower and the walls round Henry Clifford's Great and Little Parks were built; hence the name Stonybank.

The cottage housed gamekeepers and woodmen, but for a period of at least 50 years, say between 1891 and 1945, it was the home of successive Barden schoolteachers. The last of these teachers was Mrs Ellen Dunckley who, with her daughter Dora, was a 'paying guest' here from their arrival in Barden in 1914 until the school closed in 1931. Their hostess was Miss Anne de Maine,[147] who held the lease. The cottage had no indoor water supply or sanitation until after Miss de Maine retired and left Barden in 1930. After that, the 'tin tabernacle' or red-painted prefabricated hut adjacent to the cottage was made habitable for Mrs Dunckley, who lived there in retirement until the mid-1940s, while the cottage reverted to providing accommodation for estate employees. From here, a well defined footpath leads through the wood in Bull Copy to Barden Tower and the school. Dora Dunckley's memories of life in the cottage are included in a

*The glorious view from Stonybank across the valley. to Simon's Seat.*

*Dora by the gate to Stonybank.*

---

[147] Anne de Maine was a well-educated woman, who was a Methodist local preacher. Although she spelled her name differently, she claimed to be related to the Demaine family living at Catgill and The Arches Farm in Bolton Abbey. She kept a white pony in her stable at Stonybank, and she employed a maid, Annie Holmes, who walked daily to Stonybank from the cottage where she lived with her parents, on the side of the road to Storiths.

## CHAPEL AND SCHOOL

small book entitled *The Story of Barden School, its patrons, pupils and teachers*. This book was written by Brontë Bedford-Payne and Heather Beaumont, and published in 1997.

*Right, view of Stonybank Cottage and below the 'Tin Tabernacle'. Photographs taken in the late 1990s during Dora Dunckley's last visit to Stonybank.*

### Obituary of Dora Dunckley
Written for Bolton Abbey parish magazine, March 2003, by Brontë Bedford-Payne:

There are few folk now living in Barden who will remember Dora Dunckley, who was born in 1909 and lived to 'a ripe old age' until her death on 11 October 2002. She was the daughter of the school mistress who came to teach at the little school by the Tower in 1914 and remained until the school closed in July 1931.

Dora retained a keen zest for life, combined with an especial interest in birds, wild flowers, grasses and mosses, and a deep sense of devotion to the place she always referred to as home. This was the former gamekeeper's cottage at Stonybank in Barden, where she and her mother lived with Miss Ann de Maine for more than fifteen years as paying guests. During this time they shared an unheated bedroom with access to a cold water tap supplying a water trough adjoining the earth closet in a small courtyard.

Eventually Mrs Dunckley and Dora were able to move into their own more comfortable home in what Donald Wood has referred to in his book *Bolton Abbey the Time of my Life* as the 'Tin Tabernacle'. This was a hut painted red, with a corrugated iron roof, built alongside the cottage hitherto occupied by Miss de Maine. Access to their quiet home has never changed. It is reached from the schoolhouse by means of a grassy path leading up the hillside, through the woodland of Bull Coppice (beech trees during Dora's youth). It was here that the Revd. Cecil Tomlinson, after taking afternoon tea with Dora's mother and Miss de Maine, taught her to observe birds and wild flowers. There is a more direct approach from the lane above Low House Farm, but this was rarely used betwixt school and home.

Dora was a pupil at Barden School, where she made many friends with whom she kept in touch until they all grew too old and frail. Her best friend was Barbara Lister who lived at the Tower, and it was with her that Dora played in the 'oak room', where toys and games were stored in one of the capacious cupboards in the old oak dressers lining the walls. Their haunts included Bull and Springs Coppices where they romped among the great boulders, dammed streams and gathered wild daffodils for house-bound friends to enjoy. Other friendships were forged with the large number of clever children of the head gamekeeper, Stephen Birch, who lived at Barden Low Reservoir.

With her mother and her friends, Dora attended both the Wesleyan chapel and the chapel at the Tower and, on summer Sundays, they walked through the woods past The Strid to the Priory, where some Barden children sang in the choir. In 1920, having won a county minor scholarship to Skipton Girls' High School, Dora became a boarder and later went to Froebel Teacher Training College. In retirement her mother remained at Stonybank until 1944, becoming the parochial representative for Barden. Both she and Dora retained their long friendship with the Rector at Bolton Abbey, the Revd. Cecil Tomlinson, and with his first and second families. Dora's ashes are interred alongside his gravestone. It was a privilege to form a friendship with Dora, and to publish some of her memoirs, drawn from the regular flow of letters she wrote between 1990 and her death in October 2002.

**The Lister Family in Barden Tower**

The Lister family certainly lived and farmed at Barden Tower from the mid-eighteenth century, but I have uncovered no evidence to support hearsay that they lived in the Tower at the time of the battle of Flodden Field in 1513. A halberd remaining in the 'oak room' has been ascribed to this battle, and therefore to have belonged to a Lister who supported 'the Shepherd Lord', but Arthur Raistrick considered that it was of Cromwellian design, and more likely to have survived from use during the Civil War 1642-45.

The following notes have been compiled from a number of sources to suggest how the Lister family came to Barden Tower, where they came from, and the origin of the Christian name, Sylvester, but it has not been possible from these sources to draw up a clear family tree. The name Lister appears to have been introduced to Barden through the marriage in 1753 of Jane Simpson of Barden Tower to a certain Thomas Lister. The Lister family were well established in Coverdale and in Kettlewell. It seems likely that the Simpsons who are known to have lived at Barden Tower in the late seventeenth and early eighteenth centuries came from Eastwood Head in Howgill, Thomas Simpson 1692-1713 of Barden Tower being listed in The Saxon Cure for Barden Dale.[148]

---

148 Watkins, Peter, *Bolton Priory and its Church*, Watmough Holdings plc, 1986. 'The Saxon Cure was interpreted as a term referring to the Tithe List for Bolton Priory… the historian Thomas Whitaker, 1805, thought the term was in use because there was a church at Bolton in Saxon times, but Prof. Hamilton Thompson (Thoresby Society, 1928) dismissed the notion as mere conjecture'.

## THE LISTER FAMILY

It is possible that the three sets of initials carved onto the outer stonework of the small banqueting tower relate to members of this family:

T+S
IB
I S 1793

John Simpson 1689-1754, the nephew of Henry Simpson, is thought to have been the Steward for the 3rd Earl of Burlington(1694-1753), and as such, not only has his will survived,[149] but also his headstone, inscribed Gentleman. It lies flat, close to the west wall of the ruined north transept of the Priory church at Bolton Abbey.

John Simpson and his wife Sarah had four daughters, Elizabeth (Buck), Ann (Robinson), Sarah (Pollard) and Jane, who married Thomas Lister. An extract from the will of John Simpson[150] dated 1754 is as follows: '…for the goodwill I have unto my son-in-law Thomas Lister, I give unto him the entire tenant right I have to my farm in Barden.'

In April 1774, Thomas and Jane Lister's son John, 1754-93 married Elizabeth Hebden who was born in 1752/3, who was the grand-daughter of Sylvester Hebden of Ripley, and daughter of Mary and Sylvester Hebden of Appletreewick.[151] Their son Sylvester Lister was born in 1777 and died in 1853. In 1803 Sylvester married Ellen Demaine, born 1779, who was the daughter of George Demaine and Frances, (née Benson of Barden), the grand-daughter of George and Ann Demaine of Barden, and great-grand-daughter of George Demaine of Barden.

In 1808 another John Lister, born at Barden Tower moved to Fleensop in Coverdale, where he married Ann Foster(1824/5-1903) of Middlesmoor, Nidderdale. John died in 1893, while Ann outlived him for another ten years. Their sons William, John and Sylvester Lister went to school in Horsehouse, Coverdale. Their descendants still live in Gammersgill, and others still own Fleensop.

Sylvester Lister (1821-1900) and his wife Sarah Jane (1831-1903) were tenants at Barden Tower from 1850-98. They had two grandchildren both of whom died in infancy and are commemorated on a headstone at Bolton Abbey (Sylvester Hebden Lister 1900-1 and Sylvia Richmond Lister , 20 January to 18 March 1905).

Sylvester Lister (1851-1923) and his wife Margaret Ann (1855-1909) lived at Watergate. Sylvester Lister, (1869-94) son of the above, lived at Barden Tower. He shares a headstone with his sister Florence who died in childbirth and her husband Thomas William Smith who died on 21 October 1933. Sylvester Lister (1866-1928) and his wife Annie née Foster (1868-1919) had three daughters Ruth, Barbara, and Esther.

From *Craven District Household Almanac*, 1928-9

He (Sylvester Lister) was one of the best known and respected farmers in Upper Wharfedale. He died in April 1928 in his 62nd year. The last of the Listers who have farmed at Barden Tower for three centuries, he was a noted angler and sportsman, following in the footsteps of his father who was the most capable exponent of the gentle art in the North of England. He had a fine tenor voice and sang as a chorister at Bolton Abbey. He is survived by three daughters.

---

149 The Borthwick Institute of Historical Research in York
150 ibid
151 ibid

# BARDEN IN WHARFEDALE, THE PLACE AND ITS PEOPLE

Esther Lister and her husband James Boothman lived and farmed at the Tower until they died in 1972 and 1975 respectively, their tenancy being followed by their two sons, Sylvester and David Boothman (1930-84). It is said with pride that the Lister branding-iron with the initials JL continued to be used on the horns of their sheep for some time after the death of these brothers, by which time the farm land had been re-distributed to Barden Scale.

Shown below is a postcard stamped commercially on the reverse E. M. Lister, Barden Tower, for Esther, one of the three daughters of Sylvester and Annie Lister who took in 'summer visitors' as paying guests; her ham and egg teas served to passing trade in the 'Oak Room' were famed 'far and wide.' The card shows a fireplace draped with a shawl, surmounted by a heavy wooden mantel-piece on which are displayed candlesticks and pottery ornaments; these include a pair of white china dogs, such as would be traded by pedlars calling at cottage doors during the nineteenth and early twentieth centuries.

In both postcards, several pieces of historic oak furniture can be seen, namely: Two oak dressers, dating in style from the seventeenth century, are ranged along the wall which separates the room from the chapel. A large collection of blue and white serving dishes and some pewter dishes stand behind rails on open shelves supported by drawers and cupboards with brass handles. Alongside the dressers is a well-stocked, glass-fronted bookcase, standing on a tall-boy. Also in the room, lying on a gate-leg oak table is the halberd mentioned in all accounts of Barden Tower as having been wielded at the battle of Flodden

*Two postcards showing the interior of the oak room in 'The Priest's House'.*

## THE LISTER FAMILY

Field in 1515.[152] A heavily carved oak arm chair is placed alongside.

Hanging on the ceiling beams is a man's soft cap, a shot-gun and the antlers of a stag which had probably been shot in the Forest of Barden. It was here that the famed Sylvester Lister had hung his fishing rods. The ceiling beams are roughly hewn and probably date from the original building of circa 1515.

Walter Scott's postcard from the 1930s (lower of the two opposite) shows a 'modern' fireplace, without the great oak mantelpiece, but otherwise, the furniture, the beams and other artefacts are largely the same, even the candlesticks and the blue/white china, only the china dogs and the shotgun are missing. The halberd and antlers are here shown fixed to one of the beams.

### Tower Field

*An artist's impression of the house which stood in the grounds of Barden Tower*

Foundations for a long, narrow building can be seen in a field on the north side of the Tower; these earthworks indicate where a house once stood. The survival of a painting and a drawing confirm the former existence of a substantial house, as described below:

The painting of the house, above, is now owned by the great-grand-daughter of Edwin Dynely Williamson who was the last Master for the old Barden School before it closed to make way for the new Barden Church of England National School. He had been appointed to teach at the school in 1865, and it is likely that he and his family lived in the house until it was demolished in 1872. It is said that the stones were re-used in the building of the new

---

152 This halberd is now on display in the Upper Wharfedale Museum, The Square, Grassington. Note, Arthur Raistrick considered that it was more likely to date from the Civil War 1642-45

school in 1872-5.

On the gable end of the house, the painting shows the remains of a stone archway. This exists to the present day, while the background scenery could be interpreted as fields and woodland on the side of the valley below Simon Seat. A fine pen and ink drawing of the north side of the Tower, also shows Dynely Williamson's house nestling in a hollow between the road and the Tower. This drawing is signed: Thomas Maquiad, (Butterworth and Heath) but undated.

It was in Tower Field that autumn lamb sales took place. A dense gathering of farmers crowded round the grassy ring, while the auctioneer checked his book for a small flock of Swaledale sheep being herded past him. Hurdles of wood and wire were erected for the pens and later taken down and stored for another year in the barn behind the field.

After walking through the Dales in the 1930s in search of material for their books, Ella Pontefract and Marie Hartley wrote nostalgically about their visit to one of these sales and the dalesmen whom they met that day; they closed their chapter with the words 'so dales voices echo round the old decayed tower of Barden as we leave it...'[153]

---

153 Pontefract, Ella and Hartley, Marie, *Wharfedale*, 1938, London: J. M. Dent and Sons Ltd.

## Barden Scale

The cluster of barns, the farmhouse and the Keeper's Cottage now forming the small hamlet known as Barden Scale is situated on the west side of the valley of the river Wharfe, on a small bluff of rising ground at 550 feet above sea level. The farm is bordered on the south by Barden Beck, which in medieval times formed a natural boundary between the ancient Forest of Barden and the monastic estate of Bolton Priory.[154] On the north, the farm is bounded by Hare Head and Black Park. Although the derivation of the name Scale is Old Norse it is possible that a small Anglo-Saxon settlement took place on this favourable site soon after the seventh century, but there is no evidence to support this suggestion. The name implies that it developed from the ninth century onwards as a summer residence, or a shieling associated with transhumance, placed between the in-by land of meadow and pasture, and rough grazing land.

After the Norman Conquest and the subsequent building of Skipton Castle, a hunting chase was established in Barden, which was, at that time, within the royal Forest of Skipton.[155] The Scale would have been a most favourable site for the lodging of officers such as the verdurer, and the regarder who would be occupied in coppicing and maintaining the forest, and in preserving the deer and other game. It is listed in the manorial accounts for 1437/8[156] as one of the twelve Forest Lodges; it held a commanding position overlooking the primary lodge at the Tower, with its complex of gardens, fishponds, barns, stables and workshops and other support structures. In a northward direction, lay the Lodges of Hole House and Drebley, Gamsworth, Howgill and Eastwood, and from The Scale, they may have been visible above the tops of the oak trees which then formed a dense canopy above the floor of the forest. In the same way, the coney warren and the warrener's house (now Holme Farm) would have been visible across the river, on the opposite hillside. It is reasonable to assume, therefore, that Barden Scale was a pivotal point for observation of movements and communications between all these sites, each one of which was of significance in the management of the Forest by the Court Leets held in the Tower.

The Scale lies directly on the path of the early packhorse way which passed through the valley between Bolton Abbey and Burnsall. This routeway is shown on the eighteenth century estate maps[157] (see chapter 3, 'Routeways Through Barden') and it was of great importance for the development of trade between the markets of Wharfedale and Nidderdale in the east, and those in the north-west beyond Kirkby Lonsdale. With the passage of time, the trampling of feet of men and animals and the grind of cartwheels, the road has become a hollow way through the settlement, where it is intimately associated with the barns and out buildings, their entrances opening directly onto it. The hamlet at Barden Scale also lies at an important junction with another early road which came over Hare Head and Black Park, heading directly from Skipton Castle through the settlements of Halton East, Embsay and

---

154 Since the Dissolution in 1538/9, the estates have been united under the common ownership of the Cliffords and their descendants.
155 In 1310 Edward II granted the Honour of Skipton to Robert de Clifford.
156 Stephen Moorhouse, *The Archaeology of Yorkshire,* 2003, Yorkshire Archaeology Society occasional paper no 3.
157 Map drawn by Ed. Beckwith in 1730, and re-drawn by Matthew Oddie in 1778.

## BARDEN IN WHARFEDALE, THE PLACE AND ITS PEOPLE

Eastby towards the focus of the medieval chase at Barden Tower. Traces of this road can be found in the western bank at the side of later walls and revetments, where in the early eighteenth century, a turnpike was constructed between Skipton and Pateley Bridge.[158]

Along this old road from Skipton came not only trade, but also, from 1485 onwards, Henry, 10th Lord Clifford, and his court from Skipton Castle, while, a hundred years later, in 1588 came George, 3rd Earl of Cumberland, with his wife, Margaret 'great with child".[159] This child was destined to be their daughter, the redoubtable Lady Anne Clifford, whose diaries tell us the occasions on which she stayed at Barden Tower,[160] although these visits were not to be until after 1643, when, by inheritance she came into possession of her estates. Other prestigious visitors who wound their way between the barns at the Scale on their way to Barden Tower came from their residences at Londesborough and Bolton Abbey. These included Lady Elizabeth Boyle, daughter of Francis Clifford 4th Earl of Cumberland, and wife of the 2nd Earl of Cork and 1st Earl of Burlington, whose rightful inheritance of Barden was so staunchly contested by Lady Anne.

All passed by or through on their way to visit or take up residence in the Tower, accompanied by their trains of servants and followers. These visits would have brought with them a certain measure of prosperity for the local peasantry, including the possibility of lowly employment in the Clifford demesnes and in the hunting chase, and also in baronial households in the castles of Skipton and Appleby. Lady Anne's diaries show how these opportunities opened up a chance to travel to these castles, and to marry into a wider world than had hitherto been known in Barden.

---

158 See chapter 3 'Routeways'.
159 Stone inscription on the wall of Barden Tower 1588
160 Spence, Richard T., *Lady Anne Clifford*, 1997, Sutton Publishing, Stroud and Clifford, D. J. H., *The Diaries of Lady Anne Clifford*, 1990, SuttonPublishing, Stroud.

# BARDEN SCALE

## The Cruck Barn at Barden Scale[161]

*The cruck barn in 1952, when it was still thatched with ling and its walls were in a very poor state of repair.*

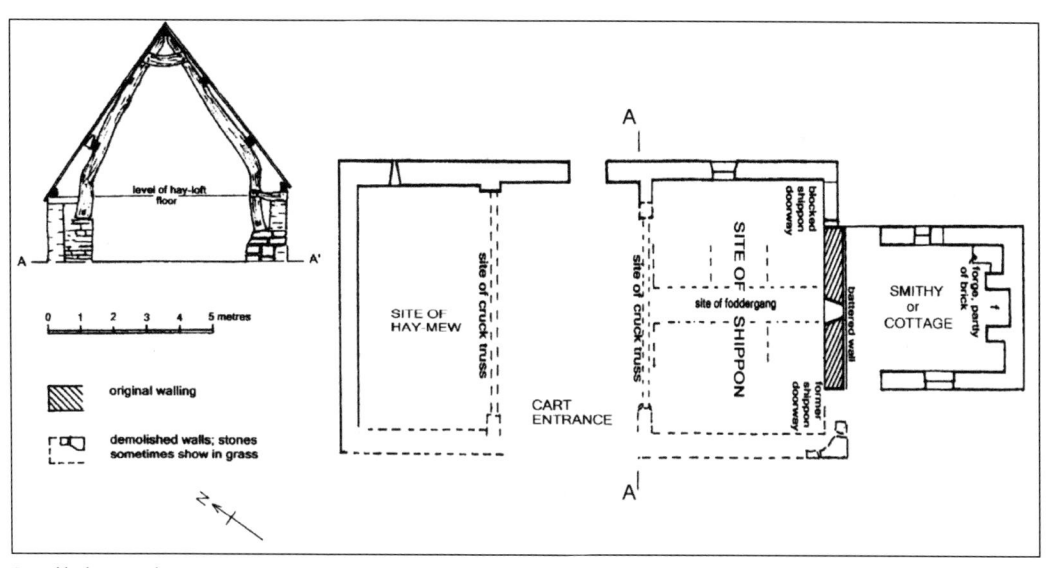

Until the early 1950s a cruck barn stood to the west of the road to Skipton. It was known as the High Laithe, and it appears on the 1st edition OS map. It is shown against a boundary with a ditch, suggesting that it could have been part of Henry Clifford's early sixteenth century 'planned' landscape around his Lodge at Barden Tower. On other Yorkshire maps Scale does not appear until Cary's 1793 map, when it is marked 'barnscales'. By 1810 it had become Bardenscales, with Barden Tower separate. Greenwood's map of 1838 shows only Scale House. The barn is shown on an estate plan of about 1860, but with a shape not

---

161 Alison Armstrong, Yorkshire Vernacular Buildings Study Group report, 1993.

compatible with a map dated 1900 and on-site observations in 1993. By 1952, it was still thatched with ling and its walls were in a very bad state of repair.

The barn had two crucks dividing it into three bays each being between eleven and sixteen feet long. It is said that the length of a bay was the width of four oxen. The longest bay served as a mistal to house twelve cattle, six tethered on each side of a central fothergang.

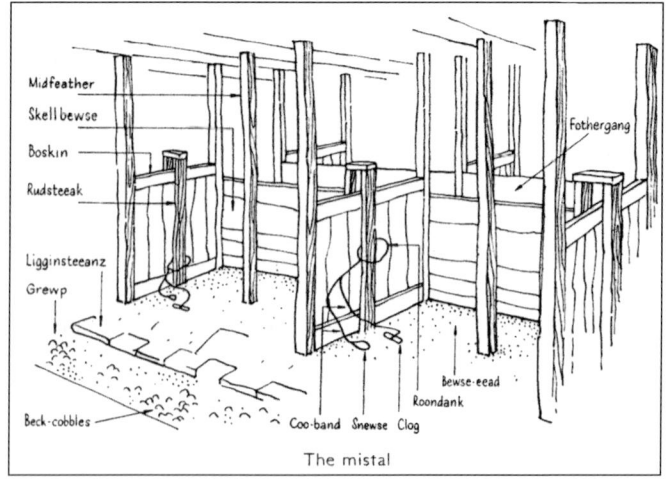

The mistal

In the middle of the south wall was a pair of large doors raised above the level of the side wall to allow for entry of loaded wagons, and in a corresponding position in the north wall was a smaller winnowing door. The floor space between these two doors was used for winnowing to fan the grain free of chaff. A cruck was made by selecting a slightly curved tree trunk, splitting it lengthwise and adzing the two halves to a roughly rectangular section. The feet of the crucks were sometimes set on large stones, or stylobates to prevent them from rotting and the beams were then set up as an arch. Held together by a collar beam and half way down by a tie beam, they took on a strong, roughly A-shape.

In 1952, the Duke of Devonshire gave the barn to Shibdon Hall Folk Museum, Halifax. It was re-erected and mentioned in a guide book 1954, but that same year the ling caught fire, and within a short space of time the crucks were alight, and the barn was gutted beyond repair.

The following notes have been added by Arnold Pacey: 'As with most cruck buildings, the thatched roof sloped steeply to low eaves, with a gentler slope to a high lintel over the cart entrance, high enough to admit a loaded cart. The cruck barn at Barden Scale appears to have been reconstructed, perhaps in the eighteenth century, to make the building both higher and wider. Before they were dismantled for removal to Halifax, the crucks stood on stub walls that raised them considerably higher than would be normal in a cruck structure. The stub walls, together with the front and back walls of the barn were of relatively thin construction suggesting a date in the eighteenth century or even after 1800. It appeared that they had been rebuilt outside the original walls to make the building much wider than the width of the cruck frame would have suggested.

'By contrast, the short wall across the north east end of the barn is very thick and battered (that is, its outer face slopes so that the wall becomes thinner towards the top). This was a characteristic of some local sixteenth century walling, particularly in cruck barns.

'The crucks themselves were of irregular shape with sharp elbows. If the curve of the tree trunk was at all irregular, as was the case here, the irregularities show in the finished structure. Splitting a single trunk should mean that the two crucks in a pair match one another, but here the base of one cruck blade had been trimmed to make it significantly shorter than its fellow, so the two halves did not quite match.

'A barn containing a shippon cannot function without a water supply for the cattle. The site of this barn is very close to a culvert or aqueduct through which water from Barden Moor was supplied to medieval fish ponds in the park associated with Barden Tower, and it is possible that a trough near the barn was filled from this, but nothing now remains.'

**The Smithy**
At the eastern end of the cruck barn stood a small building which was a smithy or blacksmith's shop. It would seem a natural site for a smithy, at this important junction of roads, for not only was coal extracted from a field in Tower Close, nearby Cinder Hill, but the remains of a medieval iron smelting industry or bloomery have been found in an area extending from the Moor Gate alongside the wall which bounded the Little Park.[162] The Demaines of Barden Scale have been recorded in the rent books from 1603 onwards as being locksmiths and gunsmiths.

*The cruck barn and the smithy at Barden Scale in 1947.*[163]

**The Sheep-washes or Dubs**
Sheep need washing before their fleeces are clipped, so many farming communities had a shared wash-dub for carrying out an activity which required more man-power and organisation than those for the everyday farm jobs. Skilfully built groups of small, walled enclosures can be found around water-courses on the outskirts of most villages or clusters of farms in the Yorkshire Dales, no matter how remote. These were an integral part of the life

---
163 Walton, J., *Homesteads of the Yorkshire Dales*, 1947, Dalesman Publishing Company, Clapham.

of a hill farmer until the introduction of purpose built, concrete troughs in which the sheep were dipped in chemical baths.

*The sheep wash at Broadshaw, Bolton Abbey, by kind permission of Kate Mason.*

## SHEEP WASHES OR DUBS

The Demaines followed by William Banks from Barden Scale, the Atkinsons from Low House Farm and the Listers from the Tower shared their sheep-wash at the foot of Broad Park, where a bridge carries the road to Skipton over Barden Beck. Their tiny walled enclosures can still be seen, where the sheep were held until each in turn was pushed down a slope into the pool which had been formed by damming the stream as it came off the moor. One or two farm men would stand waist deep in the pool, dressed in layers of old clothes, and then grab each sheep as it floundered to duck its head and body under the water. Then, with a final push, the sheep scrambled up another slope to another pen, water pouring from its fleece and running back into the pool. When this pen was full, the flock was released into the surrounding fields, or onto the open moor, where they immediately resumed grazing.

*Sheep wash pens for Barden Scale.*

Finally, the sheep were segregated into separate flocks before being driven by the farmer and his black and white collie dogs to the farmyard to which it belonged. Each sheep was identified by the marks burnt into one of its horns, and a 'splodge' of dye (either blue or red) applied to the fleece.

### The House at Barden Scale

This farmhouse is one of a few remaining seventeenth century stone houses built in the vernacular style in Barden on the site of a Forest Lodge, the others being Littlegate and Fold Farm at Drebley, and Crossfield in Howgill. As discussed in the chapter on buildings their features indicate that each was built as the home of a 'yeoman farmer',[164] albeit a tenanted leaseholder who did not own his property.

*Barden Scale.*

A collection of un-signed estate drawings dated 1871 for alterations, improvements and extensions to *William Demaine's house in Barden* show that although it was not enlarged

---

[164] Raistrick. A, *Buildings in the Yorkshire Dales*, Dalesman Publishing Co. 1976, Clapham, Lancaster.

beyond its four walls, many changes took place. The plans show how a new staircase was installed, (possibly to replace a circular stone staircase, until then in situ in a classical position to the rear of the housebody and parlour.) At the back of the house, at first floor level, is a large room labelled wool chamber. (Comparable with large first floor wool chambers at Drebley and the remote farmstead of Broadshaw, near Bolton Abbey). At the same time, a kitchen and dairy were added, with steps leading down to a cellar underneath the parlour, together with a thin wall from the front door to the staircase at the back, which partitioned off the housebody and kept in the warmth, as at Drebley and Littlegate. These alterations considerably reduced the living space in the old housebody and the parlour.

*Above, Crossfield, Howgill and below Fold Farm, Drebley.*

At the same time as the alterations were in progress within the house, enclosure of a yard adjoining its west gable was carried out. This now forms an un-heated scullery through which runs a stone drainage channel in the old flagged floor, but it has formerly formed a direct entrance from the roadway for horse-drawn carts and wagons; it may have been where the beer had been brewed.[165] From here, a doorway leads to a living room, with a fireplace and cooking range, and a wooden staircase from which further bedrooms are approached. As can be seen from the plan dated 1871, there is no communication between this end of the house and the 'polite' end, other than through an opening which forms a doorway between the scullery and the new kitchen.

---

165 In 1728 Geo D'Maine de Scale had a brewhouse, from estate survey Bolton manuscript.

# BARDEN SCALE

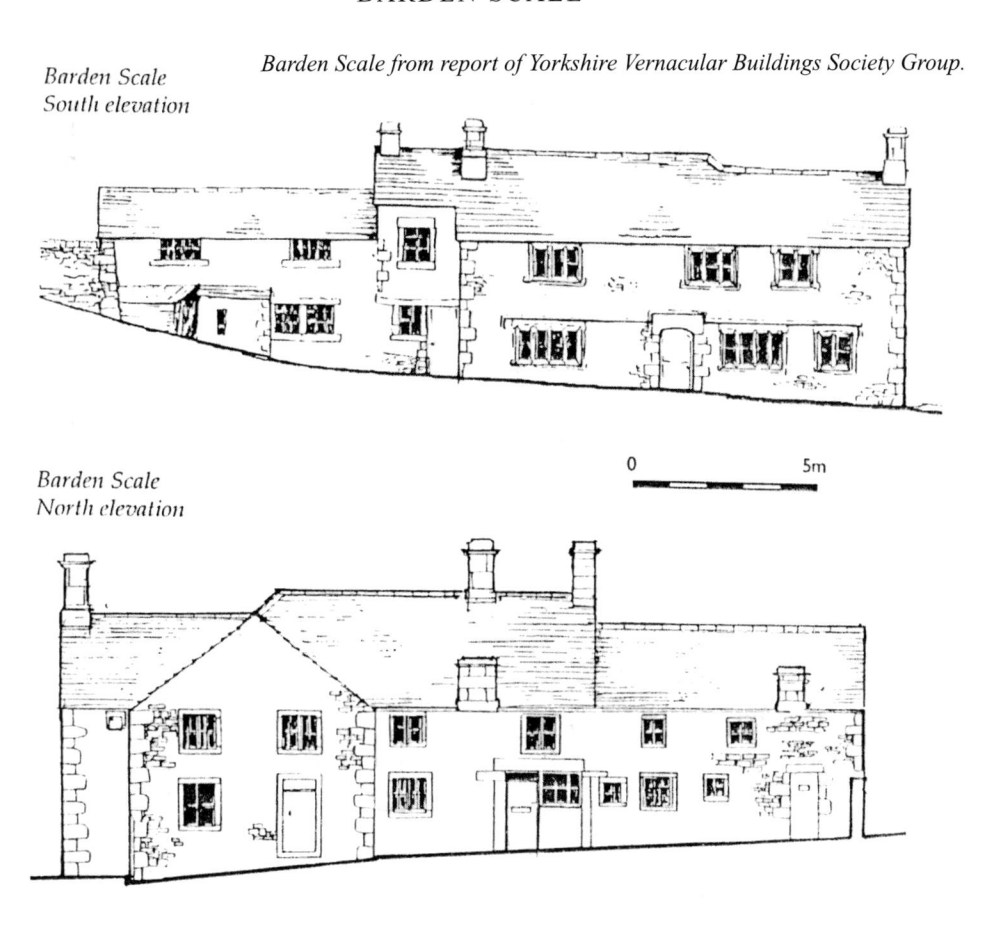

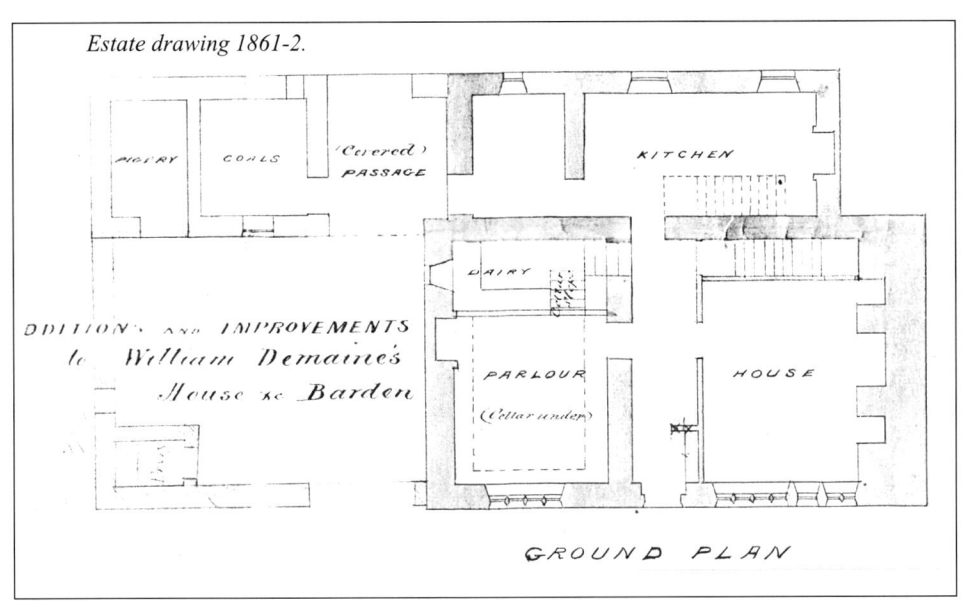

*Barden Scale from report of Yorkshire Vernacular Buildings Society Group.*

*Barden Scale South elevation*

*Barden Scale North elevation*

*Estate drawing 1861-2.*

## Barns at Barden Scale

Members of the North Yorkshire Vernacular Buildings Study Group surveyed the hamlet in 1997.[166] The report, published in their 'Bulletin' the following year, and reproduced in part here, indicates that the barns themselves may date from before 1750, and there appears to have been a major re-building around 1800. One member, Kate Mason, pointed out that there are many purpose built features in the barns, such as the use of stone setts or cobbles where horses were stabled and would have slipped if flags had been used.

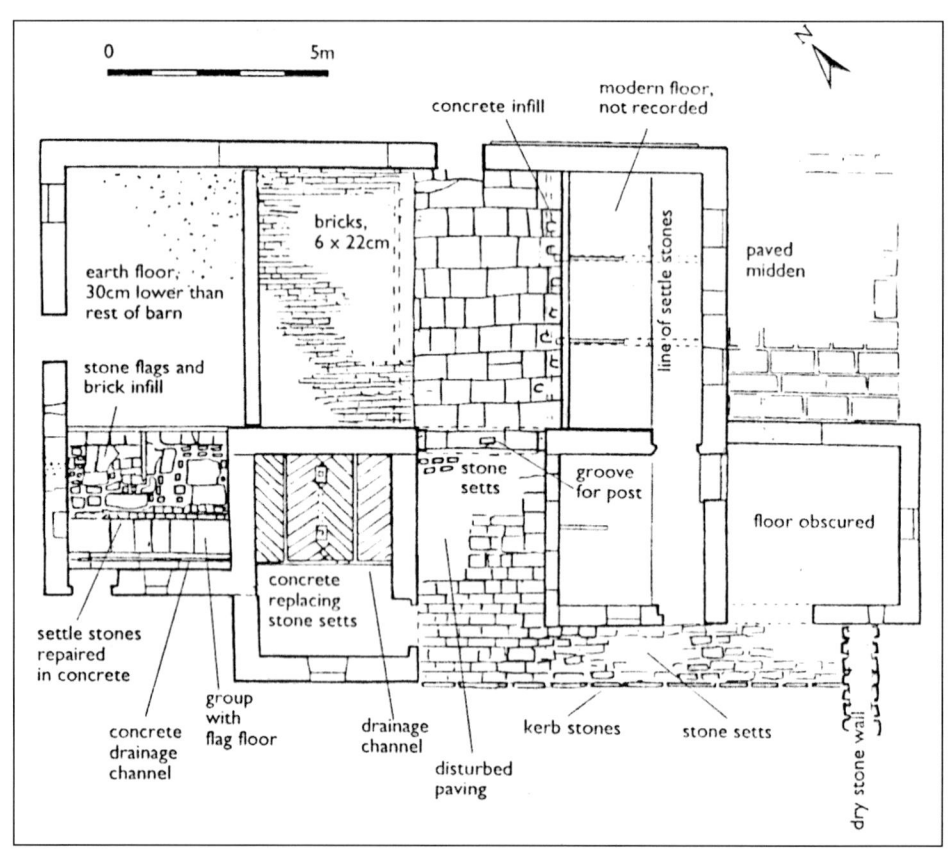

Barden Scale, situated as it is at the important junction with the only roadway up and down the valley and the road to Skipton would have been a hive of activity, where stabling of packhorses, hospitality and brewing of beer were carried out. The close proximity of the roadway winding its way between the large barns, the cottages and the farmhouse is an indication that Barden Scale was a 'stance' or overnight stand ... a stopping place for packhorse trains, where ponies could be loosed and grazed overnight, while food and sleeping accommodation were provided for the men. The brewhouse mentioned in the 1778 survey may have been associated with this, while the presence of the Smithy attached to the High Laithe in Bentlands, on the Skipton Road, would fulfil a critical place in the life of the busy

---

166 Yorkshire Vernacular Buildings Society Group reports October 1997: 1547/1549/1552, Plans and drawings 1871, Chatsworth Estate Settlement.

hamlet. The suggested traditional role of Barden Scale as a stance[167] revived when game sports became a major feature in the cycle of life on the Bolton Abbey estate. Each year, when the grouse season opened on 12 August, because the hamlet lies close to the entrance to the Great Park at Moor Gate, it was convenient for the Duke's shooting parties to assemble at the Scale, and to return there at the end of their day on the moor.[168] Here, the waggonettes would bring not only provisions, but also ladies and children of the party staying at Bolton Hall who often joined the guns for tea at Brass Castle, the shelter huts near the Low Reservoir.[169] It also became the custom for Mrs Dunckley, the school mistress, to gather the Barden children to stand by the Moor Gate where they would have a chance to see the Duke with his most illustrious visitor, King George V, who was for many years an annual guest at Bolton Abbey. It was well known that he rode a white pony named Jock, who was brought specially from Sandringham each year.[170] The excitement amongst the children would rise as they heard the jingling of harness and the voices of the keepers long before they saw the party coming over the brow of the hill.[171] In the evening, ponies needed on the moor the next day were left to graze overnight in the fields around the farm, while the blacksmith would be 'to hand' in the smithy.

The cottages at Scale housed estate workers, who turned out in force on such occasions,[172] the dog-kennels and pheasant coops being seen in the garth attached the cottage which housed the gamekeeper for Barden Moor.

Horse drawn transport through Wharfedale was slowly replaced by motorised vehicles, but not until well after the First World War. At first, open-topped charabancs were seen, carrying the first 'day trippers' up the dale, and eventually a public bus service was established between Ilkley, Bolton Abbey, Barden Tower, Burnsall and Grassington. The operation of such a service meant that relatively large motorised vehicles negotiated their way in both directions, several times a day on the narrow road between the houses and barns of Barden Scale. The chamfered north east corner of the house, being part of the 1871 building would have been an early precaution taken to minimise damage to the stonework, and to ease the passage of moving vehicles.

In the early 1970s a bypass was constructed on a new length of road to the east of the tiny hamlet and a gate was fixed across the road between the barns, to discourage unauthorised traffic passing through. In what has become a lay-by on the side of this new section of road, local men were employed in the early years of the century, dressing stone for gravestones and for sills and lintels and other items needed for buildings on the estate. It may be that the nearby medieval stone quarry (shown on Oddie's map 1778) provided a ready source

---

167 A 'stance' in this context describes where overnight provision with rough grazing was made for trains of packhorse ponies and their pack men.
168 Memories of Dora Dunckley of Barden School.
169 Brass Castle consists of two thatched stone huts, containing fixed wooden tables. One hut was for the keepers and beaters and suchlike, while the other for the Duke and his guests.
170 Donald Wood, *The Time of My Life*, 1996, p.115 and photograph.
171 Memories recorded and quoted in *The Story of Barden School,* 1997, by Brontë Bedford-Payne and Heather Beaumont, Prontaprint, Durham.
172 See section about Gladys Inman at Keeper's Cottage, Drebley.

of supply for these stones. (It was said, by the school mistress, that some of these men died of silicosis).

Close by this place was the pinfold where stray sheep were impounded until claimed by their owners. The modern lay-by now offers an excellent stand (not a stance!) where keen birdwatchers can erect their telescopes and view birds of prey soaring over Barden Moor and over the ancient enclosure of the coney warren on the other side of the valley. This activity perpetuates the dominance of the early medieval situation of Barden Scale in overlooking features and settlements in the valley.

**Who lived at Barden Scale?**
According to the nineteenth century writings of Edmund Bogg[173] (page 168) 'the De Maines took part in the Conquest' but Harry Speight the antiquarian historian also wrote[174] 'The De Maines anciently wrote their name after the province in Normandy. There do not appear to have been any Demaines in Wharfedale as early as 1378, when the first Poll Tax lists were drawn up.'

Barden Scale was mentioned in the rental of 1603, for George Clifford 3rd Earl of Cumberland, when it was leased to William Thompson and Ellin his wife.[175]

The names of generations of the Demaine family who lived at Barden Scale appear in the estate lease books dating from 1603 onwards, for instance, in 1665, at the time when Lady Anne Clifford was restoring the Tower, George Demaine of Barden Scale in his will,[176] bequeathed 'to my son John Demaine all my instruments tools and instruments stencils wholefull belonging to my trade of Locksmith', and in 1696 a John Demaine is also listed in the estate lease book as having been a locksmith.

The Demaines of Barden Scale were closely related to the Demaines at Catgill in Bolton Abbey, and in Storiths, and to those at Hole House, Barden, and Littlegate, Drebley, but records do not show any links with those at Fold Farm, Drebley. Some have headstones in the churchyard at Bolton Abbey, the last memorial being for Miss Sarah Demaine, born in 1873 and died in 1949. Sarah was the only child of William Demaine 1835-1921 and his wife Margaret, née Ward, who came from Kirkby Malzeard, and was closely related to the Wards of Hough Mill and Holme Farm. She was married to William Demaine in Rylstone Church. When their daughter Sarah was eleven years old they adopted a child named Willie, but a tragedy occurred when he died, aged 32, after falling through some wooden slats above a shippon in one of the barns. His dates 1884-1916 are recalled on his headstone in the churchyard at Bolton Abbey.

William Demaine, father of Sarah, was a Foundation Manager for the new Barden School when it was built in 1875, and he remained in an influential position in the parish for the rest of his life. After his death in 1921 Sarah lived alone at Barden Scale whilst employing Phyllis Hustwick of Holme Cottage to work in the house, and William Banks formerly of Malham and of Drebley, as her farm manager. In October 1930 she decided to wind up her

---

173 *A Thousand Miles in Wharfedale*, 1904.
174 'The history, antiquities and scenery of Upper Wharfedale', 1900.
175 Yorkshire Archaeological Society: DD121/29/23.
176 Borthwick Institute, York.

lease on Lady Day, 25 March 1931. William Banks, having married Phyllis, became the new tenant for the farm and also the first 'off comed 'un' to be a leaseholder at Barden Scale.

William and Phyllis married in October 1930 and, with their son Ronald, lived in the farmhouse while Sarah lived in the 'genteel' portion of the house, with her fine furniture and china, handed down from her forbears.

After Sarah's death in 1949, William Banks continued as the leaseholder, to be followed in turn by his son Ronald and then by his grandsons. Although there have been no members of the Demaine family living at Barden Scale since 1949, this continuity of tenancy demonstrates the customary tradition on the Bolton Abbey Estate of how, over the centuries, leases for the same farm have been passed from one generation to another.

*Above, William and Phyllis Banks on their wedding day and below, Sarah's eighteenth century wall cabinet containing some of her china.*

BARDEN IN WHARFEDALE, THE PLACE AND ITS PEOPLE

**A Lodge in the Forest of Barden - the Rabbit Warren**
Both Thomas Whitaker in 1805 and Stephen Moorhouse in 2003 have postulated that, of the probable dozen Lodges established within the Forest of Barden, and listed in the manorial accounts for 1437/8, the second Lodge counting northwards from The Laund, was known as Netherfyshstryhes.[177] Situated in a favourable position about 500 feet above the wet meadowland, it is likely that this Lodge became the Warrener's house during the years between 1496 and 1506, when Henry Clifford was establishing his residence at Barden Tower, and enclosing the Little and Great Parks,[178] for it was during this time that he enclosed the large area on the hillside east of the river for his Coney Warren.

Most medieval estates established breeding warrens, for the rabbit was an important source of food and skins. It has been pointed out that because there is no mention of them in the Domesday Book, and there is no Celtic or Anglo-Saxon word for the rabbit,[179] it is not a native species, but was imported from Northern Europe. The first written reference to rabbits on the English mainland occurred during the reign of Henry III, dated 17 February 1226, when the Keeper of the Royal Park at Guildford was directed to supply 20-40 rabbits for the King's larder.[180]

The wall which enclosed the warren can clearly be seen from the other side of the valley, from Barden Scale, and from the road over Black Park. Although classical pillow mounds have not been identified, it is assumed that the rabbits burrowed into the sandy hillside to breed, without the need for artificial mounds, and it is said that associated, small stone structures survive from an early date. The success of the rabbits is undoubted, for one of the entries in the nineteenth century estate rent books contains a plea for reduction in rent on account of the large numbers of them infesting the land at Holme Farm. This suggests that, once established, rabbits have continued to breed successfully in the same warren for at least 500 years as they do to the present day.

---

177 Moorhouse, Stephen, Whitaker's *History of Craven*.
178 Spence, Richard, *The Shepherd Lord of Skipton Castle*, 1994, Smith Settle, Otley
179 Fitter, R. S., *The Ark in our Midst*.
180 Helen Chapman Davies, *The Royal Park at Guildford Rediscovered*, 1992, Newsletter: Society for Landscape Studies, RCHME, Salisbury, Wiltshire.

# HOLME HOUSE FARM

*[Map titled "1867 HOLME FARM" showing numbered fields and features including Field Bottom, Cow Close, The New Inn (Watergate), Close before the Door, Far Close, Wood, Park Gate Close, Lime Kiln, Barden Bridge, High Holme, Holme Brow & Holme Top, River Wharfe, Holm Farm, Calf Garth, Close Before Door, Low Holme, Bottoms, Intake, Little Intake, Coney Warren, High Close, Park Hill, Newfoundland, First Close, Second Close, Cow Pastures, High New Piece, Low New Piece, Far Close, Ox Close, Long Strid.]*

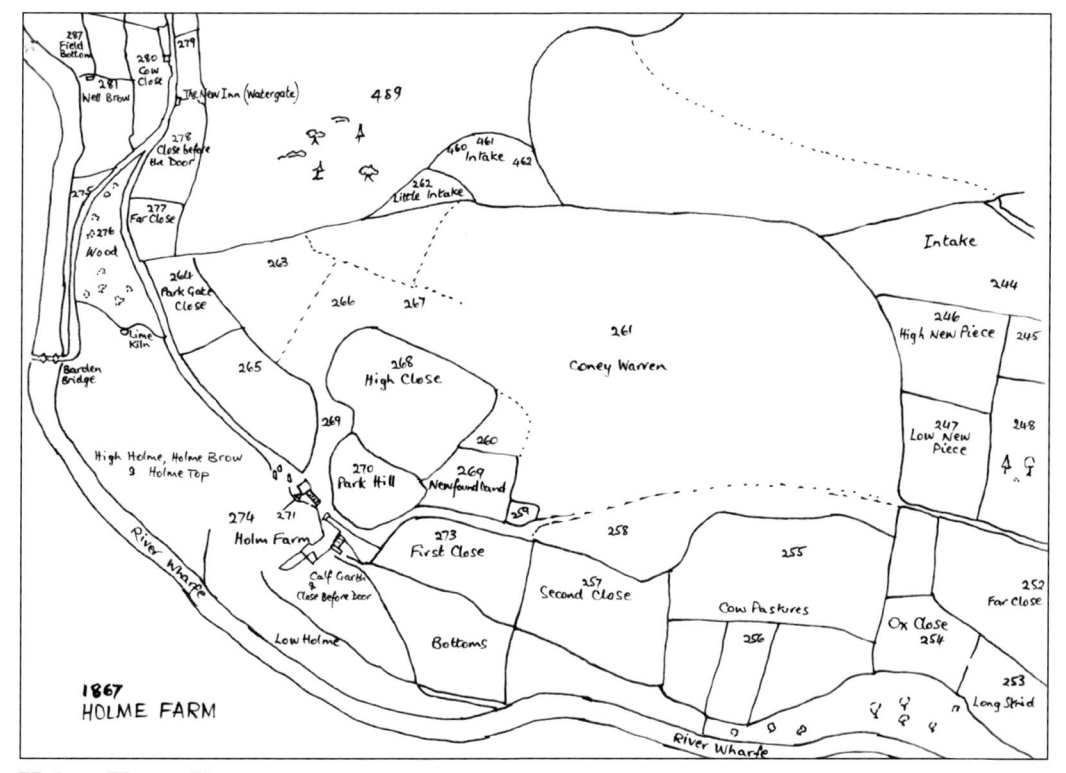

## Holme House Farm

The name Holme derives from Old Norse *holmr*, implying that the settlement here overlooks water meadows. The name does not mean that the meadowland is constantly flooded, but that it is frequently wet, as indeed it is, when the River Wharfe is in spate and overflows its banks; at such times water lies in large puddles along the flat valley bottom before draining back naturally into the river.

Although the present farmhouse and its associated cottage(s) date from the eighteenth and nineteenth centuries, their footings are doubtless built on the site of the Warrener's House. The estate map dated 1867 shows that 52 acres were enclosed for the rabbit warren, within a curving boundary wall. Within this boundary, and adjacent to the farmstead, are several Closes, two Intakes and four acres and four roods named Newfoundland. This latter field-name suggests that an area was taken from the Coney Warren and walled in at some time during the early part of the nineteenth century, when the New World was being explored. In these small, rocky enclosures on the steep hillside it is evident that bracken has been cleared to allow grass to grow for sheep and cattle to graze.

In 1867 the Victorian artist, Atkinson Grimshaw visited Barden. His painting of Holme Farm[181] shows a romanticised view of the house, the fields, and the lane, bordered not by a stone wall as it is today, but by a hedgerow. In the background, Barden Tower is shown rising from the forest of deciduous trees that would probably have surrounded it at that time, in contrast to the plantations of evergreen spruce so familiar to the viewer in the twenty-

---

181 Royle Publications Ltd

BARDEN IN WHARFEDALE, THE PLACE AND ITS PEOPLE

*Above, a copy of the painting by Atkinson Grimshaw, which now hangs in Chatsworth House, and has been reproduced on greeting cards.*[181]

first century. From the regular ridges on the field, and the sacks portrayed alongside the women, it is tempting to believe that they were harvesting a potato crop, ready for storage in one of the specially built small buildings with domed roofs found in some farmyards around Barden.[182]

This painting hangs in Chatsworth House. There are two other dwellings at The Holme. In the nineteenth century one of these, known as Bay Cottage, accommodated spinster teachers at Barden School; it was fully furnished until 1906 when the newly appointed teacher, Miss Whitely, refused to live there alone. She then became a paying guest of Miss Anne de Maine, at Stonybank, a cottage on the other side of the river, and relatively close to the school. At this time, a sale of all the cottage contents took place,[183] after which it was rented out to members of the Hustwick family, who were estate workers.

### Notes on the Ward family of Holme House and Hough Mill

In the same way as other homesteads in Barden were lived in by successive generations of the same family, Holme House was, in the eighteenth and nineteenth centuries, leased by the Ward family, who a were also millers at Hough Mill. For instance, in 1727-29 Francis Ward was also paying rent for Hough Mill and cottage, and his name appears in the estate rent book, when he was reimbursed for purchase of 'a new dusting sieve and some slates'.

By 1806, while one brother Francis, born in 1788 carried out his trade as a miller, another

---

182 Harwood Long, W., *A Survey of Yorkshire*, 1969, Royal Agricultural Society, Belgrave Square, London.
183 Barden School, Barden Box, MSS Chatsworth papers, Bolton Abbey.

## HOLME HOUSE FARM

brother James farmed at Holme, having underlet the small farm of 23 acres at Hough Mill to Francis. It seems that they were both millers, as indicated by the following notes taken from estate rent books and the Tithe Award for Bolton Abbey: 'for in 1774 James Ward paid tithes based on 30 lambs and 60 sheep.

*Holme House Farm with the Cottage and Coney Warren hill behind*

### Some names and dates for Wards at The Holme
Inscription on headstone in Bolton Abbey churchyard:
 'James Ward (1752-1828) m. Flora Ward, aged 54 died 1795, of Holme, Barden
  Francis, (1789-1812)    William, (1893-1815)'

Francis Ward born in 1789 and his wife Agnes Spence had one son James, and another named Francis who married Sarah Petty of Hazlewood.

James born in 1799 and his wife Anne born in 1803 had two sons, William born 1836 and Henry born in 1842. In 1851 they were living at Hough Mill, and it was through James' brother Thomas, who was born in 1798 that the Wards continued to live at The Holme:

Thomas Ward (1798-1878) m. Elizabeth Jackson (1804-75) of Cracoe

| William | Francis | Mary Ellen (1846-84) |
| b. 1826 | b. 1833 | m. Robert Holgate Brown (1844-1928) |

Mary Ellen, Elizabeth, Mary Anne, Sarah, Thomas, Betsy, Truman

Mary Ellen Ward, born in 1846, married Robert Holgate Brown of Kilnsey, who was born in 1844; they lived and farmed at Holme House, where their seven children were born. But in January 1884 Ellen died, aged 38 years, when all her children were under the age of twelve. A year later, in 1885 Robert, who was the Chairman of Barden School Management Committee married the schoolmistress, Agnes Biggs, who was then aged 33; she retired from teaching at the school in July of that year, to become Robert's wife, and also stepmother to his seven children. Robert died in 1928 at the age of 84, having fallen on the fire in his parlour. Barden folk were shocked to hear the tragic news.[184]

---

184 Memoirs of Dora Dunkley, Barden School, unpublished.

## Watergate

Watergate, a smallholding situated at the top of a very steep hill leading from Barden Bridge, lies at a junction with the minor road leading to The Laund, Storiths and Bolton Abbey. In the nineteenth century Watergate was a hostelry and probably an important watering place for horses and cattle. In 1851[185] the tenant Annie Thompson farmed 34 acres and was also the innkeeper; who hung out a sign on which was inscribed 'Good Ale tomorrow for nothing'.[186]

By 1867, Barden leases[187] tell us that Annie's son, Henry was the tenant, and that 'the little old roadside public house thatched and somewhat dilapidated … should be rebuilt on the other side of the road.' An artificially level bay adjoining the barnyard on the roadside is reputed to be where the original public house stood. Photographs of the old barns at Watergate show where horses would have been stabled, long before and during the time when the Thompson's kept the hostelry. The steep pitches of the barn gables indicate that they were once of cruck construction; timbers from these early cruck buildings have been re- used to form tie beams and wooden lintels over the forking hole and some doorways,[188] as shown in the group of photographs.

*Photographs showing the barns at Watergate, with steeply pitched gable ends and lintels of re-used timbers from the former cruck building.*

---

185 Census Returns.
186 Mabel Blundell-Heineman, *Appletreewick*, 1934.
187 Chatsworth manuscripts at Bolton.
188 North Yorkshire and Cleveland Vernacular Buildings Study Groups, 1980, Report No. 697

# WATERGATE

**North Yorkshire/West Riding**
(modern county/historic county)

**BARDEN**
(township)

                      Watergate Barn,           SE 0545 5774
                      Barden

---

Survey by Kate Mason and Arnold Pacey, 2 September, 1980;
report revised by Arnold Pacey using information from Brontë Bedford Payne, November 2012.

---

N.B.
This report describes the same survey as YVBSG report no. **697** but corrects some errors of fact and adds drawings of elevations.

Building type and background

This is a heather-thatched barn with corrugated iron covering the remains of the thatch. It is aligned east-west down a steep slope with the upper end facing the road. The barn belonged to a smallholding and former inn on the road from Barden Bridge to Appletreewick. In 1851 the house/inn was adjacent to the barn on the west side of the road. After 1867, the Bolton Abbey Estate rebuilt the house on the opposite side of the road.

Description

Walls are of coarse sandstone in roughly squared block laid in regular courses. There are projecting through stones and large quoins at the corners. The 60 cm (2 feet) thick walls stand on a stepped plinth. Lintels of doorways, the forking hole, and slit ventilators are of roughly trimmed stone and/or timber without chamfers or other decoration. The outhouse and dairy attached to the barn (see plan) are relatively recent.

The hay mew in the eastern half of the building was filled via a forking hole in the gable nearest the road. There is a shippon at the west end with modern cemented boskins and floors to suit 1960s milk hygiene regulations. The shippon has been extended into the central area of the barn. This has partly obstructed the cart entrance on the south side which is protected from the weather by a slight projection of the roof with stone slates rather than thatch.

On the north side there may once have been another cart entrance, though with a low lintel suggesting the use of hay sleds rather than carts. However, its width was reduced at an early date to leave only a winnowing doorway (with nice pegged door) and a window.

Roof construction

There are two roof trusses, both with tie-beams made from former cruck blades of good timber. They are only slightly curved, but do not seem to be a matching pair. There is other reused cruck timber in the building, but the principals of the truss illustrated (section A-A') do not seem to be reused. As in other local thatched buildings, rafters are closely spaced, some of them being larch poles, and fragments of thatch hang down between them. There is a dormer window to the hay mew on the north side which would have been very helpful when hay was being piled high inside.

Dating and conclusion

The quality of the stonework, with plinth and 2-foot-thick walling, suggests that the walls may date from the late 17th century. No padstones for crucks were seen. Crucks of good timber such as these often seem to date from the 16th century in this area, and a building of that date is likely to have occupied the site before the present 17th-century barn was built.

# BARDEN IN WHARFEDALE, THE PLACE AND ITS PEOPLE

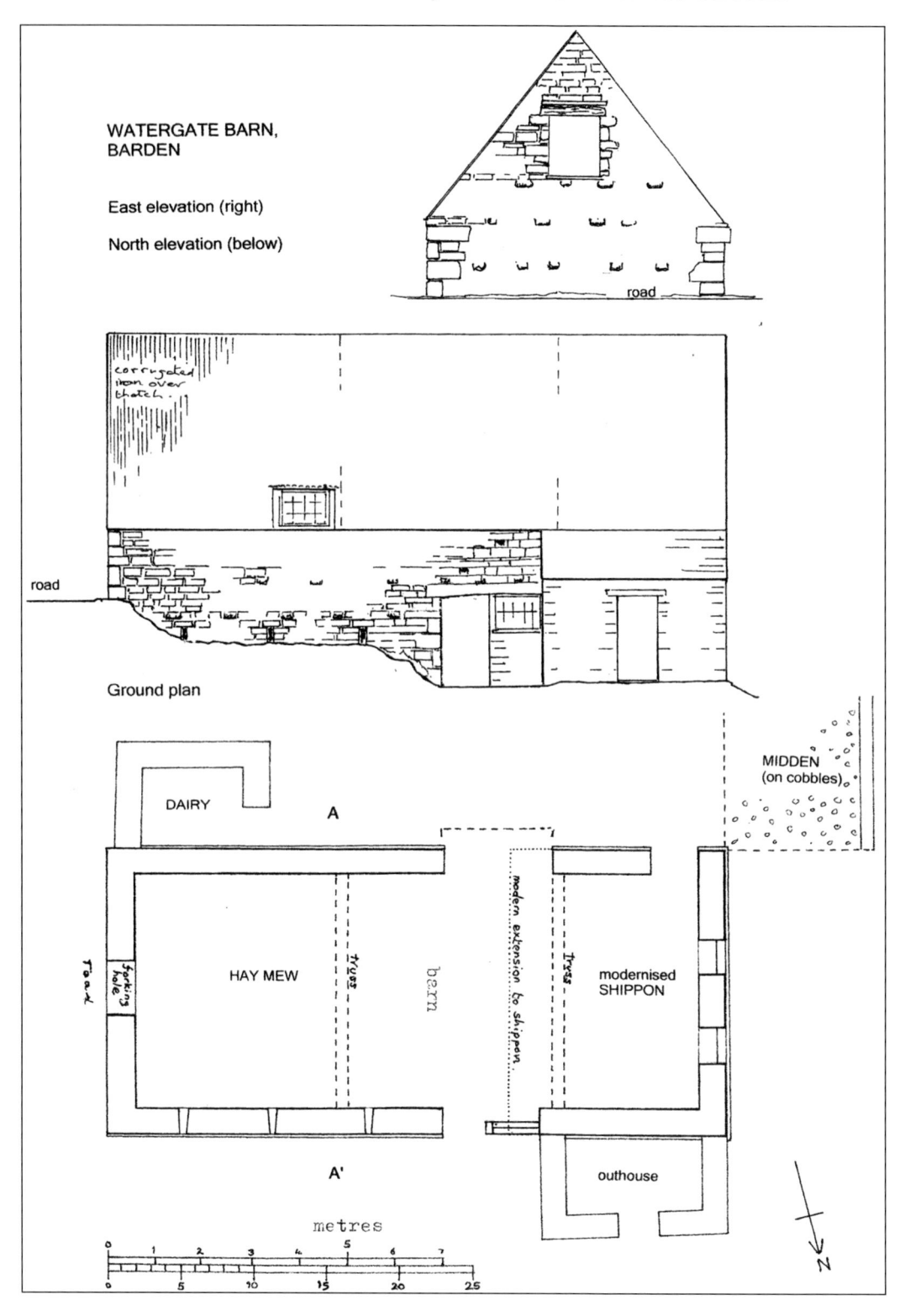

**WATERGATE BARN, BARDEN**

East elevation (right)

North elevation (below)

road

corrugated iron over thatch.

road

Ground plan

DAIRY

A

forking hole

Taak

HAY MEW

tryes

barn

modern extension to shippon.

tryes

modernised SHIPPON

MIDDEN (on cobbles)

outhouse

A'

metres

N

# WATERGATE

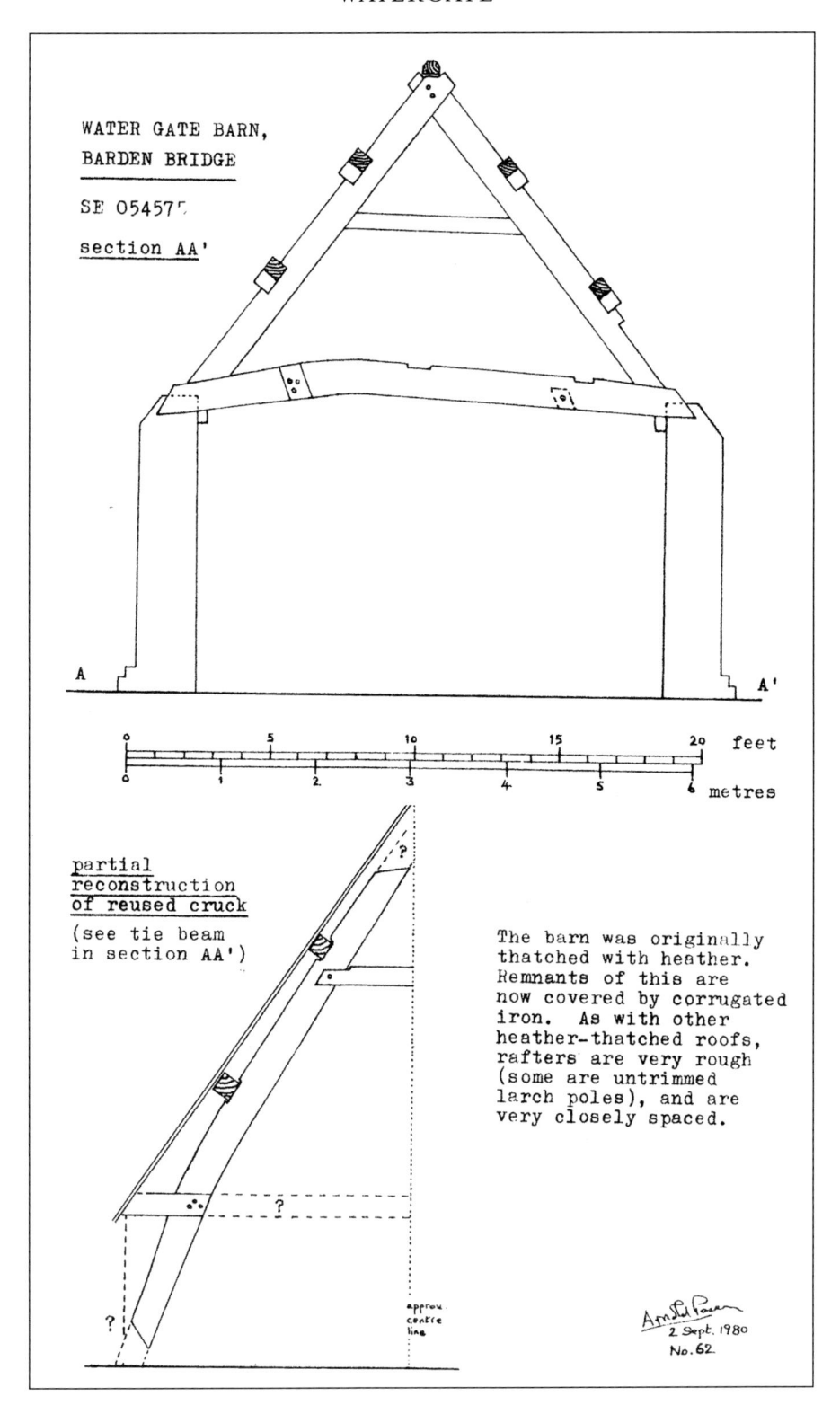

WATER GATE BARN,
BARDEN BRIDGE

SE 05457

section AA'

partial
reconstruction
of reused cruck
(see tie beam
in section AA')

The barn was originally thatched with heather. Remnants of this are now covered by corrugated iron. As with other heather-thatched roofs, rafters are very rough (some are untrimmed larch poles), and are very closely spaced.

Arnold Pacey
2 Sept. 1980
No. 62

# BARDEN IN WHARFEDALE, THE PLACE AND ITS PEOPLE

When the first edition of the Ordnance Survey map for Barden was published in 1853, the road between Hough Mill and Barden Bridge, on the east side of the valley, is shown as 'the Skipton and Pateley Bridge Trust'. This implies that it was a turnpike. It is tempting to conclude from its position that the plain cottage fronting the carriageway at Watergate was built as a toll bar, and that the small opening in the wall adjacent to the entrance door was for the purpose of collecting tolls for the Turnpike, but there is no documentary evidence to support this observation.

*Eighteenth century cottage, the Reading Room.*

By 1907 a public house was no longer marked on the map, while the old house on the east side of the road had become a public reading room, thus meeting the rising needs of late Victorian society for self-improvement. Like the old public house, it provided a social centre on the highway within easy reach of the local community. The building fulfilled this function until the early 1930s, when better facilities became available across the river in the former Barden School building.

## A working-men's Crie de Coeur

The following letter, dated 1872, reflects a growing awareness of social conditions for working men in the remote community of Barden.

Impeccably written in copperplate script, the letter is addressed to Mr Allen who was (probably?) the agent for the 7th Duke of Devonshire. The signatures are all in the same script as the letter. In style, its careful deference is noticeable, combined as it is with a determination to put forward the men's plea for 'consideration as human beings worthy of the chance to improve their working conditions.' By comparing themselves to being 'little higher than a horse and the rest of brute creation' and expressing their need 'to refresh (their) better natures' the men are hoping to secure the sympathy of their employer, whilst at the same time remaining his 'humble servants' who are dependant on his 'kind compliance with (their) request'.

The comparison with working conditions on a neighbouring estate refers to the estate at Skipton Castle, held by Sir Robert Tufton, who was a descendant of Lady Anne Clifford's elder daughter, Lady Margaret Thanet.

In 1862 plans were drawn up for building a new dwelling house at Watergate[193] to replace the old one; the architectural style is that of a 'picturesque cottage orné rather than a simple extension or replacement of the existing plain, late eighteenth century dwelling.[194] The new

---

193 Chatsworth manuscripts at Bolton.
194 See section on 'The Picturesque in Barden'.

# WATERGATE

*March 1872.*
*Barden.*

Mr Allen.
Sir

We your humble Servants, hereby beg leave to offer our united Petition, for an alteration in the time of leaving off work; and an advance of wages, namely to 3/6 per day, Summer and Winter, And that the hours of work be from 7 O'Clock Morning to ½ past 5 Evening except Saturdays at 1 o'clock afternoon. The above request will only make about 2 hours per week less actually worked, for we should not require to stop for luncheon at 4 o'clock as we do now. Our request is the same as the men have on the Neighbouring Estate of Sir R. Tufton. We the undersigned feel confident that you will be aware of the high price of provisions &c. and the privileges we are deprived off, that those have who live near a Market, or Town or more civilized part of the World, where they can hear a lecture or go to a Reading room, Mechanics institution &c and spend a leisure hour in the improvement of the mind, as it is now by the time we get home from work we must begin to prepare for bed and dream about Rising by soon after 5 in the Morning. Making ourselves a little higher than the horse and the rest off the brute Creation, Working, eating, and Sleeping away our lives, by your kind compliance with our request — we should have a few hours every week at our disposal to Refresh our better natures, Trusting that this will meet your kind approbation and Consent. We beg leave to remain your humble Servants. — John Holmes
Henry Berry
Thomas Lister
Francis Ward
Thomas Hibbid
William Holmes
John Holmes
George Holmes
Alfred Thompson
Robert Clough
Francis Whitaker

cottage was built at right angles to the original house, its accommodation separate from the earlier building. Its gabled front faces south, towards Barden Bridge and the road to Storiths.[195]

At some date, a social centre known as the Men's Reading Room was established in the old house at Watergate, but its exact date is unknown. Following the 'spirit of the times' expressed in the letter shown in this article, the Reading Room served at a time when Working Men's Institutes were being generally established throughout the country. It is worth noting that in 1855 the Mechanic's Institute in Grassington had been built by the 6th Duke of Devonshire, for the purpose of educating the huge number of miners working in his lead mines.

*Cottage built in 1871.*

The Reading Room at Watergate was certainly being used in the 1920s, when it was mentioned in the memoirs of Billy Mason (farm worker at Fold Farm, Drebley, 1929). Bernard Foster of Howgill also remembers hearsay of the room being a popular venue, especially after a billiard table was installed. It ceased to be used as a social centre after the closure of Barden School in 1931, when, as a result of another petition to the Duke, that building became available for community use; the billiard table was then removed from Watergate and installed in the former school-room on the other side of the river.

---

195 See following *Nineteenth Century Architectural Styles on the BA estate*, B. Bedford-Payne

# GAMSWORTH

## Gamsworth

The farmstead of Gamsworth is situated at 450 feet OD, on a natural river terrace on the east side of the valley, above the flood plain of the river. It overlooks the unenclosed, poorly drained land marked Gamsworth Field as shown on Matthew Oddie's map. Directly across the river lies the hamlet of Drebley, and the farms of Hole House and Club Nook.

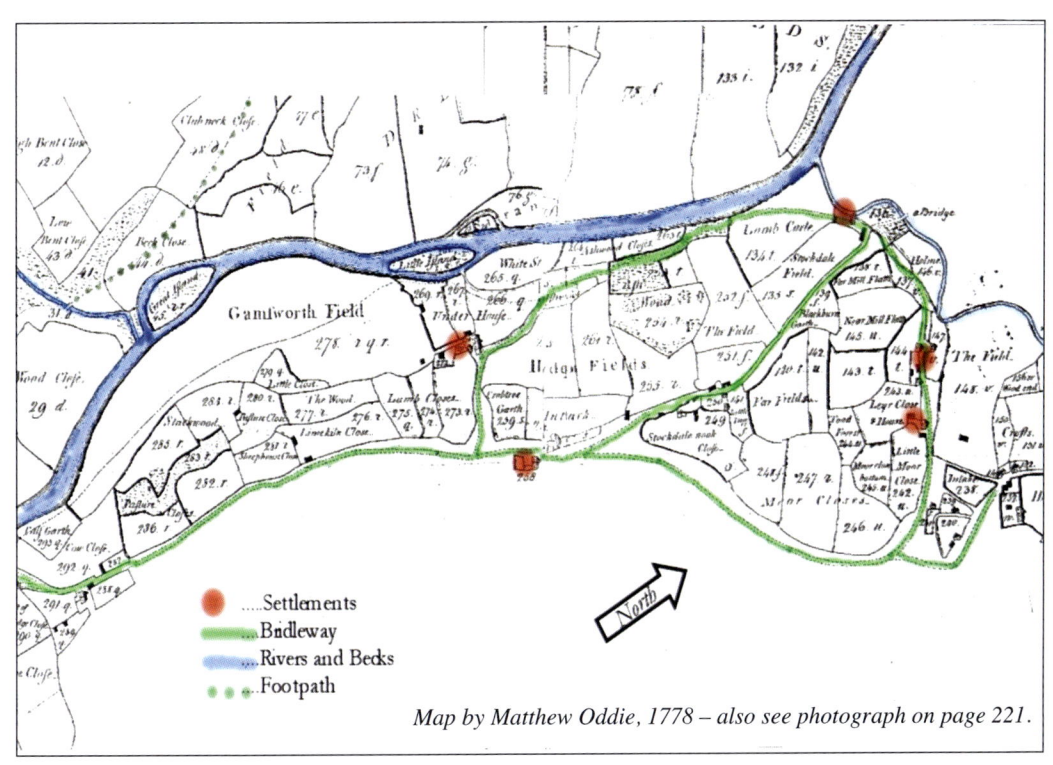

*Map by Matthew Oddie, 1778 – also see photograph on page 221.*

## Medieval Gamsworth

The name Gamsworth derives from the personal name of the Anglo-Scandinavian thane *Gamal*, who, at the time of Domesday, had a manor on the east side of Barden, and from the Old Norse name *vao*, for a wath or ford across a river. The entry in the Domesday Book reads:

> Gammalswath; 5 carucates taxable, 6 ploughs possible, Meadow 5 acre. The whole 5 leagues long, 1 league wide. Value before 1086 was 20s (at Domesday, Count Alan had it.)

## Approach to Gamsworth via the river crossing

In medieval times, the approach to the lodge at Gamsworth from the south and west would have been by means of a river crossing, or wath, the only possible place having been where Barden Bridge now stands. It is only at this point that the bed of the river is relatively smooth and shallow, where, other than in times of spate, a crossing place might have been afforded to riders on horseback and horse-drawn carts. At all other places in Barden the river is too deep and the current too strong for a ford. Although there is no readily identifiable field evidence surviving in the banks on either side to identify where a ford might have been, there

215

is a deep hollow way (now the present road) skirting the northern precincts of the Tower and leading down to the river where the bridge now stands. This was part of the ancient way which became the packhorse route through Barden, and was marked as such on Matthew Oddie's map of 1778.

In the same way as access to the seigniorial establishment at Barden Tower was by means of a private road through the Little Park, this medieval approach to Gamsworth would not have been used by the 'common people' going about their daily business in the forest. It was for access to the high status settlement of the Thane, Gamal. His presence in Barden at the time of Domesday pre-dated the building of the early forest lodge known as *le Scabbytsyke*, which, in the late fifteenth century, became the primary Lodge known as Barden Tower.

This ancient trackway leading to Gamsworth does not appear on Matthew Oddie's map, it having gone out of use many centuries beforehand, but a packhorse way was shown, by means of a double dotted line leading from Barden Bridge to Howgill, and passing at a higher level on the side of the valley in order to avoid the enclosures at Gamsworth. This was the line taken later in the eighteenth and nineteenth centuries for the Skipton and Pateley Bridge Trust turnpike. The farmstead itself was directly approached from this road by a steeply inclined walled lane, leading directly down the hillside from High Gamsworth Cottage. Although this lane is hardly a hollow way, because of the shallow depth of soil over the underlying bedrock, the sinuous course taken by the 'battered' walls, and the large boulders in its base are indications of its antiquity.

**The Lodge**

Gamsworth was listed in the manorial accounts for Skipton Castle as being one of twelve Lodges in the Forest of Barden. In 1311, when Edward II granted the Honour of Skipton to Robert de Clifford, 'the Lodge at Gamsworth with the meadow belonging was valued at xxviijs.'[196] At this lodge would have resided an official, such as a verdurer, regarder, arbarius, or a woodward.

**The Vaccary**

After the decline of the hunting chase, with a consequent demise in the need for lodge-keepers, the clearings round Gamsworth, like those round other forest lodges had become vaccaries, or cow pastures for the agistment and summer grazing of cattle from Bolton Priory. It is recorded in the Bolton Compotus that: 'forest receipts for the years 1322/23 include those for vaccaries at Drebley, Holgill, Gamsworth, Launds and Estwode, with agistments for plough cattle in the woods of Drebley and Estwode.'[197]

A vaccary such as Gamsworth was frequently D shaped in outline, with the Lodge on a spur end of land, (as at Drebley) situated on the straight side of the D. The walls which originally enclosed the vaccary form the base of many present day, rebuilt walls. These can be identified by the large boulders, derived from original field clearance which have been placed along the base of the walls on wide, raised platforms. Some of the boulders, being upright, are known as orthostats. These walls have a 'battered' or tapering profile, and they

---

196 Dawson, W. H., *The History of Skipton,* 1882, Edmondson and Co., Skipton.
197 Kershaw, *The Economy of a Northern Priory 1286-1325*, 1973, Oxford.

usually pursue a sinuous line around field boundaries, sometimes as a reversed S, possibly following the ploughed curve of a medieval cultivation terrace.

Gamsworth Field, as shown on Oddie's map, has an unfailing supply of water from a line of springs which issue from the hillside just below the Lodge. These springs are marked on later ordnance survey maps as Ashwood, Old Laithe, Pismire, Stackwood and Margaret Well. The flow of water is facilitated through low openings covered by stone lintels at the base of some walls.

After the dissolution of the priory at Bolton Abbey, the vaccaries became single farmsteads, wherein many of the walls of the medieval enclosures have survived, the lodge keeper having been superseded by a tenant farmer. Their early boundaries can be found by tracing those walls and earthworks displaying features associated with early clearings, and comparing them with present-day walls and maps dating broadly, on the Bolton Abbey Estate, from before the time of Parliamentary enclosures. These took place generally throughout the country between the end of the eighteenth century and the early years of the nineteenth century.

Amongst the features in the walls are sheep creeps, or cripple-holes; small openings in the walls through which sheep can pass from one field to another. In the early walls they are narrow in width, each having a noticeably smooth lintel, threshold and jambs, reflecting friction from the passage of sheep over many centuries. Sheep-creeps were set in roughly coursed stone walls, each standing on a broad, boulder base. Note how, in some cases, the lintel is perched somewhat precariously on the edge of the stones on either side of the hole. Insertion of probes in search of the width of the firm base-stone confirmed that the opening was originally quite narrow, when the lintel would have been securely supported on side-jambs. (A local farmer volunteered the information that a Swaledale tup had recently become wedged in one of these creeps, thus confirming that the opening had not been originally designed for large, twentieth century breeds.)

The next photograph shows another early opening, resting on a large field boulder, and now partly obscured by the growth of a tree. This type of sheep-creep, as an indication of the antiquity of a wall, can be seen only in walls surrounding early enclosures, such as those at Gamsworth and those bordering Grape Lane at High Gamsworth (Moorgaire).

Whilst considering early boundaries round Gamsworth, an exceptionally large boulder or free-standing orthostat stands alone in the far corner of the field above Grape Lane, along which there are other boulder walls. It is suggested that this area has long been cultivated and that Grape Lane formed part of a medieval routeway to the vaccary at Broadshaw and to the woodland pasture at Laund, near Bolton Abbey.

In contrast, the drinking trough shown in this photograph is one of several such troughs which have been placed in nineteenth century walls; there is a broad, well-supported lintel over a wide opening through which cattle and sheep from adjoining fields could reach the water. This is not, of course, a sheep-creep.

**Folklore**

Local tradition has it that in 1644, during the Civil War, Prince Rupert and his cavalry encamped on Gamsworth Field before attempting to turn Skipton into his base. This took place before the debacle of the Battle of Marston Moor. The men and horses 'foiled' the field, which was at that time full of standing corn.[198]

However, another report has it that Prince Rupert encamped in a field of ripe corn at Bolton Bridge, for an entry in the Skipton Castle accounts records the following:

Bolton, 12 July 1614, Agreed with Richard Barnvis for all that piece of ground called Hambilton, as it now putteth out to be eaten and foiled by the prince's horses as they passed through this country etc. £20.[199]

The trampling and destruction of the corn was thought to have been emblematic of the fall during battle which awaited the soldiers of that impetuous commander.[200]

---

198 Spence, Richard, *Skipton Castle in the Greta Civil War 1642-1645*, Otley: Smith Settle, 1991.
199 Dawson, W. H., *History of Skipton,* London: Skipton: Edmondson and Co., 1882.
200 Spence, R.

# GAMSWORTH

## Flooding

Gamsworth Field is an ancient enclosure, the name 'field' being derived from the Old English *feld* pertaining to open country, later divided for cultivation.[201] It is shown on Matthew Oddie's map of 1779 and again on Ordnance Survey maps dating from 1853 onwards.

This area will have always presented problems for husbandry of crops and animals because of frequent and severe flooding of the Wharfe and poor drainage from areas surrounding the line of springs. The revetting of the river banks in the photographs shows how man has endeavoured to control the river in spate, and thus to preserve the fertility of his land and the safety of his grazing animals. Careful inspection of lengths of the river bank along Gamsworth Field show where huge boulders have been manoeuvred into functional positions to stabilise the bank. These boulders may have come from the medieval quarry in Little Close, by Margaret Well. This quarry underlies the wall shown on Oddie's map, suggesting that the boulders were hewn at an early date, before Gamsworth Field was first enclosed. In contrast, further, recent revetting has been carried out, using stone, cement and concrete re-enforced with iron, as shown in the photographs.

The present farmer said that in his lifetime many of the nineteenth century walls in the flood areas of Gamsworth Field had collapsed due to the continual force of the river in spate over a period of a century or more since they were originally built. During the 1970s he had rebuilt many of them. At intervals, in two of the cross walls, he has restored the large square openings, through which water could pass without bringing down the wall, see photographs on next page. These are comparable with those smaller medieval openings already described,

---

201 Smith, A. H., *The Place Names of the West Riding of Yorkshire*, Vol. XXXVI, Part seven, Cambridge University Press, Cambridge.

through which spring water flows from one field to another). Where possible original stones and lintels have been used, although some have been replaced with improvised materials, some timber lintels coming from the now demolished barn at Low Laithe. These openings are not to be confused with 'cripple holes for sheep', being altogether taller and broader.

The original cast iron grids are still operating, to prevent sheep from straying between the fields. However, the farmer pointed out that these grids could collect so much debris that they impeded the passage of the water and thus could cause more damage to the walls.

**Holmes of Gamsworth**

Amongst the earliest surviving Barden leases[202] is one dated 1602, when William Hoames, Yeoman of Barden, held a messuage and tenement (not named). His sons were named James and Ingram.

In 1603 Lyonel Holmes and his wife Isabel paid rent for a tenement at Gamsworth. Their sons were William, Henry and Lyonel. The following year a lease for a messuage and tenement contains the first known reference to the corn mill at Hough as being newly built or hereafter to be erected within the manor.[203]

The family name for the leaseholders of Gamsworth was Holmes. The name of Holmes also appears on leases for Drebley, from 1641 onwards until 1929, but there appear to have been no links between the two branches of what would have originally been the same family. There were only two similarities in the use of Christian names, for those at Drebley were Humfrey, Gershom, Ingram, Henry, Jacob, whereas those most frequently used at Gamsworth were Lyonel, William and Henry, James and Ingram.

---

[202] Barden leases at the Y.A.S., Skipton, MSS DD187/77
[203] ibid.

# GAMSWORTH

*The photograph above of Gamsworth and High Gamsworth Cottage from Club Nook by John Sheard, shows:*
- *The situation of Gamsworth on a terrace above the flood plane of the river Wharfe.*
- *The cottage and enclosures around High Gamsworth which may have originated as the Lodge of Moorgaire*
- *Gamsworth Field lying between the farmstead and the river.*
- *The ancient walled lane connecting Gamsworth and High Gamsworth*
- *The walled roadway which superseded the old packhorse way and the Skipton to Pateley Trust road, following a line parallel to the river between Watergate and Hough Mill*
- *The nineteenth century cottages of Wharfe View and Wood View (on the left)*

    Another lease dates from 1624, when Lionel and Ann Holmes leased Gamsworth; their four-poster bedstead with its panelled oak headboard on which was carved ALH 1624, and on the reverse, the date 1647[204] remained for generations as a prized possession within the family. This oak board was eventually made into the lid of a needlework box, the sides of which bore the initials of its owner, Jane Holmes, and the date 1881.

    In the late eighteenth century, another Lionel Holmes, who had acquired a fair knowledge of Latin, set up a school at Gamsworth for children of nearby farms, and also for children of both sexes working at the cotton mill in Skyreholme. The following is from *The Craven Herald and Wensleydale Standard*, December 1919:

> The original house at Gamsworth was a single storey, thatched structure with a farm building attached to one end. By the middle of the eighteenth century, when Lionel Holmes lived there, it was fast falling into decay. The 'high parlour' was then removed altogether, another storey was added, and the roof slated. This did not meet with the approval of the owner, the Countess

---

[204] Whitley family papers.

Dowager of Burlington, who required it to conform with other houses in the vicinity, so Lionel thatched it on top of the slates (see full account in the above newspaper). In the time of John Holmes the thatch began to decay and fall off, so it was removed altogether. The present house is the original one that Lionel built, with later additions of barns and outbuildings.

At least two headstones in the churchyard at Bolton Abbey commemorate members of the Holmes family:
    Lionel Holmes of Barden 1777-1858 and Mary Holmes 1782-1872
    John Holmes of Gamsworth 1824-78 and Jane Holmes 1826-1914
(Note: it was probably Lionel and his son John who were the thatchers mentioned in the above newspaper report).

Jane, daughter of John Holmes and Jane (née Hustwick of Beamsley) married William Whiteley of Menston and Pool, and through her descendants there are many more records and memorabilia, now in possession of the Whiteley family.

## A group of nineteenth century estate cottages

It was not until the Victorian period that forestry and the pursuit of game as a major sport were introduced to the Bolton Abbey estate, and it was then that the need arose to house those workers and their families who were employed as foresters or gamekeepers. Labour was cheap, and wages were low, and it was necessary to provide smallholdings attached to each of these cottages, where subsistence farming and the cultivation of soft fruit and vegetables could be carried out to support the families.

During the mid-nineteenth century four such cottages were built along the roadside, (formerly the Skipton and Pateley Bridge Trust Road) between Watergate and Hough Mill; they were High Gamsworth, Ivy Cottage for the gamekeeper, Wharfe View and Wood View. Unlike the established farmsteads which had evolved on the sites of ancient Forest Lodges, three of these cottages were built on sites where there had been no previous settlement,[205] High Gamsworth being the

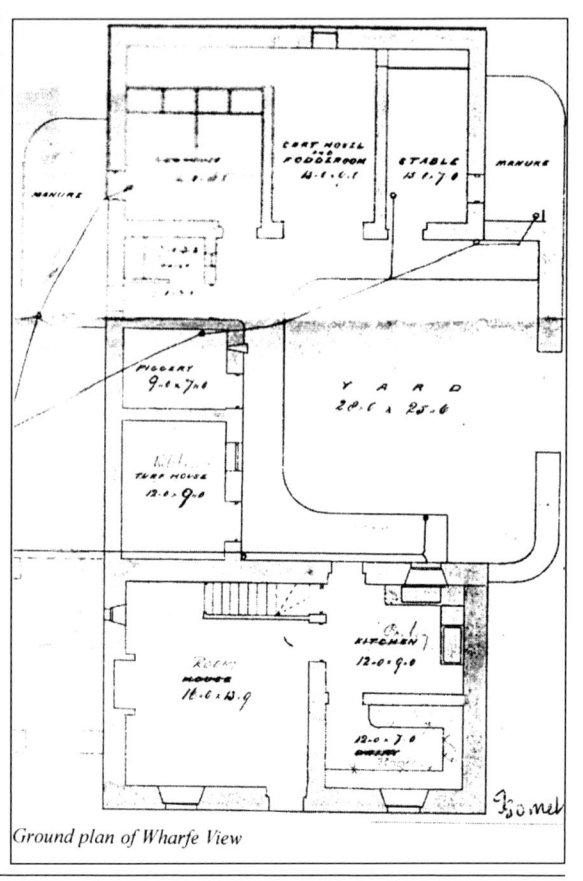

*Ground plan of Wharfe View*

[205] The map dated 1778 show outlines of un-named barns, but not dwellings on the sites where the nineteenth century cottages were built.

# GAMSWORTH

*Isometrical elevation of Wharfe View.*

*Above Wharfe View and below High Gamsworth.*

exception. In each case, a small acreage of land was taken from the farms of Gamsworth and Howgill, although the situation of the new holdings, squeezed between the edge of the thoroughfare and the valuable pasturage of the farmland, suggests that the loss of land to the tenants of those farms would have been minimal.

The style of these well-built cottages and their associated out-buildings is recognisable as mid-nineteenth century estate vernacular, although each is different in size and plan. Wood View and Wharfe View lie on opposite sides of the road, overlooking Howgill, Hough Mill and the river Wharfe as it flows through its rocky channel above the Drebley stepping stones. Drawings survive for Wharfe View dated 30 May 1862, when isometric drawings and plans for its outbuildings were drawn up for a named employee, George Holmes, who may have already been living in one of the earlier tenements built on that site.[206]

As might be expected, Ivy Cottage, for the keeper, has no pasturage, and apart from a small building where dogs would whelp and be kennelled, no provision was made for the storage of hay or a cart; neither is there a stable, nor an outbuilding where a cow might have been milked. It is evident that a gamekeeper's job was full time, and that his wages would not have supported the upkeep of a horse or a cow. There is, however, a good-sized garden and

---

206 Shown on first edition Ordnance Survey map dated 1853.

a garth in which pheasants and other game birds could be reared.

The cottage at High Gamsworth dates from the eighteenth century, although its stable yard and outbuildings are of the same period as the other three cottages.[207] For several generations it was the home of a branch of the Ideson family, who came from Old House in Howgill.

HOUGH MILL, BARDEN

---

207 The ancient site of Gamsworth Farm and the boundaries of a medieval vaccary can be detected by studying the history of Barden and the field walls; it is likely that there has long been a dwelling, known as Moorgarth on the site of High Gamsworth cottage.

**Hough/Haugh Mill, Barden** by Heather M. Beaumont

The earliest documentary references to Hough Mill which have so far come to light make it clear that it was the manorial corn mill for Barden and that tenants were obliged to have their corn ground there.

(i) For example, a lease dated 6 December 1604, granted by George, third earl of Cumberland, to William Holmes of Barden, yeoman, for a messuage and tenement situate at Howgill at Barden[1] (yearly rent of 8s.5d.) includes the following conditions:

> suit to [the] manor court of Barden twice yearly; also to, grind corn spent upon the premises at the mill of the earl either already built or hereafter to be erected within the manor.

Perhaps the wording suggests that this mill was the first manorial mill in Barden, coming with the change in management pattern, away from that of a Forest (i.e. with grazing on wood pasture for deer and domestic stock, managed by the officers of the Forest from six lodges), to the granting of tenancies and the development of arable cultivation.

(ii) A lease dated 8 May 1606 was granted by Francis, fourth earl of Cumberland, to William Lightfoot of Howgill in Barden, shoemaker.[2] For a 21 year lease he is to pay £30 'in the name of a fine' (i.e. an entry fine, payable by the tenant on any change in ownership, in this instance following the death of the third earl of Cumberland and accession of his brother), plus an annual rent of 9s.6¼d. for: 'all that water corn Mill called Hough Mill in Barden.' The obligations of manorial tenants, and the benefits to be received by the miller are then spelt out:

> …and all the suit, soken[3] mullase toll[4] service and boons of the tenants and farmers[5] within the Forest of Barden and elsewhere, to the said mill belonging and due.

The lease continues… 'all the dams, watercourses, flood hatches, etc.' The wording may indicate that the water supply to the mill was engineered and controlled or, alternatively, may simply repeat a formulaic convention.

(iii) An entry in the diary of Lady Anne Clifford (1660)[6] reads as follows:

> Towards the latter end of this summer I caused my Mill about a mile from Barden Towre in Yorkshire called Hough's Mill to be pulled downe and newbuilt up againe with stone and wood at my owne charge, for it was so ruinous as it was like to fall downe, having not bin repair'd many years before till now.

(iv) Richard Boyle, second earl of Cork and first earl of Burlington (1612-98) acquired part of the Skipton/Bolton Abbey estate following his marriage in 1634 to Elizabeth Clifford, daughter of the fifth earl of Cumberland. He did not acquire Barden until after the death of Lady Anne Clifford in 1676 and the ending of a long ownership dispute.

---

1 Yorkshire Archaeological Society, Skipton MSS, DD 187/7.
2 ibid
3 The tenant's obligation and payment to grind his corn at the Lord's mill ( Richardson, *The Local Historian's Encyclopaedia* (1986, New Barnet).
4 Money paid to a miller for grinding corn (ibid).
5 Service in kind or labour (ibid).
6 D J H Clifford, editor, 1990, Stroud, p.147.

## BARDEN IN WHARFEDALE, THE PLACE AND ITS PEOPLE

From a list of the earl of Burlington's rentals compiled for 1687: 'Hough Mill lett to John Pagett for three years from ye 21th March [or 25th Lady Day?] 1686 at ye yearly rent of £9.10s.0d.' By this time entry fines had been abolished, the term of the lease shortened, and the annual rent increased.

(v) The first earl of Burlington was succeeded by his second son, Charles (1666-1704) and then his grandson Richard (1694-1753) who inherited when only ten years old; his mother, the dowager countess Juliana (1672-1750) acted as guardian to the young heir and held Barden and part of Bolton as her jointure. New leases for her 31 tenants in Barden were prepared in 1716/17,[7] two years after the third earl came of age. This series of new leases is an early indication of the third earl's firm management of the estate at Barden, initially on behalf of his mother the countess.

On 2 May 1716, 22 Barden tenants signed a consent… 'that James Ward shall continue to farme the mill belonging to the Right Honourable Countess of Burlington…' This document, and the provisions of the agreement or lease, illustrate the arrangements under which the manorial mill operated, allowing the miller to charge dues to tenants for grinding their corn, but also protecting the tenants against extortion.

The agreement, dated 17 July 1717, is:

> between Joseph Waite Gent [agent] for and on behalf of the Rt. Hon. Juliana, Countess of Burlington… and James Ward, miller. [It concerns] All that water Corn Mill called Hough Mill… In Barden together with all ye Soke Suit Toll Moulter [Multure] dues and customs thereto belonging or therewith used and in the same manner as John Padgett… deceased held and enjoyed. And all Ways, Waters, Watercourses, Libertys, Proffits, Comodities, damms, floodgates, easements and appurtenances… belonging.

A cottage was also leased to James Ward, presumably for his accommodation. The lease is for seven years at an annual rent of £9.10s.6d., to be paid in equal portions on Lady Day and at Michaelmas. The tenant is responsible for the payment of any taxes imposed upon either the mill or the rent, and is bound to perform the prescribed services and duties. He is to:

> … sufficiently repair, maintain and amend and keep the water corn mill, dams, floodgates and all the houghs [?], working geere, utinsils and appurtenances… thereto belonging (the … Countess and her assigns are to find Milstones and Wood and repair ye Water wheel when… required.

The agreement also empowers the countess or her agent to repossess the premises if James Ward fails to pay the rent within 28 days of the due date, if he assigns the mill to another person without obtaining consent, or it he 'do unjustly wilfully and wrongfully… [take] Toll dues or moulter more than due,' or if in grinding the corn he causes loss or damage to the owners.

James Ward binds himself to fulfill 'all and Singular Covenants' in the sum of £270. The agreement is signed by J. Waite and James Ward, and witnessed by Anthon Young (a tenant in Bolton) and W. Currer (solicitor?).

(vi) In 1728 a survey of the Lordship of Barden was made by Ed. Beckwith. This

---

7 Box J., Third Earl of Burlington, Craven Estates, Barden Agreements, 1716/17, Chatsworth MSS.

comprised a listing of all the tenants and their holdings, including the names of fields, acreages and quality (e.g. good land; rushy, wet and spongy land; over-run with underwood, etc); Howgill Mill was in hand and untenanted. The survey was accompanied by a map (1730) which shows Hough Mill with its water wheel; the goit is also shown, in the position where it can be identified today, as a stone-covered channel.

(vii) Entries in the account book of Juliana, Countess Dowager of Burlington, referring to her Joynture Estate in Barden, show that in 1728 James Ward was still tenant of Hough Mill, and that in 1728-30 the drying kiln at the mill was rebuilt, following a fire. Disbursements were as follows:

November 1728
John Simpson [the tenant at Barden Tower] for the carriage of a millstone from Bolton to the Hough mill.
John Harper for 10 guage of slate for repairing that part of the new Killn in Barden which was burnt.
Thomas Killham was paid for hair cloth and thread and for slating that part of the new killn which was burnt.
Peter Demaine – paid for four days ffleighting [slating?] at the new kiln.
James Ward – for slate.
Laurence and John Holden, carpenters.
John Demaine, mason.
Payment was also made for fixing the Spindle Hock and Trundle Loads at Hough Mill, for new rope and thread and for carpentry for that which was burnt up.

In 1729 George Thompson was paid for supplying ale to the workmen when the new roof of the kiln which was burnt was laid up. Payment was made in 1730 to the following workmen:

John Read – for graving and drying ten cartsful of peat for the new mill.
William Hebden – for work done at the new mill.
Joshua Breare – for mason work done at Hough Mill.
John Simpson – for leading ten cartsful of peat for the new kill(n).
John Holden, carpenter – for work done at the new kill(n).
William Hustwick and partners – for mason work at the newhouse built out of the old kill(n) in Barden. [Note: this would seem to provide a date for the building of a house attached to the mill.]
Edward Demaine – for taking off the thatch and removing the walls of the old kill(n) and getting 95 cartloads of stone for the new house.
Thomas Killham – ? yards of hair cloth for the new kill(n) in Barden.

(viii) New seven year leases were prepared for Barden tenants in 1738 and 1745, with another agreement that James Ward may continue as miller. Lady Juliana died in 1750, when Barden properties 'reverted' to the third earl of Burlington.

(ix) In 1753, on the death of the third earl of Burlington, Barden and the rest of the Bolton Abbey estate passed to the Cavendish family, through the marriage of Charlotte Elizabeth Boyle to William, Marquis of Hartington, who became the fourth Duke of Devonshire. A rental of 1776 shows Hough Mill held by Francis Ward at £22.5s.0d.

(x) A report on Hough Mill, dated 20 May 1797, prepared by Richard Atkinson and addressed to Mr James Collins, Knaresborough (agent to the fifth Duke of Devonshire) reads:

> Part of the walls are bulged in several places, all the slating is very bad and must be stripped and part of the roof repaired. All the floors are so bad as to require new ones. All the wheels about the mill ought to be new if effectually done. The walls of the kiln are very good but the slating is bad and full of soot with drying with seeds. He wants the kiln new lathing and covering with pot tiles that he may dry with cinders. I am afraid the whole will cost a great sum…

(xi) A valuation of 1806 suggests that some refurbishment had been carried out:

> Hough Mill and drying kiln slated, in midling repair, with the land between the mill goit and the stream below. Corn Mill near the road, with a constant supply of water.[8] The blue stones and machine for dressing flour has been put up by the tenant [Francis Ward].

In a rental of 1860 Hough Mill is described as: 'lately rebuilt with a drying kiln, garden and yard between the goit and the stream, £15.'

(xii) Plans and elevations dated 1862[9] show the house with mill and drying kiln attached, and a new extension comprising kitchen, dairy, turf house, etc. Other plans dated 1865 show new farm buildings, courtyard style, separate and to the west of the house/mill complex.

(xiii) A rental of 1867 names the tenant as Thomas Ward Almack:

> Small farmhouse, recently repaired, with water corn mill attached with two pairs of stones; of little value owing to the small quantity of corn grown in the neighbourhood. Water wheel machinery belongs to the tenant. Buildings for saw mill erected but not yet completed. Farm buildings new. Saw mill not included in the valuation, (land 23 acres 3 roods 25 perches; rent £32).

By this date improvements in transport, including the railway which had reached Skipton, probably meant that corn and flour were brought in, and the growth of cereals (always problematic) had virtually come to an end. The change in function from corn mill to sawmill was typical of both area and period (e.g. Hartlington, Burnsall[10]).

(xiv) Hough Mill ceased operation in 1889 when dams supplying mills in Skyreholme broke, presumably disrupting the water supply lower down the valley. The two dams, above and below Trollers Gill, had been constructed in 1830-34 to serve two textile mills; after 1868 the mills were converted to the manufacture of paper/board.

**Water Supply to the Mill** researched by Les Bloom (UWFS) and Heather Beaumont (also incorporating relevant information from the survey of the mill (and kiln) from the survey report prepared by Arnold Pacey).

Documents providing information about the watercourse are:

(i) Estate maps, i.e. the 1778 copy by William Oddie of the 1730/1 original by Ed. Beckwith; the latter is to be checked to ensure that the later version is a true copy in respect of details pertaining to the mill.

(ii) Ordnance Survey six inch map dated 1896.

---

8 Confirmation of the relative positions of the goit and mill building.
9 Bolton MSS., Barden, Chatsworth collection.
10 H. Clark, 'Waterwheels and Mills in mid-Wharfedale', *The Dalesman*, Vol. 32, 1970, pp222-7.

# HOUGH MILL

Field observations were made on the current status of the watercourse, and any surviving features; oral evidence was obtained from Mr Donald Holme, present tenant of Hough Mill Farm.

## Eighteenth century map(s)

As already recorded, accounts for the years 1728-30 refer to repairs to 'that part of the new killn in Barden which was burnt' including re-roofing in slate; there are also records of work done 'at the new mill', and 'the Newhous built out of the old kill(n)'. Beckwith's map was therefore drawn up during a transitional phase: the mill is shown in what is probably its original position, immediately beside How Beck; Arnold Pacey believes that the site is marked by a pile of tumbled stone. The mill is shown to the west of a building lying adjacent to the road, the latter representing the site of the kiln and new house (for which 95 cartloads of stone were brought) – although the fact that there is no separate drawing to represent the house suggests it was incomplete when the original map was made.

The mill is drawn with its water wheel lying above How Beck which – as already indicated – might seem to suggest that it was directly driven by the water of the beck itself. However, a more plausible interpretation is provided by Arnold Pacey, who points out that the 1778 map also shows the mill leat passing to the north of the roadside building, with several feet between leat and building, the leat continuing to the mill building depicted on the map. Pacey offers two possible interpretations of the documentary evidence: firstly that within two years of the drying kiln being repaired the mill was rebuilt alongside it and the house; or, alternatively, the mill building referred to in the report dated 1797 was the mill on the old site, and it was rebuilt adjacent to the kiln and house between that date and 1806. From his interior survey of the surviving mill building, Pacey concluded that most of the masonry from the old mill had been reused, including the stonework of doors and windows, some of it seventeenth century (perhaps from the rebuild by Lady Anne Clifford).

## Ordnance Survey map, 1896, field observations and oral history

Marked on the map to the east of Haugh Saw Mill are 'mill race, aqueduct, sluice and weir'. The weir is shown on How Beck, just above its confluence with the larger Fir Beck. The weir apparently lay between two flat-topped mounds or hillocks which slope steeply down towards the two becks, with the How Beck flowing in a narrow gulley between them. The hillocks are probably composed chiefly of water-deposited gravels and stones, similar to others in the area (e.g. on the west bank of the Wharfe across the stepping stones leading to Drebley hamlet, and in the area between Stangs Lathe and Balker's Dub, on the west side of Fir Beck (field observations by Drs. David and Beryl Turner). It may be that the natural slopes of the two hillocks on either side of How Beck were enhanced, but the volume of water impounded must have been small, otherwise Crossfield House (seventeenth century?) would have been subject to flooding. On the day of our inspection the water levels in the becks were low following a dry spell, and it is likely that the flow in How Beck is lower now than it would have been when the mill was operational, due to afforestation on the lower slopes of Simon's Seat, where the beck rises.

We thought we could define the origin of the leat, in the bank on the western limb of a loop in the course of the beck, below the confluence; this seems to correspond to the position of the sluice marked on the map. However tree growth was such, it was impossible to confirm this, e.g. by the identification of any stone surround. The short section of aqueduct marked on the map has apparently disappeared, the area where it is shown on the map being occupied by a modern bungalow. Field boundaries have changed (cf the 1730/1778 maps) and now border the narrow lane; thus the leat can be traced running just inside the wall of the field named Holm; where it runs under the lane and into the field numbered 137v on the map (part of Mill Flatts?) it is culverted, and the covering of stone slabs are very obvious. We did not attempt to lift a slab, but prodding into the cavity confirmed the presence of a stone-lined channel about eighteen inches square. Mr D. Holme, the present day tenant of Hough Mill Farm, confirmed the existence of a similar culvert under the road and now covered by tarmac; he said that as a child he was tempted to squeeze through it. The line across the field linking the two culverted sections of the mill race is suggested by the dampness of the soil and rushes in the vegetation.

Mr Holmes also confirmed the considerable depth of the wheel pit, and the fact that the axle of the mill wheel passed between the first level of the mill building, in a basement, which also housed machinery (see the longitudinal section drawn by Arnold Pacey). Mr Holmes emphasised that both wheel pit and basement had been filled, in the interests of safety. It is very satisfying that Arnold Pacey was able to locate the opening of the tail race into How Beck.

**Conclusions**

Such evidence as we have concerning the water supply to Hough Mill suggests that the system was a simple one. It is possible that the weir across How Beck was primarily to prevent back-flow and flooding when there was a rise in water level in the Fir Beck (with its extensive catchment from Blands Beck and Skyreholme Beck), although water impounded behind the weir on How Beck may have been useful in times of shortage. The sluice marked on the map probably controlled entry into the leat which, perhaps, avoided the need for an overflow channel, as suggested by Arnold Pacey.

Mr Pacey's suggestions regarding the supply of water power, and the fall of the leat from the point where it crosses the lane (east of the mill) are interesting and helpful; the levels between the supply from the beck(s) and the commencement of the leat (and aqueduct?) have not been measured, and seem – from field observations so far – somewhat problematical.

At the present time we have nothing to add to Arnold Pacey's consideration of the size of the wheel, the level at which the water was fed, and whether it was breast-shot or back-shot. Further documentary studies are planned to obtain data on the acreage of arable land in Barden at different dates in the eighteenth and nineteenth centuries, to confirm the impression that there was a fall in the amount of corn grown, and to see how this relates to the development and decline of the mill. It is planned that data from the mill at Bolton will also be collected for comparison.

# HOUGH MILL

**Hough Mill, Barden** (map reference: SE 059592)
An eighteenth century estate map showing the earlier site of the mill, a little below the present tail-race discharge point on Howgill Beck. Reproduced courtesy of the Chatsworth Estate (Bolton Archive).

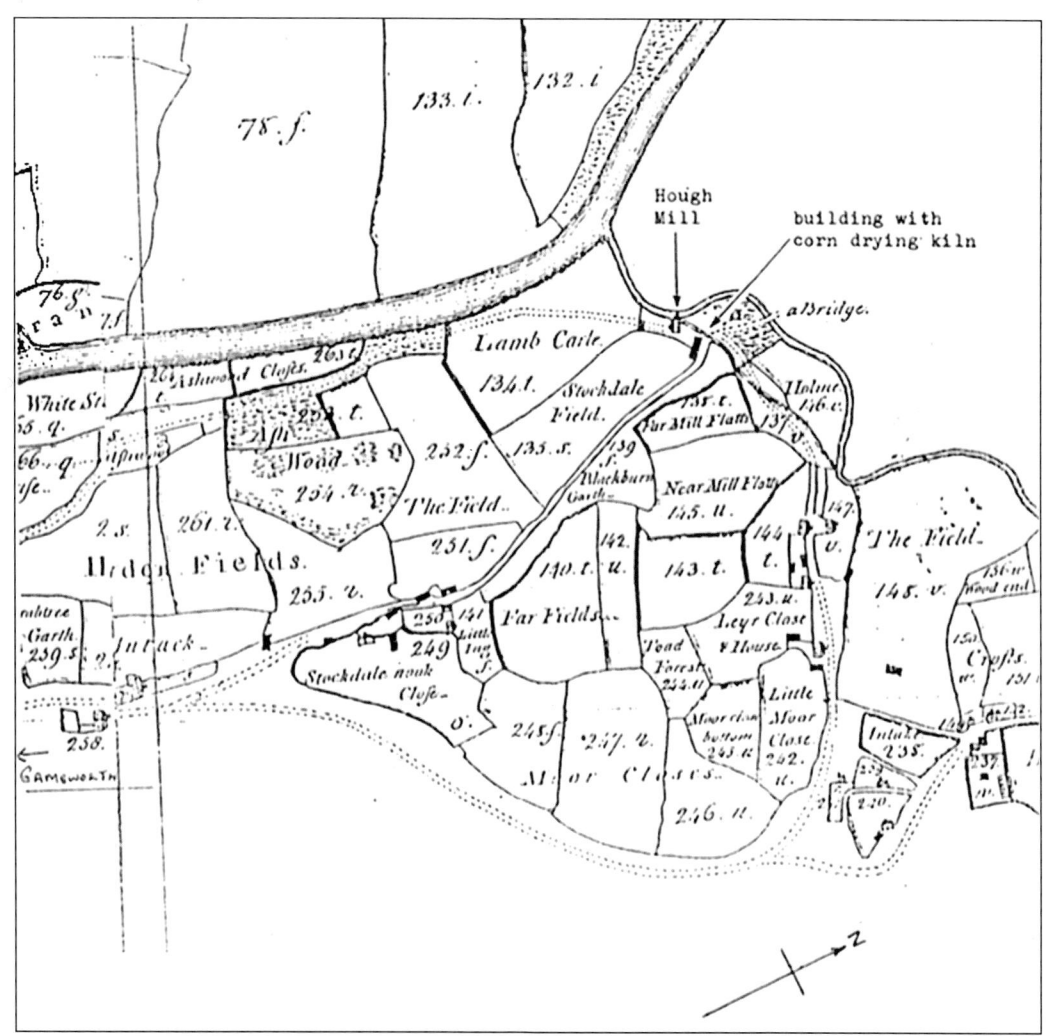

**Thoughts on the mechanical engineering of Haugh Mill, Barden**
by Les Bloom

The celebrated paper 'An experimental enquiry concerning the natural powers of water and wind to turn mills, and other machines, depending on a circular motion' given by John Smeaton to the Royal Society in 1759 and published in 1760 is clearly what Arnold Pacey refers to in his scholarly report and drawings. Les Bloom thought he should look at the mill machinery with Smeaton's 'hat on'.

Based on Arnold Pacey's report and drawings there are two limiting factors:
(i) The water wheel could only be say 15 feet in diameter (breast-shot for my money).

(ii) The spur wheel could only be say 5 feet in diameter (recess in north wall).

Moving on to Smeaton's guide lines and millwrights' rules of thumb there are three more limiting factors:

1) The peripheral velocity of the wheel should be between three and five and a half feet per second.

2) To determine the optimum speed of flour grindstones, the trick was to divide 5,000 by the stone diameter in inches to give the revolutions per minute.

3) The ratio of the 'speed step up' of the pit wheel to wallower should be between 2.5 and 3.5 to 1.

Taking careful note of Arnold Pacey's drawings which are to scale where appropriate and working within the above parameters, the following possible design evolved:

a) Water wheel 15 feet diameter operating at six rpm would have a peripheral speed of

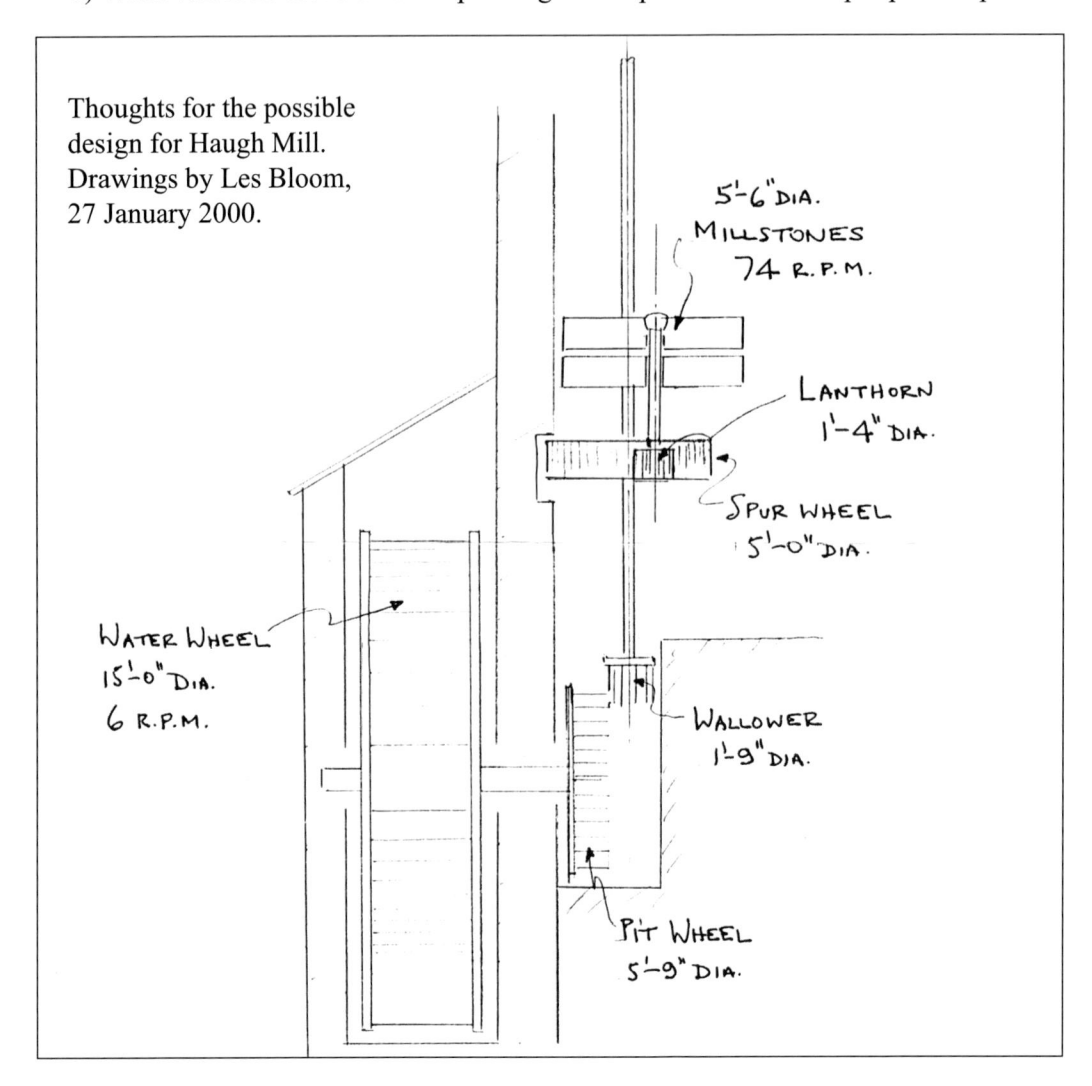

Thoughts for the possible design for Haugh Mill. Drawings by Les Bloom, 27 January 2000.

# HOUGH MILL

4.71 feet per second (i and 1 above).

b) Pit wheel 5 feet 9 inches diameter and wallower 1 foot 9 inches diameter = ratio 3.285 (3 above).

c) Spur wheel 5 feet diameter (ii above) lanthorn 1 foot 4 inches diameter = ratio 3.75.

d) Therefore speed of the 5 foot 6 inches diameter millstone would be:

6 rpm x 3.285 x 3.75 = 73.96 rpm (which is just less than the 5,000 divided by 66 inches = 75.75 rpm as it should be – see 2 above).

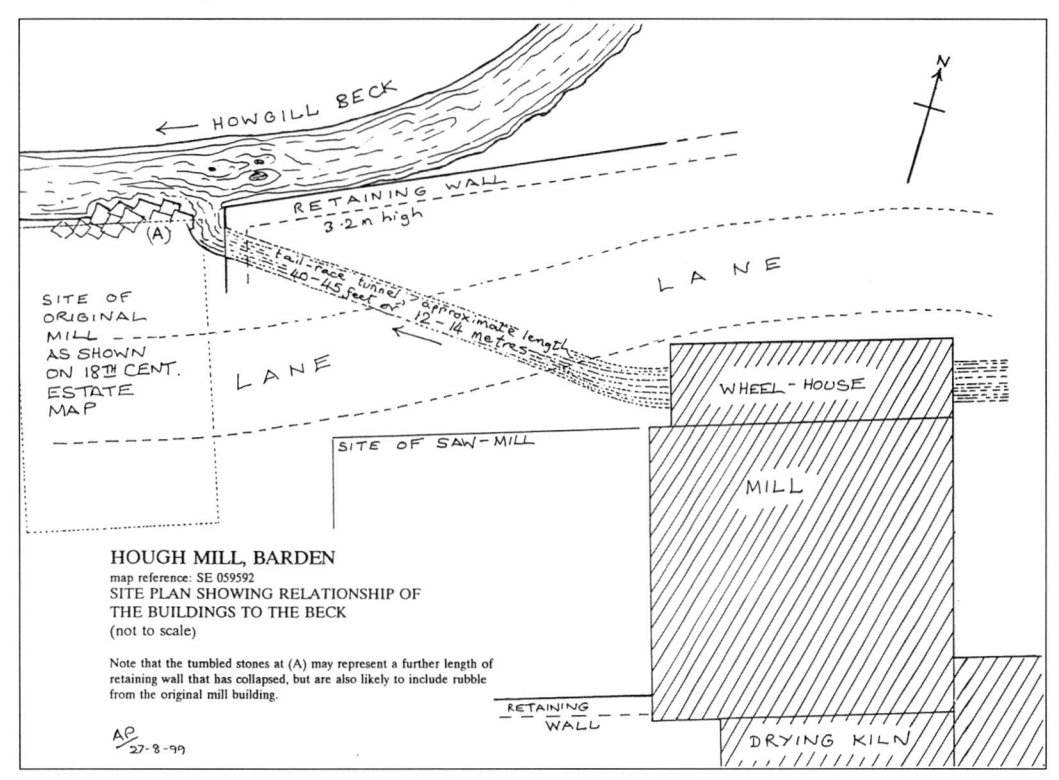

**HOUGH MILL, BARDEN**
map reference: SE 059592
SITE PLAN SHOWING RELATIONSHIP OF
THE BUILDINGS TO THE BECK
(not to scale)

Note that the tumbled stones at (A) may represent a further length of retaining wall that has collapsed, but are also likely to include rubble from the original mill building.

AP 27-8-99

## Description of site

Hough Mill is located on a steep, north-facing slope that has been formed into steps or terraces above Howgill Beck by a series of retaining walls. The lowest of these retainign walls rises 3.2 metres from the dry-weather water level in Howgill Beck to form a wide terrace on which stands the former mill building, with a land passing between its north end and the beck. The tail-race from the mill passes under the lane in a tunnel which opens to the beck under a lintel set low in an angle in the terrace wall (see site plan above).

The existing ground floor in the mill is a little higher than ground level in the lane, and a careful estimate is that the floor level is close to four metres above dry-weather water level in the beck. I shall refer to this as Level 1, since the term 'ground floor' could be confused with ground-floor levels in other buildings on the site. The mill building butts onto a second retaining wall on which stands the former corn-drying kiln. This has two floors: one from which the kiln was fired (called Level 2 in these notes), and the other corresponding to the actual drying floor, now used as a garage (Level 3).

This top level of the site corresponds to ground-floor level in the adjoining house, and is again formed by a retaining wall, with some excavation on the south side of the house necessary to form a level site. At almost no point, therefore, are the buildings seen on a natural ground surface. Some stand on excavated ground, and others rise from a back-filled surface behind retaining walls, with necessarily deep foundations.

The north end of the mill is located in a back-filled area, and it is probable that a deep wheel-pit could be formed there with relatively little excavation by building up the walls from the underlying rock, then back-filling around them to create an evenly graded surface for the lane.

**Description of building exterior**
The buildings are of coursed rubble stone with dressed quoins and window and door openings of varying styles and dates, some of them seeming out of context. Door openings in the mill at Levels 1 and 2 are consistent, though, in having a very broad chamfer in each jamb (90 to 100mm). One of these doorways is a former cart entrance on the east side with a segmental arch (also chamfered).

There is a small blocked doorway on the west side with a basket-handle lintel which, with its broad chamfer, could be of late seventeenth century date, and there is a wide doorway with a modern timber lintel set rather low. Above the basket-handle lintel are two iron tie-plates which formerly secured the end of a heavy beam carrying the millstones.

Alongside the cart entrance on the east side is a small stable, more recently adapted for other livestock (and a bicycle). Door and window openings have no chamfer and appear to be nineteenth century. The stable is logically placed close to where horses would be needed for moving wagons.

The drying kiln has one very distinctive doorway on the west side. It has a flattened ogee-pattern lintel, and there is a narrow chamfer on lintel and jambs (quite different from the apparently earlier broad chamfer on other doorways). This is likely to be the work of Joshua Breare, a stone mason who is recorded as working on the site in 1730.

I leave it to others to describe the house and outbuildings, and to discuss other details, such as the apprently re-used seventeenth century window in the north gable wall of the mill. Also on the north wall of the mill is the remains of the wheel-house which seems to have had a lean-to roof whose line along the wall of the mill is clearly evident. The relatively low level of this roof confirms that the water-wheel was set low in a deep wheel-pit.

**Description of building interior**
The mill machinery has been removed and part of the Level 1 ground floor has been used for livestock, with a loose box and manger along the north wall. In the south-west corner is a small fireplace with monolithic stone jambs and a stone lintel (a 'three-stone fireplace'). This has nothing to do with the drying kiln but was presumably for the comfort of the miller. We were told that there was formerly a chimney on the corner of the building, and the plans have been drawn to show a flue in the thickness of the wall. Wall thickness throughout the mill building is consistently close to 0.6 metres (just under two feet).

The most striking feature of the south wall inside the mill is the rough stonework of the retaining wall on which the drying kiln stands, with much neater stonework from Level 2 upwards. There are straight joints (s.j. on plans) distinguishing the stonework of the kiln from that of the mill at every level. A related straight joint can be seen from inside the stable on the east side of the building. These joints show unambiguously that the drying kiln represents an earlier phase of construction to which the mill building was added.

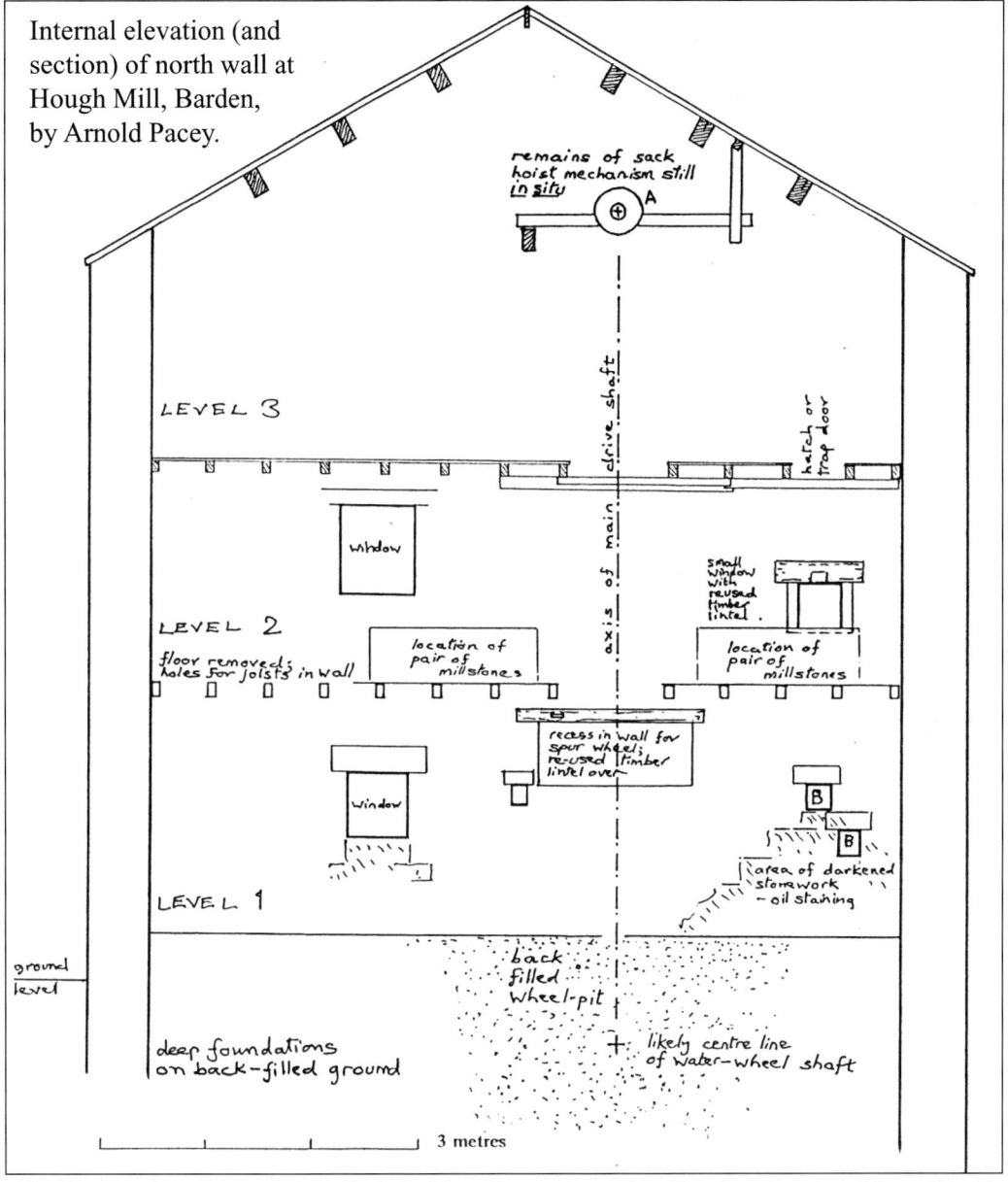

*This drawing shows a section through the building close to the north wall and an elevation of the wall itself. The location of the millstones has been reconstructed, but other features shown still exist.*
*A... is a wheel forming part of the sack-hoist mechanism, still in situ.*
*B... are two holes in the wall for a control mechanism used in cutting off or opening the supply of water to the water-wheel; the wall below seems to be stained with oil.*

## Interpretation regarding dates of construction

It was at first extremely puzzling to find this clear evidence that the mill was added to the earlier drying kiln, because it seems clear that the kiln was reconstructed in 1728-30, yet the later mill contains masonry which must be earlier than that. Some door and window detail may be seventeenth century, yet the evidence that it is in a post-1728 structure is overwhelming.

This puzzle was so niggling that I felt it necessary to revisit the site to check that I had not misinterpreted the straight joints or other evidence – but the solution came quickly when I examined the eighteenth century estate map. This maps shows what seem to be the existing buildings alongside the road, but it also shows the mill leat passing to the north of them, with a gap of several feet between the leat and the buildings. Therefore there cannot have been a water-wheel in the buildings at the time. The leat runs instead to a different building, alongside the beck some ten or twenty metres further west and it is clear that this was the watermill, i.e. in a building that was quite separate from the present drying-kiln building.

My difficulty here is that I am not sure of the date of the estate map – 1730 or 1778. If the date is 1730, then the map could have been made at a time when work had just begun on rebuilding the mill on the new site next to the kiln. Then the documents can be interpreted by saying that the drying kiln was rebuilt in 1728, and within two years the mill was being

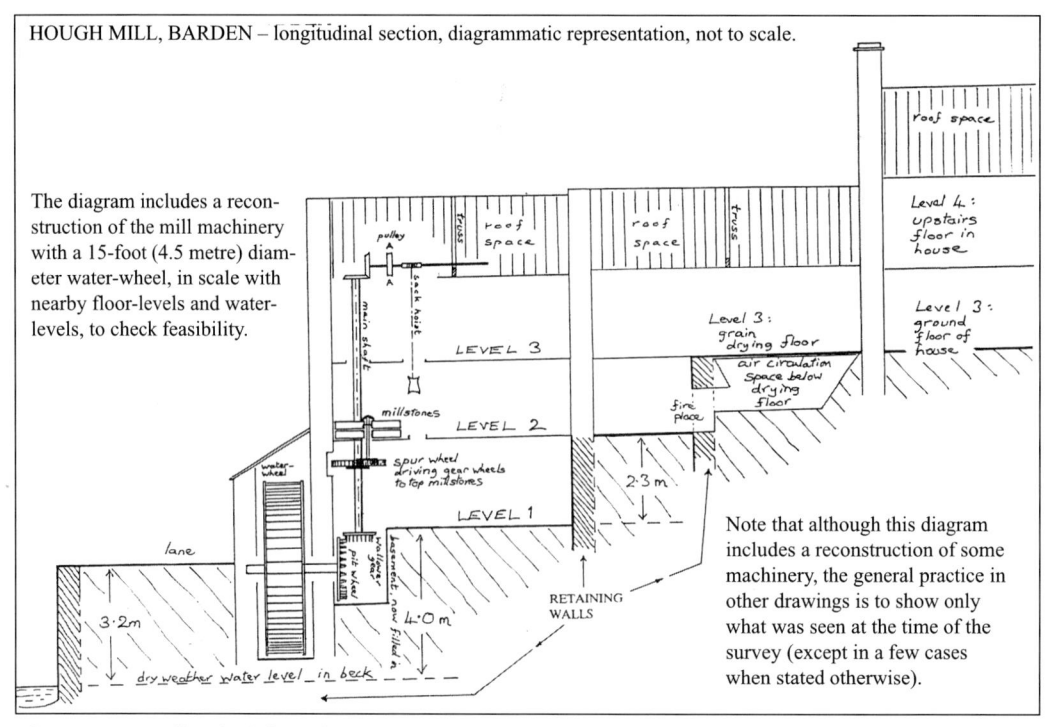

*The retaining walls which form the site into a series of steps are emphasised by close hatching, and although this is not a scale drawing, an effort has been made to represent the heights of these walls in correct proportion with the dimensions of the buildings. It is impossible to say where the original ground surface was, and hence hatching cannot be used to distinguish undisturbed from back-filled ground. Water-level in the beck is represented at lower left.*

## HOUGH MILL

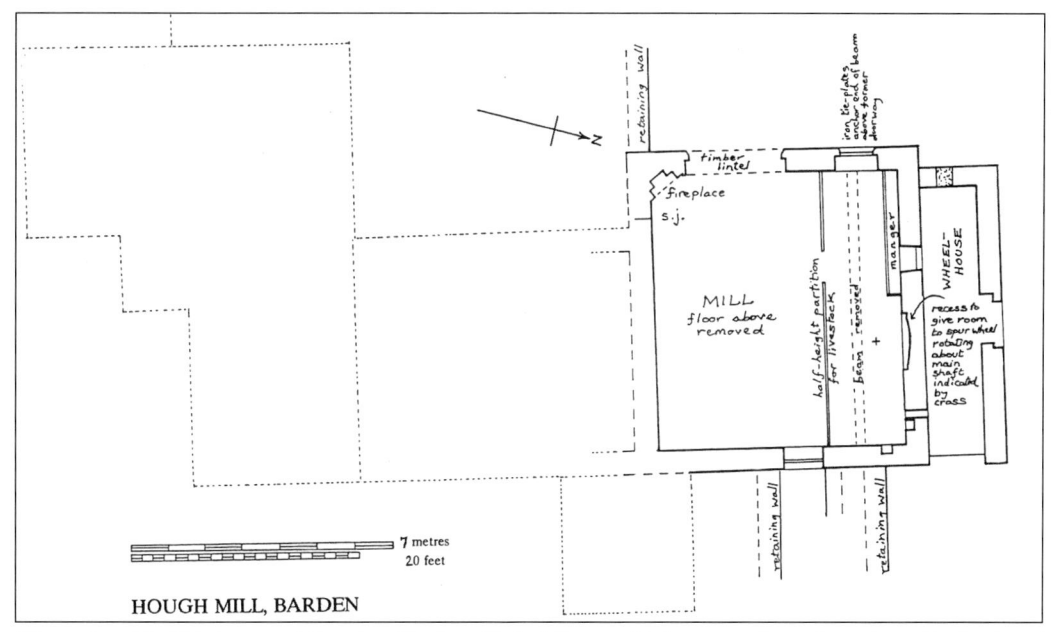

*Plan at Level 1. This is ground floor level in the mill; buildings on higher ground are shown in outline by dotted lines. The original of this drawing is to the same scale as the 1862 estate plan.*

added alongside. That would explain the reference to a 'new mill' in the 1730 payments to John Read and William Hebden. However, if the map dates from 1778, then the building described in 1797 as having bulging walls must have been the old mill, and the building described in 1806 was the reconstructed building.

My conclusion, therefore, is that either in 1730 or around 1800, the mill was totally reconstructed on a different site from where it had first been, but re-using most of the masonry from the old mill, including the stonework of doors and windows.

There were two advantages in rebuilding on the new site. One was that the top floor of the mill, where grain-cleaning processes were carried out, was now on the same level as the drying-floor in the kiln. Thus grain could be delivered by cart direct to the kiln, and from there all processes would either be on the level, or via gravity from hoppers to the millstones below. The second advantage was probably that water from the original leat could be used at a higher level by making a wheel-pit in the manner described above, so more power would be available for driving the mill.

The mill building had two floors when last in operation, but the one on which the mill stones were located has been taken out, probably to facilitate removal of the mill machinery. Nonetheless, a plan of this floor at Level 2, can usefully be drawn, showing by dashed lines the positions of beams and joists supporting the floor above.

The plan at Level 2 is also of interest in that, on this level, there was a door from the mill into the room from which the drying kiln was fired. For this purpose there was what looks like a large farmhouse fireplace with a timber lintel. At the back of the fireplace though, is a brick arch leading into the warm air circulation space under the drying floor. This also may have been brick-lined. We could stick a probe 1.2 metres into this space, where we encountered an obstruction, and it is likely that the voids have mostly been filled up to make a solid floor for the garage above. The valuation of 1806 suggests that the then tenant, Francis Ward, had been modernising the establishment, and if it was he who had installed the brickwork, he could have obtained the bricks from the kiln known to have been operating near the present site of Bolton Abbey Station.

Returning to the mill, the beams and joists of the top floor remain, but most of the floorboards have gone. Enough remains, however, for the location of hatches and the position of the main vertical drive shaft in the mill to be recognised. This shaft would extend from the basement to the top floor. In the basement (probably just below Level 1), it would be made to rotate by gears driven by the water-wheel. It would then drive the millstones via a spur-wheel and other gears, and on the top floor, Level 3, would drive the sack-hoist and any grain cleaning machine there may have been.

This vertical drive shaft was aligned close to the north wall, as one can see from the pattern of floor joists shown on the Level 2 plan. Close to where the shaft turned and above Level 1, is a horizontal recess in the wall about 1.5 metres from the floor. This indicates the position of the spur-wheel, a large gear-wheel fixed to the shaft and needing extra clearance to rotate where it was close to the wall.

This large main gear-wheel was standard in all mills, and is the wheel from which the millstones on the floor above were turned, through gears. Because this was a standard feature of which there can be no real doubt, I have shown the position of the millstones on the cross-section of the building. Other drawings show only what remains in the building.

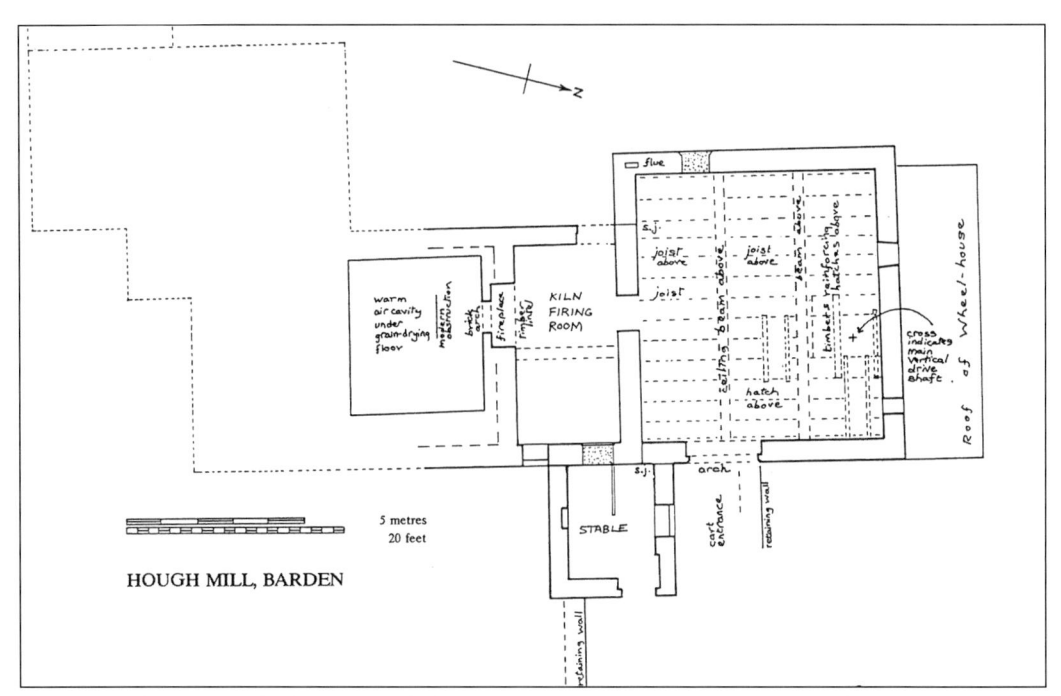

*Plan at Level 2. This is the floor on which the millstones were situated in the mill and from which the drying kiln was fired. Buildings on higher ground are shown in outline by dotted lines.*

## HOUGH MILL

Four items of mill machinery have survived, mostly in the roof space above Level 3. They are as follows:

1) part of the sack hoist, detached from its mountings on rafters above, but almost in its original position. This comprises a long wooden shaft or axle (labelled on the plan at Level 3), a pulley or drive wheel (marked A-A on the plan), and part of the device for putting the sack-hoist in 'neutral' gear.

2) a large wooden pulley-wheel with iron spokes, possibly used to drive a grain cleaning machine, but not now in its original position.

3) a basket-work cradle or funnel, probably part of a grain-cleaning machine, or perhaps for a de-husking machine for use in processing oats (since this was an oat producing area).

4) on the ground floor is a 32-tooth gear wheel with wooden teeth.

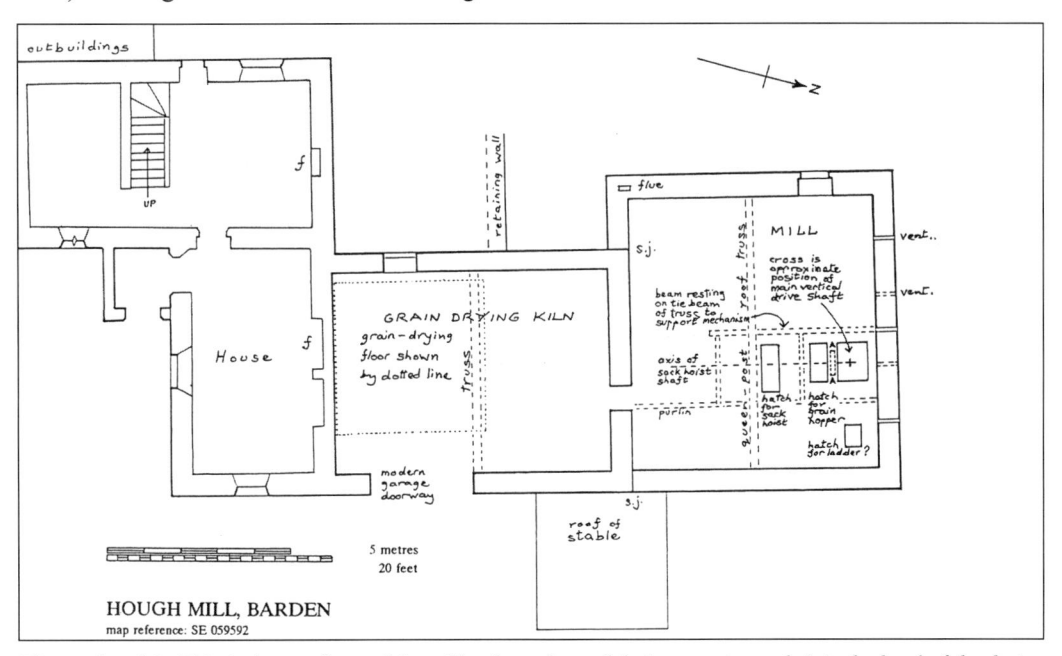

*Plan at Level 3. This is the top floor of the mill, where the sack hoist was situated; it is the level of the drying floor in the kiln building, and it is the ground floor level in the house. The interior of the house was not seen. It is shown in outline on the basis of what appears on the 1862 estate plan, and the scale used in the original version of this drawing is the same as on the estate plan.*

The few surviving bits of machinery are constructed from a mixture of wood and iron such as one might expect from around 1800. Later, more iron would have been used (compare the all iron back-shot waterwheel at Hartlington Mill).

This confirms the impression given by documents that a major reconstruction took place after 1797, and that the tenant in residence in 1806 was modernising the equipment. There is reference then to, 'Blue stones and machine for dressing flour'. This suggests an attempt to produce quality flour. Local millstone grit millstones (from Addingham Moorside?) would not be consistent with quality production because gritstone 'cut up the bran too finely for clean dressing out' (Martin Watts, *Corn Milling*, 1983).

If the miller invested in a machine for dressing flour, he needed also to invest in millstones from outside the area, in order to produce flour capable of being dressed. Blue stones (Niedermendig lava) were a type of millstone regularly imported from Germany, particularly into northern England, precisely for that reason.

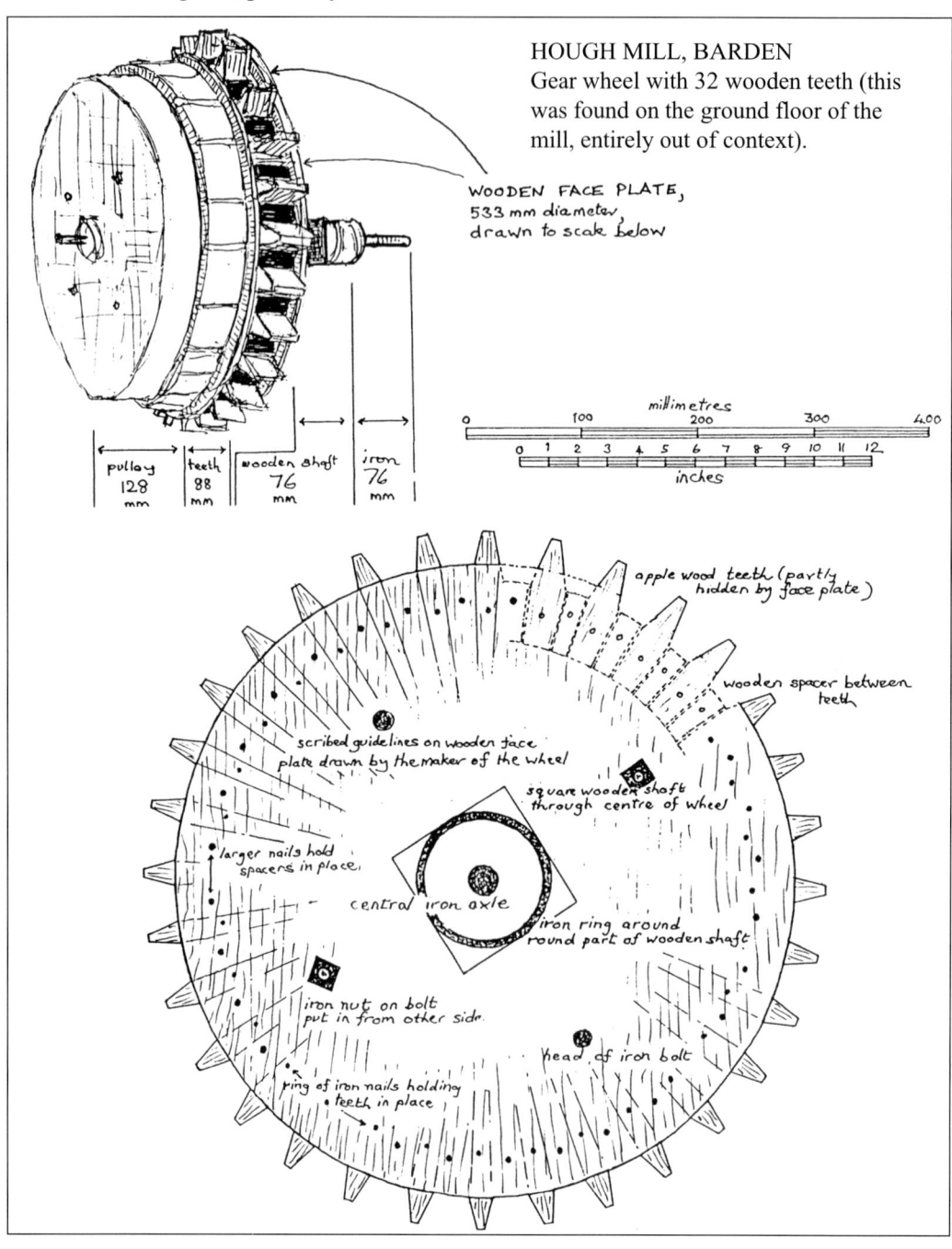

**HOUGH MILL, BARDEN**
Gear wheel with 32 wooden teeth (this was found on the ground floor of the mill, entirely out of context).

WOODEN FACE PLATE, 533 mm diameter, drawn to scale below

pulley 128 mm | teeth 88 mm | wooden shaft 76 mm | iron 76 mm

- apple wood teeth (partly hidden by face plate)
- wooden spacer between teeth
- scribed guidelines on wooden face plate drawn by the maker of the wheel
- square wooden shaft through centre of wheel
- larger nails hold spacers in place
- central iron axle
- iron ring around round part of wooden shaft
- iron nut on bolt put in from other side
- head of iron bolt
- ring of iron nails holding teeth in place

# HOUGH MILL

*[Diagram of four water wheel types with handwritten annotations:]*

*under shot* — Very unusual after c. 1790

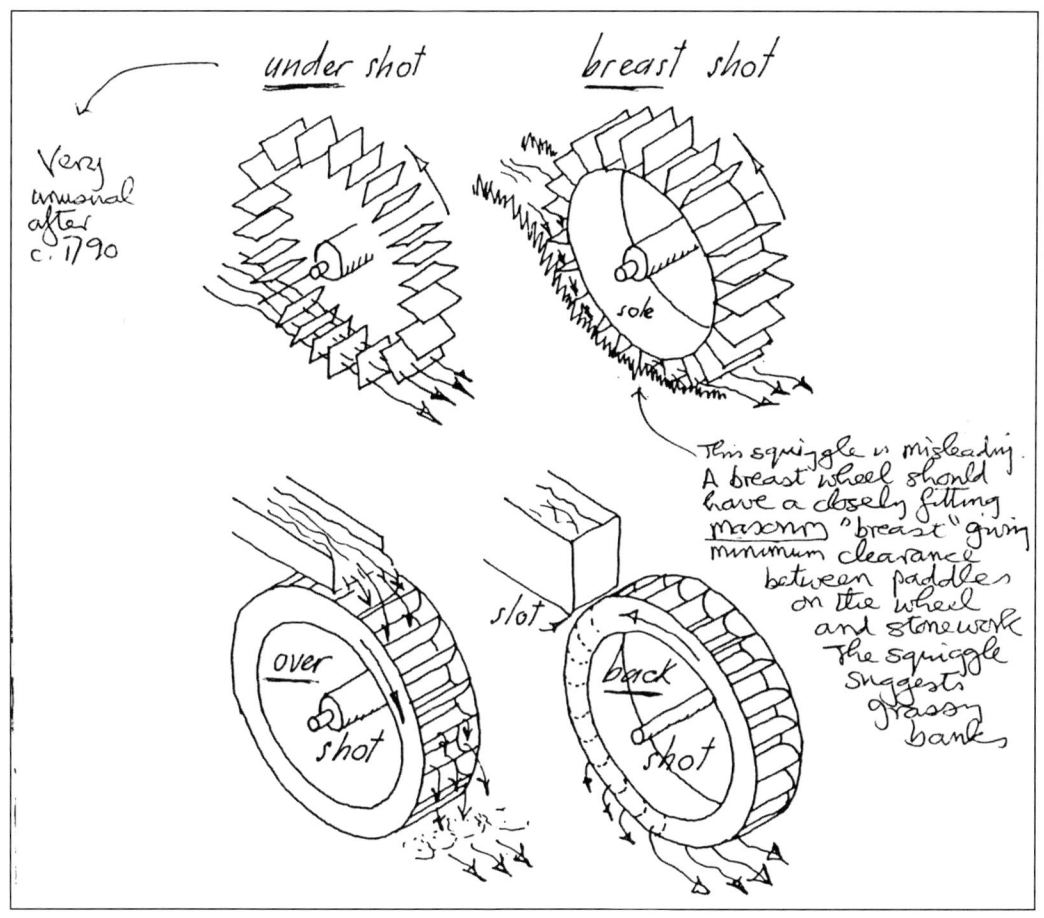

*breast shot* — sole — This squiggle is misleading. A breast wheel should have a closely fitting masonry "breast" giving minimum clearance between paddles on the wheel and stonework. The squiggle suggests grassy bank.

*over shot*

*slot — back shot*

An alternative explanation for the basketwork cradle noted earlier may be that it was covered with 'bolting cloth' – cloth through which fine flour could be sifted – and this was then part of the dressing machine of 1806. I have not seen enough dressing and grain cleaning machines to be sure what kind of equipment it was part of.

## Water power

A complete perspective on the machinery likely to have been used here is not possible without some comment on the type and position of the water-wheel driving it. To gain some insight on this, it was necessary to estimate the level at which water was supplied to the mill, and the level of the tail race.

The leat (goit) has been totally buried in the vicinity of the mill, but the stone slabs which cover it can be seen 100 metres to the west. Using a surveying instrument known as a dumpy level, we established that the top surface of these slabs is 1.1 metres above the present floor level in the mill. Water levels in the leat may have been up to 0.5 metres below the top of the slab, and the gradient of the leat could easily be 0.5 to 1 per cent. Therefore, it is likely that water reached the mill somewhat below the existing ground floor level (Level 1).

Since this at about 4 metres above the beck at the point where the tail-race discharges, the head of water available to drive the waterwheel was significantly less than 4 metres, and possibly in the range 2-3 metres. Thus the waterwheel must have been set very low relative to the present floor level. For example, a 4.5 metre diameter wheel might have its shaft (axle) more than one metre below the present floor level, which is why no sign of it can be seen in the rubbish-filled wheel pit. Such a wheel would probably have been breast-shot, under-shot wheels having been discredited since about 1760 by Smeaton's famous demonstration of their inefficiency.

Another thought is prompted by the drawing showing a cross-section of the mill close to the north wall. This drawing includes evidence of how the flow of water onto the wheel was controlled (i.e. how water was shut off when the miller wished to stop the wheel). Holes in the wall and oil stains on the right-hand side of the illustration show the position of these controls, and this suggests water approaching the mill in the leat a little above Level 1 (rather than a little below). They also suggest a 4.5 metre diameter back-shot wheel rather than a breast-shot one.

I have discussed the 1806 evidence of quality wheat flour production with Kate Mason and she reminds me that, following the enclosure of the Forest of Knaresborough, wheat production in that area increased dramatically, and grain was sold for milling into surrounding areas (she has evidence from Skipton). This may be what prompted a miller in an oat producing area such as Wharfedale to invest in a flour dressing machine.

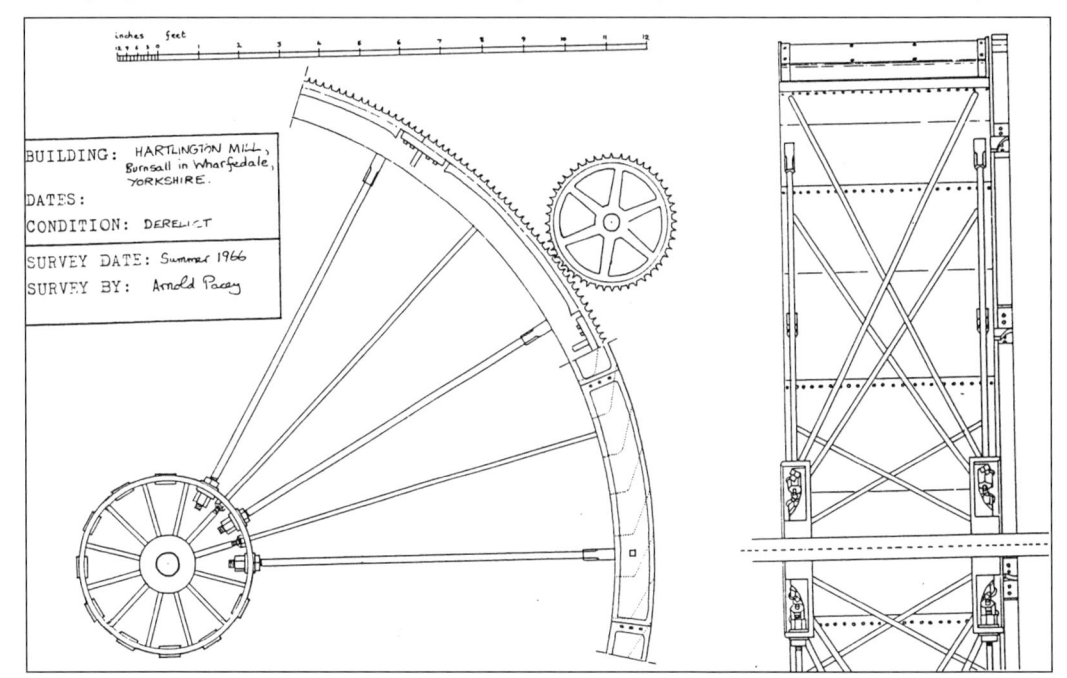

The 1717 agreement with James Ward, miller, quoted by Heather Beaumont says that the miller is to 'repair, maintain and amend and keep [the] water corn mill, dams, floodgates and all the houghs.' According to my dictionary, a hough, heugh or hoe is 'a hanging descent, a precipice… the steep face of a quarry.' Thus, as I remember Plymouth Hoe, that is a hanging descent to the sea with a retaining wall. So I guess that in 1717, there may have been a retaining wall on the site of the present one alongside the beck supporting the leat on its approach to the old mill on its former site. The retaining wall on which the corn drying kiln stands may have already existed.

There is some graffiti in and around the kiln-firing room: 1862 WW (or WV?); HP 1848 WH and WW 1866. Outside the building, around the former doorway in the north west corner: HL WW; TI (and diagrammatic forms like it, one high on a quoin).

**Conclusion**
The original Hough Mill was located somewhat to the west of the existing buildings, but was supplied with water by the same leat (goit).

Construction of the present buildings dates mainly from two phases: circa 1728-30 and circa 1797-1806. The drying kiln and a possible initial phase of the mill belong to the first dates; re-equipment of the mill and addition of most of the top storey certainly belong to the second date, and it is possible that the whole mill was built then, using old stone from the original mill in its bottom two storeys.

The sawmill added during the 1860s and now demolished seems to have led to few changes in what survives, although a drive must have been taken from the water wheel to the saw mechanism. Architectural studies may allow us to decide more precisely which stonework belongs to what period.

It is of interest to note that in a valuation of the mill dated 1806, there is mention that '…the blue stone and machine for dressing the flour has been put up by the tenant' (Francis Ward). From this time onwards, milling was carried out using the infinitely finer blue stones which came from Germany. It is therefore poignant to find a complete millstone still lying perfectly formed but fast in its bed-rock on the moor, a short distance up the hillside above Gamsworth.

**Howgill**
Flowing down the east side of the valley the Firs Beck forms a major tributary to the river Wharfe at its confluence near Hough Mill and the stepping stones leading to Drebley. A. H. Smith suggests that the place-name Howgill derives from the Old Norse *haugr*, meaning a hill or a mound, and the Old West Scandinavian *gil* meaning a ravine, while Margaret Gelling suggests that the name derives from the Old Norse *holr* for a hollow ravine.[208] These descriptions are not born out geographically, for the valley is pleasantly open, with gently rising hills on either side.

**Approach to Howgill from Hough Mill**
From the road bridge by Hough Mill a walled, sunken lane leads to the hamlet of Howgill, the track being paved in places to enable travellers to get a grip as they negotiated its steeper parts. From its appearance, it is evident that this narrow hollow way between Hough Mill and Howgill cannot have carried wheeled vehicles and that it has always been trodden on foot, or by ponies in single file. There was an alternative approach, however, as can be seen from the 1st edition Ordnance Survey map dated 1853, which shows a track labelled 'Bridle Road' branching from the Trust road near High Gamsworth; at this point a trough is clearly marked. It passed a second trough as it skirted the wall separating Lower Fell Plantation from the former medieval vaccary of Howgill.

Walls drawn on Beckwith's map of 1731 confirm that by the time of his survey the area had been enclosed and cultivated. This ancient bridleway entered the hamlet precipitously, by a network of green lanes, some branching towards the old houses and barns which now stand in semi-ruins on the hillside. At this point it is joined by the lane leading from Hough Mill to continue as a broad, walled lane, formerly with gates, up the valley of the Firs Beck. Built into the wall near Howgill Lodge, is a stone milestone showing, with a hand and four fingers the direction and distance to Pateley Bridge.[209] This milestone probably pre-dates the small, almost round stone which lies at its foot, on which is inscribed a cross, and the points of the compass.[210]

On its way north-eastward to the watershed the lane then threads its way through a cluster of barns and the farmhouse of Eastwood Head in much the same manner as the packhorse route threaded its way through the barns and cottages at Barden Scale. Finally, after passing

---

208 Smith A. H., *The Place-Names of the West Riding of Yorkshire*, Vol xxxvi part seven, 1962, Cambridge University Press. And, Gelling, M, *The Landscape of Place-Names*, 2000, Stamford: Shaun Tyas
209 Guideposts are the product of 1697, during the reign of William and Mary, when parliament authorised Justices of the Peace to order the erection of guideposts at remote cross roads to direct travellers. It is not possible to relate each stone to a specific date, but most of them would have been inscribed within a few years of the parliamentary edict.
210 Similar stones have been found by Barden Bridge, and by Bow Bridge, Linton. All three stones lie on roads interlinked with turnpikes.

Arnegill and Lamberts it reaches Dalehead, where the farmstead built in 1806 had facilities for stabling horses in its extensive outbuildings. From here, a network of tracks leads over the watershed to Greenhow, Pateley Bridge, and Knaresborough and over the green track between Howgill lane, Skyreholme and Stump Cross.

**Howgill Farm**

Forest receipts preserved amongst the Clifford papers include those for 1332-3, for vaccaries at Drebley, Holgill, Gamsworth, Launds and Estwode, and in 1505-10, Howgill is included in the Bolton Compotus when 'Bolton hired a vaccary at Holgill in the forest of Barden and agisted its cattle there.'

Beckwith's map of 1731 and Matthew Oddie's map of 1778 both show an area of land between Stockdale Nook and the scattered houses of Howgill which was clearly divided into fields and encircled by a wall. It is likely that this was the vaccary mentioned in the receipts and the Bolton Compotus, with its Lodge now succeeded by the Victorian farmhouse standing in a classical position on the straight arm of this D-shaped area.

Although mostly rebuilt in the nineteenth century, it is still possible to find some earlier walls composed of large boulders standing on substantial banks, corresponding to the walls shown on the maps dating from the eighteenth century. The bridleway shown on maps respected the field system by passing outside the boundary walls and following a course between them and the encroaching nineteenth century plantations. To the present day, the route of this old packhorse way can still be followed on foot from an entrance gateway to the woods on the road above Gamsworth farm.

Fields within the former vaccary were sub-divided when, in the nineteenth century a new road was driven between Wharfe View near (Stockdale Nook) and Howgill Farm; my records have not revealed the exact date for this road, but although it is not shown on the geological map surveyed 1849-50, nor on the first edition Ordnance Survey map of 1853, it appears on the Ordnance Survey map dated 1896.

In 1806 the tenant of Howgill farm was Thomas Wilkinson. He rebuilt the dwelling house at his own expense, in a style comparable with the houses at Dalehead and Club Nook. As can be seen from the photograph, it now has a slated roof and large sash windows which followed the addition of the eastern extension later in the century.

The farm buildings date from the Victorian period, comparable in style with others built on the estate in the 1860s, with a barn and shippon, stable and loose boxes. The pigsty retains its integral feeding trough with the hennery over. Pre-dating the farmyard is a 'potato cellar' driven into the rising ground of the garth, as discussed in the section on storage cellars.

*Left, Howgill farmyard; below the gable end of the pigsty with hen loft above and the opening to the pig trough in the outside wall, specially designed to take buckets of swill.*

A small stone cottage standing by the entrance to the yard remained in use until late in the twentieth century. It still has its cast iron cooking range, but no staircase, a ladder having probably been used for access to the upper floor. A small barn is built onto the gable wall of this cottage, where a pony and trap could have been kept, together with hay stored in the roof space. In 1867 the tenant was Mary Ann Wilkinson.

**Old house at Howgill**
The ruins of a house are situated in a field on the hillside, adjacent to the old bridleway from Dalehead which continued along the edge of the forestry plantation below Simon Seat. This house was the home of the Ideson family, although they also leased 'a messuage with appurtenances at Moorgaine near Gamsworth.'[211] On the hillside immediately above the old house is a small, two storey building, the lower storey facing west towards the house, and containing stone alcoves in which potatoes or cheeses might have been stored.

Unique in Barden, this building is an example of the ingenuity of man in making use of a steep hillside, in that the upper storey, facing east onto one of the bridleways, is open-fronted and large enough to stable a pony or store a small trap, a cart or a sledge, together with field implements such as hay rakes and forks.

The following headstones in Bolton Abbey churchyard preserve the memory of the Ideson family:[211]

David Ideson 1845-1914 whose wife Ann born in 1845, came from Wooddale in Coverdale.

Mary Ideson 1832-1906 of Howgill, wife of Francis Ideson of Barden, who, with Nathan Ideson born in 1851 of Howgill was mentioned in the Barden District Almanac 1882.

Charles Ideson 1849-1928 and his wife Sarah 1851-1915. Their son, John Thomas 1885-1918 was a prisoner of war in Germany. His name is on the Barden Roll of Honour (now hung in the Boyle Room at Bolton Abbey). His children included the following: Rennie, Phyllis, Mary, Charlie, Tom and Dennis.

*The ruinous remains of the house, with its fireplace arch still in position and below bridleways around the old house at Howgill.*

---

211 In the Skipton Castle papers, leases for Idesons date from 1603.

Mary married Billie Mason, whose memories of farming in the 1920s appear in the Fold Farm, Drebley chapter. They lived at High Gamsworth until 1939, then farmed near Bolton Abbey, at the Deer Park, and at Broadshaw until they bought Low Hall, Appletreewick, where their son Matt Mason now farms. Other Idesons appear in the nineteenth century census returns, from which it appears that the family farmed a relatively small acreage in Howgill, High Gamsworth and Barden Scale, augmented by employment as estate woodmen.

### Howgill Old Barn

This unusually large barn (which could originally have included a farmhouse), situated on the hillside overlooking Howgill and now derelict, contains a central area for storage of hay and implements including carts, with a shippon at each end. Over the doorways to these shippons each lintel bears the date 1666 and the initials H + S. The other barns shown on the photograph were probably built during the mid-nineteenth century at the same time as others in Howgill. The barn yard itself is enclosed and supported on the hillside by a huge, randomly built wall which also forms a remarkably stout revetment; again a unique feature in Barden.

### Simpson of Howgill

Barden leases and Craven rentals dating from 1602 onwards show that Henri and Humfrey Simpson occupied substantial holdings in Howgill, as shown by entries in 1604, when Edward Simpson of Barden, husbandsman, East side, leased a messuage, leyhouse, garden, three Closes of land including Higher Close, Medwards Close, Pasture Spring and Calf Close – 'calf' meaning small.

From the leases drawn up in 1603 it seems that Simpsons were already farming at Eastwood at that date, for Humfrey and Agnes Simpson are listed as paying over rent for tenements there, while in 1604 an Entry Fine of £30 was paid for Eastwood Head by their son, Henri Simpson. Henri also paid rent for one messuage and diverse grounds in Howgill, formerly belonging to the late Edward Keddies.

In 1650 Thomas Simpson, husbandman, held the lease for a messuage and tenement at Arngill Head, with permission to take in and improve from commons and moors adjoining. By 1666, the date on Howgill Old Barn lintels, members of the Simpson family were listed not only at Eastwood Head, but also at Arnegill Head, 'with permission to improve and take in from the commons and moors adjoining.'

In 1692 the name of Thomas Simpson who died in 1713 appears on the tithe list, known as the 'Saxon Cure for Barden', his place of residence being Barden Tower. He died in 1730.

John Simpson, 1689-1754 the nephew of Henry Simpson, yeoman, was possibly the Steward for the 3rd Earl of Burlington. In 1728 his name is listed in the estate accounts for lease of land at Barden Tower, and payment for work on the Tower. His will is lodged at the

# HOWGILL

*The barns high on the hillside above Howgill. Note the substantial wall which shores up the level farmyard in which the barns stand.*

Borthwick Institute in York, and his headstone in the churchyard at Bolton Priory is inscribed:

> Here lieth the body of John Simpson, late of Barden Tower, gentleman, who departed this life the 4th day of April, in the year of our Lord, One Thousand Seven Hundred and Fifty four in the 65th year of his age.

In May 1681, John Simpson is likely to have been the Steward for the Earls of Burlington at Barden Tower when an inventory of goods was drawn up and delivered to him.[212] A sandstone panel is fixed to the wall of a barn in the lane adjoining Howgill Lodge. The graceful style of lettering with serifs is typically eighteenth century. It is inscribed H T+ S 1750.

John Simpson was the nephew of Henry Simpson, yeoman, and probably the agent or steward for the Dowager Countess of Burlington, who was the mother of the 3rd Earl of Burlington, of Londesborough.[213] The estate lease book for 1728 lists John Simpson as leasing land and being paid for work at Barden Tower. In 1754 he drew up his Will,[214] bequeathing his right to the lease of the farm at Barden Tower to Thomas Lister who had married his daughter Jane.

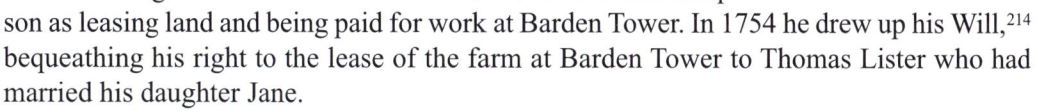

> Item: for the Good Will I have unto my son-in-law Thomas Lister, I give unto him all the Tenant right I have to my farm in Barden after my decease, by the Will and Consent of My Lady Dowager of Burlington or her Agent.

---

212 List of Goods in Barden Tower 1681. Barden Box: Bolton MSS.
213 Barden was the jointure of the Dowager Countess of Burlington.
214 The Borthwick Institute of Historical Research in York.

In addition, bequests of £100 each are made to three other daughters, Elizabeth, Anne and Sarah, and £10 each to a grandson and grand-daughter, while the servant Mary Hardwick was to receive £20. It is evident that John Simpson was a man whose substance warranted the description of Gentleman as inscribed on his headstone.

**Eastwood Head**

The farm of Eastwood Head lies at about 650 feet OD, on the east side of the Firs Beck, in Howgill; The favourable situation of this settlement can be seen from the opposite side of the valley, at High Skyreholme, and also from the New Road along the east side of Appletreewick Pasture. The farmstead lies beside the old bridleway as it winds its way through the valley towards Dalehead, and sits on a small terrace between pasture land bordering the beck, and heather covered moorland which rises steeply to the rocky outcrop of Simon Seat at 1,329 feet OD.

Evidence for early medieval settlement can be found in the stone walls enclosing some of the fields. These walls are built on mounds and follow an irregular course across the landscape, with large clearance boulders, or orthostats in the base. They are markedly different from straight walls built during the late eighteenth and early nineteenth centuries, at the time of Parliamentary enclosure.

Documentary evidence for these early enclosures appears in the Skipton Castle accounts for 1322/3 when receipts of income from Bolton Priory were issued by the Cliffords for agistment of cattle in a vaccary at Eastwode in Barden Forest '…there were vaccaries at Drebley, Holgill, Gamsworth and Estwode, with agisment for plough cattle in the woods at Drebley and Estwode.'[215]

A study of field-names[216] sheds light on the history of the area. Since most of the names derive from pre-conquest Saxon or Norse, it is likely that Eastwood was settled during that time, and that the area was wooded.

The name Eastwood describes the position of this settlement, i.e. east of woodland, where the fields bearing names such as Ley *leah* are of Saxon origin and imply that the area was first settled and cleared of woodland during the seventh and eighth centuries. The name Field *feld* implies that the cutting down of trees was followed by open land which was later divided for arable cultivation. The greater number of names deriving from Old Norse implies that the area was favoured by Norse pastoralists who settled in Craven during the ninth century These names are as follows:

Beck – ON *bekkr* for a stream flowing through an open valley (as opposed to a ravine)

Carr – ON *kjarr* is associated with marsh and brushwood and, as expected, these enclosures are found mostly adjoining the Firs Beck.

Garth – ON *garor*, a small enclosure in close proximity to the farmstead.

Holme – ON *holmr*, an area re-claimed after recent flooding, or a water-meadow.

Ing – ON *eng*, a waterside meadow.

---

215 *Victoria County History*, London, 1907, reprinted 1974, Vol. 1, p510.
216 Smith, A. H. *The Place-names of the West Riding of Yorkshire*, 1959, Vols xxxv and xxxvi, Cambridge University Press.

# EASTWOOD HEAD

Intake – ON *intak*, refers to assarts, or land taken in for cultivation, e.g. from the rough fell below Simon Seat.

Close – OFr enclosure. These enclosures date from the post-conquest period, after the establishment of the hunting chase in Barden by the Norman-French Lords of Skipton Castle.

Ley – OE *leah*, a clearing in a wood, later pasture meadow.[217]

Ridding – OE *rydding* describes an area cleared of woodland.

## Early seventeenth century leases for Simpson of Eastwood, also Rowland, Lambert and Frances Ellis[218]

1602/3: Agnes Sympson, widow, daughters Jane and Janet, sons Edward and William Sympson leased a tenement at Eastwood Head. Paid rent: 8s 4d, Over Rent:1s 6d (Craven Rental).

1603: The name of Henri Simpson of Howgill appears on the List of Freeholders in Barden Forest. This list records the rents of the tenants in Barden East side by Indenture and Warrant. He paid '13s 4d for one messuage and divers grounds, late of Edward Keddies'.

1604: October 8th Rowland Lambert of Eastwood Head in Barden Eastside, yeoman, surrendered his warrant for '…all that messuage and tenement situate within the territories of Eastwood Head.'

1604: December 6th Henri Simpson paid an Entry Fine of £30 for the lease of Eastwood Head, the 'principal farm' being occupied by Humphrey Simpson, father of Henri.

1610: The lease of Eastwood was held by Frances Ellis widow.

## The Holdens of Eastwood Head

Leases were held by the Holden family from 1602 onwards, the first being Richard Holden whose property was described as 'one decayed house and barn and turf house, meadows and arable containing nine acres. Also, two intakes called Burnetts, containing 20 acres situated in Barden and Appletreewick.' He also paid rent for a tenement which included 'Moregate, Gamsworth, Lodge Close and over-rent for Eastwood Head and Burweth.' After his death in 1650, his son Lawrence and his wife Frances were the lease holders.

1692 The Saxon Cure for Barden Dale[219] lists the names of Richard and John Holden

1756-85 Lawrence Holden was the leaseholder, he paid an annual rent of £25 for two houses and £21 for 70 acres.

Lawrence Holden and his brother John were carpenters who worked at Hough Mill, and also at Barden Tower, where they 'sawed one rood of boards for this house' i.e. the house attached to the chapel (now known as The Priest's House)

Nineteenth century Holdens were at Eastwood Head, Dalehead and Low Hall Appletreewick, for instance in 1806 John Holden was the tenant and appears on the list of gate-holders for Barden East.

In 1808 during the reign of King George III, an indenture for a pauper apprentice was sealed and delivered in the presence of Thomas Atkinson and William Demaine, Churchwardens and Oversees of the Poor. It was drawn up between Benjamin Brown, a poor child

---

217 Gelling, M. and Cole, A., *The landscape of Place-Names*, 2000, Stamford, Shaun Tyas.
218 Bolton MSS.
219 Saxon Cure was the tithe list for Bolton

of the Township of Barden and John Holden of Barden who died in 1821.

**Nineteenth century Holdens**
In 1807 William Holden (1776-1862) married Ann Inman, (1768-1810), daughter of Thomas and Elizabeth Inman of Howgill. Their marriage licence is preserved in the Craven Museum, Skipton but Ann died three years after their marriage, at the age of 32. She was buried in the churchyard at Bolton Abbey, where there is a headstone. Her brother James Inman died in 1834 and shares her grave, but when her husband William died in 1863, he was buried in a separate grave, with his own headstone.

William farmed 74 acres at Eastwood Head, but by 1845, the lease was held by John Holden who was unmarried. He and the widower William shared the house, and the 1841 census returns record that they had a 32 year old housekeeper named Hannah Bell, who came from Colne. John Holden then married, and he and his wife Mary had three sons. The eldest, George William born in 1855 farmed at Eastwood Head with his wife Margaret until his death in 1909. In 1904 Margarethad died; her funeral cost £14 13s and in 1910 her headstone, erected in Bolton Abbey churchyard, cost £27. George had two brothers, John Thomas (1859-89), who farmed at Low Hall, Appletreewick and James Lawrence (1862-1927), who later farmed with his wife Margaret at Dalehead.

Headstones in Bolton Abbey Churchyard:
William Holden 1783-1862 and his wife Ann Inman 1768-1810
John Holden 1813-81 and his wife Mary 1821-1904
George William Holden 1855-1909 and his wife Margaret Ann 1857-1904
John Thomas Holden 1859-89 of Low Hall, Appletreewick
James Lawrence Holden 1862-1927 of Dalehead

**The house and buildings at Eastwood Head**
The present house and buildings at Eastwood Head date from the mid-nineteenth century, but the Estate rent book, family history as outlined above, and two earlier datestones preserved and built into the walls is evidence to show that earlier buildings were demolished to make way for those we see today. For instance, a stone bearing the date 1688 has been preserved, re-fixed into the wall supporting a short flight of steps leading to the hen-loft above the pigsty, while one of the stones forming the jamb for a barn doorway has been re-positioned upside down, and bears the initials and date LH 1734 for Lawrence Holden. Between 1860 and 1867 John Holden built a new house, to plans drawn up in 1862.[220]

In the Craven Museum in Skipton there is a box of papers containing amongst other things notes from a diary 1856-63, and an account for money spent on decorating the new house built in 1867.

A bill dated 1865 for the interior decorating of the newly built house throws a clear light on the care taken over its quality. For instance, expenses were incurred for 65 dozen diamond window panes, painted with two coats of white, just as we see them today. The sitting room was varnished, as was the paper lining the staircase walls and passageway, while the

---

[220] Note: Drebley House was built at the expense of the tenant, Henry Holmes, whose initials are inscribed on the lintel over the front door, H.H.1830.

# EASTWOOD HEAD

*The house at Eastwood Head and, right, the steps leading to the hen loft above the pigsty with the 1688 date stone.*

mahogany handrail was grained. The impression gained is that this house, which was built at the expense of the leaseholder himself, and not by the Duke of Devonshire, was intended to be both substantial and prestigious. It not only faces south west to catch the sunlight, but it has a dominating position over the old bridleway as it winds its way up the valley from Howgill to Dalehead. It is a house fitting for members of this family, who served as Guardians of the Poor in Barden and were Representatives on the Court Leet.[221]

Whilst the house was being built, rent books for 1867 state that the farm buildings were not in very good repair, and so it is likely that the large hay-barn (comprising storage room for hay, some 'loose boxes' and shippons) was built at the time when John Holden carved his initials and the date on one of the wooden cart-entrance doors – J.T.H.1871. This barn, another across the lane, and the functional stone buildings attached to the north side of the new house are comparable in style with those at Howgill Farm, and Drebley on the other

---

[221] In 1870, the Court Leet was held 'at the house of Thompson of Barden, the ancient seat at Barden Tower being uninhabitable and now in ruins.'

side of the river, where the 'model' farmyard was being built during the same period. At Eastwood, however, there is no courtyard, the buildings being arranged in a dog-leg fashion, fronting onto the lane, as do the much older buildings at Barden Scale. Historical precedents for a right of way for the old bridleway would have had a bearing on the situation of these new farm buildings, some of which, if not all, stand on foundations for older thatched barns. Significantly, where there is a limited area of well-drained level ground as here, on the side of the valley, it would have been practical to re-use old sites and footings.

*Above, south elevation and below, east elevation.*

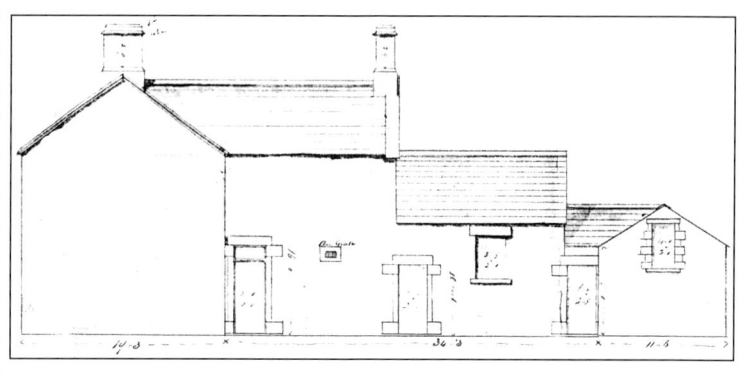

## Nineteenth century farming at Eastwood Head

William Holden 1783-1862 was the collector of land taxes for the Parish of Barden; his notebooks have been preserved at Skipton Museum, Craven, recording the names of Barden tenants with whose money he was entrusted. He also managed the church rates, and payments for the use of the highway.

Excerpts from his diary entries date from 1856. They record the shearing of sheep, ploughing, sowing of seeds, and leading of hay and harvest. He also writes about hiring extra help for hay time, how much it costs and for how many weeks, giving the precise dates. Hay-time was always between the end of July and the 20 August.

He mentions extremes of weather, when a great storm in December 1860 began about Christmas time and went on until well into February 1861. During this time 'of tremendous cold and wind, when it snowed on 9 February so fast that people could not stand nor lookout for their sheep. Many hundreds were overblown.' He goes on to describe snow in the following May, when hundreds of newly shorn sheep starved to death, and then, in 1862-3 'a tremendous white frost killed the potato tops, and lay on the bracken as thick as a skin, or a sheet'

# EASTWOOD HEAD

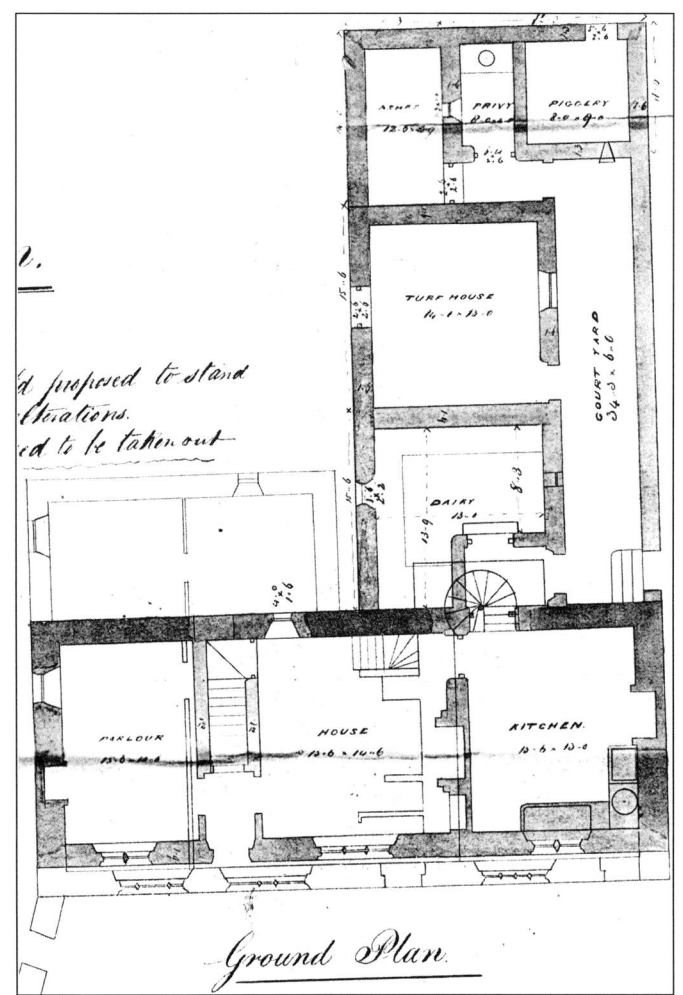

The mention of potatoes is a reminder that they were a major crop in Barden in the nineteenth century, and that special buildings were necessary for their storage and protection against frost and severe winter weather. There is just such a building at Eastwood, as described in the section on storage cellars. It is driven into the hillside on a plot of rising ground adjacent to the lane. By 1941, 'a quarter of an acre of potatoes, main crop and second earlies, together with a quarter of turnips and swedes for fodder'[222] were being grown at Eastwood Head, where Marion Holden was the leaseholder. The continued production of these staple crops may well have been imposed by food shortages experienced during the Second World War.

---

[222] Ministry of Agriculture and Fisheries Agricultural Return, 4 June 1941.

### Sedgwick of Dalehead

Dalehead with its nineteenth century farmhouse and out-buildings, did not become a separate entity until after 1806, when the intakes shown on an estate map of that date had been established. These lands were incorporated into the farm of Dalehead together with land formerly belonging to the two adjacent small holdings of Lambert's and Arngill Head. Rent books show that William Benson was the lessee in 1797, and by 1806 George Sidgwick held the lease.

When did George Sidgwick come to Barden? By 1795 he held pew number six in the church at Bolton Abbey, and by 1806 he was at Dalehead with his wife Martha (née Dodgson of Skipton, born in 1781). He was the son of Francis Sidgwick, a Wensleydale hosier, and Isabella Hunter who came from Dent. The establishment of a new farm on the Bolton Abbey estate, together with a new house on virgin territory, was a unique event. In addition, it was leased to new tenants who were not descendants of long established Howgill families. The Sidgwicks were in fact 'off comed 'uns' who settled, reared a family, and remained for several generations.

In 1806 specifications were drawn up 'for the building of a farmhouse at Dalehead, to be occupied by George Sidgewick.' In 1850, his son John 'was admitted to the tenancy in favour of his father, who had resigned in 1847' and proved to be 'an intelligent, improving tenant, building new walls at his own cost.'[223]

One of the daughters of George and Martha Sidgewick was born in 1811, and named Elizabeth. She appears in the 1881 census as living on her own means as head of household in Halton Gill. She was at that time aged 79 and single.

---

223 Bolton M.S.S. Rent book, 1867.

# 7
# Social History in Barden

**The Story of Barden School, its patrons, pupils and teachers**
Brontë Bedford-Payne and Heather Beaumont
In 1997 Her Grace, Deborah, the Duchess of Devonshire wrote a foreword to the book about Barden School in which she said, 'Through this book my family and I have learnt a lot about a part of the country which is so much loved by us. I am delighted to have this chance to commend it to a larger readership.'

Barden School lies close to the ruins of medieval Barden Tower. It stands:

> ...at what is perhaps the most beautiful highway-corner in all England... backed by a friendly belt of woodland, rising to the moors and fronting the grey tower... while... below tower and school, the road winds down to the bridge, ... takes Wharfe in its long stride, and climbs to the pine forest and moors beyond. Forest and heath and river are part of the children's lives as they go to school and home again.'

The elements of this scene, described by the romantic writer Halliwell Sutcliffe in his 1929 book *The Striding Dales* and largely unchanged over several centuries, have been experienced by many generations of children. Although the present building dates from the latter part of the nineteenth century, the history of a school in Barden began almost 500 years ago. The first known reference is from 1510, when a school was attached to the household of Henry Lord Clifford, the 'Shepherd Lord', at the Tower. There was probably a break through the later sixteenth and seventeenth centuries, but evidence suggests the continuous existence of a school in Barden from the mid-eighteenth century. Records from the late nineteenth and early twentieth centuries are plentiful.

For much of its history the school was largely dependent upon the patronage of the noble owners of the estate of which Barden was a part; first the Cliffords of Skipton Castle then, from the late seventeenth century, the Earls of Cork and Burlington followed in the mid-eighteenth century by the Dukes of Devonshire.

There are no records to suggest that the later Cliffords (1st to 5th Earls of Cumberland and Lady Anne Clifford) were patrons of a school in Barden.

There are instances, however, of schools being run on the initiative of individual tenants. An estate rental for neighbouring Bolton Abbey shows that, in 1603, Ingram Lister, Clerke, paid rent of 1s 8d for a house and garden in Barden, 'and for another house which he useth for the scoole.' The word 'Clerke' probably denotes his status as an educated man, or cleric. After the Reformation the clergy and others who wished to practise as schoolmasters were obliged to give evidence of religious orthodoxy and, from 1604, all schoolmasters had to be licensed by their bishop. In Barden, Lionel Holmes, 'who had acquired a fair knowledge of Latin', set up a school at Gamsworth Farm (near Howgill), which he occupied in 1624.

From 1704, following the death of the 2nd Earl of Burlington, income from the estate at Barden became the jointure of the Dowager Countess Juliana. A few years before Archbishop Herring's Visitation, she was much exercised over a matter concerning the school. In February 1739 her agent Henry Simpson wrote to Thomas Hawkswell, his representative at Bolton Abbey, that the Countess had:

> ...ordered me to tell you that she would have Jackman ousted of ye profession of Barden School, (although) in... no way prejudicial to Mr Petyt's charity, and... for ye good of ye Tennants children.

At a meeting of the trustees of Mr Petyt's charity, it was agreed that no more money should be paid to Jackman so that, as Henry Simpson put it, 'you may take such method to oust Jackman as shall be thought advisable by ye learned in the Law...' By 1740 Mr Coates had become schoolmaster at Barden, at a salary of £10 per annum (the sum granted by the trustees of Mr Petyt's charity).

Perhaps because of its historical foundation, but also to serve a scattered population, the school has always been situated at the 'centre' of Barden township, close to the Tower and the bridge across the Wharfe. Nevertheless, children from outlying farms and cottages had to walk two miles or more, to and fro, each day. During the late nineteenth and early twentieth centuries they came from Laund House and Waterfall Cottage on the road to Storiths, and from Drebley hamlet off the Burnsall Road.

Up to the 1870s and the implementation of the Education Act, Barden School maintained its independent status, supported by the Dukes of Devonshire and other local benefactors. It seems that the site of the school changed several times during the first half of the century. A rent book entry for 1806 refers to a cottage near Barden Tower, 'underlet to John Pickersgill for a school.' The suggestions then follows:

> If a larger piece was laid to the garden and some addition made to ye cottage and rented immediately to His Grace, it might be of great service to the tenants of Barden who, at present, suffer much inconvenience in the want of a more commodious school for the children.

A note made by the Revd. William Carr (the Duke's agent) confirms that this was done. An estate map of the same date shows that John Pickersgill held School brow, a small enclosure just north of the Tower precinct. A building named Park School, on School Brow, appears on the First Edition Ordnance Survey map, published in 1853. Thus, some time between 1806 and 1853, the school moved from a domestic dwelling to premises that were purpose-built.

From 1860 onwards a problem was posed by the large but temporary population engaged

## SOCIAL HISTORY IN BARDEN

in the construction of two reservoirs on Barden Moor. The first report by Mr. Codd (1871) concerning school accommodation in Barden includes a reference to about 200 temporary workers being employed. Between 1860 and 1870 a make-shift school was held in a farm for the children of navvies working on the lower reservoir, but this seems to have been discontinued.

As a first stage in the implementation of the 1870 Act, inspectors from the Education Department toured the country in order to report on schools already in existence and make recommendations about future provision, in order to fulfil the newly-established requirements and meet the needs of each community. As a result, a new school was built in Barden on a site closer to the Tower than the previous school. Stone is said to have been taken from a house in the Tower precinct, demolished in 1872 and previously tenanted by the schoolmaster, Dyneley Williamson.

The school opened on 14 February 1876 and was able to accommodate up to 50 children. It was registered as a voluntary or National School (Church of England) and was in receipt of government grants, while also retaining the patronage of the Dukes of Devonshire. The exterior of the new school building departs from the vernacular tradition of Upper Wharfedale. With its steeply-pitched roof, porch, bell-cote and decorative barge-boarding, it has features in common with a large number of schools built all over the country in the 1870s. Although the architect's plans for Barden School included a cottage for the teacher, the latter was never built. The lack of accommodation was to present problems in the future.

*Two photographs of the school children in the early 20th century.*

# BARDEN IN WHARFEDALE, THE PLACE AND ITS PEOPLE

The school log book (1876-1931), which every principal teacher was required to keep, provides details of the organisation of the school, its staffing and day-to-day life, as well as its educational achievements, assessed annually by HM Inspectors. These records show that, as the approach to education gradually became more liberal, the little school prospered: new freedoms were exploited, and the children blossomed. This is confirmed by the testimony of some of those who attended the school during the long regime of its last headmistress, Mrs Dunckley; academic achievement is demonstrated by the number who gained scholarships to local grammar schools. Past pupils have also provided graphic accounts of childhood in Barden during the early twentieth century; they show what life was like in this isolated rural community that was also an integral part of a great estate, situated in an area of natural beauty. The log book entries convey a lot of details about the life of the school and its pupils, as well as the personalities of the teachers. The records also convey the impact of national policies in education on this small, rural school and show the generally beneficial effects of new trends in educational philosophy and organisation.

In April 1878, when the upper reservoir was under construction, the Rev. Charles Bellairs (Rector of Bolton Abbey and correspondent of the managers of Barden School) wrote an eloquent appeal to the Inspector, requesting help to meet the educational needs of the children living on the two remote sites:

> Sir… I beg to lay before you the following circumstances, and to ask if you can render any assistance. There has lately come into this parish a colony of navvies for the purpose of making a reservoir for the town of Bradford which is 20 miles from us. These navvies are located in two separate groups of huts on a desolate moor, called Barden Moor and the groups are three miles apart, and there is no way of getting from one group to another except along the train road made for a temporary locomotive. It may therefore be said that there are two distinct and separate colonies. Each colony has about 200 navvies, besides women and children, and the children of school age, at each colony may be said to be, in round numbers, about 30. The work is not likely to last more than three years when the whole thing will break up, the huts will be removed and the moor will be as desolate again as it was before the navvies came. These huts are from four to six miles from the parish church and there is no school within from two to four miles, and even if the children could go to one of these schools (i.e. at Barden or Burnsall) there is not sufficient accommodation.

A note in the Inspector's hand reads: 'I think we can only write as follows… while fully appreciating the desire to make provision for the navvies, the Education Department has no power to make any grant for such a purpose.' He points out that under the terms of the Act it would be difficult to establish a school board or to compel ratepayers to provide schools. The problem must have been common for navvies on Victorian construction projects all over the country.

During the reign of King George V and Queen Mary the Royal couple often stayed at Bolton Abbey with the Duke and Duchess of Devonshire. People working on the estate and the schoolchildren were aware that the King and Queen came to stay each year in August for the grouse shooting. Although the King stayed at Bolton Hall, Queen Mary slept in the Royal train in the siding at Bolton Abbey station where she was more secluded. On Sundays when the Royal party attended morning service and the Priory Church was

## SOCIAL HISTORY IN BARDEN

certain to have a substantially increased congregation.

Queen Mary regularly travelled up the valley from Bolton Abbey to Parcevall Hall where she visited her godson, Sir William Milner. It was a true 'royal progress' in her chauffeured limousine, and an occasion none of the families on the estate would miss if they had a chance to be by the roadside to see her drive past. Children were taken, the girls in their best frocks, to stand with their mothers, aunts and grandmothers, by the lane ends leading to their farms. Often they stood for a long time before the Queen came, thus making sure they did not miss her; as she passed they might see a gloved hand raised in acknowledgement.

There were some who had a closer association with the King, namely the keepers and loaders of the guns who were in attendance on the moors each day. During the season many of the younger men went as beaters, driving the birds before the guns, but this was an arduous job for which only the fit and eager were employed. Reg Harper said: 'I did not care to see the keepers and beaters being servile, with hats in hand, awaiting the King's smallest command; I have never forgotten how, on one occasion the King swept his arm in the direction of one of the men, saying, 'No need to do that my good fellow, I am only a man like yourself."

Another special visitor, whom Reg Harper and Dora Dunckley each observed separately while walking in Bolton Woods, was Mary, Princess Royal, when she was being courted by the Earl of Harewood. Although the woods were closed to the public on Sundays, anyone living on the estate could walk there freely in order to reach the Priory Church, and so the children noticed the aristocratic couple, seated on flat rocks near the Strid. Shortly afterwards their engagement was announced and Barden children were amongst those given a day's holiday from school.

Between the two world wars the girls remembered walking to school wearing laced boots, iron-shod clogs and leggings. Groups of children walking to school were aware of each other across the valley. As the Drebley children passed the Wesleyan chapel, they could hear the Idesons of High Gamsworth clattering down the hill from Watergate, their clog-irons striking on the loose surface of the road and their shrill voices echoing across the river... Apart from those who walked to school, a few children were lucky enough to possess a bicycle. One of these was Winnie Davies from Waterfall Cottage, who sometimes allowed her younger brother, Reg, to ride on the handlebars... There were two children at The Riddings who travelled to and from school driving their father's pony and trap. Chris and Margaret Hagar came spanking down Cinder Hill each morning, turned into the Tower yard, and left their pony to graze in the Lister's croft while they were at their lessons. The Ideson family remembered the little Shetland pony, and also a donkey which sometimes pulled the trap.

Following the end of the First World War groups of severely injured ex-servicemen commonly walked the roads between the workhouses at Skipton, Settle and Pateley Bridge. Most were looking for work as navvies, building the reservoirs of Upper Nidderdale and the associated conduits laid across Wharfedale for Bradford Corporation. Many of them were scarred and lame – men whom the children dreaded meeting, especially on the lonely and secluded road to Storiths between the fir trees and past Coney Warren. They felt intimidated by their roughness, and would go to great lengths to avoid them. On one occasion, when Reg and Winnie saw a group of these men seated on a 'rustic' seat by Posforth Bridge, brewing a can of tea, they climbed a high wall beside the road and crept along behind it, until they reached the safety of home.

Local communications and transport improved to such an extent during the tenure of Mrs Dunckley that some children travelled daily to the Girls High School or to Ermysted's Boys Grammar School in Skipton. Not only the station at Bolton Abbey, but also the advent of privately owned motor transport offered opportunities hitherto beyond the reach of tenant farmers and estate workers in Barden. In addition, a significant improvement in the marketing of milk in the 1920s provided the hill farmer with a secure and regular income, however small. Thus the standard of living rose minimally, enabling some parents to encourage their children's academic achievements.

It was perhaps only within the confines of the schoolroom on annual prize-giving days that the tenants' wives actually saw and possibly met members of the Cavendish family, who were the focus of so much awe and respect. The children were taught to curtsey or bow when receiving their prizes, and the whole school spent a great deal of time in learning the songs with which they would entertain their visitors. Small, wistful details survive, concerning the clothes worn, and there are memories of the behaviour of the Duchess's children or grandchildren, especillay when they joined in the dancing after tea, or went out to play with the tenants' children in the yard. It was not unknown for rough 'horse-play' to take place, resulting in a push towards the water trough, according to Sydney Binns!

For the greater part of the year life in Barden was relatively humdrum and uneventful, chiefly influenced by the season, the weather and the farming pattern, church festivals, and the school calendar, as recorded faithfully in the school log book. Some families arranged outings to such annual events as Appletreewick Fair, or a day-trip to the seaside, but there were very few major holidays.

## SOCIAL HISTORY IN BARDEN

The visits of Royalty and the Duke and Duchess and their family were occasions when each child had the opportunity to share in the excitement and pride of living on the estate. Invitations to attend special events at Chatsworth, such as the coming of age of the Marquess of Hartington, a marriage, or an anniversary, were accepted by only a few representatives of the tenants until improved travel by charabanc or coach became feasible. After this, invitations were issued to all and accepted with alacrity by as many as could leave their familiar environment for a brief glimpse of the family and the great 'parent' estate in Derbyshire.

After the school closed on 10 July 1931 the building was used as a village institute. However, in 1993 it re-opened to accommodate some of the pupils attending the Montessori school, based at nearby Strid Cottage in Bolton Abbey township. So, once again, the shouts of children at play issue from the grassy slopes below Barden Tower, re-echoing the cries of earlier generations who also came to school on this historic site.

### Social Life in Barden, 1930s

Due to the scattered nature of the farms and hamlets in which they lived, and the division of the township by the river, children in Barden had little opportunity to meet once school hours were over. Nevertheless, in recalling their childhood, many speak with nostalgia of the freedom of roaming the fields, river banks and moors, either alone or with one or two companions.

Dora Dunckley and Barbara Lister were close friends and often spent time together. Barbara lived at the Priest's House at the Tower and was Dora's nearest neighbour and the youngest of three daughters. In contrast to the cramped accommodation at Stonybank Cottage, Barbara's home offered endless space for imaginative play, either in the 'oak room' or outside around the barns and precinct of the ancient building.

Acutely aware of their natural surroundings, these two girls became protective about the few holly trees which carried berries for decorating the chapel at the Tower for Christmas, keeping an eye on strangers who might attempt to raid them. In Springs Wood, between the Tower and the river, grew wild daffodils, known to only a few; Dora and Barbara climbed the wall and picked small bunches which they took to sick or elderly people, whom they knew would share their delight in these early wild flowers. They also treasured the sight of cowslips growing in a steep field below Watergate. Each year their mothers arranged bowls of moss and spring flowers on their windowsills. Dora became a keen and competent naturalist:

> I learnt to identify many birds around my home at Stonybank, including the pied flycatcher, redstarts nesting along the walled lane and a nightjar which could be heard quite clearly at dusk, sitting in an oak tree. I was also familiar with the corncrake, a regular summer visitor, nesting in the field below the Wesleyan chapel. I noted the rarer visits to our bird table of the lesser spotted woodpecker, and in the time before dustmen collected rubbish, I found a robin's nest in an old kettle in the wood… The great dome of sky above the moors was sometimes lit by the Northern Lights and, on darker nights, shooting stars were observed, together with those in the constellations. We had been taught how to identify some these by the Appletreewick school teacher, Miss Clayton.

## BARDEN IN WHARFEDALE, THE PLACE AND ITS PEOPLE

Nearer home, glow worms were seen on several evenings. They were on the bank of Gillbeck Wood as we walked up the lane from Low House Farm. A plague of caterpillars of the small ermine or the brow-tailed moth occurred in Gillbeck Wood in the early 1920s. It was impossible to go into the wood without trampling on them, and the sound of their rasping could be clearly heard. They devastated a large area, eating every leaf.

A quiet walk from Club Nook Farm is also recalled by Dora, when she once saw an otter at play at the point where Gill Beck flows into the Wharfe. One of her friends saw a stoat, swaying on its hind legs to mesmerise a rabbit. Some evenings, when she called at Club Nook to collect supplies of fresh yeast and milk, she remembers watching Frank Almack, seated on a three legged stool in the shippon, hand milking. On one occasion, he squirted the milk from the teat straight into her mouth!

The family of Thomas Birch, the head gamekeeper, were friends of the Dunckleys. On warm sunny days in the school holidays Dora and her mother loved meeting them for a picnic on the moors. The two of them would walk up the hill from the back of Stonybank Cottage, through a well-used gap in the wall and so into the Broad Park. Following tracks through the heather, they came to a 'promenade' to walk along, which was part of the pipe track from the reservoir, although this could be a perilous experience in high winds: once or twice, Dora needed to be shielded by her mother for fear she would be blown off.

Their favourite picnic spot lay beyond the low reservoir in a sheltered place known as Brass Castle, where shooting parties gathered for refreshments. Mrs Birch and her children walked from Park House, while Barbara Lister and Janet Potts, who sometimes joined the picnic group, walked up the track from Barden Scale. Mrs Birch carried on her arm a large basket: this usually contained currant teacakes, sandwiches spread with meat paste, ginger biscuits and sponge cakes filled with raspberry jam, everything covered with a snowy white teacloth. While she spread out the tea on the grass, cropped short by sheep, the children played and paddled in the stream or explored the two thatched huts used on shooting days. One was for the Duke's party and the other for the keepers; the beaters remained outside on the heather. Inside one of the huts there was a rough wooden, curved table bearing many initials and even a roughly hewn gaming board, reminders of wet days when the men had to while away the time.

Reg Harper was generally a solitary child who roamed freely from his quiet home at Waterfall Cottage, within Bolton Deer Park. Favourite haunts were the Nab, where the last of the deer grazed during the 1920s, and the Valley of Desolation at its foot. He learnt how to stalk the deer amongst tall bracken fronds until he was almost upon them before they became aware of his presence and bolted away. Sometimes he would venture farther, across the open breezy fell to the rocks of Simon's Seat. In summer walks along the riverside, Reg saw and envied stronger boys, able to swim in deep pools of the Wharfe; occasionally he observed foolhardy visitors who recklessly leapt across the Strid, where fatalities are not unknown.

The plantations around Barden School were busy areas for the powerful Clydesdale horses when they worked amongst the trees, and Reg has never forgotten watching them. As he stood in the school yard, looking over the wall into Bull Coppice, he could see and hear them straining at the heavy chains as their names were called: Dick, Touch, Bob and

## SOCIAL HISTORY IN BARDEN

Charlie. When the time came to fell the ancient beeches, he can recall the scream and whine of the saws and winches, and the crash of the falling trees, combined with the sight of the huge tripods and the towering horses with their gleaming harness.

On Sundays, Barden families did not take part in games or any other form of recreation, nor in knitting, handicraft, or any activity that could be construed as work. This resulted in considerable boredom for the children, but the tedium was relieved by attending Sunday schools and services at both the Wesleyan chapel and the Anglican chapel at the Tower. Gladys Inman was one of the children who learnt to play the organ to accompany hymns.

People walked to evening services at the Wesleyan chapel, carrying their lanterns in the darker months of the year. As the time for each service approached, little lights from these lanterns could be seen moving erratically up the lanes and along the roads from the farmsteads, meeting others to form larger groups as they neared the bridge. The lanterns were extinguished and left in the chapel porch until after the service, when they were relit in readiness for the return journey. When this close-knit community held their Harvest Festival at the Wesleyan chapel, Dora said:

> It was known as Our Autumn Highlight, for which masses of food was brought in. After the service the offerings were taken down the outside flight of stone steps to the room below the chapel, where Alec Birch of Club Nook auctioned it on Monday evening and mother took charge of the money, as usual.

There were sufficient numbers of Barden children for a horse and trap to be provided to take them to Bolton Abbey for special events, such as the singing of a Cantata at Easter. Dora's account recalls the warm friendship amongst them all, as they packed themselves under their rugs, with the lantern lit for the journey, and how Mrs Lister would be waiting at the gate of Tower Close to greet them when they returned.

Some children, including Sydney Binns of Watergate were members of the choir at the Priory Church, and also sang in the chapel at Barden Tower on Sunday afternoons. The annual choir outings with the Revd. Cecil Tomlinson were a great event, especially when the day ended at Harry Ramsden's Fish and Chip shop. On these occasions the rector went for a pint of bitter while the boys indulged in their treat. In 1927 seven boys went on a visit to Ripon Cathedral and Studley Royal, but those who were not in the choir had to attend school as usual.

Parties were held in the schoolroom at the end of every Christmas term; after the school closed in 1931 they were held in the 'schoolroom' beneath the Wesleyan chapel. Everyone brought food, and parents as well as children took part in the games, since it was an occasion for the whole community to enjoy a social gathering. It was always considered easier when such events were arranged for moonlit nights, so that people could walk to the chapel without having to use their paraffin lamps.

Cricket matches at Beamsley were an annual event, when the Cavendish family team played the village team, after which a huge tea was served by the ladies... Cricket was also played by Barden folk in the flat field adjacent to the bridge, where a small pavilion was erected on land belonging to Holme House Farm.

# BARDEN IN WHARFEDALE, THE PLACE AND ITS PEOPLE

**A letter to a niece from Herbert Chester, 14 March 1937**

When I wakened up early this morning I heard a howling round the house, so I got up and decided to light the fire before I went round the barns. I stepped out into a white world and as I came back with a shovel full of coals the wind blew my hat over the coal house. As I paused to watch it the coals were all blown away off my shovel, so I ran for shelter and then for my hat; putting it firmly on my head I took it off again quickly for it was full of wet snow. It took me something like an hour and a half to get round the barns for I could hardly make any progress facing the driving snow, nor see where I was going.

The trees were all laden with frozen snow, and in the howling tempest you could hear many old trees come crashing down. The old silver birch near Bumby barn with all those clumps like crows' nests came down with a tremendous crash crushing the wall and smashing the gate to matchwood. The wireless aerial and the telephone wires were hung like cart ropes nearly touching the ground with their weight of frozen snow.

Jim being away made matters worse, but we managed to water the cows, and then, being uneasy about the sheep, I went up on Tuesday morning with Cecil (Demaine) to get the sheep off the moor. We found a lot with very little food or shelter, and made a paddled track back for their return journey home. I had the first big drove with Bobby (the sheepdog). Coming down the lane one sheep got entangled in the telephone wires. I ran to catch it, Bobby came to help and was caught by one hind leg with another loop round his tail; the more the sheep pulled the harder did Bobby yelp and bite at the wires. It was a most exciting four minutes and when I had released the sheep, I had to hold Bobby down and stop him from biting until I sorted out all the tangles. Then we had an almost fruitless search for stray sheep, and what a wilderness the moor did seem, knee deep in snow.

One day I found myself at the top of Waterford Ghyll, overlooking Sandybeck Bar. There was a keen wind drifting the snow and all the landmarks near at hand were blotted out, when suddenly I dropped overhead in snow. I let out a startled cry, for the pain in my feet warned me that I was sinking into icy water, so I scrambled out in a hurry, took off my shoe, poured the water out and wrung out my stocking as well as I could. I set off to run to get warm again but Jack Frost was there behind me and on in front lay five or six miles of deep snow before I reached my warm fireside again. I heard a train puffing down there in the valley and, as I felt in my pocket I thought yes, I had plenty of money to buy stockings, but there were no shops and everyone was far away.

Well, if you cannot buy what you want you must make it, and I knew that Jack Frost was going to win, for my foot was going asleep. I did not run any further but sat down under a crag and took off my shoe and stocking and, after drying my foot with my handkerchief I rubbed it with my mittens. Taking off my overcoat I said, 'Come on, Johnny, you pop in there where it's warm, inside the sleeve, while I make you a new dry stocking.' I found the upper half of the old one was dry, so I took out my pen knife and cut it half way up the leg. I tied a piece of string round to keep my toes in, but it wasn't very comfortable so I thought I had better sew it. Having no needle, I made holes with my pencil and threaded string through. The result was a good dry stocking, so I beat Jack Frost after all. Now we have had some warmer days, the snow drifts are getting less, but there is a big one under Simon's Seat. On 14 April the swallows will come so spring is not far away and we have lots of lambs and chickens.

*What we call the beginning is often the end.*
*And to make an end is to make a beginning.*
*The end is where we start from.*

                T. S. Elliot Four Quartets 'Little Gidding' 1942

# Bibliography

Bedford-Payne, Brontë and Beaumont, Heather, *The Story of Barden School, its Patrons, Pupils and Teachers*, Prontaprint, Durham, 1997.
Bedford-Payne, Brontë, *People and Places in Upper Wharfedale,* Summers Barn Publishing, Grassington, 2007.
Bedford-Payne, Brontë, Hough Mill in Barden 1604-1889, compiled for the Upper Wharfedale Field Society, 2010.
Bedford-Payne Brontë, *The Turnpike from Skipton to Cracoe and Sandybeck Bar*, compiled for the Upper Wharfedale Field Society, 2012.
Bedford-Payne Brontë, *Charles Kingsley Christian Socialist*, North Craven Heritage Trust, 2011.
Smith, A. H., *The Place-Names of the West Riding of Yorkshire*, Cambridge University Press, 1958.
Gelling, M. and Ann Cole, The landscape of Place-Names, Stamford: Shaun Tyas, 2000.
Spence, Richard T., *Skipton Castle and its Builders*, Smith Settle, Otley, 2002.
Spence, Richard T., 1994 *The Shepherd Lord of Skipton Castle,* Smith Settle, Otley, 1994.
Moorhouse, Stephen, *The Archaeology of Yorkshire*, Occasional Paper no 3: The Anatomy of the Yorkshire Dales: deciphering a medieval landscape, 2003.
Rackham, Oliver, *The History of the Countryside*, *Wooded Forests*, Nicholson and Weidenfeld, 1995.
Beaumont, Heather, Tracing the Evolution of an Estate Township: Barden in Upper Wharfedale, *The Local Historian,* Vol. 26, No. 2, 1996.
Moorhouse, Stephen, *The anatomy of the Yorkshire Dales: deciphering the medieval landscape,* Yorkshire Archaeological Society Occasional Paper No 3, ed. T. G. Manby, S. Moorhouse and P. Ottaway, 2003.
Whitaker, T. D., *The History and Antiquities of the Deanery of Craven*, Manchester and Skipton, 1878, republished 1973.
Winchester, Angus J. L., *The Harvest of the Hills, Rural life in Northern England and the Scottish Borders, 1400-1700.* Edinburgh University Press, 2000.
Bogg, Edmund, *A Thousand Miles in Wharfedale*
Clifford, D. J. H., *The Diaries of Lady Anne Clifford,* Sutton Publishing, Stroud, Gloucester, 1990.
Dawson, Harbutt, *History of Skipton,* Edmondson and Co., Skipton, 1882.
Holmes, Martin, *Proud Northern Lady*, Phillimore, Chichester, Sussex, 1975.
Pontefract, Ella and Hartley, Marie, *Wharfedale*, J. M. Dent and Sons Ltd, London, 1938.
Sutcliffe, Halliwell, *The Striding Dales*, Frederick Warne, London, 1929.
The West Riding War Agriculture, Technical Development sub-committee 'information'. Vol. 2, No. 5, October 1943
*The Yorkshire Post* articles: 16 June 1952 'Bold venture in the dark days rewarded' Percy Illingworth and 14 August 1954 'Wharfedale farm where old and new are contrasted' Richard Joy.
Newspaper cuttings undated but probably from the 1940s, e.g. 'A day in the Yorkshire Dales. Down on the farm'.
'Agricultural Adventures' and 'Mr Hudson, the Minister of Agriculture, in the Hills, Skipton' transcript of the BBC Home Service broadcast from Manchester, 30 January 1944.
*Country Magazine*, ed. Francis Dillon, pub. Audrey Jones.
Further material and family memorabilia was added by Herbert Chester's niece, the author.